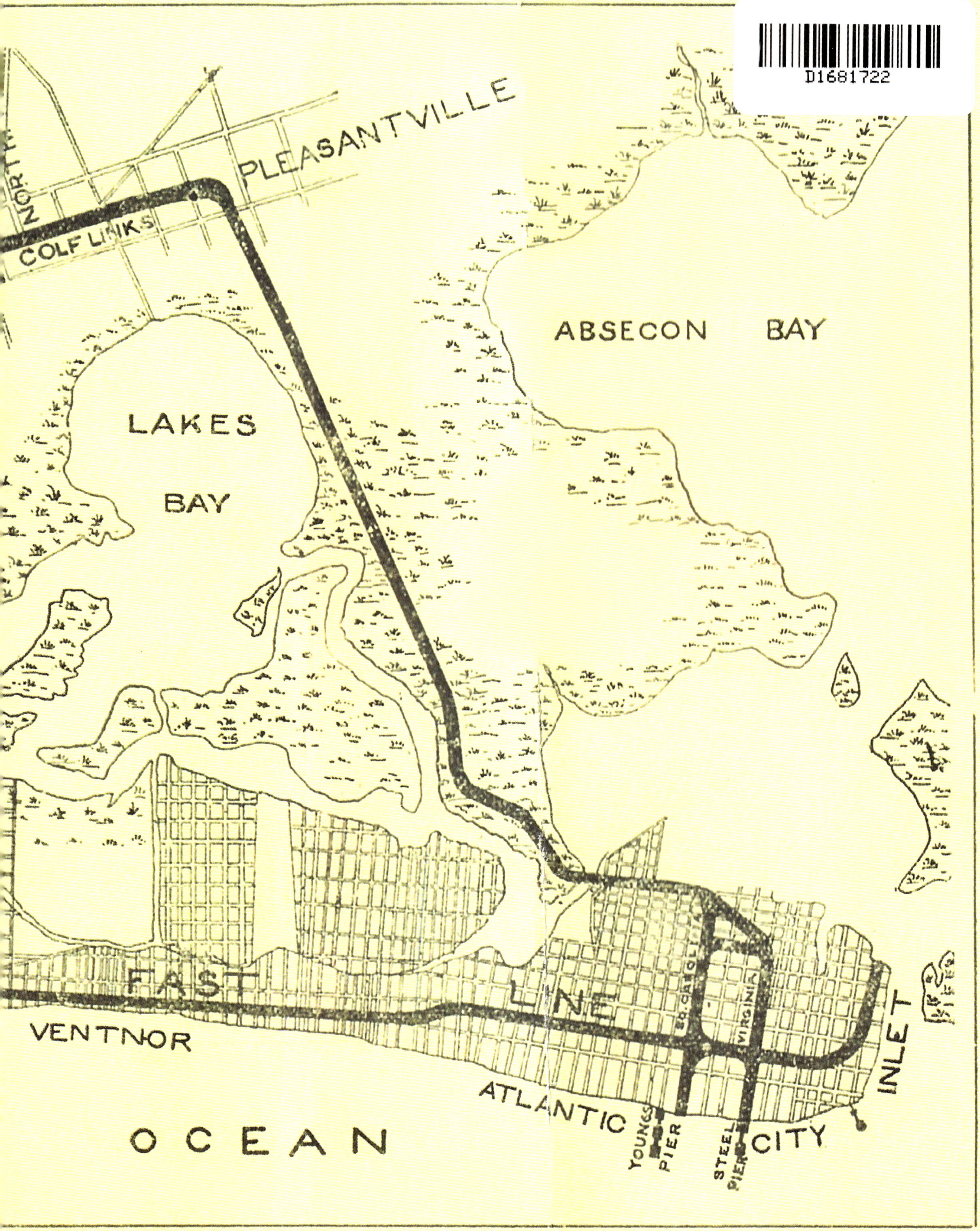
NORTH
PLEASANTVILLE
GOLF LINKS
ABSECON BAY
LAKES BAY
FAST LINE
VENTNOR
ATLANTIC CITY
OCEAN
INLET
SO. CAROLINA
VIRGINIA
YOUNGS PIER
STEEL PIER

Trolleys to the Boardwalk

A History of Atlantic City Trolleys 1854-1955

James N.J. Henwood

Bulletin 151 of the Central Electric Railfans' Association

Trolleys to the Boardwalk

A History of Atlantic City Trolleys 1854-1955

By James N.J. Henwood

Bulletin 151 of the Central Electric Railfans' Association

ISSN 0069-1623

©2021 by the Central Electric Railfans' Association
An Illinois Not-for-Profit Corporation
Post Office Box 503, Chicago, Illinois 60690, U.S.A.

CERA DIRECTORS 2018

Lenard Marcus*	Michael Lehman
John Nicholson	Andrew Sunderland
Joseph Reuter*	David Zucker
William Reynolds	(*Deceased)

All rights reserved. No part of this book may be commercially reproduced or utilized in any form, except for brief quotations, nor by any means electronic or mechanical, including photocopying and recording, nor by any informational storage/retrieval system, without permission in writing from the publisher.

Trolleys to the Boardwalk was designed by Curt Schultz, Curtis Digital Production was coordinated by John D. Nicholson

CERA Bulletins are technical, educational references prepared as historic projects by members of the Central Electric Railfans' Association, working without salary due to their interest in the subject. This bulletin is consistent with the stated purpose of the corporation: To foster the study of the history, equipment and operation of the electric railways.

Library of Congress Cataloging-in-Publication Data

Names: Henwood, James N. J., author.
Title: Trolleys to the Boardwalk : a History of Atlantic City Trolleys 1854-1955 / James N.J. Henwood.
Description: Chicago, IL : Central Electric Railfans Association, 2019. | Series: Bulletin of the Central Electric Railfans' Association, 0069-1623 ; 151 | Summary: "The history of passenger transportation to Atlantic City, especially the development of the Atlantic City & Shore Railroad, an interurban built by the Pennsylvania Railroad"-- Provided by publisher.
Identifiers: LCCN 2019021623 | ISBN 9780915348527 (hardcover)
Subjects: LCSH: Street-railroads--New Jersey--Atlantic City--History. | Local transit--New Jersey--Atlantic City--History. | Atlantic City & Shore Railroad--History. | Pennsylvania Railroad--History.
Classification: LCC TF725.A83 H46 2019 | DDC 388.4/60974985--dc23
LC record available at https://lccn.loc.gov/2019021623

CONTENTS

Acknowledgements v

Preface vii

Introduction viii

CHAPTER 1
Building a City by the Sea, 1854-1955 2

CHAPTER 2
The Horse Cars to Electric Cars: Local Transportation Lines, 1865-1900 8

CHAPTER 3
The Atlantic City & Suburban Traction Company, 1902-1929 22

CHAPTER 4
The Atlantic City & Shore Railroad Take Over Area Transit Operations, 1900-1910 42

CHAPTER 5
The Decade of Turmoil, 1910-1920 64

CHAPTER 6
The Return of Prosperity, 1920-1930 82

CHAPTER 7
A Decade of Difficulties 100

CHAPTER 8
Trolley or Bus? The Pennsylvania Railroad Decides, 1935-1940 118

CHAPTER 9
Wartime Challenges, 1940-1945 134

CHAPTER 10
The Pennsylvania Railroad Bows Out, 1944-1945 156

CHAPTER 11
The Atlantic City Transportation Company, 1946-1950 168

CHAPTER 12
The Final Years of Rail Service, 1950-1955 186

CONTENTS (cont.)

CHAPTER 13
Scenes from the Atlantic City & Shore..196

CHAPTER 14
A Selected Roster of Equipment 214

Bibliography 230

ACKNOWLEDGEMENTS

No book is possible without the aid of many people. I have been exceptionally fortunate to benefit from the assistance of a number of institutions and individuals.

Foremost among the former is the Hagley Museum and Library in Greenville, Delaware. Hagley contains an extensive collection of the records of the Pennsylvania Railroad, the Reading Company, and John McShain, all of which were immensely useful in writing this history. The staff at Hagley is outstanding, and I am indebted to archivist Christopher Baer, whose knowledge of railroads is profound. Also, very helpful was librarian Marjorie McNinch, whose skill and kindness were of great help.

Also indispensable in providing source material were the New Jersey Archives and the State Library in Trenton, and especially librarian Bette Marie Epstein. Both institutions house important documents that added greatly to my knowledge of the development and operation of the railroads and transportation lines in the Atlantic City region.

Useful as well was the collection in the library of the Electric City Trolley Museum in Scranton, Pennsylvania, and the assistance of its very capable and energetic curator, David Biles. In a similar manner, Edward Lybarger, archivist of the Pennsylvania Trolley Museum in Washington, Pennsylvania, provided access to the museum's excellent photograph collection. Not to be forgotten is the aid and assistance of the Motor Bus Society Library, ably administered by Tom Jones and the staff.

Other institutions which provided useful records and information were the Historical Society of Pennsylvania in Philadelphia, the University of Scranton Library, the Kemp Library at East Stroudsburg University, the Pennsylvania Archives in Harrisburg, and the library of the Railroad Museum of Pennsylvania in Strasburg. The staffs of these organizations extended every help and courtesy and made the writing of this history possible.

Many individuals provided help, advice, items from their collections, and other assistance that increased my knowledge and whose contributions, in various forms, were indispensable. Foremost among them is Jeffrey Marinoff of Ventnor City, New Jersey, who opened his extensive collection of documents and photographs to the author's use. Also extremely helpful and generous in providing me with numerous documents, photographs, and items from his large collection was John Nieveen of Ocean City, New Jersey. Both he and Jeffrey Marinoff suggested that I write this history, and their continuous help and encouragement over the span of many years gave needed incentive to finally complete the task.

Another major contributor to the work was the late LeRoy O. King, Jr. of Dallas, Texas. He possessed a vast knowledge of Atlantic City trolleys and an outstanding collection of documents and photographs, some taken by his father in the early years of the century.

Fred W. Schneider of Lancaster, Pennsylvania, a well known expert and author on electric traction, shared his extensive knowledge and provided his collection of photographs, timetables, and other items. A friend of many years, he helped select the photographs and write the captions. I am indeed grateful for his continuous assistance.

The late John D. Denney, Jr., of Columbia, Pennsylvania, was another knowledgeable and experienced writer and researcher who provided me with all his files and photographs on Atlantic City, including those he gathered many years ago. He was particularly helpful in offering his materials on the Atlantic City & Suburban Traction Company, and that chapter is much richer because of his contributions. His kindness and generosity will not be forgotten.

Among those who provided photographs was Richard Allman, M.D., of Villanova, Pennsylvania, who made the extensive David Cope collection available, as well as the work of other prominent photographers. He constantly encouraged me, and his assistance added much to the book. Also generous in sending photographs and information were F. Paul Kutta of West Chester, Pennsylvania; the late Ronald DeGraw of King of Prussia, Pennsylvania; Robert L. Long of Stratford, New Jersey; David Biles of Emmaus, Pennsylvania; the late John Brinckmann of Winchester, Virginia; the late George Krambles of Oak Park, Illinois; Craig Knox of Kennesaw, Georgia; James Kranefeld of Lansdowne, Pennsylvania; William D. Volkmer of Plantation, Florida, and Donald Wentzel of Millville, New Jersey. All these gentlemen were of great assistance in providing visual and other records of the trolleys.

The late Robert J. Wasche, a long-time employee of the Atlantic City Transportation Company, offered not only photographs but also information about the company and its operations. His contributions were of great value in telling the story of the ACTC years. Also generous with information and advice was Joseph M. Canfield of Weaverville, North Carolina.

Accompanying me on many of my visits to libraries and helping in making notes were several people. Prominent among them was John G. Muncie, of Pawleys Island, South Carolina, professor emeritus of history at East Stroudsburg University, and good friend and colleague for 35 years. His help made researching much quicker and more pleasant that it would have been, and his proofreading caught a number of errors. Helping too with research was Matthew Schenk of Allentown, Pennsylvania, a good friend and former student of the writer, and Christopher Muik, also of Allentown.

Wendella M. Ricker of Haverford Township, Pennsylvania, enabled the writer to arrange a meeting with Sister Pauline McShain, the daughter of John McShain, and Mary Tompkins Sowney, former secretary to Mr. McShain, both of Bryn Mawr, Pennsylvania. They expanded my perceptions of the man who guided the Atlantic City Transportation Company. Joseph F. Eid, Jr., of Brick, New Jersey, and the late Barker Gummere made available their excellent article on Atlantic City from their book, Streetcars of New Jersey, and the roster that appears here is largely their work. Their contributions made my work easier and I extend them my sincere thanks.

No railroad book is complete without maps. I am extremely fortunate to have the aid of Gary Kleinedler of Allentown, New Jersey, and Andrew Maginnis of Lansdale, Pennsylvania. The former drew the many excellent computer-generated maps found in these pages, and the latter provided his hand-drawn system and related maps. Their contributions have greatly enhanced the visual understanding the region's rail lines.

Frederick A. Kramer of Newtown Square, and Samuel James of Wynnewood, Pennsylvania, assisted in various ways, including invaluable advice and aid in selecting photographs and writing captions. Mervin E. Borgnis, who has written extensively on his memories of Atlantic City traction, added to my knowledge and understanding of the complex system. The late Richard G. Prince made available items from his collection.

The contributions and assistance offered by all these people and institutions were vital in the writing of this history, and simply put, it could not have been done without their generosity, help, and friendship. My thanks to them all. Any errors or omissions are my own, and I ask forgiveness from anyone I may have overlooked.

PREFACE

My curiosity and interest in the Atlantic City trolley lines began in the 1940s, when I accompanied my family on one-day trips to Atlantic City during the summer season. Lacking an automobile, we took the train from Philadelphia to the resort. Although a good part of the day was spent on the beach and on the Million Dollar Pier, we often managed to take a ride on one of the Brilliners, whose fare of seven cents was one-half cent cheaper than Philadelphia fares. Our visits continued as I grew older, and I always rode the Atlantic Avenue cars just for the enjoyment of it. My last ride was in November, 1955, shortly before the line's abandonment, while on leave from the Army.

As the years passed, I always retained an interest in Atlantic City, even though we now favored Ocean City for seashore visits. While writing a short history of the long-gone Ocean City Electric Railway, I met John Nieveen and his friend Jeffrey Marinoff, who urged me to write the history of the much larger Atlantic City system. They opened their collections to me, and I agreed, having no idea how complicated the story was and how long it would take me to write it.

As I undertook research, many questions occurred to me which I have tried to answer. How and when did these lines begin? Who owned them? How were they managed and operated? Were they profitable? How did they evolve over the years? How important were they to the region? Why were they eventually abandoned and converted to buses? How did the community regard them? How well did private enterprise firms meet the need for local transportation? In the following pages, I attempt to answer these and other questions and to draw some conclusions.

This is one of the most detailed account of local transit in the Atlantic City region to date, but many questions remain unanswered. Some of the files of the two operating companies are extant and in private hands, and their owners generously offered to make them available. I have used parts of them, and they have added significantly to my knowledge of the companies' affairs.

I have also relied heavily on the extensive Pennsylvania Railroad Collection, as well as the Reading Company Records, and the papers of John McShain, all housed in the Hagley Museum and Library. Archivists there have written research guides that enable the historian to examine them systematically and to extract vital information. The same can be said for the other archives and libraries mentioned in the acknowledgements.

Still largely unknown are the inner workings of the engineering and operating firm of Stern & Silverman. Most of what is known comes from references in the PRR Collection, but the company's papers were probably destroyed when the firm was dissolved. The company was closely held by a small group of investors and managed over its existence by William Stern, Isaac Silverman, and Leo Isenthal. For almost forty years, it controlled the Atlantic City & Shore Railroad, which ran the Atlantic City trolley lines. Although there were only two major lines, their history is surprisingly complex, and I have attempted to unravel it in the following pages.

Atlantic City and its environs are far different today from what they were a century or more ago. My hope is that residents, visitors, and all interested parties will gain a greater understanding and appreciation of the evolution of the transportation network, the problems it faced, its strengths and weaknesses, and its importance to the communities it served. It is also a study of local transportation when it was conducted by privately-owned, tax-paying corporations, which were interested in earning profits.

James N. J. Henwood
Newtown Square, Pennsylvania

A Geographic Note:
Atlantic City is situated on an axis of southwest to northeast. Many, but by no means all, of the sources signify directions by referring to the Atlantic Avenue Line as running east when heading to the Inlet and to the west when going to Longport. Others describe the Inlet section as the north, and Longport as the south. I have chosen the latter terminology.

INTRODUCTION

Nature has blessed New Jersey with a string of barrier islands along the Atlantic Coast that were magnets attracting residents and visitors from inland points to the salubrious air, crashing waves, sandy beaches, and the indefinable appeal of the ever-changing seashore. Southern New Jersey in particular grew rapidly after the arrival of the railroad in the mid-nineteenth century.

Of the many resorts that developed along the coast, Atlantic City, located on the northern part of Absecon Island, soon became the dominant one. Situated only 60 miles due east from Philadelphia and easily reached by competing railroads whose trains raced each other over the flat terrain, Atlantic City overshadowed the others and developed an urban and cosmopolitan atmosphere that attracted the masses. Never elite or high-toned, Atlantic City was a working man's resort that offered a variety of activities and pleasures that could be enjoyed by all.

As the city grew, it developed some less desirable characteristics too, including crime, municipal corruption, gambling, drinking, and other vices that appealed to some and repelled others. Regardless of their motivations, the crowds who descended on the city each summer needed local transportation to reach their hotels, boarding houses, restaurants, places of amusement, and of course the beach.

The Camden & Atlantic Railroad and its related land company laid out the city's street grid. The railroad initially extended from Pennsylvania Avenue to the Absecon Inlet, which it reached by a long, gentle curve to the west. In time, the tracks were extended over eight miles to the southern tip of the island, at the Great Egg Harbor Bay Inlet. A broad artery, named Atlantic Avenue, was developed on both sides of the tracks, which became the profitable Atlantic Avenue & Longport Division of the railroad, operated by electric cars after 1889. By virtue of its role as the original developer of the city, the railroad claimed ownership of its right-of-way, without the need for franchises from city officials. This caused resentment on the part of local politicians and the press who were often hostile to the railroad and its operations.

In 1905, the Philadelphia engineering and construction firm of Stern & Silverman decided to build an interurban electric line between Atlantic City and Ocean City, using mostly trackage rights on the Pennsylvania Railroad's Newfield Branch, between Atlantic City and Pleasantville, and on the Somers Point Branch, to that point on the Great Egg Harbor Bay, which would be crossed by a long trestle into Ocean City.

Stern & Silverman incorporated the Atlantic City & Shore Railroad to operate the route, which was advertised as the Shore Fast Line. Impressed by the Stern & Silverman management, the Pennsylvania Railroad leased its Atlantic Avenue & Longport trolley line to them in 1907. Both agreements would expire in December 1945. At that time, the Pennsylvania Railroad and Stern & Silverman sold their lines to the Atlantic City Transportation Company, which converted the Shore Fast Line to buses in January 1948, and the Atlantic Avenue & Longport Line to buses in December 1955.

The challenges, problems, achievements, and difficulties of operating this small but often busy transit system are described in the following pages. Some attention is given to the Atlantic City & Suburban Traction Company, a less successful enterprise which preceded and paralleled the Shore Fast Line for much of its route. The reader is invited to draw his own conclusions, which may differ from the author's, about the management and operations of these lines and to decide how successful private managements were in meeting the transportation needs of the region.

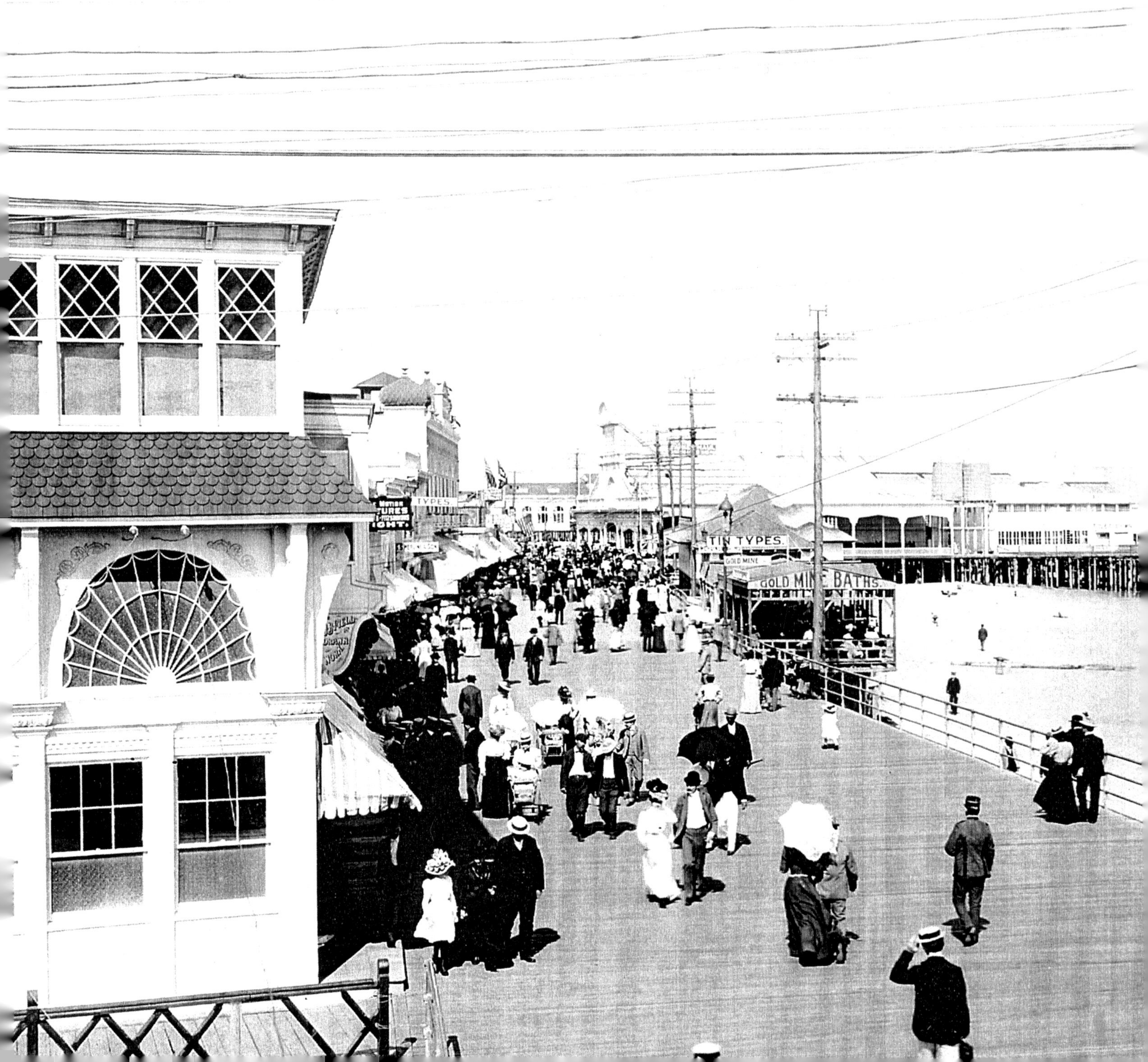
TYPES
TIN TYPES.
GOLD MINE
GOLD MINE BATHS.

CHAPTER ONE

Building a City by the Sea
1854-1885

Absecon Island

Stretching down the southern coast of New Jersey, like a string of pearls, are a series of barrier islands, separated from the mainland by narrow but fast-flowing channels. Virtually deserted and remote in the early nineteenth century, they in time grew into a chain of seaside towns attracting millions of visitors seeking relief from summer's heat and doldrums, even to the present day. Prominent among them was Absecon Island, the site of the future Atlantic City.

Located 55 miles southeast of Philadelphia, Absecon Island is about nine miles long, whose width varies from less than a mile to about two miles. It was called Absegami, or "little sea water," by the Lenape Indians, who occasionally visited it. The first settler, Jeremiah Leeds, built a cabin in 1783, but few followed him. In 1850, there were only seven houses on the island, but significant changes were about to occur.

The Pioneers

The population of the United States was slightly over 23 million people by mid-century; Pennsylvania had about 2.3 million, and New Jersey about half a million. National attention increasingly focused on a growing dispute over whether slavery be permitted to expand into the new territories west of the Missouri River. In southern New Jersey, a group of entrepreneurs was planning a railroad to the ocean. Their goal was to open the area to more rapid growth and lead to the establishment of a city by the sea they hoped would be a source of traffic and profits.

These developers were men who owned glass and iron factories and large tracts of land. They envisioned Absecon Island as a source of sand, as a port providing shorter access to Philadelphia than the 108-mile voyage up the Delaware River, and as a place with potential for recreation and development. Among them were Samuel Richards, the owner of a glass works near Berlin; Joseph Porter, who made glass at Waterford in Camden County; and a physician, Jonathan Pitney, of the village of Absecon in Atlantic County. They proposed to construct a railroad from Camden, reachable by ferries from Philadelphia, through Camden and Atlantic counties to Absecon Island, where they would establish a town to be named Atlantic City. After considerable difficulty, the group led by Dr. Pitney secured a charter from the state legislature on March 19, 1852, for the Camden and Atlantic Railroad (C&A). The company was organized on June 24, 1852, in Philadelphia. A civil engineer, Richard B. Osborne, and a contractor were hired to survey and build the road.

After overcoming numerous problems and skeptics, the line was completed in June 1854, except for a bridge over the Beach Thorofare, a narrow but deep channel separating Absecon Island from the mainland. A special train opened the line on July 1, 1854, and regular service began three days later. The same promoters who had organized the Camden and Atlantic Land Company in 1853 purchased the northern half of the island. These men also obtained a charter from the state creating the city of Atlantic City, effective May 1, 1854.

Facing Page: By the end of the nineteenth century, Atlantic City had become a popular summer resort and acquired a respectable number of permanent residents. The development of railroads in this area had made it possible. The twentieth century was just beginning when this view was snapped from the Luray Hotel. The new hotel didn't last long into the new century, being destroyed by fire in April 1902. LeRoy O. King, Jr. collection.

Above: Southern New Jersey at the time of Atlantic City's development.

James N.J. Henwood

Establishing a New City

Osborne laid out the street plan for the new town. Streets paralleling the Atlantic Ocean were named after oceans and seas, beginning with Pacific, then Atlantic (eventually to become the major commercial street), Arctic, Baltic, Mediterranean, Adriatic, Caspian, and Magellan. These streets ran roughly in a north-south direction, between the ocean and the Beach Thorofare, the irregular channel separating the island from the mainland. Cross streets, extending approximately from east to west, were named after states, grouped roughly geographically, from the New England states on the northern end of the island to the Mid-Atlantic states, the southern states, and then the western states, ending with Texas and California, which included the 27 states then in the federal union. The original limits of the city were from Absecon Inlet on the north to California Avenue. Atlantic Avenue, the principal street running down the island, was 100 feet wide, with 60 feet in the center reserved for the railroad right-of-way and 20 feet on each side for roadways.

The Camden and Atlantic Railroad in Atlantic City

The promoters hoped to develop the city as a seaport, a dream never to be realized. They planned to build five piers at Absecon Inlet, at the western end of Maine Avenue. The railroad line extended from the Thorofare bridge, diagonally across the town to Atlantic Avenue, near Pennsylvania Avenue, and then up Atlantic Avenue to Massachusetts Avenue. Soon the track was extended along a gentle westerly curve between Massachusetts Avenue and Maine Avenue, to end at Caspian Avenue at the Inlet. A long shed between North Carolina and South Carolina Avenues served as a depot. The track on Atlantic Avenue was extended by 1866 from Pennsylvania Avenue down to Georgia Avenue. By 1875, it was further extended to the southern tip of the island at Great Egg Harbor Inlet and Bay. The 100-foot width of the street was maintained for its entire length, and it soon became the site for stores, hotels, and commercial establishments.

To accommodate the growing number of summer riders who were taking one-day trips to the shore, the Sea View Hotel Company, a railroad subsidiary, built an Excursion House on Pacific Avenue at Missouri Avenue, at a cost of over $30,000. This, and subsequent similar structures, provided a place for day or weekend visitors to gather. They contained dining rooms, locker and bathing facilities, ballrooms, and amusements, and they helped to attract a growing number of visitors to the city.

As the appeal of the seaside resort spread, the city developed and gained more permanent residents. From 687 people in 1860, and 1,043 in 1870, the population reached 5,477 in 1880. Stimulating this expansion was the arrival of two more railroads that provided competition to the Camden and Atlantic, drawing more visitors to the city.

A Second Railroad Enters the City

By early 1876, some of the directors of the Camden and Atlantic Railroad became dissatisfied with the company's

Above: *To meet growing demand for local service in Atlantic City, Brill constructed car 6827 shown here, with a baggage door, useful for handling the large trunks of visitors to the shore who normally stayed a few weeks. The Camden & Atlantic would later be absorbed into the West Jersey & Seashore consolidation of the seashore railroads.* Robert L. Long collection

conservative management. Resigning, they incorporated a rival line, the Philadelphia and Atlantic City Railroad (P&AC) in March. To save money, the managers decided on a 3-foot, 6-inch gauge track. Construction of the 54.6-mile narrow gauge line was rapid. Ferry connections were established between Philadelphia and Bulson Street in Camden. The line approached the shore resort through the towns of Hammonton, Egg Harbor, and Pleasantville. It entered the city slightly to the south of the Camden and Atlantic line and built a station at Arkansas and Atlantic avenues. A short branch ran down Mississippi Avenue to the beach by 1878.

Cape May, on a route that carried it through Glassboro, Newfield, Vineland, and Millville. The PRR was taking an increasing interest in southern New Jersey, and in 1875 it gained control of the West Jersey Railroad through stock ownership. Anxious to penetrate the lucrative Atlantic City market, the PRR authorized West Jersey vice-president General William Sewell, a Civil War veteran and prominent South Jersey resident, to organize the West Jersey and Atlantic Railroad (WJ&A) in 1879. Essentially a branch of the West Jersey, the WJ&A extended from Newfield on the Cape May line 34 miles, through Richland, Mays

Above: A Camden & Atlantic horse car sits on a transfer table at the builder's shop. The letterboard near the roof displays the car's route, from the Inlet to the Excursion House at Missouri Avenue. Fred W. Schneider, III collection

Opened with great fanfare in 1877 and offering cheap fares, the P&AC soon developed financial problems and fell into bankruptcy. In 1883, it was purchased by the Philadelphia and Reading Railroad (P&R), standard-gauged, and began offering vigorous competition to the Camden and Atlantic.

A Third Railroad Arrives in Atlantic City

Still another railroad sought to tap the Atlantic City traffic. This one was sponsored by the West Jersey Railroad, controlled by the powerful Pennsylvania Railroad (PRR). The West Jersey was chartered in 1853 to build a line 81.5 miles from Camden to Cape May. Progress was slow, and not until 1863 did it reach

Landing, and Pleasantville, to Atlantic City, where it erected a station at New York Avenue. Opened in 1880, the company built a new Excursion House at Georgia Avenue and soon attracted considerable patronage.

At Pleasantville, Philadelphia and Atlantic City officials had organized the narrow-gauge Pleasantville and Ocean City Railroad in an effort to boost traffic. In 1880, a seven-mile branch to Somers Point was built. Located on Great Egg Harbor Bay, steamboats of the Atlantic Coast Steamboat Company carried passengers across the bay to the new Methodist resort town of Ocean City. The aggressive WJ&A also passed through Pleasantville and acquired control of the Somers Point line in 1882. It was standard-gauged and connected to the WJ&A, and thereafter operated as a part of that system. Soon, an intense rivalry for dominance in the Atlantic City market developed between the Pennsylvania Railroad lines and the Philadelphia and Reading.

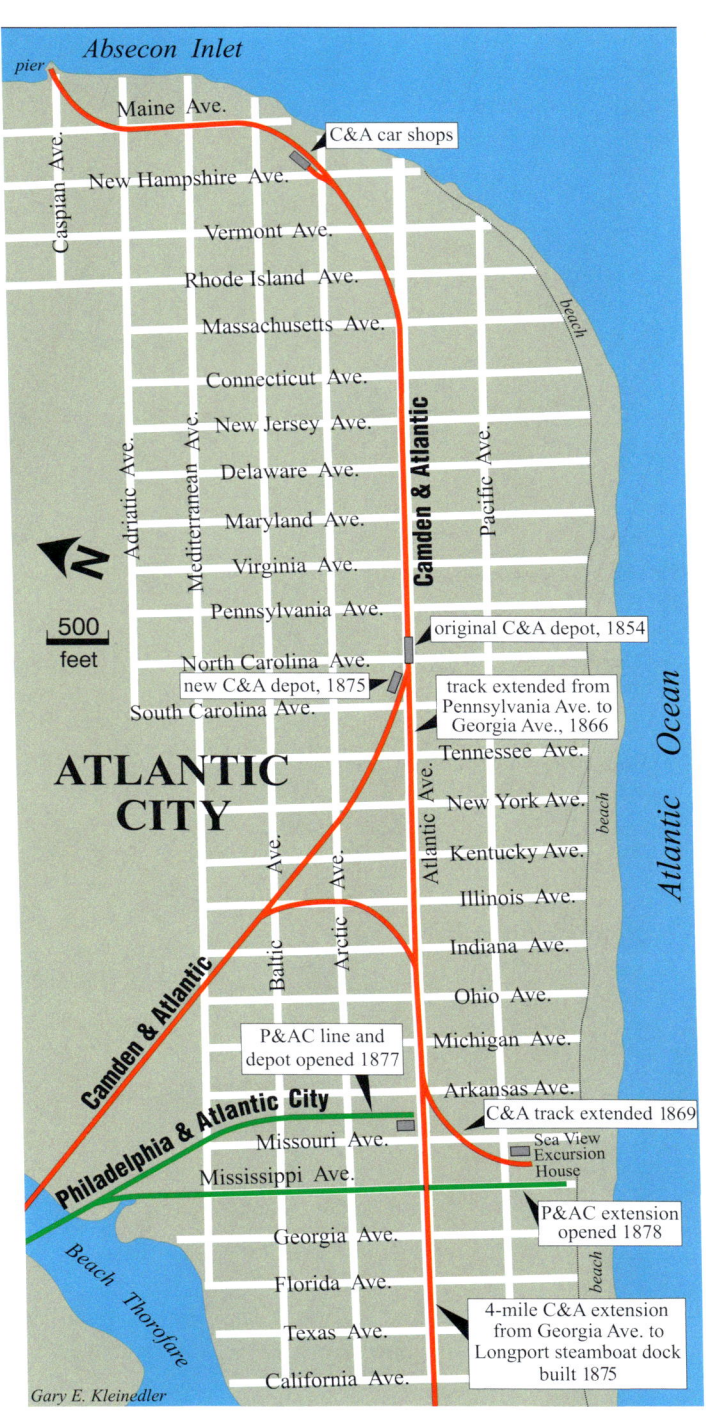

Above: *Railroads to Atlantic City in 1881.*

Facing Page Top: *A new coach for the West Jersey Railroad for probable use on the steam-powered dummy trains to Longport or Somers Point sits on a J.G. Brill flatcar ready for shipment. The flatcar still uses the link-and-pin method of coupling.* Historical Society of Pennsylvania, Fred W. Schneider, III collection

Facing Page Bottom: *Throngs of summer visitors promenade, as best they can, up and down the Boardwalk in a view from the early twentieth century.* Detroit Press Co. collection at the Library of Congress

CHAPTER ONE | 1854-1885

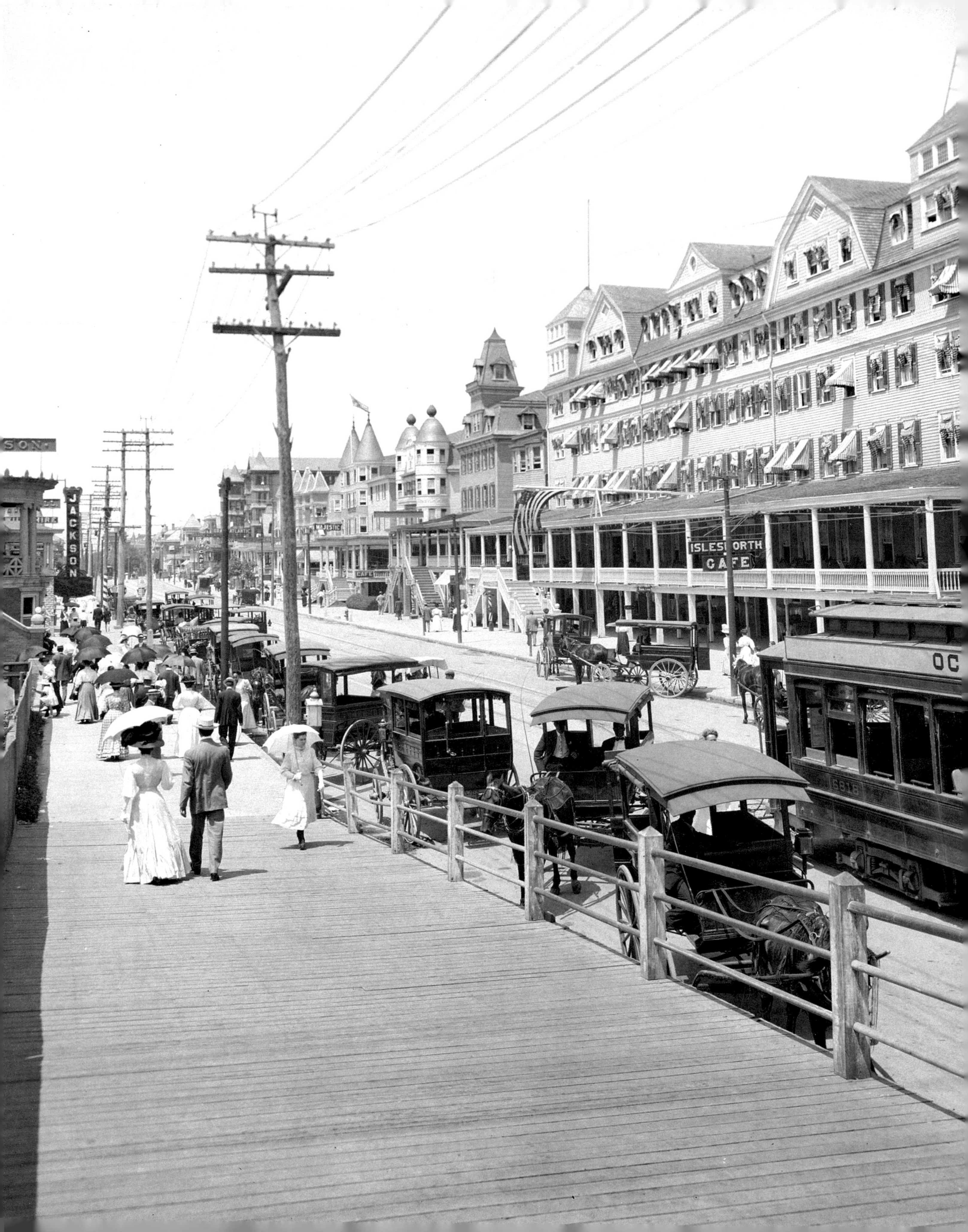
JACKSON
MAJESTIC
ISLESWORTH
CAFE

CHAPTER TWO

From Horse Cars to Electric Cars: Local Transportation Lines - *1865-1900*

The Need for Transportation: Roads, Canals, and Railroads

It is difficult for present-day readers, blessed with private automobiles and modern highways, to realize the primitive state of local transportation in the latter half of the nineteenth century. People of means could afford horses, stables, and carriages, as could some public officials and businessmen. It was possible to rent hacks and wagons, like modern taxicabs, by those able to afford them. But public transportation in the form of omnibuses, or large covered carriages, were found only in big cities. Elsewhere, people had to rely on friends or relatives to get about, or they simply walked.

Even those with conveyances faced difficulties. Outside of the cities, the condition of the roads was abysmal, and in towns such as Atlantic City the streets were largely unpaved and usually covered with loose stone or gravel. Mud and dust were common problems, depending on the season and the weather, and pollution from animals was always present.

The reason for the neglect of roads can be traced to the federal Constitution of 1787, which established a central government of specific, limited powers listed in the document. For the first half of our national existence a great political battle raged between those who interpreted the Constitution loosely and those who felt it must be read strictly as it was written. Since transportation was not mentioned in the document, it was often the focal point of the struggle between these two factions.

As the nation grew and pushed beyond the Ohio and Mississippi valleys, there were ever more forceful demands from the public for improved means of travel. With the federal government unable to act, except in a few exceptional instances, it fell to the states and private enterprise to do so. From this came the turnpike road movement and the era of canals. Turnpikes were privately-owned road companies, chartered by the state governments, usually with some form of graded or paved surface, such as macadam, that charged a toll for those wishing to use them. Canals were much more expensive to construct and maintain. These were sometimes built by private, state-chartered companies, or by the states themselves. The first great canal, the Erie, spanning New York between the Hudson River north of Albany and Lake Erie at Buffalo, touched off a mania of canal building in the eastern half of the country. Ironically, while the states and private companies were spending millions of tax dollars constructing canals, a new and far superior form of transportation appeared: the railroad.

Facing Page: A view down Virginia Avenue with a view of the Islesworth Gardens Hotel on the right. Atlantic City & Shore 6818, a 1904-05 Brill semi-convertible car, begins its journey to Ocean City. Date of the photo would have to be after July 4, 1907, when trolley service into Ocean City commenced. Detroit Press Co. Collection at the Library of Congress

This Page: This view of the Boardwalk dating to 1895 is quite a contrast to the view in the previous chapter. The weather in Atlantic City was seasonal and this affected the number of visitors to be expected. This could possibly be an early spring photograph, when tourists began to trickle back to the seaside resort. Detroit Press Co. collection at the Library of Congress

9

The railroad had many advantages over the turnpikes and canals, including cheaper construction costs, the ability to traverse difficult terrain, higher speeds, and all-weather operating ability. While some of the earlier carriers were built by state and local governments, private entrepreneurs, quick to recognize the potential for profits from a public desperate for better transportation facilities, soon took over. As railroads spread across the country, the canals and turnpikes languished and gradually went out of business. So superior were railroads that intercity road building virtually ceased. Most states let local jurisdictions, such as counties and cities, build and maintain highways, with the result that outside of larger cities, roads were neglected and generally in a deplorable condition.

Railroads linked cities and states, but they did not usually address local transportation needs. However, the underlying principle of rail travel, the inherent efficiency of an iron wheel on an iron rail, was recognized. Local entrepreneurs in large cities were soon gaining franchises, or licenses, to lay track in city streets and to operate cars on them pulled by horses or mules. While slow and crude, coupled with the concomitant health problems created from the droppings of the animals, the horse car gave town dwellers their first relatively cheap, available means of local transportation, and their popularity spread.

The Growth of the Seashore Region

Atlantic City was a town created and developed by railroads. Its tracks already lay in what was becoming its main commercial artery. A demand for local transportation developed as the city grew. After traveling from Camden to Atlantic City, the poet Walt Whitman recognized the impact of the railroad when he wrote in 1877:

> *The whole route has been literally made up and opened up to growth by the...railroad. That has furnished a spine or vertebrae to a section previously without any . . . [The railroad] sets in motion every indirect and many direct means of making a really substantial community...bringing information and light into a dark place, opening up trade, markets, purchases, newspapers, fashions, visitors...*

Population figures reflected the wisdom of Whitman's observation. Philadelphia counted 565,000 residents in 1860, reported 847,000 in 1880 and 1,294,000 in 1900. New Jersey's population jumped from 672,000 in 1860 to over 1,883,000 in 1900, increasing by 25 percent or more each decade. The four coastal counties of the state doubled their population between 1850 and 1885. Atlantic County had 14,000 people in 1870 and over 46,000 thirty years later. Atlantic City claimed 5,477 in 1880, 13,055 in 1890, and 27,838 in 1900, a phenomenal rate of growth. Railroads facilitated this population increase, and during this period, their mileage in the state climbed from 560 in 1860 to 2,257 in 1900.

Above: *Railroads serving Atlantic City by 1881.*

The Introduction of Horse Car Service

The railroad offered quick and cheap access into the new resort, stimulating an increasing need for local public transportation within the city. Recognizing the potential for profit, two brothers from Absecon, Samuel and John Cordery, received a franchise from the Camden and Atlantic (C&A) in 1865 to run horse cars along Atlantic Avenue over the railroad tracks from South Carolina

Avenue to the Inlet. They purchased two cars and four horses; each man operated one of the vehicles, serving as conductor and driver.

Whether the summer service was profitable is impossible to say, but it was short-lived. The operation was taken over by William G. Bartlett, a Philadelphia merchant, who substituted mules for the horses. In the winter, the mules were turned loose in the sand dunes of lower Absecon Island where a resident recalled, "in the spring they came up looking fine." Apparently, the railroad was dissatisfied with the arrangement, for in 1869 it terminated the lease and took over the operation itself. Bartlett, however, remained actively involved in transit ventures on the island for many years. When the Sea View Excursion House opened at Pacific and Missouri Avenues in the same year, a connection was built from the C&A line into the city, through Illinois Avenue to Atlantic Avenue, and then to the beach at Missouri Avenue, permitting trains to reach that facility directly. The horse cars down Atlantic Avenue were also extended to the Excursion House.

The Atlantic City Passenger Railroad

Attracted by the possibilities of making money, a group of local and Philadelphia investors was granted a charter by the General Assembly of New Jersey on February 10, 1869. The bill, titled "An Act to Incorporate the Atlantic City Passenger Railroad Company," authorized the company, with the consent of the Common Council of Atlantic City, to construct a line and begin operations. Among the entrepreneurs were Ezra J. and William G. Bartlett. Ezra was a partner in the firm of Bartlett and Shepherd, Ship Chandlers and Grocers, of 304 North Front Street in Philadelphia, while William resided in Atlantic City. The company was authorized to sell $100,000 in stock, but only $25,000 in shares was issued.

The new company planned to build a line from the Inlet to Missouri Avenue via Pacific Avenue, which paralleled Atlantic Avenue and which was a block closer to the ocean. In 1874, the City Council authorized the building of a line along Atlantic Avenue to Ohio Avenue, and then by Pacific Avenue the remaining three blocks to the Excursion House at Missouri Avenue. Knowing the C&A would bitterly oppose this intrusion into their Atlantic Avenue domain, the company attempted to lay a track on the seven blocks between Massachusetts and North Carolina Avenues. But A. K. Hay, president of the C&A, was informed of the work and quickly obtained a court injunction from the chancellor to halt the construction, and it was never completed.

Except for the required annual meetings and occasional changes

Above: LeRoy O. King, Sr. captured car 497830 on film in the early twentieth century. Apparently a former horse car, it has been reduced to maintenance of way service and given a number in the Pennsylvania Railroad's six-digit category for such equipment. LeRoy O. King, Sr. photo, LeRoy O. King, Jr. collection

James N.J. Henwood

in the membership of the board of directors, nothing further was attempted until 1900, when on August 6, William G. Bartlett, the president, formally accepted in the name of the company an ordinance passed by the borough council of Pleasantville granting it a franchise to build and operate an electric trolley line along the Shore Road in that town. Evidently, it was impossible to raise the capital to do this; in its 1901 report to the state, the amount of stock outstanding was noted as $1,950, a sharp reduction from the $25,000 listed in previous years. After 1903, there is no further record of the company's existence.

The C&A Horse Car Department

During the period when the Atlantic City Passenger Railroad was struggling to construct its line, the Camden & Atlantic formally decided to recognize it was engaged in local transportation. In the spring of 1875, it established the Atlantic City Horse Car Department. Service was operated during the summer season, with four cars and 16 mules, costing $5,225. A total of $7,286 was collected in fares that apparently covered at least some of the cost of operations. More cars were purchased, creating a fleet of five closed and three open cars in 1876. Sharing the same tracks as the steam trains was problematic at best, causing erratic service and frequent delays. About the same time, the C&A stopped running most trains to the Inlet and built a new, enlarged station on private ground at South Carolina Avenue. The original station structure in the middle of Atlantic Avenue was moved to New Hampshire Avenue where it served as a stable and barn for the Horse Car Department. In 1877, an additional track was constructed from

Right: *Early Atlantic City horse car railroads, 1865-1876.*

Below: *Steam dummy 44 with a two-car train consisting of open coach 6861 and closed coach 6859 on the West Jersey & Seashore Railroad's Somers Point branch. Dummy locomotives were given a passenger car-like shroud to make them seem less threatening and more acceptable to nearby property owners. Railways to Yesterday Library photo, Fred W. Schneider, III collection*

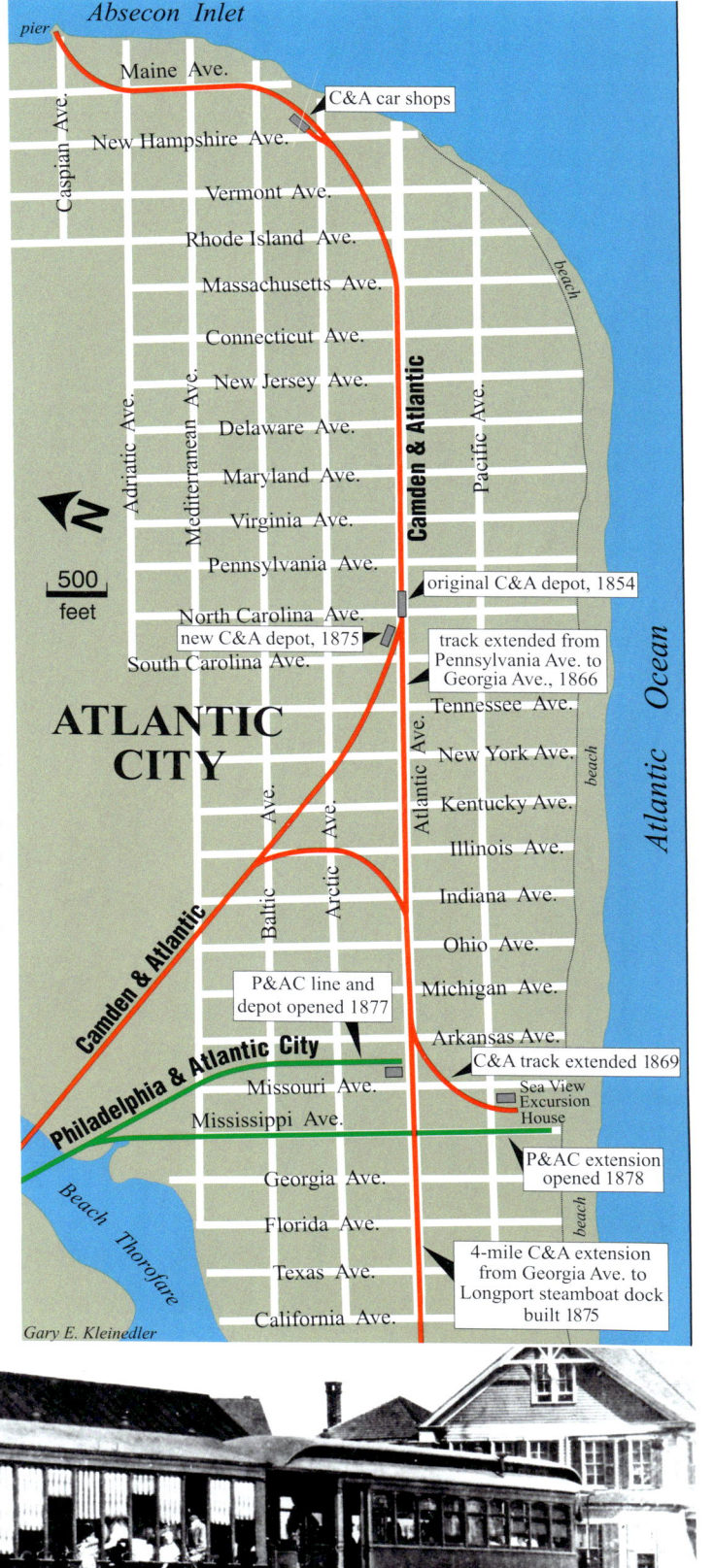

Massachusetts to Pennsylvania avenues, a distance of six blocks. The main track had been extended south to Georgia Avenue earlier.

The South Atlantic City Branch

Well aware that the development and sale of land was highly profitable, the directors of the C&A Railroad and its associated land company had received legislative approval in 1861 to build a branch railroad down the island from the main tracks at South Carolina Avenue to its southern tip at Great Egg Harbor Inlet. Not until its meeting of September 25, 1875, did the board of directors act on this authority. They adopted a map of the branch railroad that had been filed with the New Jersey secretary of state, and they planned to operate the extension with small steam locomotives, commonly called "dummies." These were regular steam engines covered with a passenger car type body placed over the boiler that attempted to disguise the machine and make it appear less threatening to pedestrians and horses. In 1877, the C&A began to grade a roadbed and lay track south on Atlantic Avenue.

Residents along Atlantic Avenue strongly opposed more noisy steam trains in the middle of the resort's main street, as did Mayor W. Wright. The city attempted to block the railroad by passing ordinances which called for a $100 fine for each car operated, and another which threatened employees with a $50 fine and a 20-day jail term. The railroad argued it had legal authority, granted in 1861, to extend its tracks, while the city claimed it controlled the avenue and that the railroad was "a public nuisance." The company took the city to court, and after much wrangling, a settlement was reached in 1881. Under its terms, which were specified in a city ordinance, the railroad was granted the right to build and operate its line on the whole length of Atlantic Avenue. The company promised to extend its tracks to the southern boundary of the city and to

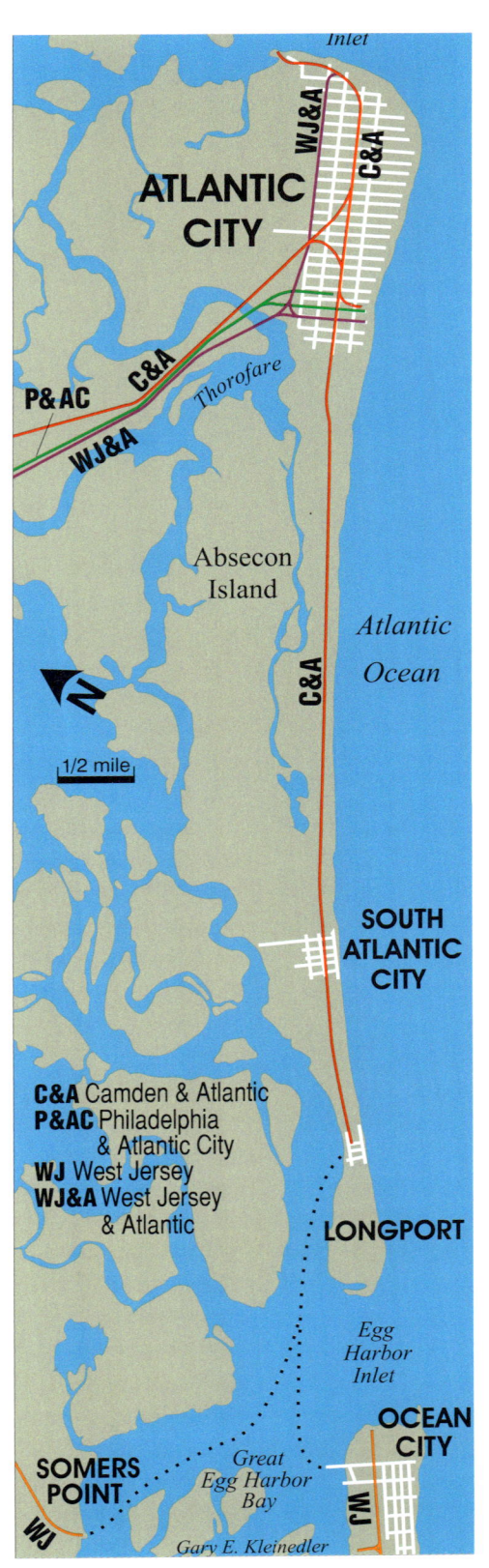

Left: Absecon Island railroads

keep them in good condition. They were to be planked or paved between the rails and immediately outside of them. In addition, the company agreed to provide sand and gravel, at the city's request, to cover Atlantic Avenue from curb to curb. The railroad also agreed to pay an annual fee of $50 for each horse car. Finally, the city in turn granted the C&A a transportation monopoly on Atlantic Avenue.

Basically, the city was forced to recognize that legally it could not nullify the railroad's rights on Atlantic Avenue south of California Avenue, since it was owned by the C&A. The city's claims to control Atlantic Avenue were also questionable. The fact that the city's existence was a direct result of the arrival of the railroad and depended on it for its prosperity also strengthened the company's hand.

Development of Lower Absecon Island

Free at last, at least for the time being, of municipal attempts to control its property, the C&A resumed its expansion down Absecon Island. In 1881, the track was extended 4.6 miles from Florida Avenue through the future town of Ventnor to South Atlantic City (later called Margate). At the time part of Egg Harbor Township, the area was mostly sand dunes, pine trees, bayberry bushes, and a few houses. To attract potential buyers, a Philadelphia real estate promoter, James V. Lafferty, built a giant wooden and tin elephant, later named "Lucy," which still stands (in a different location). Regular steam trains began operation, only on Sundays, on December 18, 1881. By 1883, they ran all year.

With the advent of the railroad, development followed. In 1884, the railroad laid out the street plot in Margate. At the same time, the tracks were extended another 1.3 miles to the village of Longport. A final half-mile of track was built in 1888, including a loop near the inlet into Great Egg Harbor Bay. In the same year, the C&A Land Company conveyed two blocks fronting on Atlantic

Avenue at Portland Avenue to the railroad company, which built a station there. The board of directors of the land company named the area Ventnor in 1889, after a similar seaside resort on the Isle of Wight in England. In 1903, the town was separated from Egg Harbor Township and incorporated as a city. It became primarily a residential community, with a boardwalk free of commercial establishments, and with recreational facilities available. South Atlantic City was renamed Margate and incorporated in 1897. It too grew rapidly with rail service available.

The southern tip of Absecon Island had been acquired in 1857 by James Long, who did nothing with it. Around 1882, he sold it to friend and promoter, M. Simpson McCullough, who named it Longport in honor of his friend, and because of its potential as a port, with considerable frontage on an arm of Great Egg Harbor Bay. The arrival of the railroad stimulated growth, and in 1889 it was incorporated as a borough and became a residential area.

The Pennsylvania Railroad Increases in Presence

A momentous event occurred in 1883, when the powerful Pennsylvania Railroad gained control of the Camden and Atlantic. The PRR already controlled the West Jersey Railroad and its affiliated West Jersey and Atlantic, which had reached Atlantic City in 1879, via Newfield and Pleasantville. The rapid growth of the seashore resort and the potential for more profits from freight and passenger trains attracted the attention of PRR executives under the presidency of George B. Roberts. His administration, from 1880 to 1897, was marked by continued growth and modernization of facilities, leading the carrier to immodestly call itself "the Standard Railroad of the World." The direct and shorter C&A route from Camden to Atlantic City gave the PRR a superior line and eliminated competition, which was always desirable to managers of any enterprise. From this time forward, the PRR was to be a major player in Atlantic City transportation affairs, a situation made stronger by the popularity of the resort and its proximity to the railroad's headquarters in the new Broad Street Station in Philadelphia.

The Electric Railway Arrives

Another profound change took place in the 1880s: the invention of a practical electric railway car. For some time, a number of inventors had been experimenting for a way to apply the newly developed energy force of electricity to traction, which they felt would be superior to steam or animal power. The invention of the dynamo, or generator, made such a quest more intense. The principle of electric traction was recognized, but the practical difficulties of applying an electric motor to a moving locomotive or car were daunting. A number of ingenious men made contributions, including Belgian-born Charles J. van Depoele, who in 1886 built a car powered by a "traveler" or "troller," which ran along overhead wires and sent energy via a cable to a motor on the car's platform. He electrified a horse car line in Montgomery, Alabama, and in November of the same year he successfully energized the Scranton Suburban Railway's line to Green Ridge Street. Although the lines were plagued with problems, he had shown that an electric railway could effectively operate.

The Pennsylvania Railroad Decides on Electric Traction

The PRR management was alert to the advantages and possibilities of electrifying the C&A's Atlantic Avenue horse car line. Considerable discussion ensued, in the press and among city officials, concerning the merits and dangers of this new and mostly unknown form of energy. Thomas A. Edison had perfected the electric light in 1879 and was already contracting to build power plants to provide illumination of city streets and buildings. In 1882, Atlantic City began the process of installing electric street lights. Power contained within wires was one thing, but the idea of having railway cars propelled by this invisible but potent force alarmed many people. Some felt stepping on the rails would result in electrocution, and others feared the cars would emit sparks and electrical discharges. Still others were concerned about the placement of poles to support the overhead wires.

To help settle the matter, Aaron O. Dayton, the superintendent of the West Jersey Railroad and the Camden and Atlantic Railroad, both PRR properties, arranged a trip to Scranton, Pennsylvania, to inspect the van Depoele trolley line running there. Early in May, 1888, a group of 16 people, including the mayor, some members of the city council, and other officials left Atlantic City in a private car. After arrival in Camden and an overnight stay in a Philadelphia hotel, they resumed their trip to Scranton the next morning, via Trenton, the Belvidere-Delaware line, and the Lackawanna Railroad, arriving in the late afternoon. After dinner, the party rode the four-mile Scranton Suburban line and inspected the poles, wires, and power plant. The local citizens spoke highly of the line and reported there were no problems with the wires or service. Suitably impressed, the party returned to Atlantic City the next day.

In the following spring and summer, much discussion raged about the possibilities of electrification. So tense were the emotions on the question that the editor of the Journal, a supporter of the idea, was physically assaulted on the street by a prominent hotel owner, who opposed the concept. In July, the *Journal* published an editorial pointing out that the PRR was willing to spend over $50,000 for the electrical plant and other improvements, and that electric cars could be extended to Longport. The city council deliberated through the fall, and finally, in December, it passed an ordinance giving the C&A the right to erect poles and wires on Atlantic Avenue.

The next question was where to place the poles: in the center of the street or along the sides. Once again Superintendent Dayton arranged a private car junket for city officials, this time to Washington, D.C., to inspect the newly electrified New York Avenue line. The poles in town were iron and were located in the middle of the street, with arms extending over both tracks carrying the wires. Every other pole had a cluster of incandescent lights at the top. In the outskirts, wooden poles were placed along the sidewalks, which supported lateral span wires. The officials were impressed, and on returning to Atlantic City, the council's street committee specified that iron poles be placed in the center of briefly for Thomas A. Edison and then formed his own company in 1884. The next year he developed a constant speed motor and a new method of attaching it to a railway car truck, thereby solving a problem which had bedeviled inventors up to that point. In 1888, he successfully electrified the new Richmond, Virginia, Union Passenger Railway, which attracted much attention, including that of executives of the PRR.

Sprague and his engineers promptly got to work. Iron poles were erected and silicon bronze wire was hung. The rails were bonded, to provide a route for the electricity to return to the

Above: It is August 1889 and a group of men and a boy have gathered on Atlantic Avenue to inspect new electric streetcar 808. Standards of dress were more rigid at this time as only the boy seems comfortably attired for the summer heat. LeRoy O. King, Jr. collection

Atlantic Avenue. Superintendent Dayton diplomatically accepted this demand, saying the company was not concerned with cost but with "practicability, utility, and acceptability."

Frank J. Sprague Electrifies the Railway

The next step was to hire someone to equip the horse car line for electric operation. Wisely, PRR officials turned to a brilliant engineer, Frank Julian Sprague, to undertake the task. Born in Connecticut in 1857, with a natural talent for mathematics and science, he attended the Naval Academy in Annapolis, served on the *U.S.S. Richmond*, experimented with arc lights, and became interested in electric traction after riding on the smoky, steam-powered London Underground. After leaving the navy, he worked

power house. Arrangements were made with the Electric Light Company of Atlantic City to provide temporarily electric power. Six of the mule cars were fitted with two, 15 horsepower Sprague motors, sufficient to run at a speed of 15 miles per hour and to pull two trailing cars.

Nothing was accomplished easily in Atlantic City, and another contentious dispute arose with the city. The municipally-appointed street committee had ordered the new iron poles placed in the center of the street. An agreement to this effect was signed with the railroad in December, 1888. However, in March, 1889, the city council demanded the C&A light Atlantic Avenue in return for permission to place the poles, claiming that city ordinances required lights on obstructions in the street. PRR

Above: An early single-truck electric car pulls a trailer on Atlantic Avenue in the 1890s. No passengers are in sight, so this must have been a special run. Left-hand operation on Atlantic Avenue was common at the time. LeRoy O. King, Jr. collection

managers rejected this demand, with Superintendent Dayton stating, "We are not going into the electric lighting business." The council then took the case to the chancery court in Camden, while Sprague's forces continued to erect the poles.

The case was argued before vice-chancellor Bird early in April, 1889. The city demanded an injunction to stop the work, saying the street committee signed the original agreement on a Sunday, making it void, as the statues of the day prohibited "all worldly employment and business" on the Sabbath. Peter Voorhees, attorney for the railroad, dismissed these arguments and added that the railroad "virtually owned Atlantic Avenue as a right-of-way" and did not need council's permission, which the C&A sought "only as a matter of courtesy and formality." The vice-chancellor took the case under advisement, but he did not issue an injunction and the pole placement went on, down to Kentucky Avenue.

By April 24, 1889, all was in readiness, and at 3:30 P.M., the first car rolled out of the New Hampshire Avenue barn, carrying a party of dignitaries, including Frank Sprague, George Roberts, president of the PRR, General William J. Sewell, president of the West Jersey & Atlantic, Superintendent Aaron O. Dayton, and other officials. The cars had incandescent lights in the interior and one on each end platform. Other than a startled horse which ran away with its wagon, everything went well. Free rides were offered for the rest of the day, and hundreds took advantage of the opportunity. The new electric cars were a grand success.

The PRR immediately equipped 12 open cars with 16 crosswise seats, patterned after cars in service in Washington. A follow-up order was made for ten additional cars. Visitors and various street railway managers came to enjoy a ride. That summer every car was pressed into service to handle the crowds, and reportedly not one trip was missed; the new Sprague motors worked very well. The cars were carrying up to 100 people at a time; counting the trailers, 200 people were hauled. A contract was given to A. Randolph of Bridgeton to construct a power plant at New York Avenue, which was completed in 30 days. Electric wires were extended to Albany Avenue, where Pacific Avenue ended and Atlantic Avenue veered diagonally one block toward the ocean. A loop was constructed here, permitting the cars to turn back to the Inlet, as wire had been extended to that point as well. The fare was a rather high ten cents, which was reduced to five cents in 1891. The new line was no doubt profitable; clearly, the PRR made no mistake when it invested almost $71,000 in the electrification project.

The PRR Makes More Improvements

A number of other changes were underway at the same time. In 1888, regular steam train service to Longport, which had begun

CHAPTER TWO | 1865-1900

Left: Atlantic City railroads, 1900

in 1884, was withdrawn and replaced by two small steam dummy locomotives, numbered 519 and 520, which were built by the Baldwin Locomotive Works in Philadelphia. Twelve lightweight passenger cars, built by the J. G. Brill Company of Philadelphia, were purchased, to be pulled by the dummy locomotives. At the Longport loop, a small pier and pavilion were erected to provide entertainment and other facilities for relaxation. A third steam dummy locomotive arrived from Baldwin in 1892.

For the steam dummy service, a new station and a small yard were built at Tennessee Avenue, one block south of the C&A's main station at South Carolina Avenue. The dummy trains ran between Tennessee Avenue and Longport and stopped only at Arkansas Avenue, Chelsea, Albany Avenue, Halfway House, Ventnor, South Atlantic City, Lennig, and Longport. The fare was a very high 20 cents. C&A freight trains continued to run as needed, mostly at night.

Another improvement in 1889 was the opening of a new Sea View Excursion House, built on a large tract of land off Atlantic Avenue south of Albany Avenue. Intended for year-round use, the five buildings contained dance floors, restaurants, amusements, bathing facilities, and other features. They were surrounded by flower beds and lawns. The aim of the construction was to develop this area of the city and further enrich the PRR by giving visitors a pleasant destination that would require them to ride the company's new electric cars. Almost a mile of second track was laid from California to Albany Avenues, and service was extended to that point in June. The old excursion house at Missouri Avenue was closed.

Soon after the Sea View House opened, Superintendent Aaron Dayton of the C&A, who must have wondered by this time whether he was a railroad manager or a party host, arranged another junket for city officials, newspaper men, and various dignitaries. In early July, a special steam dummy train carried the group to Albany Avenue to inspect the new excursion house. Quite impressed, they proceeded to Longport, where they boarded the "smart little steamer *Ocean City*" and sailed across Great Egg Harbor Bay to Somers Point, on the mainland. Here they were entertained and fed at the Bradford House and enjoyed "the superb scenery and view of the bay," before returning to Atlantic City. These efforts by the PRR to popularize the new excursion house ultimately failed. People preferred the uptown location and attractions, and the Sea View House was closed and sold for other uses in 1899.

Still one more improvement in 1889 was the construction of the Chelsea Branch by the C&A. The new line, about 1.2 miles long, left the C&A main tracks as soon as they crossed the Thorofare drawbridge. It ran through an undeveloped section of the city, on the bay side, called Chelsea, to a junction with the Atlantic Avenue line near Albany Avenue, where a small yard was built. The aim was to carry steam trains to the new Sea View Excursion House without running on Atlantic Avenue. It would

17

James N.J. Henwood

Above: Former horse car 6815, now equipped with motors, moves up unpaved Atlantic Avenue in a scene recorded around 1900. The iron poles erected by Frank Sprague with their decorated cross arms would last for the life of the trolley line. A flat car containing workers occupies the adjacent track, while horse-drawn wagons and carriages provide the other means of transportation. Car 6815 would be scrapped in 1905. LeRoy O. King, Jr. collection

also be used by freight trains, and it would stimulate development of that part of the city.

By this time, the streetcar service was operating year-round, but the date when this began is unknown. Evidently, in periods of light traffic, the PRR tried to economize by running cars with only one man, a practice that had been followed with the smaller horse cars. Since passengers boarded the cars on the back platform, the motorman had to go into the car to collect fares, letting the car run itself. Even though the tracks were open and unpaved, the dangers were obvious. The *Journal*, which was supportive of the electric cars, rebuked the company, noting the PRR admitted that the streetcars, in proportion to the capital invested, paid better than any other investments the railroad had in the city. The editor stated emphatically the company "could well afford to have conductors." Whether because of this public scolding or because of practical reasons, two-man cars became standard.

When first introduced, the electric cars were heated by coal stoves, a cumbersome and inefficient method. In 1895, an electric heating system was installed on one car. The device worked so well that by 1898 all cars were equipped with these heaters.

Trolleys to Longport

As riding increased, the PRR recognized the steam dummy trains were unsuitable for urban service. In 1893, the entire South Atlantic City branch, from Albany Avenue to Longport, was double-tracked and electrified. Some Longport cars began their journey at the Tennessee Avenue station, where they connected with C&A trains. The extended trolley line gave a splendid view of the ocean, with the surf crashing onto the white sandy beaches. Sometimes, as in 1892, depending on the currents and storms at sea, thousands of dead clams and mussels would wash up along the tracks, causing a terrible smell. Offsetting this, however, was the sight of hundreds of sea gulls feasting on the shell fish. Eventually, workers would have to remove the remains by the wagon load. But even this activity, and the ocean itself, attracted visitors to the Longport line. Except for a few hotels and dance halls, population densities were still low in the down beach communities, so pleasure riding and sightseeing were the mainstay of the line.

In an effort to attract more sightseers and visitors, in 1894, the PRR decided to inaugurate steamboat service on Great Egg Harbor Bay, linking Longport with Somers Point and Ocean City. The latter was a smaller, more subdued resort on Peck's Beach, the next barrier island south of Absecon Island. Contracts were let for three steamboats, with a length of 70 feet and a displacement of 20 tons. In 1896, a 50 by 36-foot extension improved the Longport

CHAPTER TWO | *1865-1900*

Above: A postcard night view reveals Camden & Atlantic motor car 6855 and a trailer bound for Longport. The ultimate destination, for those who chose to go there, was Ocean City, reached by the Pennsylvania Railroad steamboats which plied the waters of the Great Egg Harbor Bay to Longport, Somers Point, and Ocean City. , Fred W. Schneider, III collection

wharf. A freight house, ticket office, and restaurant were added, adjacent to the trolley loop. Service began in late June, 1895, with the steamers *Avalon, Longport,* and *Somers Point*. In Ocean City, about 2.75 miles distant, the boats called at the 2nd Street wharf, where connections were made with the cars of the new Ocean City Electric Railway. Their cars carried visitors to the central part of town at 8th Street. The boats were coaled and laid over at the Ocean City pier. On Sundays, passengers faced a long walk, or they returned to Longport on the steamer, since the Ocean City cars did not run on that day. The city's Methodist founders frowned on

Above: The West Jersey & Seashore steam launch Longport floats serenely on the waters of the Great Egg Harbor Bay off what appears to be the Second Street Wharf in Ocean City. Steamboat service between Longport and Ocean City began in 1896 with the fleet ultimately expanded to five vessels. James Kranefeld collection

commercial activities on the Sabbath. Nonetheless, the line was busy enough to justify the addition of another steamer in 1900, the *Ocean City*, which was slightly larger than her sister vessels.

Shore visitors who planned an extended stay of a week or longer often arrived with large trunks and considerable baggage. To service them, the C&A in 1893 converted a former dummy car into combination passenger-baggage car 6826, which ran on a regular schedule from Tennessee Avenue to Longport. It was capable of carrying up to 20 trunks. Brill built a similar car, 6827, in 1895 which also served the boarding houses and hotels. By this time, a loop had been installed at the Portland Avenue station in Ventnor, and the fare zone was extended from Jackson Avenue in Atlantic City to Savannah Avenue (later Douglas Avenue) in South Atlantic City (Margate).

The Formation of the West Jersey and Seashore Railroad

A major reorganization of its New Jersey properties was undertaken by the PRR on May 4, 1896, when the West Jersey Railroad, the West Jersey and Atlantic, the Camden and Atlantic, the Chelsea Branch Railroad, and two small lines were merged into the new West Jersey and Seashore Railroad (WJ&S). This simplified the corporate structure and placed the PRR in a better position to compete with its rival, the Philadelphia and Reading's Atlantic City Railroad. At the time, the new company rostered 43 motor cars and 19 trailers on its trolley lines.

The Atlantic City Street Railway Company

At the same time the PRR was evaluating its Atlantic City holdings, a would-be competitor appeared. Probably attracted by the heavy loads carried by the Atlantic Avenue cars, a group of local investors, led by Levi C. Allerton, received a charter on July 14, 1894, for the Atlantic City Street Railway Company, valid for 99 years. The company was capitalized at $100,000, and the seven original directors, a majority of whom had to be residents of Atlantic City, pledged the entire amount, although it is unlikely they actually paid for it. Allerton subscribed for 1,598 shares himself. The company hoped to build a line on South Carolina Avenue from the Boardwalk to Arctic Avenue, which paralleled Atlantic Avenue one block to the west. It would extend along Arctic to Rhode Island Avenue, nine blocks north of South Carolina, and then go west on Rhode Island into an undeveloped part of the city at Magellan Avenue, before turning north again to a terminus at Absecon Inlet. The total distance was about two miles. Following New Jersey law, the sum of $4,000 was forwarded to the state for the privilege of building the line.

Negotiations proceeded slowly with city officials, and not until October 1899, was an ordinance approved by the city council authorizing construction, but the mayor refused to sign it. The following year the town council of the borough of Absecon on the mainland, which was anxious to have an electric railway, approved an ordinance favoring the line. But without the power to build in Atlantic City, it was of little value. In 1902, another company, the Atlantic City and Suburban Traction Company, did receive approval to build a line from Atlantic City to Absecon, via Pleasantville. This so discouraged Allerton and his friends that they sold their interests to PRR executives, led by Samuel Rea, the president of the PRR. Whether the PRR officials intended actually to build such a line is unknown, but it is more likely they were eliminating potential competition to the existing Atlantic Avenue line. In June, 1906, the Atlantic City Street Railway Company

Above: West Jersey & Shore combine 6879 poses for its builder's photo at the Brill plant in 1901. Robert Lung Collection

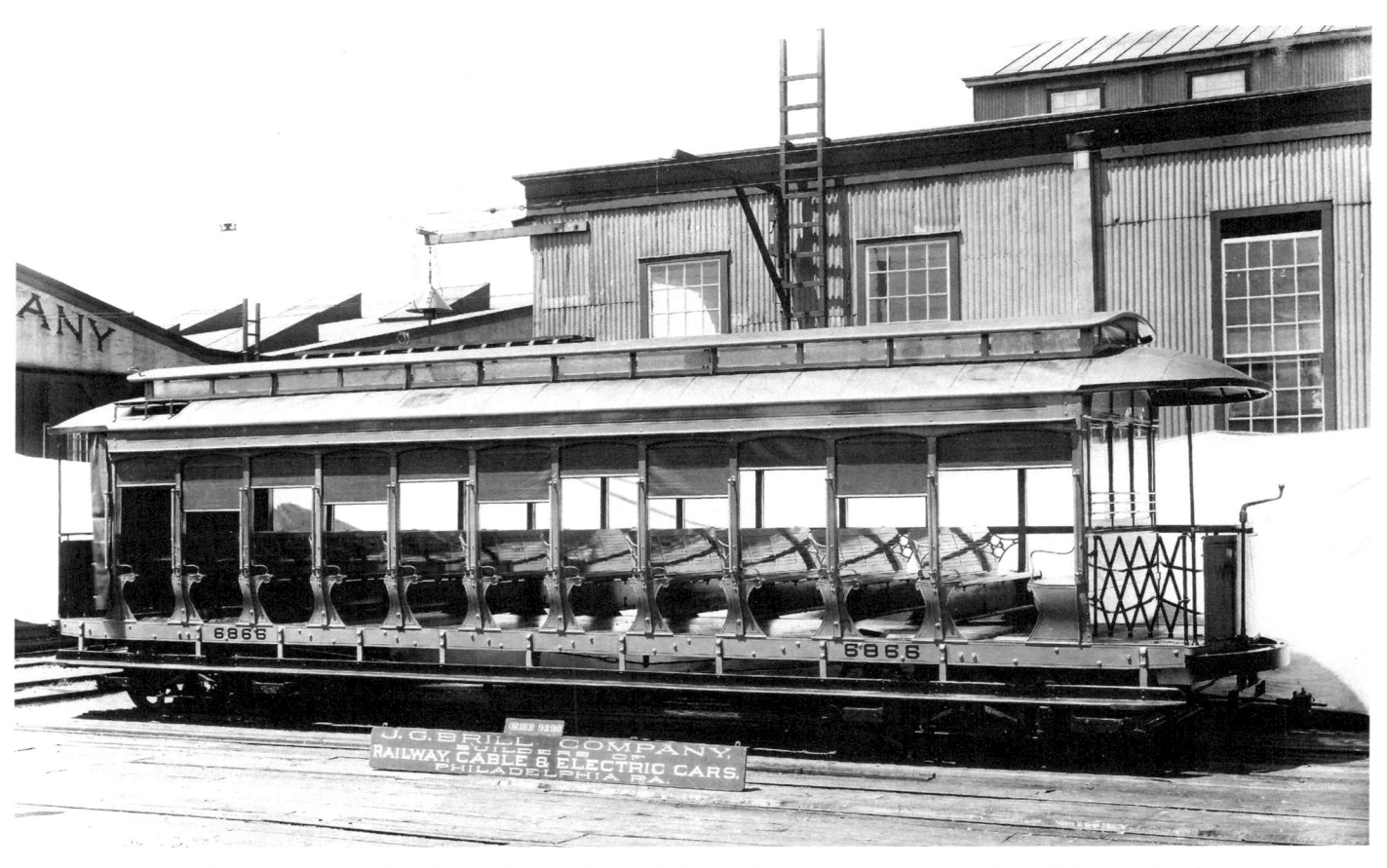

Above: Three 12-bench open cars were ordered from Brill in 1899. Car 6866 is pristine in its new paint and striping. Not seen in the photo are two Brill workers holding up a large white sheet to serve as a background for the builder's photograph. The Historical Society of Pennsylvania, Fred W. Schneider, III collection.

asked the state treasurer to refund the $4,000 payment. Upon receipt of this sum, the company was dissolved. As will be seen, other competitors would soon appear who would have a major impact on the PRR's Atlantic City operations.

The PRR Reigns Supreme

With business booming, the PRR constantly added to its fleet of electric cars, but in small numbers. In 1891, two cars were built at the railroad's Camden shops, and three used cars were purchased from the Philadelphia Traction Company. In 1892, two more used cars were acquired, from the West End Street Railway of Boston. Management favored single-end cars, which were cheaper, but they required loops to reverse direction. In 1899, four single truck closed cars were acquired, and ten large open cars were received from the J. G. Brill Company. They were 43 feet, 9 inches long, with short platforms at the front and rear, not intended for passengers. A guard rail extended the length of the car on the left side. Defying convention, the roof was covered with tin instead of canvas. With its sea breezes, open cars were ideal for Atlantic City summers, and they were used for many years. Also acquired that year was a sprinkler car, used to hold down the dust and dirt.

As the turn of the century approached, the PRR lines were in good condition, and if winters were somewhat slower, summer business was brisk. The company looked forward to the new century with optimism and confidence. But significant changes were in the offing that would affect the trolley lines and result in fundamental changes in the local transit scene. A harbinger was the paving of the first street in Atlantic City, one block of South Carolina Avenue, from Atlantic to Arctic Avenues, in 1890. Various tinkerers and inventors were working to develop an internal combustion vehicle that would run on its own wheels. These machines would begin to appear in quantity in coming years and pose the biggest threat the young electric railway industry would face.

But railway executives were unaware of this future danger. In 1902, the first successful challenge to PRR dominance would appear in the form of the Atlantic City and Suburban Traction Company. Although ultimately a failure, the Suburban opened the door to other entrepreneurs ready to challenge the PRR's monopoly of local transportation.

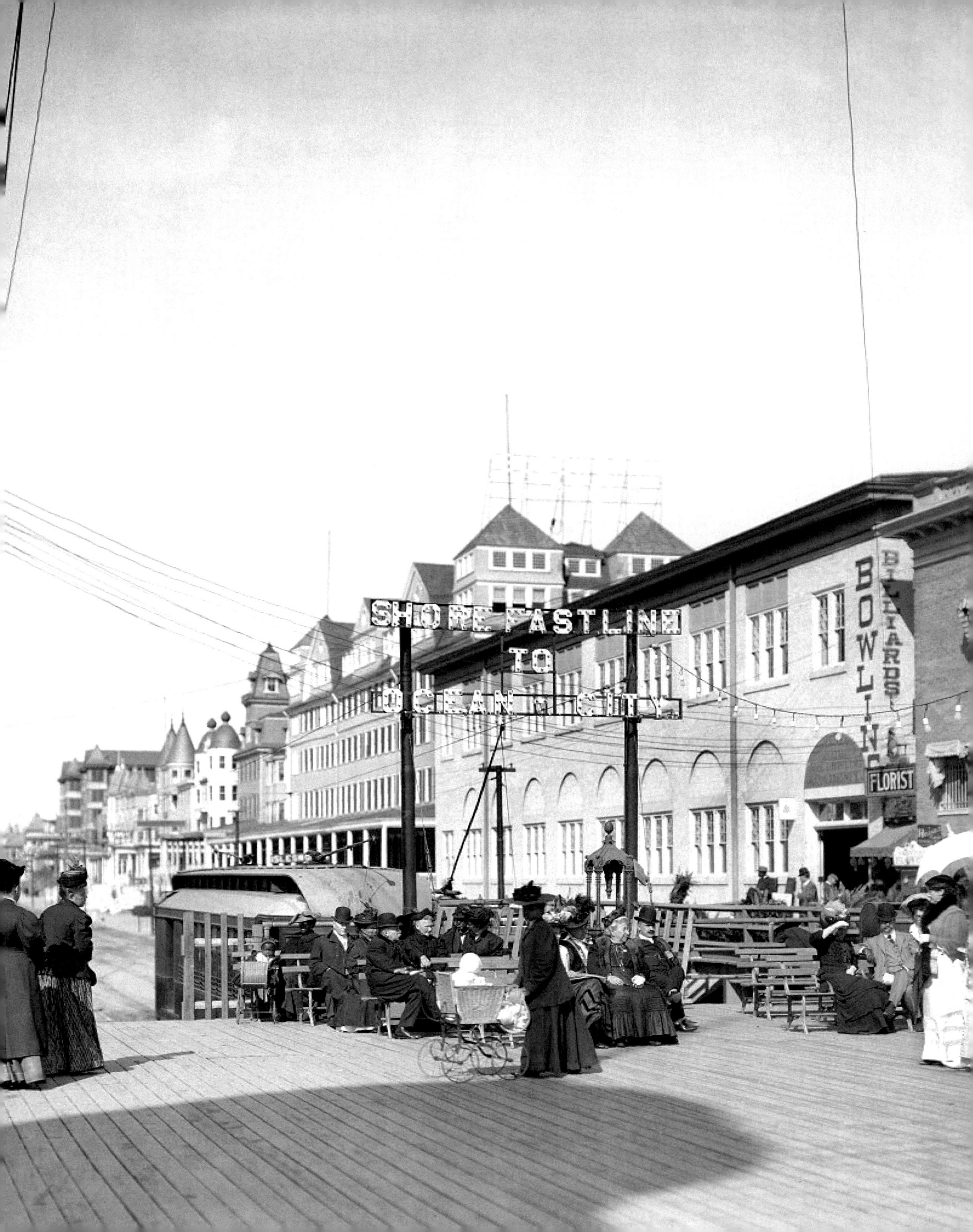
SHORE FASTLINE
TO
OCEAN CITY
BOWLING
BILLIARDS
FLORIST

CHAPTER THREE

The Atlantic City and Suburban Traction Company - *1902-1929*

The Pleasantville and Atlantic City Turnpike or Plank Road Company

Although the Atlantic City and Shore Railroad was to become the prime local passenger carrier soon after its 1906 incorporation, it was preceded a few years earlier by another company which offered service between Atlantic City and several mainland communities. This was the Atlantic City and Suburban Traction Company, later known as the Atlantic and Suburban Railway. Its antecedents went back to the mid-nineteenth century.

After the establishment of Atlantic City in 1854, interest in building a road to Absecon Island from the mainland developed. The small farming and fishing villages of Absecon and Pleasantville were located west of Absecon Island, separated from it by about five miles of salt marshes, partially covered by tidal flows and small streams. Neither the state nor local governments were interested in building a connection to the new seashore resort, so on March 14, 1864, a group of enterprising local entrepreneurs secured a charter by a special act of the legislature for the Pleasantville & Atlantic Turnpike or Plank Road Company. The leading investors were David, Simon, and Lucas Lake, members of a prominent and wealthy family of the area.

The idea of a plank road was soon dropped and a gravel artery was substituted. The company acquired a right-of-way 100 feet wide, extending 5.5 miles from Pleasantville to the Beach Thorofare and then via a drawbridge into Atlantic City. The road as built was 30 feet wide; pools and ponds were filled in, and eight inches of gravel were spread along the surface. Four small bridges spanned creeks, and a large drawbridge was erected over the Beach Thorofare, which cost $9,000 and required a watchman to operate it. Progress was slow, and the road was not opened until 1876. Tolls were five cents per mile for wheeled vehicles, and three cents for horses and mules. For a number of years, the turnpike was the only road to Atlantic City. In 1880, the new West Jersey and Atlantic Railroad built its line through Pleasantville to the resort city. It intersected the turnpike in the salt marshes and established a grade crossing there.

By the 1890s, stimulated in part by the bicycle craze, a movement developed for improved free roads. In 1892, the New Jersey legislature passed the State Aid Road Act, whereby the county Boards of Chosen Freeholders could propose the building of improved, paved roads. If approved by the state Commissioner of Public Roads, the state would pay one-third of the cost of the improvement. By 1900, Atlantic County had 30 miles of gravel roads and three miles of stone roads. In 1901, an additional 19 miles of road were built. Neighboring Cape May County had 14 miles of improved roads in the same year.

In 1903 and 1904, Albany Avenue Boulevard, 60 feet in width, was built between the Boardwalk at Albany Avenue west to Main Street (the Shore Road) and Verona Avenue in Pleasantville. This public road, which closely paralleled the turnpike, immediately attracted most of the traffic between the two towns, severely reducing turnpike revenues. By then, however, ownership of the company had changed, and much of the turnpike right-of-way had become the route of a new electric trolley line linking the seashore resort with the five mainland communities bordering the marshlands.

The Mainland Communities

At the turn of the century, five small communities, carved from Egg Harbor Township, lined the bays, waterways, and marshlands that separated them from Atlantic City. From north to south, they were Absecon, Pleasantville, Northfield, Linwood, and Somers Point. Residents wanted better transportation to the seashore resort than was provided by the limited service of the steam railroads.

Absecon, located five miles west of Atlantic City, was a seaport at the time of the American Revolution. Incorporated as a city in 1902, it was a station on the Camden and Atlantic line to the seashore. In 1900, it had 530 residents, some of whom worked in Atlantic City hotels. Pleasantville was the largest of the towns, with a population of about 2,200 people in 1900. Settled in the eighteenth century by whaling captain William Lake, its residents engaged in farming and oystering, and, with better transportation, it would become a residential community for seashore workers.

Facing Page: A view of the Shore Fast Line's terminal on Virginia Avenue at the Boardwalk. Two trolleys are in the terminal with one, poles changed, readying to depart. It's 1908 and service to Ocean City has been in operation for a year. Detroit Press Co. Collection at the Library of Congress

Above: *The Atlantic City & Suburban Traction Company and its routes to Absecon and Somers Point.*

Northfield, known as a builder of schooners, was incorporated as a city in 1905. Linwood was incorporated as a borough in 1889, and its populace of 495 engaged in farming, fishing, and shipbuilding. Somers Point, another farming and fishing community, was founded in 1693 and was the oldest settlement in Atlantic County. It was incorporated as a city in 1902.

The Atlantic City and Suburban Traction Company

Collectively, these small communities did not seem to hold much promise for supporting a trolley line, but their proximity to Atlantic City, their potential for growth, and the exuberance of the promoters made them the locale for the Atlantic City and Suburban Traction Company. Two Pennsylvanians, Edward R. Sponsler of Harrisburg and C. Taylor Leland of Philadelphia, joined by Albert M. Jordon of Atlantic City, applied for a charter for the new line under the 1893 act governing the incorporation of traction companies. A certificate of incorporation was granted on February 19, 1902, giving the company authority to sell $500,000 of capital stock, divided into 10,000 shares of $50 each. Sponsler and Leland each pledged to buy 4,995 shares, with the remaining ten claimed by Jordon, and the group opened an office in Atlantic City.

The first step was to determine a route to the mainland. It quickly became apparent that a ready-made right-of-way was available. The owners of the turnpike sold their company to the Suburban. Surveys were run, and a route in the rough form of a "T" was located. The stem began in Atlantic City at the Boardwalk and Florida Avenue, then an unpaved street quite removed from the business area. It ran west along Florida, crossed the Chelsea branch of the West Jersey and Seashore (WJ&S), to the end of the turnpike and its bridge over the Thorofare. The municipal government imposed several requirements: 90-pound girder rail must be laid; iron poles used to support the overhead wire; the company must pave Florida Avenue; speed could not exceed 10 miles per hour; the railroad crossing had to be flagged; the company must pay $500 per year for lighting the avenue, and free transportation had to be provided for city officials. Despite these onerous conditions, the promoters optimistically accepted them.

The line followed the southern shoulder of the turnpike through the meadows, crossing the streams on six bridges. At the point where the WJ&S's Newfield line crossed the turnpike, the trolley route veered slightly to the left, avoiding the railroad crossing, and paralleled the railroad into Pleasantville. The distance from the Boardwalk was 5.37 miles. At Pleasantville, the line split into two branches. One turned north in the center of Main Street (the local name for the Shore Road) into Absecon, where it reached the Camden & Atlantic tracks. It avoided this crossing by turning left onto Charlotte Street, on private right-of-way, and ran several blocks to the railroad station, a distance of 2.7 miles from Pleasantville. The second branch ran 7.25 miles down the unpaved Shore Road from Pleasantville, through Northfield and Linwood to Somers Point, where the track turned east down New Jersey Avenue a short distance to Bay Avenue, and then south five blocks to end on the western shore of the Great Egg Harbor Bay, at the point where the WJ&S Somers Point branch terminated.

The track layout at Pleasantville was complicated. The line entered the city on West Jersey Avenue, crossed Franklin Avenue, and reached Main Street, where the Somers Point branch turned south. A station was built on West Jersey Avenue, midway between Franklin Avenue and Main Street. Immediately to the north of West Jersey Avenue lay the tracks of the WJ&S's Newfield line, and one block further north were the parallel tracks of the Reading's Atlantic City Railroad main line. Neither of these companies would tolerate a grade crossing by the trolley line. Consequently, on entering Pleasantville, Absecon branch cars

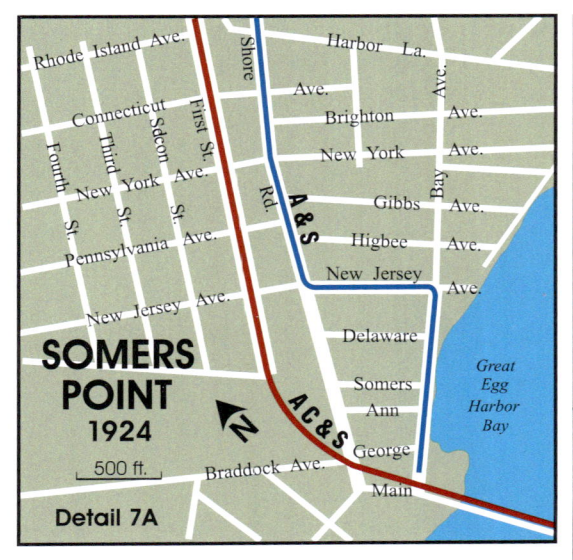

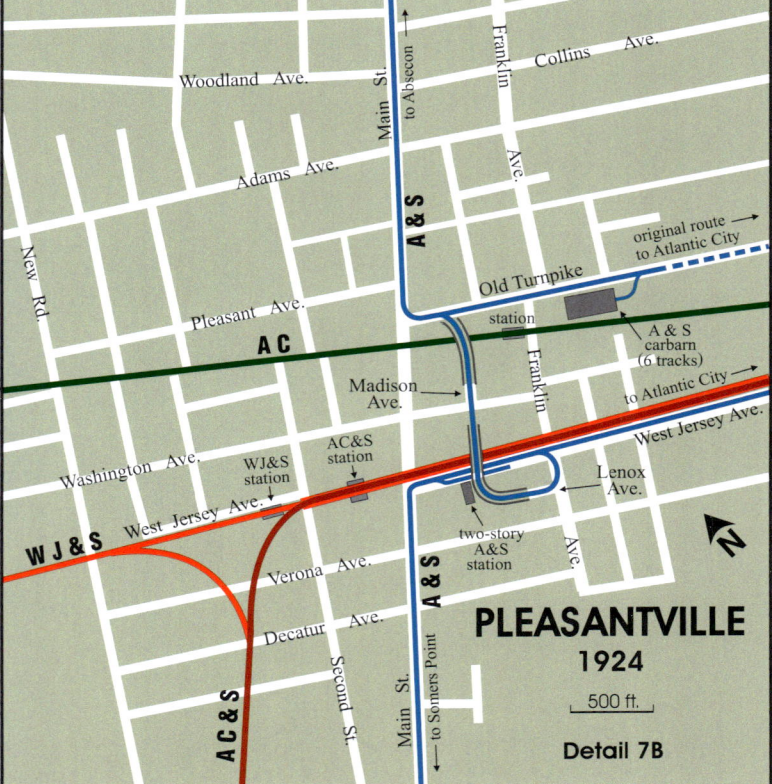

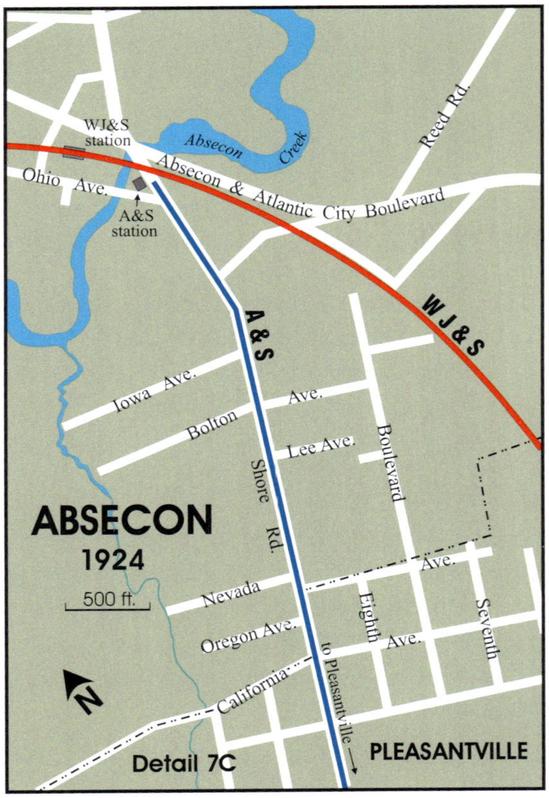

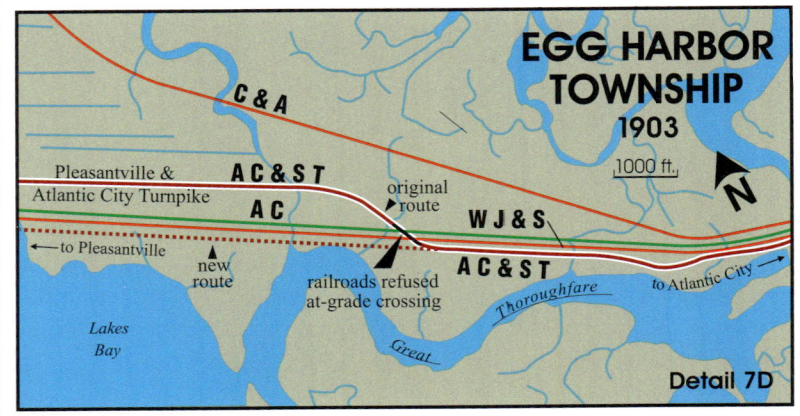

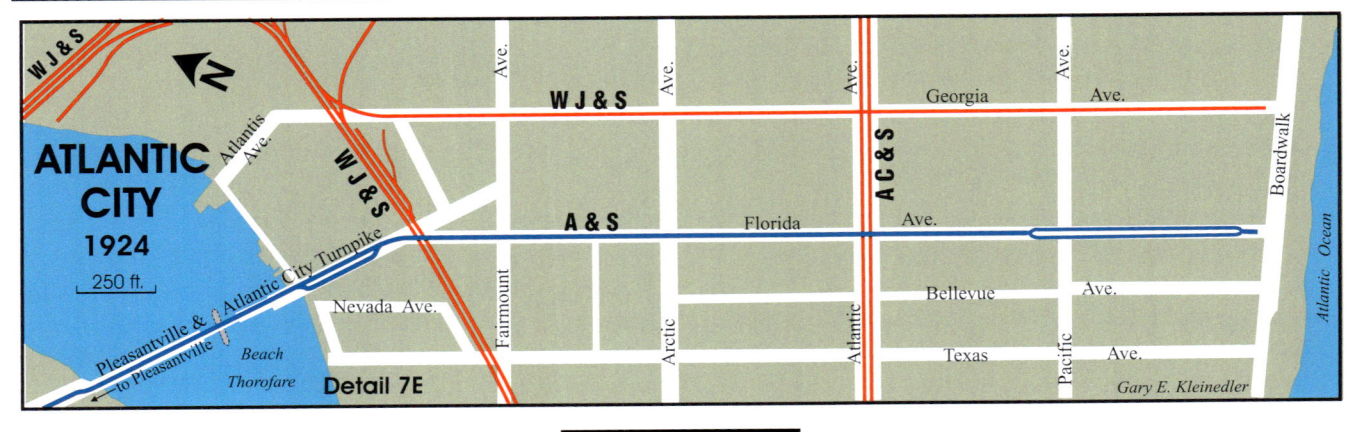

CHAPTER THREE | 1902-1929

Map 7A-E. Details of Atlantic and Suburban Railway

Detail 7A — SOMERS POINT 1924

Detail 7B — PLEASANTVILLE 1924

Detail 7C — ABSECON 1924

Detail 7D — EGG HARBOR TOWNSHIP 1903

Detail 7E — ATLANTIC CITY 1924

Gary E. Kleinedler

25

turned from West Jersey Avenue, a short distance down Franklin Avenue, then turned west and climbed a trestle, turning north again and stopping at the Suburban's station, which had an upper level platform. In roller coaster fashion, the track crossed the WJ&S line on 150 feet of reinforced truss and plate girder spans, dropped down to street level to cross Washington Street at grade, and immediately climbed a second trestle, with an 83-foot girder span, over the Reading's tracks. Descending to ground level, it turned west onto the Pleasantville end of the old turnpike road, going a short distance to Main Street, where one final turn to the north sent them to Absecon.

A carbarn, power house, and shops were built off the turnpike just east of Franklin Avenue, which was accessed by a track on the turnpike from Main Street. The car house was 180 by 70 feet; the power house was 73 by 48 feet and the boiler room was 73 feet by 35 feet. Line poles were of chestnut, about 30 feet tall. Trolley wire was 4.0 copper, and a signal system controlled by the motormen gave some measure of protection.

Franchises had to be secured from each of the towns, and they all contained a number of requirements. The location of the tracks, turnouts, and line poles was specified. T-rail of 80 pounds to the yard was required, although the company used only 70-pound rail. The top of the rails had to be level with the gravel surface of the Shore Road, and at street intersections, a thick wooden plank had to be placed to permit vehicles to cross the tracks. The company had to maintain eight inches of gravel across the entire surface of the Shore Road and to lay a macadam surface between the rails. Cars were to run at least every hour, from 6 A.M. to midnight on weekdays and slightly later on Sundays. It is perhaps an indication of the inexperience of the promoters that they readily accepted these conditions, which involved continuous expense that the company would not be able to meet; consequently, it would soon wear out its welcome.

Constructing the Line

The Suburban was a single-track operation, with turnouts or sidings at various points where cars going in opposite directions could pass each other. The turnouts were 300 feet long and ranged from one-half to a mile apart. There was one in the meadows between Atlantic City and Pleasantville, one between Pleasantville and Absecon, and ten between Pleasantville and Somers Point. They spanned much of the width of the Shore Road. The only double track was about 500 feet in Pleasantville. Overall, the company operated 6.5 miles of private right-of-way, across the meadows and on a short stretch in Absecon.

Construction got underway in 1902 and continued for much of 1903. It soon became apparent that more money was needed. The board of directors met on August 4, 1903, and passed a resolution increasing the capital stock from $500,000 to $750,000, and authorizing the sale of 5,000 additional shares at $50 each. This was approved by the required two-thirds of the stockholders. Most of the outstanding shares were now owned by the Atlantic Coast Construction Company, which had been formed by President Edward Sponsler and Treasurer C. Taylor Leland. The promoters could now profit by building the line they had advocated, which would be left with the problem of paying the bills. Other stockholders were C. Taylor Leland, Eli Chandler, and Sponsler's bank, the West End Trust Company, which held 1,500 shares. At the same time, a bond issue of $750,000 was floated, paying five percent and redeemable in 30 years.

An order was placed with the J. G. Brill Company of Philadelphia for eight, 15-bench "Narragansett" type open cars and for seven semi-convertible cars. Both types were mounted on Brill 27-G trucks and were propelled by four, 30 horsepower motors per car. They were painted red with black numbers. The closed cars were numbered consecutively from 1 and the open cars from 11.

By the late summer of 1903, construction of the line was almost complete and plans were underway for the formal opening. Delivery of the new cars was in progress; most were stored in the car house and one was running on the line when, on September 16, a violent storm, accompanied by severe winds, struck the Pleasantville area. The high winds blew in the walls of the new carbarn and lifted the heavy slate roof and supporting girders and dropped them on the cars. The roofs of the cars were damaged by the mass of slate and metal, although the bodies remained intact. The roof was also blown off the adjoining power house, but fortunately the electrical equipment suffered only minor damage. No one was hurt. Some of the new cars had not yet been delivered, and the damaged ones were returned to Brill for repairs. Work began immediately rebuilding the car and powerhouses, which were ready the next month.

Another incident took place in mid-October when a disgruntled landowner, whose property abutted the turnpike near the Thorofare, cut down eight of the wooden line poles and erected a fence to stop the trolley from running across what he claimed was his property. The court promptly resolved this issue in the company's favor.

The New Line Opens

The first official car ran on October 22, 1903, on Florida Avenue from the Boardwalk to the Thorofare drawbridge, carrying a band, company officials, and local dignitaries. The following day car number 5 left the Boardwalk at 4 P.M. on the first trip to Pleasantville, operated by C. Taylor Leland, the company treasurer, and William A. Sponsler, the superintendent of construction. A large crowd, estimated at 500, gathered to witness the event.

At first the Suburban attracted considerable business, partly from the novelty of a new line, and partly from the easy access it provided mainland residents to Atlantic City. It attracted shore

CHAPTER THREE | *1902-1929*

Above: A stock certificate from the 1903 offering of shares in the Atlantic & Suburban Railway Company. The operating and financial history of the line in years to come would confirm that this was not exactly a blue chip investment. John D. Denney, Jr. collection

Above: AC&ST Co. car 6, one of the original Brill semi-convertible cars built in 1903, pauses at a stop in Atlantic City on September 6, 1909. Although it is carrying a respectable load of passengers, the company had failed financially and was then in the process of being reorganized and taken over by the Stern & Silverman organization. LeRoy O. King, Sr. photo, LeRoy O. King, Jr. collection

visitors going to golf courses in Northfield and Linwood, or those just seeking a pleasant diversion and ride through the towns of the Shore Road area. There were three zones, with a fare of five cents for each one. Tickets were sold at a rate of six for 25 cents. Cars ran directly from Atlantic City to Somers Point and took 55 minutes for the outbound trip and slightly less for the inbound run. The Absecon branch was served by cars which connected with the through Somers Point cars at Pleasantville; they required 13 minutes for the one-way ride. During the summer, traffic was brisk; cars ran every 7 ½ minutes, but during the long winter period, headways were 30 minutes. The frequency of service and the many stops attracted passengers who had formerly patronized the WJ&S's dummy train, which ran infrequently on their Somers Point Branch. The dummy train was soon withdrawn. For the moment, the Suburban enjoyed a period of popularity. Special cars were chartered by various groups for picnics and trolley parties, sometimes accompanied by bands and the car strung with lights.

The Suburban was well situated to serve the residents of the small towns along the Shore Road, but its location in Atlantic City was less desirable. Florida Avenue, still unpaved, was well south of the commercial center of the city and relatively remote. Aware of the forthcoming competition from a new electric railway in 1906, which would operate from Virginia Avenue in the business and entertainment center, the managers of the Suburban developed plans for a major expansion of trackage in the resort city. They hoped to lay new rails on Arctic, Missouri, Pacific, and Tennessee Avenues, serving both the WJ&S's and Reading's stations and reaching the hotel and business area. This grandiose proposal was probably an act of desperation on the part of the Suburban, which was already faltering financially. Not only did the Suburban lack the funds for the costly expansion, but it would also arouse strong opposition from the PRR, and the city was unlikely to approve, especially since the Suburban had yet to maintain Florida Avenue, as required by its franchise. In any event, the project was quietly dropped, and nothing more was heard about it.

An unusual operation was conducted in March 1906. A house was being moved a short distance along the Shore Road parallel to the trolley line. Horses pulled the house to the track, where a trolley car was substituted, hauling the house slowly down the

Above: LeRoy O. King, Sr. captured AC&ST open car 12 on film at the same location as the photo of car 6. The few passengers on board was more typical of ridership on the Suburban. The line suffered from low population in towns it served and had stiff competition from the adjacent Shore Fast Line. The open cars were a pleasant ride in warm weather, but they represented a capital investment that was idle for the majority of the year. LeRoy O. King, Sr. photo, LeRoy O. King, Jr. collection

CHAPTER THREE | 1902-1929

Above: AC&ST line car 339 sits on the Pleasantville trestle which carried Absecon branch cars over the tracks of the Somers Point branch, the West Jersey & Seashore, and Atlantic City Railroad's lines from Camden to Atlantic City. The roller coaster-like track arrangement in Pleasantville avoided crossing other lines at grade but added considerably to the cost of building the line. LeRoy O. King, Sr. photo, LeRoy O. King, Jr. collection

road. Linemen removed and replaced the span wires, one by one, and the trolley wire was moved to one side, sliding along the edge of the house. The operation was completed successfully.

Troubles Begin for the Suburban

While the company might be applauded for aiding a home owner, it was under attack elsewhere. The local government in Atlantic City was threatening to remove the line's tracks from Florida Avenue. Under its franchise, the Suburban was required to pave between its rails, and it had failed to do so, despite repeated warning from city officials. On the mainland, in an effort to increase revenue, the company proposed to haul freight along the Shore Road. The towns emphatically rejected this plan, and there was grumbling over the difficulties the location of the tracks presented to carriages and wagons, especially at the passing sidings.

But much greater challenges were facing the company in 1906. The Pennsylvania Railroad had electrified its Newfield line, from Camden through Newfield and Pleasantville to Atlantic City. More importantly, the PRR had made an agreement with the newly incorporated Atlantic City & Shore Railroad (AC&S), which opened a new interurban line linking Atlantic City and Pleasantville, Northfield, Linwood, and Somers Point, using mostly PRR tracks, including the newly electrified and double-tracked Somers Point branch. The next year, after building a mile of trestles across Great Egg Harbor Bay, the line entered Ocean City. The new line, using the trade name Shore Fast Line, closely paralleled the Suburban route and offered superior service and equipment.

The Suburban Enters Receivership

Even before this new threat materialized, the Suburban was faltering financially. Built mostly with borrowed money in the mistaken belief that any new electric railway would prosper, the line was burdened by heavy construction costs, expensive franchise requirements, a territory of relatively undeveloped small towns with sparse populations, and a busy season of only a few summer months. In the face of these conditions, on February 1, 1907, the company defaulted on the five percent interest payments due on its $750,000 bond issue of 1903. In addition, the firm had a floating debt of $100,000, had issued $27,000 in car equipment bonds, and had signed a $15,000 contract to pave Florida Avenue, as required by its Atlantic City franchise.

After a receiver was appointed, the bondholders formed a committee and agreed to defer interest payments for two years. They also bought shares of preferred stock, to the value of 12 percent of their bond holdings. Unsecured creditors were forced to accept shares of the $50 par value preferred stock in lieu of the money due them. The current officers and directors resigned and

James N.J. Henwood

Above: *The motorman of AC&ST car 2 uses a switch iron to turn a switch on what appears to be on Shore Road in Pleasantville on September 7, 1910. The light passenger load was all too common on Suburban cars. Shore Road was unimproved at the time, a condition which made riding the Suburban cars an attractive option. LeRoy O. King, Sr. photo, LeRoy O. King, Jr. collection*

were replaced by the creditors' committee.

These steps enabled the company to keep operating until a more permanent solution could be reached. As a preliminary step, the line was sold at auction on October 31, 1908, to the first mortgage bondholders' committee for $91,000. Several weeks later, on November 28, 1908, the bondholders sold the rail line and the turnpike company to the newly formed Atlantic & Suburban Railway Company for $150,000 of capital stock and $650,000 of four percent, 20-year bonds. This would enable the firm to retire the original bonds, but it did not change the fundamental problems facing the line: too little traffic and competition from the Shore Fast Line.

Stern and Silverman take over the Suburban

New officers were elected. They included Robert Wetherill of Chester, Pennsylvania, the former chairman of the bondholders' committee. Joining him on the board of directors were William Blakeley and Richard Wetherill of Chester, John S. Block of Atlantic City, and Garnett Pendleton of Upland, Pennsylvania, a Philadelphia suburb. They lost no time in seeking the obvious solution to their problem: sell the new Atlantic & Suburban and the Turnpike or Plank Road Company to the Atlantic City & Shore Railroad. Like most entrepreneurs, the Stern & Silverman combine did not welcome competition, even if it were weak, and they were amenable to eliminating it if they could.

On December 10, 1908, Robert Wetherill wrote to Samuel Rea, third vice-president of the Pennsylvania Railroad in Philadelphia, informing him the Suburban was anxious to sell its property "…for a good guarantee for the bond interest." He added that gross receipts of the line for the past year had been $65,700, which he expected would increase, as the sale of six tickets for 25 cents had been discontinued. This information was passed on to Stern & Silverman, whose offices in the Land Title Building were less than two blocks from the PRR's Broad Street Station offices. On February 25, 1909, William Stern, president of the AC&S, wrote to Rea telling him that negotiations were underway for the purchase. Stern proposed to pay $650,000 in the AC&S's 30-year, four percent bonds for the same amount in the new Suburban company's bonds, and one dollar for its stock, which obviously had no value. Under its lease agreement with the PRR, the AC&S needed the consent of the PRR-controlled West Jersey & Seashore Railroad to consummate the purchase.

Stern kept Rea informed of the details of the proposed buyout. In addition to the payment of the bonds, after one year, the AC&S could abandon whatever parts of the Suburban's line it wished. Stern planned to abandon the Suburban route across the salt marshes from Pleasantville to near Meadows tower in Atlantic City and to have both companies use the PRR's Newfield branch between those points. In a report to James McCrea, president of the PRR, on March 18, 1909, Rea recommended the railroad's board of directors give its consent to the purchase. He noted that "We have always regarded the Suburban Company's line across the Meadows as an absolute waste of capital." He added that the Shore Road route from Pleasantville to Somers Point would have to be abandoned "in time" because it was very slow and impeded highway traffic.

The PRR disliked competition as much as Stern & Silverman, and approved the purchase by the end of March, subject to the requirement in its lease to the AC&S that all its passengers and

CHAPTER THREE | 1902-1929

baggage continue to be routed over the Shore Fast Line. However, completion of the purchase was delayed for over two years because a New Jersey law forbade a steam railroad from owning any street or other railway company not necessary to its own operations. In a judicial challenge, the New Jersey Court of Errors and Appeals rejected the completion of the purchase. In response, Stern & Silverman formed a new holding company, incorporated in Delaware, called the Atlantic City & Shore Company, which then bought all the Atlantic City & Shore Railroad Company stock, in exchange for its own stock. As a holding company and not as a railroad, the Shore Company could also hold the stock of other lines, including the Suburban. While these disputes were underway, the PRR formally rescinded its earlier approval of the purchase of the Suburban, but apparently it later re-approved it when the holding company took over. Not until the end of 1911 were these complex transactions completed.

These intricate financial maneuvers enabled the Suburban, and its affiliated turnpike company to continue operating, even though they were marginal at best and frequently reported losses. They also enabled the original bondholders of the old Atlantic City & Suburban Traction Company to emerge relatively well, although the stockholders lost everything. In 1910, in the midst of these dealings, an additional issue of $100,000 first mortgage, five percent bonds had to be floated to pay the company's share of the cost of paving the Shore Road. Furthermore, 150,000 shares of Suburban capital stock, at $50 par were issued, all held by the AC&S Company. Stern & Silverman appointed new officers, including H. E. Kohn, president, Robert Wetherill, vice-president, John M. Campbell, secretary, and R. A. Cole, superintendent.

Social and Economic Changes

As the first decade of the century progressed, profound changes were underway in American society, which would affect even the struggling Suburban line. Population growth was rapid overall, but uneven in places. The nation had over 92 million inhabitants in 1910, and an additional 14 million were recorded in 1920. New Jersey's population jumped from 2.5 million in 1910 to 3.1 million ten years later, an increase of 24 percent. In the same decade, Atlantic City's population grew by only ten percent, to 50,700. On the mainland, Pleasantville had 5,880 residents in 1920, an increase of 34 percent in the decade. Northfield grew by 30 percent and had 1,120 people in 1920. Growth in the other towns was less impressive. Linwood increased by six percent, to 638 people in 1920. In the same period, Somers Point and Absecon were static, with only 843 and 702 residents respectively. The population base to support the Suburban's routes was still distressingly small, and this was a significant factor in the company's struggle to survive.

More ominous for the future of the line was the arrival of the automobile as a serious and more convenient mode of transportation. The car, earlier only a curiosity, had developed into a reliable and practical machine by 1910, and it began to appear in ever larger quantities. In that year, 100,000 automobiles were produced; by 1914, over 500,000 were rolling out of the factories, and by 1917, almost 2,000,000 cars were manufactured. Motor vehicle registrations increased proportionally.

Along with the rising tide of motor vehicles came the construction of a network of paved highways to support them. The state began to assist the county freeholders by designating certain routes as state roads and paving them. Among them was the White

Above: Shortly after abandonment in 1929, a photographer snapped this view of the plain, unappealing terminal on Florida Avenue and the Boardwalk. This section of the Boardwalk was south of the more heavily traveled upper section and did little to attract passengers. The modest terminal consisted of a single track and a short stub siding for a spare car. LeRoy O. King, Jr. collection

Horse Pike, which ran from Camden to Absecon, and which was extended across the salt meadows to Atlantic City in 1919. Over 21 miles of the Shore Road were graded and graveled by 1917, and it was designated a state road in 1923. In the same year, the state purchased a private toll road that had been built across Great Egg Harbor Bay from Somers Point to Ocean City in 1912. Federal aid for road construction began with the passage of the Federal Aid Road Act of 1916, which appropriated $75,000,000 for road building and required the states to establish highway departments to receive the funds, amounting to 50 cents for each dollar expended. The principle of federal-state partnerships in road construction was thus established. These publicly-funded projects were a significant factor in the weakening of privately-owned transportation companies such as the Suburban.

Financial Troubles of the Turnpike or Plank Road Company

Not only were the electric railway lines affected but also the privately-owned toll roads, such as the Pleasantville & Atlantic Turnpike or Plank Road Company, which was owned by the Suburban. It was capitalized with $15,000 in stock and a $40,000 first mortgage bond issue, all of which were held by the Suburban. The stock had little value and no interest had been paid on the bonds. Traffic was minimal on the poorly maintained road, and the company suffered an average loss each year of the decade of about $700. A toll house was located at the drawbridge over the Thorofare, and a watchman employed to lower it for the occasional traveler. Tolls ranged from five cents to 25 cents, but an average annual income of only $500 was realized. Since it was a public utility, now subject to state regulation, and since it provided a right-of-way for the Suburban across part of the meadows, the company had to maintain its precarious existence throughout the decade.

Another problem which affected virtually everyone during the second decade of the century was inflation, bought on by the economic instability generated by the World War. The index of wholesale prices stood at 100 in 1913; by 1916 it had jumped to 124, by 1918 to 196, and by 1920 to 243. Electric railways reeled under the pressure of ever rising prices and the difficulties of obtaining state approval of fare increases. Taxes increased as well, especially in New Jersey, which was notorious for having the highest taxes in the nation levied on railways. This expense had to be added to the cost of operating a struggling transit line in a rapidly changing environment.

Inspections and Complaints about the Suburban

Despite these challenges, the Suburban carried on. Not everyone owned an automobile, and well over half of American households depended on public transit. An inspection of the property by the Public Utilities Commission in 1911 pronounced the road to be "in good condition." The report presented detailed statistics on track, rail, bridges, buildings, overhead construction, and power. Aside from the short timber trestles in the meadows, the only bridges were over the steam railroads in Pleasantville, and the 194-foot draw span over the Beach Thorofare. The carbarn, shops, powerhouse, and the Pleasantville station were the only structures of note.

Another inspection by state officials in 1914 noted that over 4,000 ties had been installed and that three miles of track through the marshes had been raised and surfaced. About 60 line poles along the Shore Road were rotting at the base, and the paving, with a substance called Amesite, was in very bad condition, with the portion contiguous to the rails dangerous to vehicular traffic. The inspectors recommended replacement of the line poles and repair of the paving, but they pronounced the cars to be "in very good condition," and the track and roadway to be "in splendid condition."

While the company was getting high marks from the state, some of the line's patrons were not so pleased, especially since the Stern & Silverman management had raised the fares in July, 1910. The cost of a ride from Pleasantville to Atlantic City doubled from five cents to ten cents, which was the same fare charged by the parallel Shore Fast Line. Not surprisingly, certain riders felt the new management had stifled competition, and they filed a petition with the PUC, against both the Suburban and the AC&S in September 1911, protesting the higher rate.

In the subsequent hearings, the Suburban explained its line was divided into four fare zones, with overlaps, three of which, on the mainland, charged five cents per zone. The remaining zone was from Pleasantville to Atlantic City, where the fare had recently been doubled. Strip tickets, in packages of 50, were sold for eight and one-third cents each, and monthly commutation tickets in books of 60 rides, cost six and one-half cents each. The rival West Jersey & Seashore steam trains charged 12 cents between the same points, and the Reading charged 13 cents. In view of the line's bonded debt, lack of dividends, and limited income, the PUC ruled the fare increase was "just and reasonable" and they dismissed the petition.

Cooperation with the Shore Fast Line

Since they were under common ownership by the Atlantic City & Shore Company, the Suburban maintained cordial relations with its rival, the Shore Fast Line. One example was an agreement made in 1915, whereby each line would accept the other company's strip tickets for passage between Pleasantville and Atlantic City. Settlement was made each month, when the carriers would exchange tickets and be reimbursed. This sensible arrangement gave passengers the option of using whichever route might be more convenient.

At other times, when a disruption occurred on one line, the other company would honor all tickets from its opposite carrier. Such was the case in February 1920, when ice on the Shore Fast Line tracks sent passengers to the Suburban. In all these cases, the issuing line reimbursed the other company for the amount paid for each ticket.

CHAPTER THREE | *1902-1929*

Above: *Equally as informal was the "terminal" of the Absecon branch on Charlotte Street, a short distance from the Shore Road. AC&ST car 2 lays over awaiting its return trip to Atlantic City. The unpaved road was typical of the time.* Sam James collection

Pressed by wartime inflation and continuous deficits, the Suburban applied for a fare increase in May 1918. The ten-cent fare between Atlantic City and Pleasantville would increase to 12 cents, and the five cent zone fares would jump to six cents. Six trip tickets would rise from 50 to 60 cents. No changes were requested for the multiple trip commutation tickets, which remained a bargain at six and one-half cents per ride between Pleasantville and Atlantic City. Conscious of the company's heavy bond indebtedness and operating losses, the Public Utilities Commission granted the request in July.

During the decade, a few equipment changes were made. In 1909, the new Stern and Silverman management was sufficiently optimistic that it ordered three new semi-convertible cars from the J. G. Brill Company, of the same style as the line's original cars. They were numbered 8, 9, and 10. A decade later, traffic had declined to the point that the five open cars were sold to the AC&S, where they were renumbered and continued to operate in Atlantic Avenue summer service until 1939.

Life Along the Line

By the second decade of the century, the novelty of the electric cars had worn off. There was less interest in trolley parties and special runs, especially after the start of the war in Europe, and more so after the United States entered the conflict in 1917. A terrible influenza epidemic at the end of the war further dampened spirits.

Nevertheless, the Suburban offered good service. In the summer, cars ran on a half-hour headway from Somers Point to Pleasantville and across the meadows to Atlantic City, from early morning until midnight. The Absecon branch was served by two cars, usually running on a half-hour frequency from Pleasantville to the northern terminus next to the PRR's Absecon station. Passengers going to and from Atlantic City changed cars at Pleasantville. In later years, headways increased to 60 minutes in the evening.

George Washington Pine, a retired conductor, recalled in 1971, when he was 93, that summer headways could be as close as seven minutes, with Sunday loads particularly heavy. He remembered the big open cars running from Florida Avenue to Pleasantville carrying as many as 100 people. Crossing the meadows at high tide could be an adventure, especially if the motorman did not run slowly. Splashing in places could short out the motors.

Operations were sometimes informal. Mrs. Anna Hand, an elderly resident of Northfield, recalled that cars stopped anywhere along the Shore Road at the convenience of the passenger, unlike

Above: A Suburban car rolls down Shore Road in Somers Point approaching New Jersey Avenue where it will head east to Bay Avenue. It will then turn south for a few blocks until reaching the end of the line on the shore of the Great Egg Harbor Bay. In this 1908 scene an automobile, a growing menace to trolley lines, is parked ahead of a horse and wagon whose owner is likely in the Braddock grocery store to the left. John D. Denney, Jr. collection

the Shore Fast Line cars, which stopped only at designated stations. Dr. Morgan A. Johnson, a dentist in Absecon, had vivid memories of the Suburban during his youth. Living at the time on Main Street, Pleasantville, he had a cousin, William Martin, who wore the number one on his motorman's cap, and who was a boarder in the house. Known as "Spide" to his friends, Martin rose at 4 A.M. daily and then walked a mile down the Shore Road to the carbarn on the turnpike to prepare for his first run on the Somers Point-Florida Avenue route, leaving at 6 A.M. At lunchtime, he took an Absecon-bound car to his house, where a hot meal was waiting for him. Exactly one-half hour later, he left the dwelling and catch the same car, now headed to Pleasantville, and return to his duties. Spide took advantage of the country clubs along the Somers Point line. When he saw a golf ball near the track, he stopped his car to retrieve it, thus insuring he always had plenty of golf balls on hand for his personal use.

One story about the line concerns a dishonest conductor who was suspected of pocketing some of his fares. Company spotters who rode on his car were unable to detect any malfeasance, since he rang every fare on the register. Apparently by accident or by carelessness, one day he opened the briefcase he always carried, and the company agent saw therein another fare register, a duplicate of the official one mounted in the car. The culprit would switch registers on one trip each day, and keep the receipts recorded on his personal one. Needless to say, he was promptly discharged.

Jack Steelman, who grew up along the line, commented on crossing the meadows on the big Brill semi-convertibles. The loud motors and gears, along with the rough track, gave the impression of speed, but at most the cars managed to run about 40 miles per hour. Informality reigned. On one occasion, he witnessed the motorman leave the controller open while he went into the car to talk to a young lady. Aside from the uneven rails and low spots, there was little danger of hitting anything on the isolated right-of-way in the meadows.

The Atlantic City terminal was simplicity itself. The single track ended at the Boardwalk, where there was also a storage siding for a spare car. A small ticket office was perched on the edge of the Boardwalk, and the agent doubled as a starter, who would announce the next departure and make sure no one boarded the spare car by mistake. At the time the locale was relatively isolated, and there was not much foot traffic.

Financial problems increase

However informal the Suburban might have been, its financial returns made increasingly grim reading for the management.

CHAPTER THREE | *1902-1929*

Except for 1911, when it earned a meager $3,300 profit, the line lost increasing amounts of money for the remainder of its corporate life. In 1915, a loss of $13,800 was noted, which jumped to over $20,000 in 1918, and to over $32,000 in 1922. The last years were especially difficult; annual losses between 1923 and 1928 averaged about $48,000. Even in its last year, 1929, when it ran for only four months, $11,675 was lost.

The operating ratio, which indicated the percentage of the annual expenses in relation to operating income, climbed ever higher. In 1911, the ratio was about 64 percent, but in later years it reached 74 percent, leaving only 26 percent to pay taxes, interest, depreciation, and other ongoing expenses. By 1922, the operating ratio was an alarming 92 percent, and thereafter it exceeded 100 percent, meaning that revenues did not even cover the direct expense of running the cars. By 1927 and 1928, a ratio of 139 percent was recorded, and in the short year of 1929 a record high of 173 percent was reached.

Nothing the management did seemed to stem the flow of red ink. Since the Stern & Silverman takeover, the company was encumbered with $691,000 in bonded debt in the form of two separate bond issues. All the bonds were owned by the Atlantic City & Shore Company, the holding company which controlled the AC&S Railroad and its related companies. All the Suburban's $150,000 in outstanding stock was in the coffers of the AC&S Company. On paper at least, interest on the bonds was paid by the Suburban each year through 1926, but no real money was paid because of the heavy losses. The AC&S Company used these securities, which were essentially worthless, as collateral for its own 1910 issue of $591,000 five percent bonds. It was in Stern & Silverman's interest to keep the Suburban afloat as long as possible to support the AC&S Company's bonds, and their officers remained firmly in control throughout this period. This may explain why the Suburban was able to survive as long as it did, despite its heavy and relentless losses.

The Suburban Struggles Through the 1920s

In its final years, the Suburban continued its close relationship with its ostensible rival, the Shore Fast Line. In July 1921, when the Shore Fast Line experienced overhead wire trouble near Somers Point, Suburban conductors accepted AC&S hat checks from passengers on a stalled car as the equivalent of a 21-cent fare. These were sent to the AC&S offices in Atlantic City for reimbursement. Sometime after 1921, the Suburban closed its power plant in Pleasantville and thereafter it purchased its power from the AC&S. When a new door was needed at the Pleasantville station in 1921, AC&S carpenters fashioned one for the Suburban's use. In December, AC&S workers made repairs to the Suburban's crossing of the Atlantic Avenue line at Florida Avenue at a cost of $104. The Suburban's Florida Avenue tracks between Atlantic

Above: This photo of Birney car 21 was taken in 1922 at the J.G. Brill factory in Philadelphia. The small four-wheel car was not comfortable to ride, but was cheaper to operate than larger cars. The letterboard is barely long enough to display the major towns served by the line. Boarding passengers were admonished to "Please have exact fare ready." Not even the economy of these cars could save the Suburban. LeRoy O. King, Jr. collection

Avenue and the Boardwalk were repaired and rebuilt by AC&S laborers in October 1922, at a cost of $140. No doubt it was easier and cheaper to employ trackmen from the AC&S than for the Suburban to employ its own workers.

The final equipment changes were made in 1922. M. T. Montgomery, who had replaced R. A. Cole as superintendent in that year, was permitted to buy six new Birney-type cars from the J. G. Brill Company numbered 21 to 26. These small, lightweight, four-wheel cars with only two motors were then the rage of the industry, since they promised cheaper, more efficient operation and closer headways. Designed for one-man operation rather than the usual two-man crew, they had such features as "dead man control," which cut the power and applied the brakes if the motorman's hand left the controller handle. With their lightweight and smaller motors, they were easier on the track and drew less power. Passengers, however, found them uncomfortable, with smaller seats and less leg room, and they gave a bouncy, uneven ride, especially over poor track. The Suburban placed them on the Shore Road service, especially to Absecon. While they may have operated over the meadows to Atlantic City, it is unlikely they did so very often. At the same time, several of the older semi-convertible cars were modernized, with new electrical equipment, steel pilots, fresh "Brunswick green" paint, with cream-colored window frames and maroon doors. Among them were numbers 4, 5, 8, 9, and 10.

Partly because of resentment by crewmen about the use of one-man cars, the company experienced a short, futile strike in the fall of 1923, by which time the last superintendent, Paul R. Goldey, was in charge. One-man operation of some runs made by the large, older cars led to the walkout, with the men charging the practice was dangerous. The strike ended when the company agreed to a one-month "truce," during which two men were placed on all cars, except the Birneys on the Pleasantville-Absecon run. Later, one-man operation of cars during periods of light traffic was evidently established. One unwelcome effect of the short stoppage was Pleasantville mayor Charles Johnson's decision to issue permits for buses to operate between his town and Atlantic City. However, no evidence exists that they did so.

Desperate for more money as losses increased, the company won a partial fare increase in April 1920. Zone fares went from six cents to seven cents, and the charge for a ride from Pleasantville to Atlantic City rose to 14 cents. These modest increases did little to reduce the losses, and in September 1924, the company applied for additional raises. In hearings in Atlantic City in October and November, Superintendent Goldey presented evidence about the annual shortfall. He claimed the proposed increases would not

Above: In a 1910 scene that typifies the Suburban, a lone car rolls down an empty Shore Road in Launch-haven near Somers Point. Only one dwelling offers the possibility of potential riders, while a real estate sign touts 50 by 150-foot lots for sale and boasting the town has the "finest harbor on the coast." Today the area is fully developed and the Shore Road is a busy highway. John D. Denney, Jr. collection

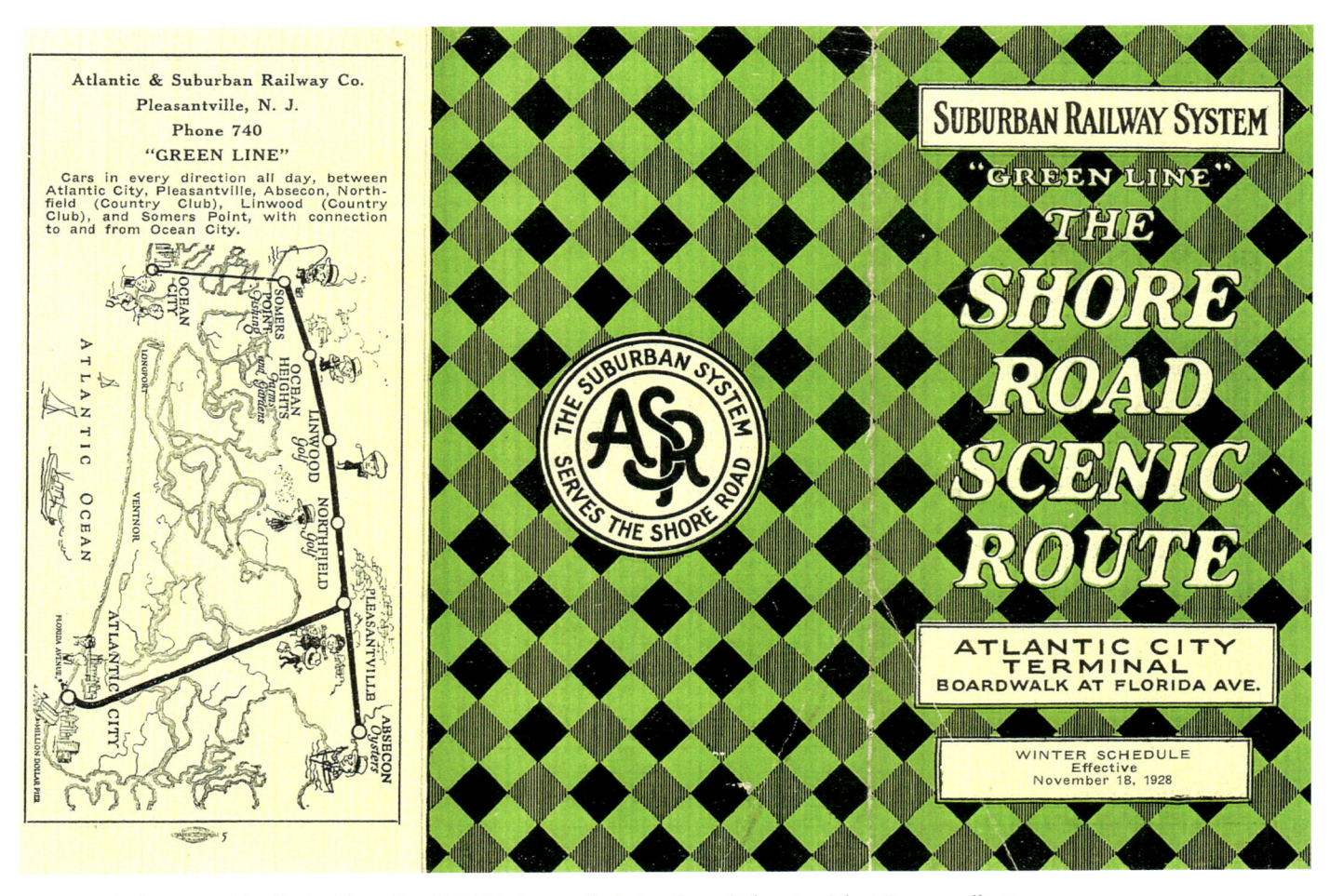

Above: Suburban timetable effective November 18, 1928, five months before the end of service. John Nieveen collection

eliminate them, but that greater increases would probably drive away so many riders the receipts would fall even more. Some objectors argued that community residents wanted abandonment of the line, especially between Pleasantville and Atlantic City, where the Shore Fast Line or buses could substitute for the cars. Faced with the stark reality of the poor financial health of the Suburban, the PUC approved the increases in January 1925. Zone fares were now eight cents and the Pleasantville-Atlantic City segment cost 16 cents. Commutation and strip tickets were raised proportionately.

What proved to be the last proposal to extend the Suburban was made early in 1925, when residents of Mays Landing, the seat of Atlantic County, urged the company to build a line to their town from Pleasantville. They claimed the lack of a local trolley line had impeded the growth of the community, and such a line would relieve growing traffic congestion on the road to Atlantic City. With the Suburban rapidly sinking into insolvency, Stern & Silverman turned a deaf ear to this plea.

Instead of expanding, the Suburban was retrenching. In 1924, Philander Betts, the chief inspector of the Board of Public Utility Commissioners, spoke before the Chambers of Commerce of Cape May County and Atlantic City. He urged the replacement of cars with buses between Pleasantville and Absecon and the abandonment of the Suburban's duplicate service across the meadows. In June, 1925, the Suburban discontinued rail service to Absecon, and buses replaced them. In the same year, the Common Council of the city of Absecon granted a franchise to the Absecon Bus Company to provide direct service to Atlantic City via Absecon Boulevard at a fare of 20 cents. The ordinance specifically permitted the city to grant a bus franchise to the Suburban for its route to Pleasantville.

The company staggered through 1928, and it was increasingly clear it could not survive much longer. In June, a broken overhead wire struck a car, slightly injuring two passengers who received compensation of $100 and $225 respectively. Essential repairs to equipment continued to be made. In 1928 and early 1929, several orders were placed with the Brill Company for hardware items and with the American Car and Foundry Company for new 26-inch and 33-inch wheels for various cars. Only four cars were licensed for Atlantic City service in 1928: 4, 8, 9, and 10, which cost the company $400.

The Suburban Applies for Abandonment

By the summer of 1928, the Stern & Silverman management recognized the inevitable and threw the company into bankruptcy,

Above: Service was frequent on the Suburban, but ultimately it couldn't overcome the faster schedules of the Shore Fast Line Route or the convenience of the private automobile. John Nieveen collection

filing suit seeking its dissolution. Paul R. Goldey was appointed receiver on July 25, and hearings were scheduled to determine if abandonment was justified. An income report for December showed there was only one outcome that could be expected: total abandonment. A total of 49,000 fare zone passengers were carried, the bulk of them between Absecon, Pleasantville and Atlantic City. Only 6,700 went to Linwood and 1,000 to Somers Point. A total of $3,600 was collected, but expenses far exceeded that amount.

At the hearings before the United States District Court for the District of New Jersey, held in Trenton in March 1929, the hopeless condition of the Suburban was revealed. Receiver Goldey testified he had managed to pay salaries and repair costs but only a portion of the power bill. The company owed the AC&S over $4,800 for power; no taxes or interest had been paid, and there was only $2,600 in the company's bank account. The two mortgages, totaling $691,000, were impossible to redeem, as was a judgment of $3,000 against the line held by the Guarantee Trust Company of New York. Continuing to operate the line would only increase the losses and further depreciate the value of the remaining assets.

Goldey sought authority to sell all the company's property to the highest bidder, first at a private sale, and then at a public sale. He listed the property the firm owned, which consisted of several small plots in Pleasantville and one in Atlantic City, the carbarn and shop buildings, the right-of-way across the meadows, and the trestles in Pleasantville. Also listed as assets were the franchises from the towns, the track, ties, overhead wire, line poles, shop equipment, office supplies, and the cars. Six of the semi-convertibles were in operating condition, but four were not. The six Birneys and two work cars were available. Finally, the stock and bonds of the Pleasantville & Atlantic Turnpike or Plank Road Company were listed. Most of these materials had minimal or no value, there being no market for most of it. As for the mortgages and judgment, Goldey said they should be written off as total losses. Whatever was realized from the sale would be divided among the creditors, which really meant the AC&S Company, which held the worthless stock and bonds of the Suburban. In the face of this evidence, the court ordered the property to be sold.

Goldey was authorized to continue to operate the railway, but no longer than 90 days from March 25, 1929. He immediately arranged a private sale of what could be salvaged to the one logical buyer: the AC&S Railroad. An inventory of the equipment was

CHAPTER THREE | 1902-1929

prepared. The AC&S bid $675 for the lot, which Goldey promptly accepted and which the court approved. The Suburban was permitted to use what it needed until the final day of operation, set for Tuesday, April 30.

What the AC&S did not buy was offered at a public sale in Pleasantville in April. The real estate, most of the cars, evidently sold for scrap, and other items, realized about $14,000. When Goldey paid the back taxes and interest due the municipalities, franchise taxes, the overdue power bill, and other expenses, less than $8,000 remained, to be divided among the creditors. The towns and Atlantic City agreed to assess the company only one-third of their annual taxes and fees for 1929 and the franchises were surrendered. Semi-convertible Brill car number 10 was sold to the PRR's Atlantic City fleet, where it became a rail grinder and was renumbered 499200.

Ironically, while the Suburban was winding up its affairs and being legally dissolved, the turnpike road company struggled on. As a regulated utility, it could not simply be abandoned, but like its former parent, it suffered financial losses most years of its existence. The stock and bonds of the company were transferred to the PRR's West Jersey & Seashore Railroad in 1930. The office was moved to the AC&S's Inlet car barn, whose managers handled the affairs of the company.

The only positive development for the turnpike company had been a 1923 agreement with the Atlantic City Electric Company, permitting it to run its power line along the right-of-way to service a meat-packing plant near Pleasantville. For this the company received $500 a year. The tolls collected annually usually totaled about $500, but expenses, on the average between 1909 and 1937, were $1,250 a year.

The company had $15,000 in stock outstanding and $26,000 in mortgage bonds, which were worthless and held by the West Jersey & Seashore Railroad. When the railroad assumed the burden of owning the turnpike, it forgave $41,000 in unpaid interest. Good public roads to Atlantic City were now available, so only a few local travelers used the turnpike, but the Thorofare drawbridge had to be maintained.

For reasons that are obscure, the PRR waited until 1938 to divest itself of this antiquated, money-losing mode of transportation. At that time, Leo R. Isenthal, president of the turnpike company (and also president of the Atlantic City & Shore Railroad), filed a petition with the Public Utility Commission to abandon the property. In a lengthy document, the company noted its continuous losses, the decrepit condition of the road and bridges, the availability of alternate paved public roads, the fact that dividends and interest had never been paid, and that an

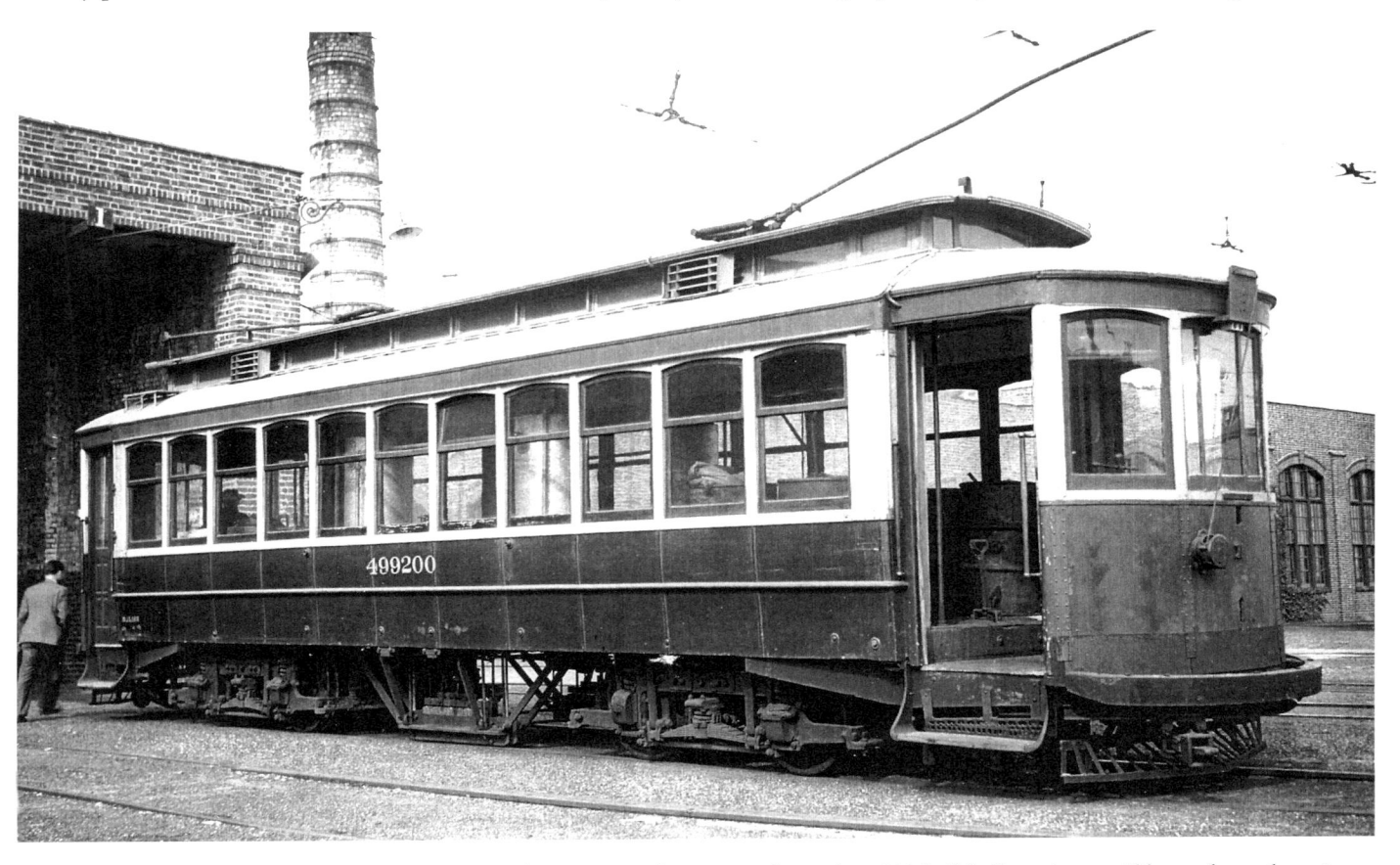

Above: Upon abandonment of the Suburban in 1929, Atlantic City & Shore acquired one of its 1902 Brill-built semi-convertible cars for work service where it ran as a salt car and rail grinder. Renumbered to 499200, it's shown at the Inlet carbarn on October 12, 1938. LeRoy O. King, jr.

engineering study had shown it would cost over a million dollars to rebuild the turnpike to modern standards. The West Jersey & Seashore promised to cancel a debt of $750 owed to it, and the Pennsylvania-Reading Seashore Lines agreed to forgive the $1,850 debt due it. The West Jersey & Seashore would also write off the $26,000 in bonds it held. The turnpike company promised to cede its land east of the Shore Road to the city of Pleasantville. Faced with this catalog of compelling reasons, the PUC approved the abandonment, and the turnpike company, which had been chartered in 1864, was formally dissolved on September 29, 1939.

It took several more years to finally close the books. Small parcels of land, such as the right-of-way in Atlantic City from the Thorofare to Baltic Avenue, had to be sold. The city paid $200 for this strip, and toll gate lot in Pleasantville was sold for $100. Taxes still had to be paid, and not until 1945 were the last transactions completed and the turnpike laid to rest.

The Suburban was born in a period of enthusiastic optimism regarding electric railways. The turnpike gave it a right-of-way, but one that was decidedly inferior to that of the parallel PRR Newfield branch, which was soon electrified and used by the faster and more modern Shore Fast Line cars. When the Suburban failed in 1907, Stern & Silverman, abetted by the PRR, bought control in order to eliminate competition. With the benefit of hindsight, it would have been better to let the Suburban continue on its own; in all probability it would have been abandoned before 1929.

By the time of the Great War, the Suburban had lost the support of many residents of the mainland towns. Traffic was always heavier on the northern section of the route, from Pleasantville and Absecon; Linwood and Somers Point provided minimal fares. The tracks and passing sidings, in the middle of the Shore Road, were increasingly regarded as obstructions, by automobile and truck drivers. Buses seemed to offer a better alternative, and the Shore Fast Line continued to provide frequent service. After abandonment, AC&S buses were substituted, but so low were the passenger loads that they were soon reduced to a few daily runs. An exception was the Pleasantville-Absecon route, which continued to offer connecting service to the Shore Fast Line cars.

When the Suburban was still new and prosperous early in the century, it was confronted with a strong competitor whose route closely paralleled its line, and which offered superior service and accommodations. The Atlantic City & Shore Railroad, using the trade name Shore Fast Line for its Atlantic City-Ocean City interurban, lasted almost 20 years longer than the Suburban, but it quickly discovered that mainland service offered few rewards. The story of the AC&S offers an interesting contrast to that of the Suburban, as the following pages will demonstrate.

Selected Suburban Financial Data

Year	Operating Revenues	Operating Expenses	Interest Due	Net Income	Operating Ratio
1911	$95,994	$67,825	$24,868	$3,301	64%
1915	80,141	54,471	28,532	(13,806)	74%
1918	88,368	77,804	30,906	(20,164)	80%
1921	148,460	145,719	30,956	(26,251)	87%
1925	106,553	123,160	30,871	(46,269)	107%
1927	80,254	120,676	5,015*	(44,042)	140%
1928	54,301	82,440	5,018	(32,452)	139%

*Interest on bonds written off

Source: Public Utilities Commission of New Jersey

Facing Page Top: One of the line's five 15-bench open cars delivered from Brill in 1902, rests outside the carbarn on September 7, 1910. These cars had a center aisle which made fare collection much easier for the conductor. LeRoy O. King, Sr. photo, LeRoy O. King, Jr. collection

Facing Page Bottom: AC&ST car 2 in service on September 19, 1905. This car was one of seven delivered by Brill in 1902. LeRoy O. King, Sr. photo, LeRoy O. King, Jr. collection

CHAPTER THREE | *1902-1929*

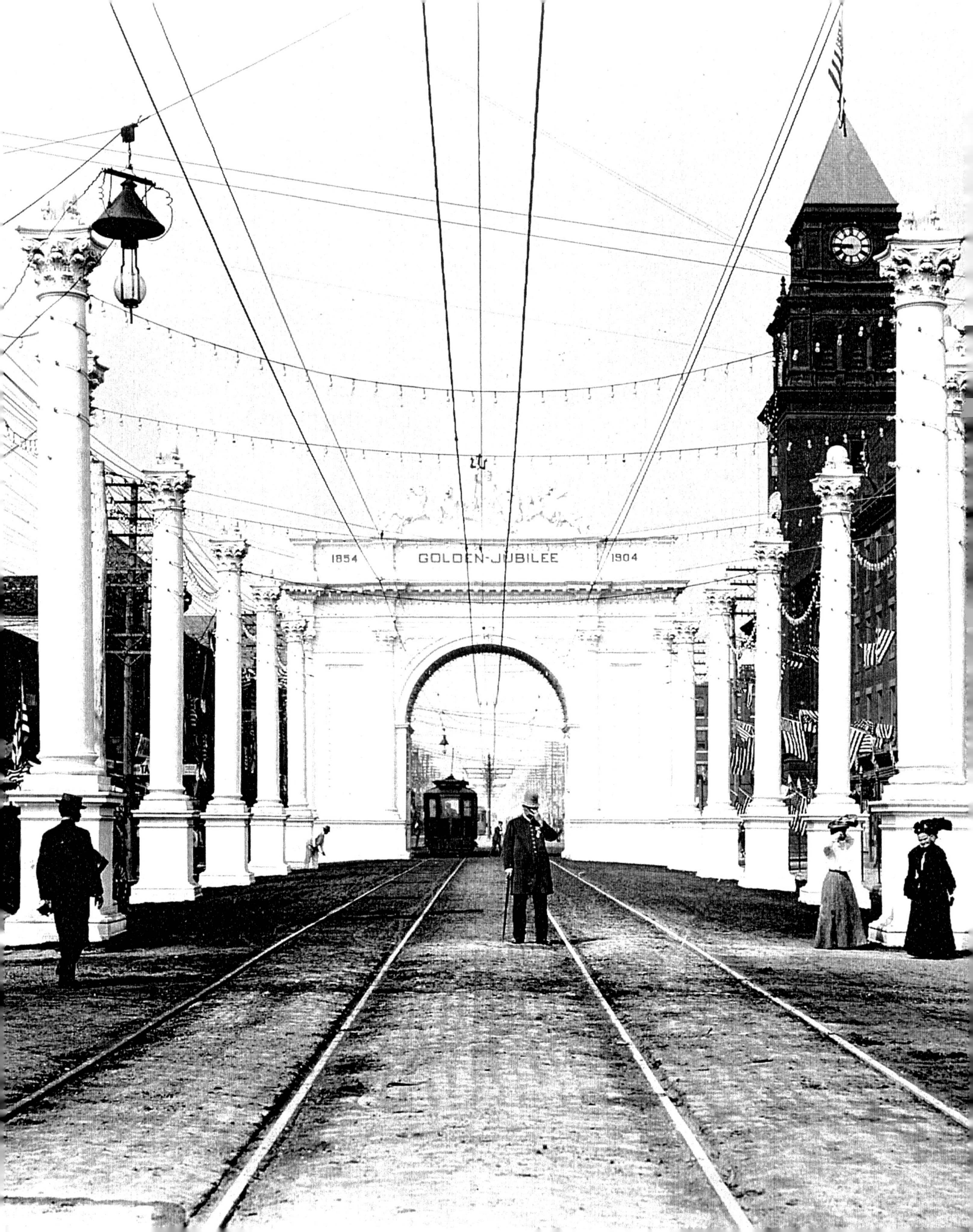
1854
GOLDEN-JUBILEE
1904

CHAPTER FOUR

The Atlantic City and Shore Railroad Takes Over Area Transit Operations - *1900-1910*

Population Growth in the Atlantic City Region

While promoters were planning to build the Atlantic City and Suburban Traction Company to connect the resort with adjacent mainland communities, the nation entered the twentieth century. Many changes were in the offing on the political, economic, and social levels. The first decade of the century marked the high point of freedom from highway competition for electric railways and the last stage of their unfettered expansion. New entrepreneurs were attracted to the industry, hoping to tap expanding markets and to make lucrative profits from the business of carrying people to various points by building new and improved trolley lines.

Continued rapid growth marked the initial decade of the century. The republic, which had over 76,000,000 people in 1900, boasted a population of over 92,000,000 ten years later, an increase of 22 percent. Pennsylvania gained 1,300,000 people and New Jersey 654,000 in the same period, increases of 22 percent and 45 percent respectively. Philadelphia, a major source of the summer crowds that flocked to the resort beaches, saw its population jump from about 1,294,000 in 1900 to 1,549,000 in 1910, an increase of 20 percent. Atlantic County grew by 25,000, to about 71,900, an impressive increase of 55 percent. Atlantic City recorded over 46,000 residents in 1910, an increase of 18,000, or a notable 66 percent in ten years. The communities of Ventnor, Margate, and Longport, which had fewer than 100 residents each in the previous census, reported 490, 129, and 118 people respectively in 1910. Pleasantville, with 4,390 persons in 1910, doubled its population. None of these figures reflected the summer months, when many thousands of visitors would need transit service. It is little wonder that ambitious promoters believed that the large populations would reward their efforts to expand and build electric railways.

Facing Page: In 1904 Atlantic City celebrated the 50th anniversary of its incorporation by holding a Golden Jubilee. The seaside community had grown and prospered. Indeed, Atlantic City's future looked golden. A Golden Jubilee arch spanned the trolley tracks on Atlantic Avenue while columns lined either side. The local constabulary was on hand to maintain order and keep the traffic flowing. View is from South Carolina Avenue. LeRoy O. King, Jr. collection *Above:* Then as now, the Boardwalk and the beaches were the prime attractions of the city. In this view from the turn of the twentieth century, the Hotel Chalfonte looms over the crowds strolling on the Boardwalk or enjoying the white, sandy beach and the cool Atlantic waters. The style of the day dictated that bathers be well covered, but they enjoyed the experience then just as they do now. LeRoy O. King, Jr. collection

New Jersey Establishes a Regulatory Agency

As the Progressive Movement gained strength early in the century, New Jersey began to adopt Progressive measures of its own, at the urging of Democratic governor Woodrow Wilson. In 1911, the legislature enacted a comprehensive public utility law. It established a three-member Board of Public Utility Commissioners (PUC), which had the power to approve rates and establish standards of service. Electric railway managers such as Stern and Silverman and PRR executives would be forced to have many dealings with the PUC in the future; the days of unrestricted actions by public service corporations such as railways were over.

Atlantic City at the Dawn of the New Century

By 1900, Atlantic City had matured and taken on the characteristics that marked it for the next 50 years. Several factors contributed to its growth. It had a good location and was easily accessible from major population centers, such as Philadelphia and New York, and even inland points such as Pittsburgh and Cincinnati. The Pennsylvania Railroad advertised and promoted the resort heavily across much of its system. Service on the three lines reaching the city was excellent, especially in the busy summer season, with the run from Camden taking little more than an hour. After 1897, when the PRR opened its massive Delair Bridge over the Delaware River, direct service was offered from Philadelphia, taking a little longer and costing slightly more but avoiding the ferry crossing of the river.

As the city expanded and gained a national reputation, it built the facilities to house, feed, and entertain its many visitors. Small boarding houses, accommodating ten or twenty people, proliferated, and large boarding houses and small hotels even more. Beginning around 1890, fashionable grand hotels began to appear, attracting people of wealth and refinement. The Marborough-Blenheim, built in 1906 at a cost of $2,000,000., joined such establishments as the Breakers, the Brighton, Chalfont-Haddon Hall, the Chelsea, and in 1915, the Traymore, that could serve 3,000 people. At the same time, there were 75 hotels with 100 to 200 rooms in the city.

Many of these establishments were located along the Boardwalk, which became Atlantic City's most distinguishing feature. The first Boardwalk, a modest eight feet in width, was built in 1870, at a time when sea bathing was limited to an hour or two in the morning. It crossed pools and dunes to access bathhouses and the beaches. Each year it was expanded and lengthened until in 1879 a permanent structure was built. This became the resort's promenade and the site of stores, hotels, restaurants, numerous shops, and amusement piers. The structures were limited to the

Above: *In season the Boardwalk attracted crowds day and night as seen here. The land side of the promenade was lined with stores, restaurants, hotels, and places of amusement, while the ocean side featured pavilions and piers. The Woolworth 5-and-10-cent store was an American institution that remained popular into the 1960s.* LeRoy O. King, Jr. collection

Above: In this view taken during the off-season, strollers and rolling chairs, a popular Atlantic City feature, congregate before the Steel Pier, the longest and most popular of the ocean piers. It extended well beyond the breakers and offered many attractions to those willing to pay the admission. The pier structures would be modified several times over the years and remained a major entertainment venue into the 1950s. As the city declined in the post-World War II era, so did the pier. Today the pier, devoid of structures, is basically a long platform over the water and supports various amusement rides. LeRoy O. King, Jr. collection

land side of the Boardwalk, except for the piers, giving visitors a fine view of the beaches and ocean.

The first pier was built in 1884 and was expanded by Captain John Lake Young, who called it Young's Ocean Pier. It provided rides, games, a ballroom, restaurants, bathhouses, and a daily net haul of fish. In 1898, the longer Steel Pier at Virginia Avenue opened, with an even more elaborate array of entertainment and amusement facilities, including theatres, ballrooms, and later, a high-diving horse. In typical Atlantic City fashion, it proclaimed itself "the Showplace of the Nation," and it was easily reached from the adjacent Virginia Avenue terminal of the soon-to-be-built Shore Fast Line. In 1906, Captain Young opened his Million Dollar Pier off Arkansas Avenue. In addition to all the other facilities, it contained his three-story Italian-style villa, with 12 rooms, a conservatory, and a formal garden. Dubbed No. 1 Atlantic Ocean, it became Young's home. The Heinz Pier, Steeplechase Pier, Garden Pier, and Central Pier also extended over the breakers.

The hotels, boardinghouses, and other establishments provided jobs for many of the skilled and unskilled workers among the city's population, especially in the summer. African Americans became a significant minority; by 1905, they constituted 24 percent of the city's permanent residents. Although needed in the summer, many were destitute in the off-season, living in small structures behind the hotels in the northern section of the city. De facto segregation was practiced; in 1904, police ordered blacks off the Boardwalk amusements and confined their bathing to the Missouri Avenue beach. In September, many African Americans from Philadelphia and elsewhere traveled to the resort on special excursion trains to enjoy a holiday period after the regular season had ended.

Although Atlantic City attracted some of the country's wealthier citizens, it was by no means a Newport or Bar Harbor, nor did it pretend to be. The greatest number of visitors was from the lower middle and working classes and the resort catered to them. Small, cheaper hotels and boarding houses were readily available and the railroads frequently ran low-fare excursion trains. Some described the resort as gaudy and impious. State "blue laws" limiting Sunday activities were routinely overlooked by the municipal government and drinking, gambling, and prostitution were permitted, although amusements were closed. In an era of the six-day week, working class visitors looked forward to a brief respite from the harshness of their daily jobs, and the city, for economic reasons, did not deny them. One critical observer wrote: "Atlantic City is an eighth wonder of the world. It is overwhelming in its crudeness – barbaric, hideous and magnificent. There is something colossal about its vulgarity." The city was basically a reflection of American society and fundamentally no different from many other cities in its social attitudes.

Politically the city was dominated by the Republicans and experienced a series of local "bosses," but the party was often fragmented and disorganized. No one group controlled the town,

Above: Two Brill semi-convertible cars arrive at the Atlantic Avenue line's southern terminal in Longport. Steamers departed from the elaborate two-level pier for a cruise to Ocean City where connections could be made with Pennsylvania Railroad trains to other seashore towns. The windows of the cars could be raised high into the roof structure, thus making the cars partially open, or semi-convertible, into open cars. The track going straight was a siding for storage of electric cars or the occasional freight car. The beginning of a reverse loop is in the foreground, enabling the cars to turn and head back to Atlantic City. Railways to Yesterday Library photo, Fred W. Schneider, III collection

and business interests often prevailed. The city had a mayor-council municipal structure until 1912, when it adopted a city commission form of government, one of the reforms pushed by Progressives. But the change made no real difference in the way the city functioned, nor did it end the frequent clashes between the politicians and the electric railways. Like most cities of the day, it had ethnic neighborhoods, with middle class whites in the Inlet, Italians along Arctic Avenue, blacks in the northern quarter, and the major business establishments along Atlantic Avenue where the streetcars ran. In 1904, the city celebrated its 50th anniversary with parades, speechs, and ceremonies, and a large triumphal arch was erected over Atlantic Avenue. By 1910, the resort was calling itself "The World's Playground" and attracting well over 200,000 visitors during the summer.

The Atlantic Avenue Line Prospers

As people flocked to the city by the sea, the West Jersey and Seashore was busily engaged in carrying them about. "The trolley is a blessing . . . It has been a factor in largely increasing realty values all along its route," gushed a writer in the Atlantic Review on March 30, 1905. To keep up with demand, the company regularly added to its fleet of cars and disposed of old, outmoded models. In 1900, ten new streetcars were purchased and seven maintenance-of-way cars were added to the roster. An additional launch, the Ocean City, joined the flotilla of steam vessels navigating Great Egg Harbor Bay and a final boat, the Wildwood, arrived five years later. In 1901, twelve cars were purchased, and four more in 1903. Eight new double-truck semi-convertible Brill cars replaced eight old cars in 1904. They were called "Jubilee cars" in honor of the city's 50th anniversary celebration. In 1905, another 18 Brill cars arrived. By then, the company had 60 active cars for its single line, and it had scrapped, sold, or converted to maintenance duties 37 obsolete cars.

One problem generated by the new electric railways was electrolysis, whereby current returning to the power house through the rails "leaked" to adjacent water, sewer, and gas pipes, energizing and corroding them. To guard against this potential menace, the city passed an ordinance in 1902 requiring the railway to make tests to see the current was not being misdirected and to report by February 1, 1903, plans demonstrating how they were protecting the city's mains. Tests were mandated every February and August, and if the company did not correct any leakage, penalties were to be imposed. The solution to the problem, if one existed, was proper bonding of the rail joints to provide a clear avenue for the negative current. Evidently, the company routinely passed these semi-annual tests.

A much more expensive project was required by an ordinance passed on August 22, 1904, providing for the paving of Atlantic Avenue for its entire length within the city, and the railway company was expected to pay for much of it. On September 6, the WJ&S signed an agreement with the city promising to contribute

CHAPTER FOUR | 1900-1910

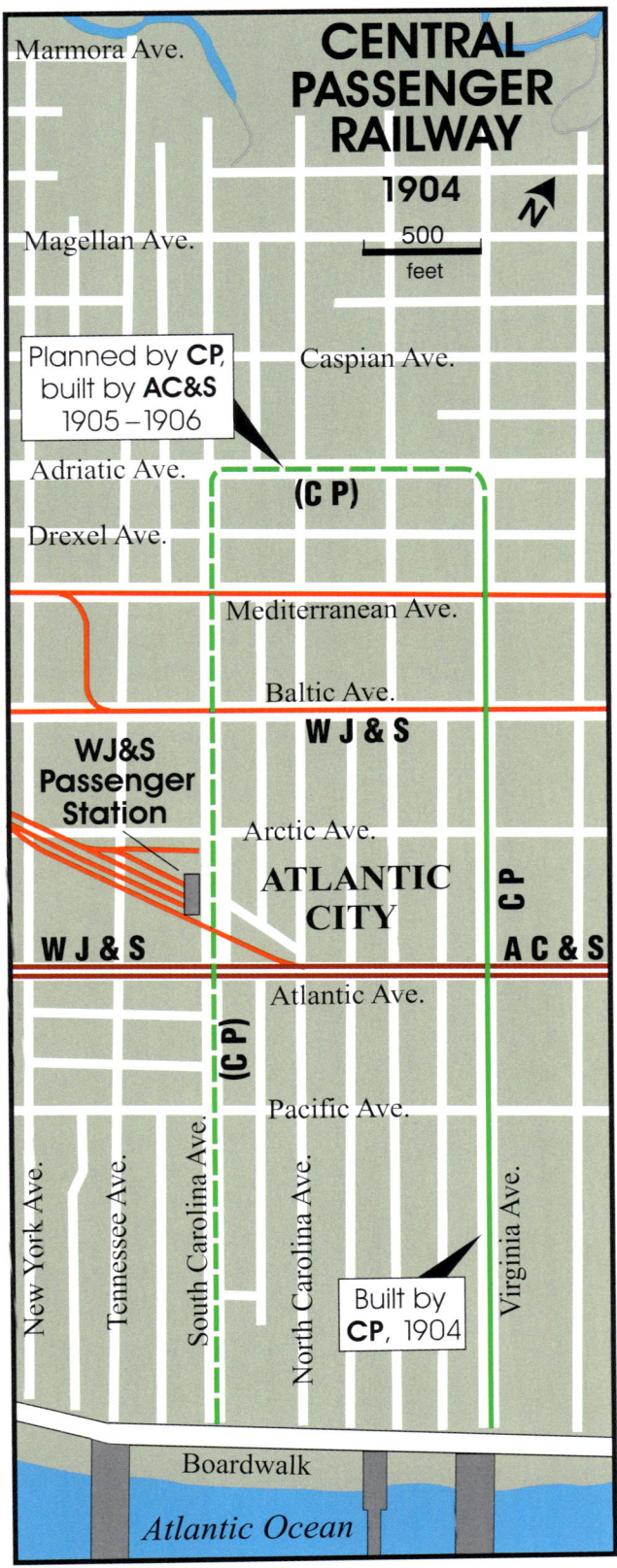

Above: Maps of Central Passenger Railway from 1904 and 1908.

James N.J. Henwood

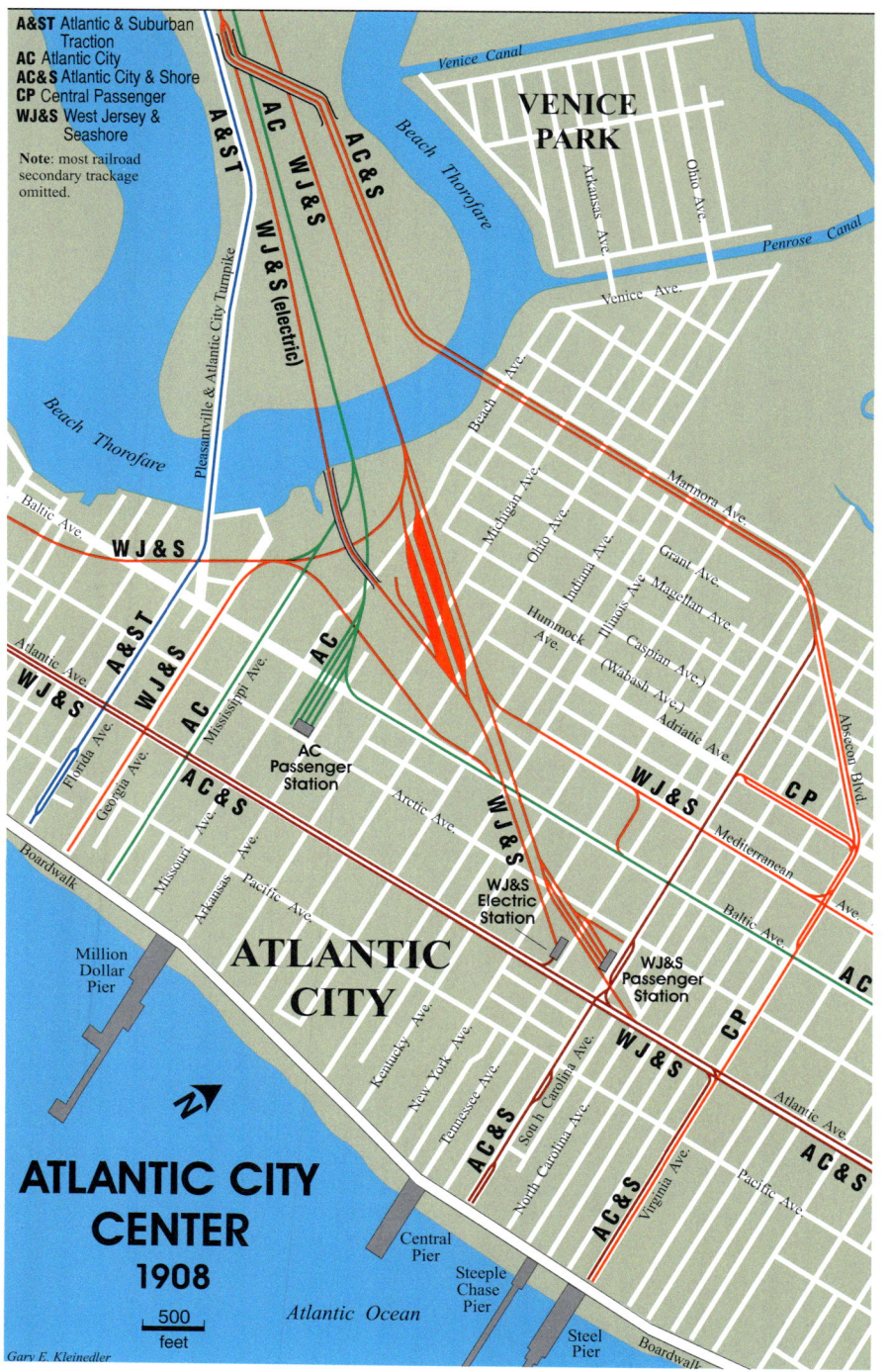

yet no public transit was available. The Central Passenger Railway, incorporated on April 21, 1903, under the street railway law of the state, proposed to remedy this deficiency. It was formed by a group of local investors, led by William McLaughlin, a newspaper publisher, who owned a tract of land near the Thorofare, which was ripe for development if it were more accessible. The company proposed to build a U-shaped crosstown line on Virginia Avenue, beginning at the Boardwalk and running west six blocks to Adriatic Avenue. It would then turn south on that street three blocks to South Carolina Avenue, and then return to the Boardwalk, a total distance of 1.8 miles. Such a route would cross the Atlantic Avenue line twice. The city granted a franchise on August 23, 1903.

Not until May 1904, did work begin in building a track on Virginia Avenue from the Boardwalk to Adriatic Avenue. Several open and closed single-truck cars were acquired, and service began on July 4. McLaughlin was more interested in developing his land than he was in running a railway, and the short line remained incomplete until December 1905, when it was sold to the new Atlantic City and Shore Railroad. It retained its corporate existence until 1945. While this small line was coming to life, events of much greater significance were underway in Philadelphia, where both the PRR and a new engineering firm were planning major changes in Atlantic City's transportation system.

The Stern and Silverman Partnership

As the field of electrical engineering suddenly developed in the 1880s, it attracted a number of capable, ambitious young men. Among them were William A. Stern and Isaac Silverman, who formed a successful partnership centered on the emerging electric railway field. The firm maintained a low profile during its existence, appropriate for a company that always kept its headquarters in the Quaker City.

The senior member of the partnership was William A. Stern. Born in 1860, he presumably had a high school education and reached his maturity just as electric lighting and power stations were being developed. Possibly he sought employment with the pioneer inventor Thomas A. Edison, but in any event, he mastered the basic principles of electrical energy and its practical applications, especially in transportation, which became his

$150,000 toward the cost and to pay an additional $5,000 annually for ten years for ongoing maintenance expenses. The company also agreed to pave and maintain its tracks thereafter. To lessen the cost, a strip of three feet was taken from the avenue and added to the sidewalk areas. By 1907, the work was completed.

The Central Passenger Railway

The Atlantic Avenue line served its locale well, but the city blocks between the ocean and the Thorofare were long, and as

Above: Central Passenger Railway car 32 is seen on March 30, 1907, at an unknown location, possibly on South Carolina Avenue. This small company, which became part of the Atlantic City & Shore Railroad, seemed to favor old, used, and somewhat dated cars for its short crosstown route. LeRoy O. King, Jr. collection

specialty for the rest of his life. In his early years, he met a like-minded young man and the two decided to form a partnership.

Isaac H. Silverman was born in Pittsburgh in 1862. After graduation from high school in 1886, he began working as an accountant, but several years later he, too, learned basic electrical engineering. He began electrical contracting work in eastern Ohio and West Virginia, and he became associated with the Edison United Manufacturing Company and the General Electric Company.

About the same time, he met William Stern and they formed a partnership, the firm of Stern and Silverman, located in Pittsburgh. In 1892, they moved to Philadelphia, and opened an office at 707 Arch Street. In the following year, they became contractors for the construction of street railway lines in Ohio, eventually working in Cincinnati and Dayton, Ohio, as well as Detroit and Mount Clemens, Michigan.

Another of their contracts was to rebuild the beachfront line of the Brigantine Transit Company in that town, north of Atlantic City on the opposite side of Absecon Inlet. The seven-mile line had no sooner opened when it was partially destroyed in a coastal storm. The owners contracted with Stern and Silverman to rebuild it. Perhaps their experience at the Jersey seashore opened the eyes of the partners to the possibilities of another electric railway in the booming region of Atlantic City.

In an illustrated brochure published around 1900, the partners declared they designed and built electric railways, and light, power, and steam plants. An additional note claimed, "We undertake the complete planning and construction of electric railways . . . When desired, securities, conservatively issued upon good properties, will be taken in payment for the construction of lines." They were successful enough and they soon moved their offices to the prestigious Land Title Building at Broad and Chestnut streets, then the heart of the city's financial district.

The Pennsylvania Railroad Electrifies the Newfield Branch

At the same time Stern and Silverman were building trolley lines, the Pennsylvania Railroad was planning a major project: the electrification of the West Jersey and Seashore's 75-mile line connecting Camden, Newfield, Pleasantville, and Atlantic City. The route carried heavy summertime traffic and it served a number of South Jersey towns. This was a daring enterprise at the time and it involved reconstructing much of the line, adding a second track, building new terminals in Camden and Atlantic City, constructing a power plant, and laying an overrunning third rail for transmitting power to new electric multiple-unit cars, and building a new bridge over the Thorofare.

Stern and Silverman's new offices were only a short distance from the Pennsylvania's headquarters in the Broad Street Station. Stern was a member of the Union League, an elite club for gentlemen immediately south of the Land Title Building. PRR executives were impressed with Messrs. Stern and Silverman and their work. They hired the partners as consulting engineers to help with the Newfield electrification. The project was approved by the Board of Directors in 1905 and work was completed by September, 1906. At the same time, the partners conceived the idea of building a high-speed electric line, linking Atlantic City with its sedate sister resort to the south, Ocean City, on an inland route that would use mostly PRR lines, under a trackage rights agreement. The new enterprise was to be called the Atlantic City and Shore Railroad (AC&S), and use the trade name of the Shore Fast Line.

The Atlantic City and Shore Railroad

The exact circumstances that led to the building of an interurban electric railway between the two seashore towns are unknown. A number of factors coalesced by 1905 that inspired its creation.

The first decade of the twentieth century was the peak of the interurban fever that was sweeping the country. New lines were being promoted in almost every state. The firm of Stern & Silverman, already established as a builder of trolley lines, was well positioned to take the lead in forming this new enterprise. The partners were experienced and respected; they were familiar with the seashore region and recognized its potential for further growth, especially during the busy summer season. With offices in downtown Philadelphia, they were highly regarded by the PRR executives in the nearby Broad Street Station.

At the same time, PRR managers were faced with changing political conditions. The Progressive Movement was well underway, and the aggressive young President, Theodore Roosevelt had already demonstrated his willingness to curb what many perceived to be the monopolistic tendencies of the railroads. Although the Reading offered some competition in serving southern New Jersey resorts, the PRR was the dominant carrier, with two lines into Atlantic City. Local transportation was also dominated by the WJ&S's Atlantic Avenue line. The PRR managers sought a method to remove them from the public eye while at the same time they could keep firm control of their properties and protect their interests in the region.

The uneasiness of the PRR's managers is shown by their relinquishing control of their rival trunk line, the Baltimore and Ohio Railroad (B&O). In 1900 and 1901, in an effort to minimize competition, the PRR purchased $65,000,000 of B&O stock,

Above: *A Central Passenger Railway open car is seen on September 6, 1910, on Virginia Avenue. By this time the company was controlled by the new Atlantic City & Shore Railroad, which used its Virginia Avenue tracks to reach the Boardwalk. Although popular with the public, open cars required a considerable investment for equipment that could only earn revenue during the summer. LeRoy O. King, Sr. photo, LeRoy O. King, Jr. collection*

CHAPTER FOUR | 1900-1910

Above: This view facing east towards Atlantic City, taken around 1910 near Meadows Tower on the Newfield branch, shows the junction of the AC&S with the PRR's line. The two outer tracks are the Newfield branch and the two inner tracks descend from the trestle and will merge behind the photographer. A careful examination of the distant inner tracks will show the extension high wooden trestles used by the AC&S to cross the other railroads entering Atlantic City. Some people found the roller coaster-type trestles unnerving and sought other means of transport. Robert Long collection

giving it control of the company. Only five years later, alarmed by Congressional and court action, and public hostility, the PRR withdrew and returned the B&O to local management. When William Stern and Isaac Silverman developed a plan to build a high-speed interurban line between Atlantic City and Ocean City, utilizing rights over the PRR's tracks between the western edge of Atlantic City and Somers Point, the PRR managers were willing to support the idea.

In October 1905, the Stern and Silverman partnership incorporated the Atlantic City and Shore Railroad (AC&S) under the New Jersey "Act Concerning Railroads" of 1903. The charter was valid for 999 years and provided for the construction of a railroad, less than two miles in length, from a point in Egg Harbor Township, near the WJ&S's Newfield line, to a location near the Beach Thorofare in Atlantic City. Initially, the authorized capital stock was only $25,000; most of it was in the name of John A. MacPeak of Philadelphia, an associate of the partners. Six other qualifying directors each held one share. The required sum of $4,000 was paid to the state treasurer's office. A survey and maps were submitted to the state in November, showing the line extending in a gentle arc from the corner of Virginia and Adriatic avenues, the end of track of the Central Passenger Railway, to the Beach Thorofare, and then on trestles over the WJ&S and Reading main lines, to the Newfield line near Meadows Tower.

In order to reach the Boardwalk at Virginia Avenue, the AC&S purchased the Central Passenger Railway in December 1905. The Central Passenger line was promptly completed under its original franchise by building a track down Adriatic Avenue to South Carolina Avenue, and then east along that artery to the Boardwalk. Soon after the Shore Fast Line began operating, outbound cars used Virginia Avenue to Adriatic, while inbound cars ran on South Carolina Avenue to Atlantic Avenue, north several blocks to Virginia Avenue, and on that street to the Boardwalk terminal.

In the same busy month of December 1905, the WJ&S signed an agreement with the AC&S and its affiliated Central Passenger Railway granting them rights to operate over the Newfield Branch, between Meadows tower and Pleasantville, and down the Somers Point Branch to its end at the Great Egg Harbor Bay. The rental payments for the Newfield trackage were four percent of the book value of the right-of-way and half the cost of maintenance and operations. For use of the Somers Point Branch, the AC&S agreed to pay five percent of the value of the property and the entire cost of operating and maintaining the line. The PRR retained the right to use the branch for freight and its own trains.

Construction of the Atlantic City-Somers Point Line

Construction got underway immediately. Tracks were laid on a private right-of-way along the median of what soon become Absecon Boulevard and then on Marmora Avenue to the Beach Thorofare, with overhead wire supported by center poles. They were replaced by third rail power as the double tracks crossed the

51

Above: A Newfield line train for Atlantic City, led by West Jersey & Atlantic Railroad locomotive 24, arrives at Pleasantville in the late nineteenth century while a Somers Point local train waits. The branch would be rebuilt and electrified in 1906 for use by the new Shore Fast Line service between Atlantic City and Ocean City. John D. Denney, Jr. collection

waterway on a steel, 110-foot drawbridge. The line then crossed above the tracks of the WJ&S and Reading on 2,500 feet of S-shaped trestles and bridges and descended to join the Newfield line near Meadows Tower. A flyover permitted inbound AC&S cars to pass above the westbound Newfield track on a trestle.

In June 1906, William Stern was dismayed to learn that the survey locating the junction with the Newfield line was "a few hundred feet" short of the actual junction point. This meant the AC&S track needed to be extended, but if the AC&S did the work, it would exceed the two-mile route specified in its charter. A flurry of letters between Stern and the PRR engineers followed, with the railroad's contractors finally agreeing to do the work at the expense of the AC&S. By the end of July, the new line was completed and ready for service.

Work was also underway rebuilding and double-tracking the Somers Point Branch. Initially, Stern wanted power transmitted by a third rail, but by March 1906, he decided on an overhead trolley method because of the many grade crossings and the dangers of a third rail in an area of a potentially rapid population growth. He also insisted on 85-pound rail on the original single track as well as on the new second track. PRR Vice-President Samuel Rea approved these measures and an appropriation of $234,000 was budgeted for the work.

By July, much of the new track had been laid, but Stern and Silverman's engineer complained to the PRR that there were many gaps, up to ¾ of an inch, between the ends of the rail sections, which interfered with the bonding. Stern and Silverman were dissatisfied with the pace of the work and pressured the PRR to complete it as soon as possible so they could begin service. By August 16, the PRR engineers reported the track was ready for

CHAPTER FOUR | *1900-1910*

Above: : *Only four years old, coach 102 rests in the Mamora Avenue yard in 1910. The wood interurban cars would be the only equipment to serve the Shore Fast Line route during its entire existence. They were updated over the years, but retained their basic features. The windows lifted into roof pockets providing plenty of fresh air into the non-air-conditioned cars. LeRoy O. King, Sr. photo, LeRoy O. King, Jr. collection* **Bottom:** *In 1905 horse-drawn wagons are the only vehicles to offer competition to the Central Passenger Railway car on Virginia Avenue and the Boardwalk. Evidently taken in the off-season as few people are to be seen. The wooden hotel is typical of the era where guests could sit in rocking chairs on the covered porches and enjoy the sea breezes. Richard Allman collection*

James N.J. Henwood

Above: When the Pennsylvania Railroad electrified its Camden-Newfield-Pleasantville line to Atlantic City, it purchased a fleet of wood multiple-unit cars to operate the branch. In a scene taken much later, probably the 1940s, two of these durable cars, lettered for the successor company, Pennsylvania-Reading Seashore Lines, are seen at the Federal Street Station in Camden. Although most of the power on the route was collected by third rail shoes (as seen here), frequent grade crossings in Gloucester required the use of overhead wire, so the cars were also equipped with trolley poles. For a short period, some of these cars ran from Pleasantville to Ocean City over the Shore Fast Line route. Richard Short collection

AC&S crews to string the overhead wire. Surfacing and ditching along the tracks were almost completed.

Power was supplied by the Westville power station of the WJ&S and transmitted at 33,000 volts AC to substations along the branch, including one in Atlantic City, which also supplied the AC&S cars. A high-tension line was carried along the Somers Point Branch on the line poles, spread 150 feet apart, which supported the overhead wires. A new brick substation was built in Somers Point, where the current was reduced to 650 volts DC by two 300-kw rotary converters. This substation provided power from Linwood to Somers Point, and soon into Ocean City. It was placed in service in August 1906.

New Cars for the Shore Fast Line

During the summer, 20 new double-end wood interurban cars were received from the John Stephenson Company of Elizabeth, New Jersey, a subsidiary of the J. G. Brill Company of Philadelphia. Eighteen were coaches numbered 100 to 117, and two were combination baggage-passenger cars, numbered 118 and 119. No. 100 was soon converted into a funeral car named *Absequam*. Painted red, the cars were 45 feet, five inches long, eight feet, eight inches wide, and were of the Brill semi-convertible type, with windows that rose into pockets under the roof to allow a copious flow of air during the warm season. Capable of a speed of 55 miles per hour, they had Brill 27-E1 MCB trucks, with four General Electric 60-horsepower motors and Type M multiple-unit control and couplers. Equipped with four overrunning third rail shoes that folded up and latched when not in use, they could also draw power through two roof-mounted trolley poles. Interiors were finished in cherry, with white ceilings, reversible rattan seats, 52 for the coaches and 36 for the combines. They were painted red and were equipped with portable arc headlights. Later modified, they served for the life of the line.

Service Begins

In the summer of 1906, the Central Passenger Railway began service on its loop line on Virginia, Adriatic, and South Carolina avenues, utilizing five single-truck cars. By August, the new Shore Fast Line was ready to inaugurate service to Somers Point, its temporary terminal. A carbarn had been erected along Marmora Avenue, between Illinois and New York avenues to store and service the cars. An inspection trip for company officials was operated on August 23, 1906, and two days later regular service began.

CHAPTER FOUR | *1900-1910*

SHORE FAST LINE

The Automobile Route

TO OCEAN CITY AND POINTS SOUTH
Crossing Great Egg Harbor Bay

Service Between **Somers Point** and **Ocean City**

Phone Superintendent's Office—1700 Bell or 872 Coast—twenty minutes before you want service and we will be at your command at SOMERS POINT OR OCEAN CITY.

STAR PRINT, 1632 ATL. AVE.

Above: *Late in 1907 this advertisement touted the soon-to-begin automobile service where electric cars could pull autos on flatcars over its Great Egg Harbor Bridge trestle between Somers Point and Ocean City. The construction of a road bridge next to the trolley line soon put an end to the experiment.* John Nieveen collection

Above: A view from the early years of Shore Fast Line's operation. A car from Atlantic City has just left the joint trackage shared with PRR as it readies to complete its run to Ocean City. Jim Kranefeld collection

Patronage was light at first, and it was not helped by a third rail failure on the Meadows, which stalled several cars. The passengers were forced to wade through mud and soggy ground to the Turnpike Road, where cars of the Suburban line carried them back to Atlantic City. Nor were Stern and Silverman satisfied. Isaac Silverman complained to the PRR engineers that the surfacing of the Somers Point line was very poor. After examining the track, the PRR agreed that the southern half of the line needed improvement. WJ&S Superintendent D. H. Lovell arranged for a work train to correct the deficiencies in October. But in the following spring when the AC&S asked that 3,000 new crossties be installed on the original track to Somers Point, the PRR flatly rejected the demand, stating the branch "was put in first class condition, every tie being renewed which should be renewed." Stern and Silverman were forced to accept this decision. Despite these problems, ridership soon increased, especially after the PRR began electric train service from Camden to Atlantic City on September 18, 1906. Passengers could conveniently transfer to Shore Fast Line cars at Pleasantville.

The Shore Fast Line Reaches Ocean City

While the Somers Point Branch was being rebuilt, Stern and Silverman were planning to construct the extension from Somers Point over the Great Egg Harbor Bay to Ocean City. The first step was the incorporation of the Atlantic City and Ocean City Railroad (AC&OC) on March 19, 1906, under the "Act Concerning Railroads of 1903." Initially the authorized capital stock was only $25,000, but it was increased to $180,000 in March, 1907.

A survey of the route, from Bay Avenue in Somers Point to 8th Street and the bay shore in Ocean City, was filed in August 1906. The required $4,000 had been paid to the state in March at the time of incorporation. The work was undertaken by the Atlantic City Construction Company, another Stern and Silverman organization, and the bridges were erected by the Penn Bridge Company. The line spanned the bay, crossing two drawbridges and a series of four trestles. Near the center of the bay, it crossed the two low-lying Rainbow islands. Here the right-of-way was built up by sand pumped from the bottom of the bay and deposited as a base for the track. Two passing sidings were located in this section. Altogether, the line stretched almost two miles from Somers Point to the 8th Street bulkhead in Ocean City.

The agreement with the PRR granting the AC&S the right to use the Somers Point Branch was amended on March 26, 1907, giving the AC&S and the AC&OC the right to connect with the WJ&S in Somers Point and in Ocean City, where the PRR-owned Ocean City Branch ran from south to north along West Avenue. The PRR station was located on West Avenue, between 9th Street and 8th Street. The railroad owned a large tract of land between those streets, extending from West Avenue to the bay, containing storage tracks and a wye for turning locomotives. A new track was laid on railroad property along the south side of 8th Street, which was connected to the end of the wye track for

CHAPTER FOUR | 1900-1910

use by the electric cars. They terminated short of the PRR West Avenue station building.

The Effort to Reach the Ocean City Boardwalk

From the 1905 incorporation of the Atlantic City and Shore, both Stern and Silverman and the PRR expected the new electric railway to run from the Atlantic City Boardwalk to the Ocean City Boardwalk, but the attempt to extend the line a little more than one-half mile from the bay down 8th Street proved to be a major challenge. Initially, the PRR managers, ever mindful of the importance of maintaining "control" over the territory through which their lines ran, expected the PRR to build the 8th Street trackage itself. In 1906, WJ&S Superintendent D. H. Lovell attempted to get city approval for the line, but property owners along the street, fearful of having steam trains rumbling down their thoroughfare, opposed the effort. By 1907, however, as the new electric line approached, the residents reconsidered, and they then favored a trolley line, with the exception of two property owners. At the same time, William Stern was anxious to have the AC&OC build this extension. Under New Jersey law, if a railroad company sought a franchise for street trackage, it must have the approval of all the abutting property owners, forcing the PRR to resort to condemnation proceedings against the two recalcitrant owners. On the other hand, a franchise could be granted to a street railway with the approval of only 51 percent of the owners.

This situation caused Samuel Rea and other PRR executives to reverse their position and approve the proposal of William Stern that the AC&OC build the line, but only from West Avenue east to the Boardwalk. The new Shore Fast Line cars would still have to use the track on PRR property paralleling 8th Street, between the bay and West Avenue, and the AC&OC would have to grant the PRR rights to run any trains they wished directly to the beach. This saved the railroad the $20,000 cost of construction and still maintain its control by virtue of its ownership of the bay-West Avenue segment.

Neither William Stern nor Isaac Silverman were willing to accept this fragmented approach, and backed by their lawyers,

Above: *An Atlantic City & Shore Railroad Company stock certificate for 100 shares, registered on April 17, 1907. At a stated value of $100 each, this was a considerable investment at the time.* John Nieveen collection

57

James N.J. Henwood

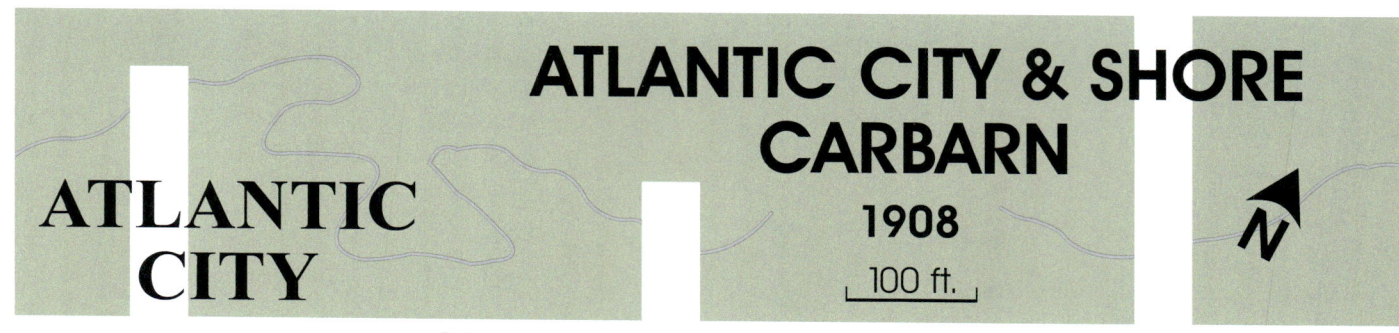

ATLANTIC CITY & SHORE CARBARN
1908

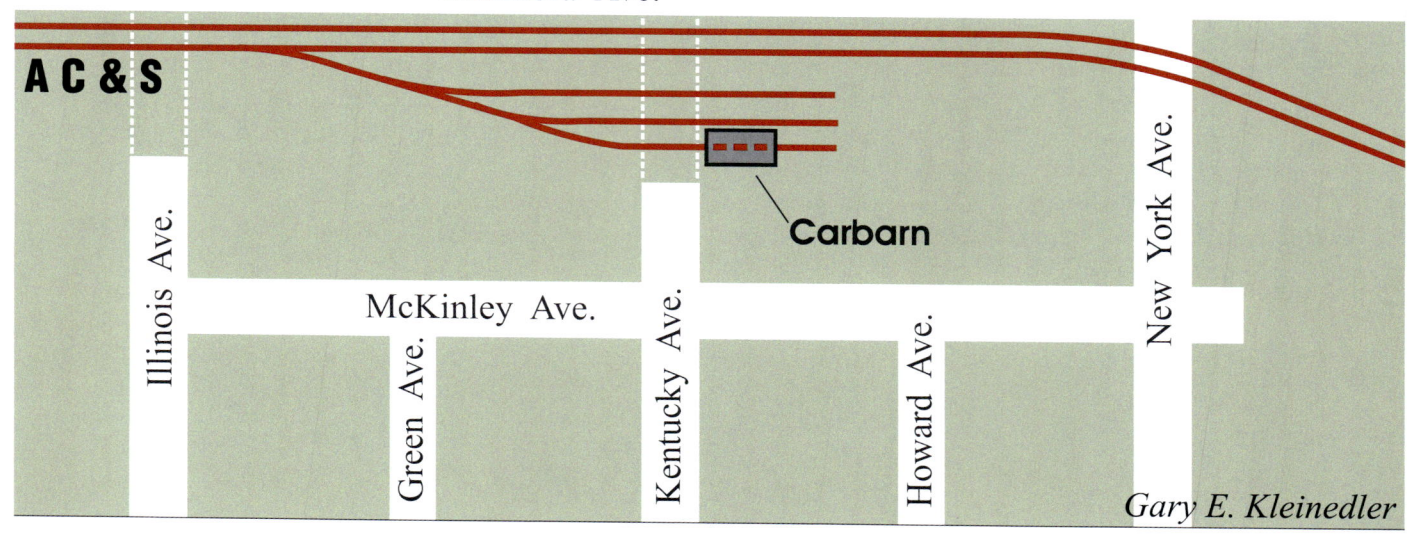

Above and below: Maps showing the carbarns of both the AC&S and the WJ&S in 1908.

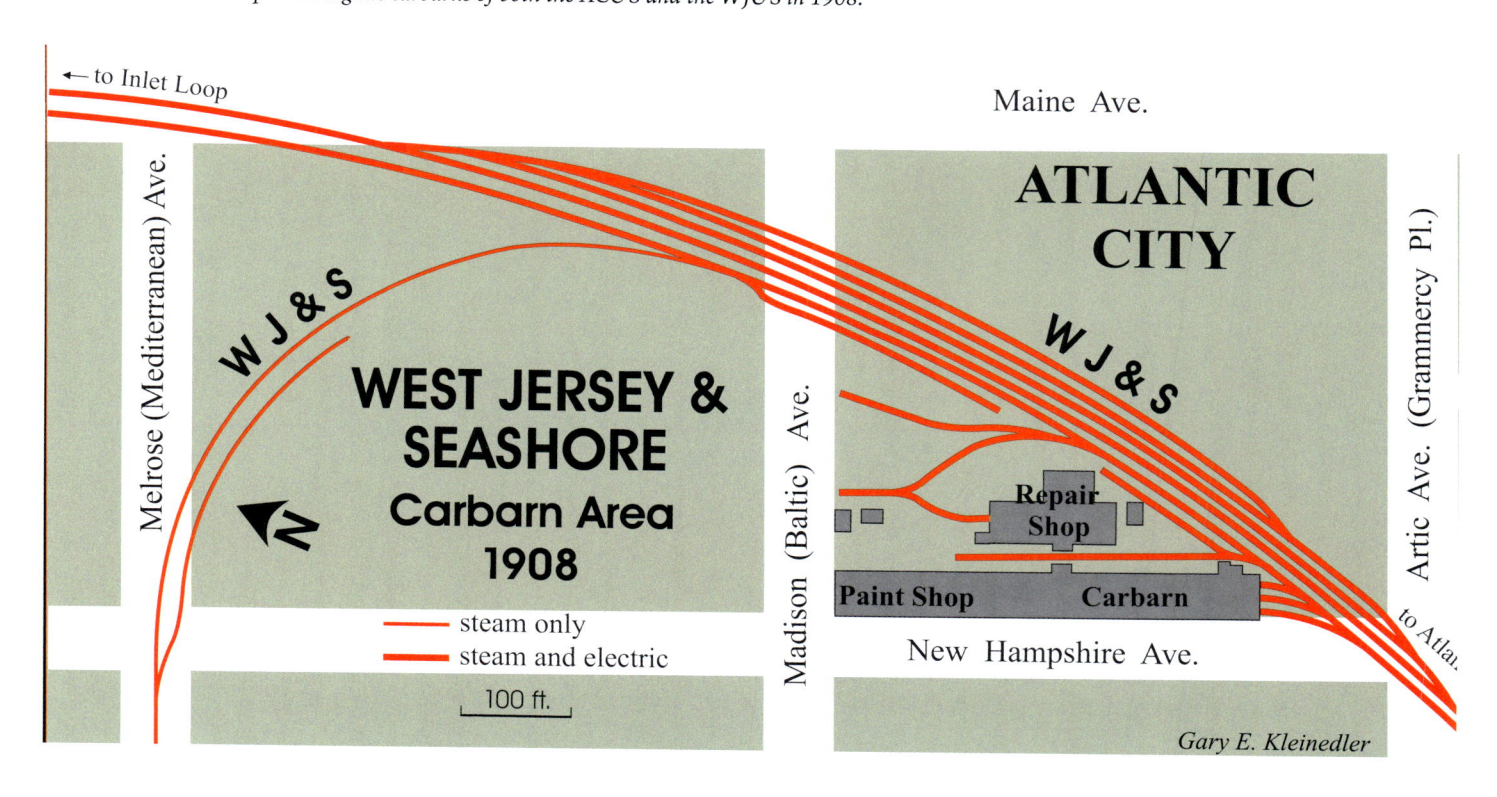

WEST JERSEY & SEASHORE
Carbarn Area
1908

— steam only
— steam and electric

Gary E. Kleinedler

58

Above: In a classic view early in the century, crowds gather outside the Philadelphia & Reading station at Arkansas Avenue. A northbound Atlantic Avenue streetcar pauses while an open landau carriage heads toward the ocean. Such scenes were common in the pre-automobile age when people traveled by train and local trolley lines were profitable. All too soon, the automobile would offer competition to both the railroads and trolley lines. Railways to Yesterday Library photo, Fred W. Schneider, III collection

insisted on the right to construct the 8th Street line from the bay to the Boardwalk. Samuel Rea understood the logic of their position and agreed with their demand, provided that the AC&OC was still obligated to use the line on the PRR property, between the bay and West Avenue. This would create, in effect, a double track section between those points which could be used as a passing siding. The Shore Fast Line was obliged to protect its cars when crossing the PRR tracks on West Avenue as well as when crossing the parallel Reading Railroad tracks on Haven Avenue; agree not to plan any other connection or extension without PRR approval, and grant the PRR the right to run its trains on 8th Street if it so desired. The prior rights gained by the PRR to cross the city streets along 8th Street as well as to cross the Reading's line on Haven Avenue, were extended to cover the AC&OC tracks, both on PRR property and on 8th Street.

The Firm of Stern and Silverman, Inc. is Created

While the construction across the bay continued and the question of the 8th Street extension was debated, William Stern and Isaac Silverman wisely decided to incorporate their firm, creating a more reliable and beneficial business structure than a partnership. The company was incorporated on January 21, 1907, under Pennsylvania's general incorporation law of 1874, to "carry on a general engineering and contracting business," with offices in Philadelphia. A capital stock issue of 1,000 shares, at a par value of $100 each, was authorized and used to acquire the property and good will of the partnership. William Stern and Isaac Silverman thus owned virtually all the stock of the new corporation. Among the associates of the founders were Leo A. Isenthal, Alvin W. From, Harry Kohn, Tilghman Johnston, and George H. B. Martin.

POLITICAL CHANGES:

THE PROGRESSIVE MOVEMENT IMPACTS THE PENNSYLVANIA RAILROAD

By the turn of the century, an emerging group of reformers, both Democrats and Republicans, who styled themselves as Progressives, were calling for fundamental changes in the way governments--federal, state, and local--reacted to the growth of the large corporations that dominated the business world. They argued that the basic democratic institutions of the republic were threatened by the immense wealth and power wielded by a relative handful of executives and bankers in vital industries, especially railroads, steel, oil, and shipping. These large corporations tended to form monopolies, crushing small businesses and competition in the process.

Although Progressives agreed that big business was a menace, they disagreed about a solution to the problem. Some wanted the federal government to break up these gigantic trusts, while others called for the creation of new federal agencies to regulate and control them. In September 1901, a dramatic political change took place when the young, dynamic Vice-President, Theodore Roosevelt, was propelled into the White House following the assassination of William McKinley. Eminently practical, highly popular, with an oversized ego, and arguably the most intelligent man ever to sit in the presidential chair, Roosevelt agreed that big business combinations were dangerous for political and economic reasons, but he felt it was futile to break them up. His solution was to create a federal agency to regulate business that would permit the public to benefit from their efficiencies and lower prices and at the same time check their abuses.

Unable to persuade Congress to act, Roosevelt decided to use the almost moribund Sherman Anti-trust Act of 1890 to attack selected trusts, which he identified as evil and led by "malefactors of great wealth," on the premise this would frighten the other big businesses and lessen the power of monopolies. In November 1901, he startled the nation by announcing the federal government planned to use the Sherman Act to dissolve a gigantic railroad combine in the Northwest, the Northern Securities Company, involving such powerful men as James Jerome Hill, president of the Great Northern Railroad, William Henry Harriman, chairman of the Union Pacific, and J. P. Morgan, whose banking house was among the more powerful on Wall Street. Shivers must have run down the backs of Pennsylvania Railroad executives, who might wonder if Roosevelt would see them as "malefactors of great wealth." This apprehension may have been a factor in the railroad's 1907 decision to end its local transportation monopoly in Atlantic City by leasing its properties to the new Atlantic City and Shore Railroad.

Letters Patent were signed by the governor on February 21, 1907, giving corporate and legal powers to the new company for a term of 99 years.

The Shore Fast Line Enters Ocean City

By late spring 1907, the bridge and trestle work across the bay was nearing completion. Test runs of cars into Ocean City and on to the track on PRR property paralleling 8th Street began in May. On June 22, a local newspaper exalted, "Atlantic City and Ocean City were joined in trolley wedlock for the first time." The official grand opening was celebrated, appropriately, on July 4, and the Ocean City Sentinel proclaimed: "To the majority of the residents of this city, there never was heard prettier music than the ugly tooting of the whistle Monday afternoon proclaiming the arrival in Ocean City of the first car over the bridge across the bay." Cars ran every 15 minutes between 9 A.M. and 9 P.M. and every 30 minutes from 6 A.M. to 9 A.M. and from 9 P.M. to midnight.

As track workers spiked rails down 8th Street, Stern and Silverman took another legal step, leasing the AC&OC Railroad to the AC&S on August 30, 1907. Under its terms, valid for 999 years, the AC&S agreed to pay all taxes and fees and give the AC&OC $500 annually for maintaining its corporate organization. It also was to pay $10,000 a year to the AC&OC, but $9,000 was to be returned to the AC&S in the form of dividends on the stock, all of which was owned by the Shore Company. In addition to paying the interest on the $180,000 in five percent bonds, also owned by the AC&S, it would pay one-third of the net profits, up to $25,000, to the AC&S. The Shore Company was given complete operating and legal authority, including the right to abandon the property. All these provisions were a case of moving funds, in theory, from one pocket to the other of the AC&S, since it owned all the stock and bonds of the AC&OC. As required by its agreements with the WJ&S, that company formally approved the lease on September 27, 1907.

The Atlantic City and Shore Leases the Atlantic Avenue Trolley Line

Perhaps the most significant indication of the growing influence of the AC&S was the agreement signed with the PRR on June 28, 1907, under which the trolley company leased for a period of 20 years the Atlantic Avenue to Longport line, the boat line on Great Egg Harbor Bay connecting Atlantic City and Ocean City, the rolling stock, the carbarn and shop equipment, office furniture, and miscellaneous facilities, thereby making it the dominant operator of the local transit lines, effective July 15, 1907. Included were 60 cars: 20 semi-convertibles, 35 open cars, two combination cars, and three open trailers.

Under the terms of the agreement, the AC&S was to operate and maintain the line, pay all taxes and insurance as well as a rental based on five percent of the value of the property, and six percent on any subsequent betterments. This amounted to $6,250 a month initially. In addition, the traction company had to pay half of its net operating profits to the lessor.

The initial impetus for this transaction probably came from Stern and Silverman. Both of the partners were in an expansive mood and were aggressively increasing their presence in the shore communities. It made economic and political sense to have one operator of the trolley lines, which shared tracks in certain places. The conservative PRR managers agreed to the arrangement, but they shrewdly kept firm control of their property and earned a healthy income while being spared the many problems associated with operating the streetcars. Relations with the towns were often contentious, and by not directly operating the line, the PRR hoped to reduce the hostile glare of Progressive politicians who consistently attacked what they perceived to be railroad monopolies.

In the annual report of the West Jersey and Seashore Railroad, President James McCrea (who was also president of the PRR) blandly noted the agreement would aid in the development of the shore territory and place operations with a firm which specialized in electric railways. A few years later, in 1910, Samuel Rea, by then Second Vice-President of the PRR, wrote that the trackage rights were granted because the AC&S "would ultimately be a competitive system, and already had on the ground an Operative Organization [sic] and outfit of sufficient experience and ability [so that] it was to our advantage to utilize the same and thus save a duplication of expense both to ourselves and the public."

Unrealized Proposals for Further Expansion

An air of optimism still prevailed in railroad circles in the latter half of the decade, and several proposals for extending service appeared. None of them were to be realized, and within a few years, the emergence of highway competition ended such hopes permanently.

In 1907, reports that a group of financiers from Buffalo, New York, were planning to build a 36-mile electric line from Millville to Ocean City caused some concern among PRR and Stern and Silverman officials in Philadelphia, but nothing came of it. In 1908 and 1909, William Stern urged Samuel Rea to permit the AC&S to operate motor cars on the PRR's Ocean City Branch between Ocean City and Stone Harbor. From there, boats would carry passengers to Anglesea in northern Wildwood. He also supported a proposed rail line from Stone Harbor to Cape May Court House, the county seat, which local entrepreneurs were promoting. Stern was anxious to strengthen the Shore Fast Line interurban by giving it better connections and by helping to develop the region south of Ocean City. Rea was interested, telling Superintendent D. H. Lovell of the WJ&S to investigate, saying "we ought to do everything possible to increase the income of the WJ&S R.R. Co." Again, nothing came of this idea.

In 1909 and 1910, the PRR conducted a detailed survey and study for a new line on Absecon Island to be built from the end of the Chelsea Branch, at Albany and Atlantic Avenues, south to Longport over a route close to the Thorofare and parallel to the existing Atlantic Avenue trolley line. Such a route would tap the communities of Ventnor, Margate, and Longport and remove freight trains from Atlantic Avenue where they were increasingly unpopular. It would permit the PRR to run passenger trains from these towns to the Newfield Branch and the Main Line west of the city, avoiding the South Carolina Avenue station. The aim was to develop further Absecon Island as well as to attract commuters who were currently using the Reading's trains. The estimated cost to build the five-mile line was $283,000. Fortunately for the PRR, cooler heads prevailed and the extravagant proposal was dropped.

Improvements and Modifications

The Stern and Silverman management made a number of improvements on its lines. In 1907, the Central Passenger Railway secured approval from the city to install about 1,000 feet of double track on Virginia Avenue, from Atlantic Avenue to the Boardwalk, at a cost of $200,000. This section was used by the Central Passenger loop cars and those of the Shore Fast Line. In the same year, the WJ&S undertook to grade, lay new rail, and pave its tracks in Atlantic City at a cost of $366,000.

Also, in 1908, the AC&S rented a new four-story brick building at 8 South Virginia Avenue, directly off Atlantic Avenue, for a waiting room and office space, at an annual rental of $840. That same year the company launched an innovative "auto ferry" service from Somers Point to Ocean City. Using a flat car pulled by one of the interurban cars, the railroad offered to carry automobiles over its trestles and bridges spanning the bay. The arrangement was cumbersome and time-consuming, and since Ocean City was already accessible via a toll road that entered the southern tip of the island, the business was short-lived. In 1908, inbound Shore Fast Line cars began to run down South Carolina Avenue from Absecon Boulevard to Atlantic Avenue instead of using Virginia Avenue. The WJ&S granted the AC&S the right to run its Ocean City cars on Atlantic Avenue from South Carolina to Virginia Avenues in return for a small additional rental. In 1910, the fare between Pleasantville and Atlantic City on both the AC&S and the Suburban was doubled from five cents to ten cents, causing many complaints.

Above: West Jersey & Shore car 6801 awaits a local run to Ventnor on April 5, 1907. The car was still fairly new, having been built by Brill in 1904. LeRoy O. King, Jr. collection

Concerned over the expense of operations, Stern and Silverman conducted two series of coasting tests in the spring of 1910. Two cars were used: one with ordinary brass journals and one equipped with ball-bearing journals. The results showed the ball-bearing car could save one-half a kilowatt hour per mile over a standard car. The engineers estimated that a car which ran 60,000 miles a year could save $190 in power costs. Despite this convincing demonstration, no changes were made to the other cars. However, a New Jersey law mandating that locomotives be equipped with 30-pound bells that had to run continuously when approaching grade crossings, did provoke a change. The WJ&S legal department concluded the law applied to electric cars as well. Consequently, in 1911, Shore Fast Line cars were equipped with electrically-operated bells, mounted on the center of the roofs at a cost of $60 each.

By this time, service on the Shore Fast Line had stabilized with cars running every 30 minutes until about 8 P.M., after which 60-minute headways were maintained until midnight. Additional cars ran southbound on Saturday afternoons and Sunday mornings, and northbound on Sunday afternoons. Connections were made in both directions for PRR trains between Market Street Wharf in Philadelphia and the Tennessee Avenue electric line terminal in Atlantic City.

Direct Service from Camden to Ocean City is Tried

The connection between the Shore Fast Line and the PRR electric trains at Pleasantville was an easy one, but some people wondered why the PRR trains could not run directly from Camden to Ocean City and return. In January, 1908, R. W. Edwards, Chairman of the Transportation Committee of the Ocean City Board of Trade, submitted a petition to the WJ&S asking for through train service. PRR officials refused, for "... practical and physical reasons." As there were no east to south switches at Pleasantville, such trains would have to reverse direction to enter the Somers Point Branch. This argument did not convince the critics, and appeals for direct service continued. In 1909, William Wallace Atterbury, Fifth Vice-President of the PRR, urged that such trains be tried as an experiment. As the 1910 season approached, the PRR managers concurred. For the period between May 27 and September 26, five through trains were operated each way to and from Camden and Ocean City. In the following year, for approximately the same period, the PRR ran two trains each way.

Early in 1912, PRR President James McCrea appointed a committee to analyze the question of through service and to make recommendations. In its May 20 report, the committee noted a projected cost of up to $175,000 to construct a wye at Pleasantville, to strengthen the Great Egg Harbor Bay bridges and trestles, and to rearrange station facilities in Ocean City. Although electric MU cars were slated to be used, the committee believed that the route had to be suitable for steam-powered trains. The writers of the report pointed out that, under the lease granted to the AC&S, that carrier had to be paid 50 cents per mile for PRR passenger trains operating over its route from Pleasantville to Ocean City. Instead of through service, the committee favored the construction at some point in the future of a new direct electric line from Mays Landing on the Newfield Line to Somers Point. Until traffic increased, it was more economical to keep the current cross-platform transfer point at Pleasantville. In 1911, over 65,000 passengers were carried to Ocean City via Pleasantville and the AC&S, but that was not enough to justify the added expense of direct service trains. The group concluded that the present arrangement should continue.

Despite this negative recommendation, the PRR continued to operate two through trains daily (except Saturday, when only one train ran) in the summer seasons of 1912 and 1913. By 1916 and 1917, this had been reduced to only one westbound train a week, during the summer season, leaving Ocean City on Sunday evenings at about 7:00 P.M. for Market Street Wharf. This minimal direct service was not resumed in 1918.

Disputes with Ventnor

On the Atlantic Avenue to Longport Line, the WJ&S and Stern and Silverman were able to settle a long-running dispute with Ventnor over the operation of its cars through that town, which bordered Atlantic City. The argument began in 1896 when the WJ&S constructed a new loop on its property along the west side of Atlantic Avenue, between Cambridge and Portland Avenues. The city officials were angered by a small freight yard on the property and by a proposal to charge an extra five cent fare for entering Ventnor. The city went to court, and in 1908, it won a decision that the loop had to be removed because the tracks entering and leaving it were far above the grade of unpaved Atlantic Avenue, making it difficult for road traffic to cross them. Samuel Rea was a moderating and reasonable influence and he urged negotiations. He recognized that underlying the complaints of the politicians were the interests of real estate developers, telling William Wallace Atterbury, "We must realize that Ventnor cannot do without us any more than we can do without Ventnor."

An understanding was reached, under which the WJ&S agreed to remove the freight spurs and to reconstruct the loop, lowering the track by six inches. The company deeded to the city its ownership of Atlantic Avenue, on both sides of its right-of-way of 24 feet, 3 inches, and agreed to build and pave 31 street crossings of its tracks. The city confirmed the right of the company to operate its rail line indefinitely and promised it would not permit another railway to use any part of Atlantic Avenue. The city also agreed to accept the Portland Avenue loop for the next ten years.

Atlantic Avenue was subsequently paved on both sides of the right-of-way. The tracks in Ventnor were covered with loose gravel and stone but were not otherwise paved. The agreement was confirmed by an ordinance in 1912, upheld by the Public Utilities Commission, and it settled for a time the disputes with Ventnor.

A Hopeful Look Forward

At the end of the first decade of the century, the AC&S had established itself as the premier transportation company in the vicinity of Atlantic City. It owned very little equipment, except for the 20 interurban cars, and most of its lines were operated under leases from the PRR. It had recently rebuilt 20 semi-convertibles as double-end cars to provide more flexibility of service. Economies were instituted, such as running alternate cars only between New Hampshire and Boston Avenues in the winter. At all times cars ran from the Inlet to either Portland Avenue loop in Ventnor or the full length of the line to Longport. The Central Passenger Railway ran its "Loop Car" on Virginia and South Carolina avenues, providing a cross-town option. The Shore Fast Line cars had established themselves, carrying commuters from the mainland towns and tourists in season who wanted to enjoy a pleasant trip through the coastal areas and the off-shore countryside.

In Philadelphia, officials of the PRR kept a wary eye on their properties along the Jersey seashore, and William Stern and Isaac Silverman continued to make all important decisions regarding the AC&S and its affiliated companies. They looked forward hopefully to even more prosperous undertakings in the near future. But fundamental changes were underway in American society and in distant Europe that would present them with unforeseen and significant challenges in the coming years.

Above: An early photo on the Ocean City end shows passengers boarding Shore Fast Line car 110 for a fast run up to Atlantic City. Like Atlantic City, Shore Fast Line trains terminated at the Ocean City Boardwalk at 8th Street. George Krambles collection

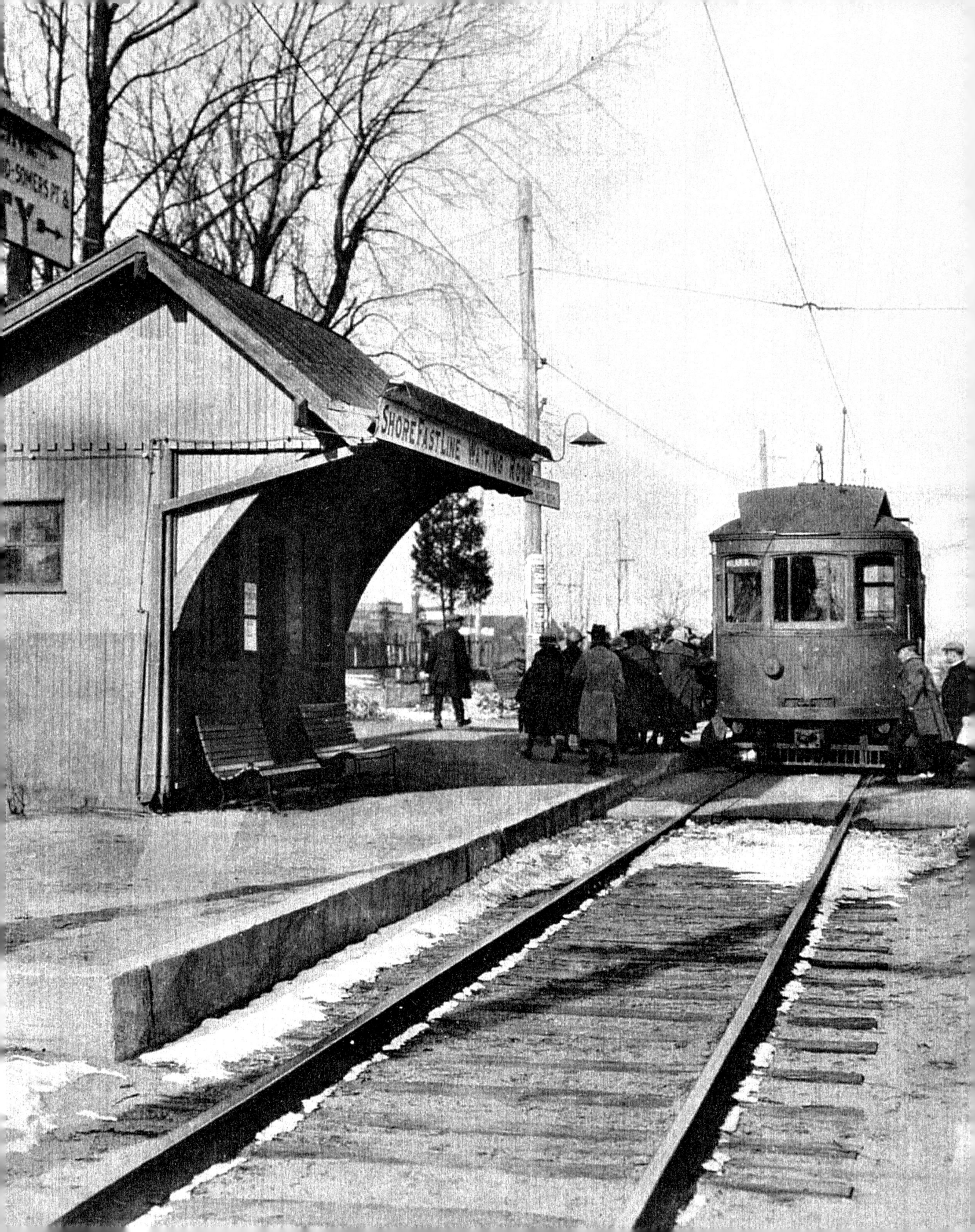
SHORE FAST LINE WAITING

CHAPTER FIVE

A Decade of Turmoil

Stern and Silverman's Atlantic City Enterprise

By the opening of the second decade of the last century, Stern and Silverman had created a complex group of interconnected companies, giving the Philadelphia firm effective control of public transportation in the Atlantic City area. At the apex was the Atlantic City and Shore Company, chartered in Delaware in 1909. This company owned a majority of the capital stock of the Atlantic City and Shore Railroad and the Central Passenger Railway. The AC&S Railroad controlled the Atlantic City and Ocean City Railroad, which owned the line from Somers Point to Ocean City. These corporations had sold bonds to finance the construction and operation of the routes and had considerable fixed interest charges. Stern and Silverman supervised operations through a superintendent stationed in Atlantic City.

By 1913, travel on the boat line between Longport and Ocean City had fallen, reducing the need for five steamers. In April, an effort was made to use the surplus boats and strengthen the Shore Fast Line. William Stern and Isaac Silverman conducted a tour from Atlantic City to Ocean City, Stone Harbor, and Wildwood for a party of local dignitaries. The purpose was to examine the feasibility of instituting a boat line between Stone Harbor, the end of the PRR branch from Ocean City, and Wildwood. Such a line was shorter and more direct than the PRR's circuitous route via Sea Isle Junction, Wildwood Junction, Anglesea, and Wildwood. Satisfied, Stern and Silverman inaugurated a summer service beginning June 28, under the Atlantic City and Shore Railroad banner, using the steamers *Ocean City and Wildwood*. The vessels ran every hour between 7 A.M. and 7 P.M. from Stone Harbor to Anglesea and return, linking the two WJ&S

Facing Page: An Atlantic City-bound car makes a stop at Pleasantville on a wintery day in the 1920s. Once passengers have been discharged and boarded, the interurban will switch onto third rail track for the continuation of its run. James Kranefeld collection

Above: In this view—probably the '30s—open car 6844 rests at the Douglas Avenue loop while the crew takes a break. This car was originally built for service on the Longport steam dummy trains and was later electrified. Charles Duncan, Fred W. Schneider, III collection

branches. The fare was 15 cents. Evidently the experiment was unsuccessful, as it was not repeated.

The following year, on September 4, the firm suffered a major blow when William Stern, the senior partner, died at age 54 after a sudden illness. Always the more aggressive of the partners, he was involved in a number of projects, including a plan to construct a rapid transit tunnel under the Delaware River. Isaac Silverman succeeded him as head of the firm and in executive positions in the several Atlantic City companies.

The death of Stern symbolized a transition in the affairs of the company and in the electric railway industry as a whole. Both had matured; the period of growth and expansion was coming to a close. The firm settled down to manage its properties and to combat the increasing forces of competition threatening the profitability and survival of the electric railways.

The Venice Park Railroad

Among the last acquisitions by the AC&S was the Venice Park Railroad, a short trolley line built to provide access to a real estate development called Venice Park, in the northwestern part of the city. Surrounded by waterways and embracing about 40 acres, it was conceived as a potential Venice by the developer, the South End Real Estate Company.

The Venice Park Railroad Company was incorporated under the New Jersey steam railroad act on May 4, 1909. It was capitalized at $10,000, although only $2,000 was subscribed by the initial investors, mostly New Yorkers, led by W. Russell Osborne. The line began on Ohio Avenue, at Marmora Avenue, where it met but did not connect with the Shore Fast Line route. It followed Ohio Avenue to the Penrose Canal, a short waterway branching off the Thorofare and crossed it on a bridge. It continued on Ohio Avenue in Venice Park until Central Avenue (later renamed Kuehnle Avenue), where it turned left onto Central, ending at Riverside Drive, paralleling the Beach Thorofare. The length of the route was slightly more than one-half mile.

In October 1909, the Venice Park Railroad made an agreement with the AC&S, whereby the Shore Fast Line was to build feeder wires and sell electric power to the short line for three cents per kilowatt hour. A second-hand, single-truck car was procured from the Union Railway of New York City. No fares were charged, in order to stimulate sales in the development.

By 1911, the Venice Park Railroad was controlled by local investors, including Louis Kuehnle and George F. Joly, Jr., purchasers of the development in the same year. The lack of a direct connection to central Atlantic City and the Boardwalk was a serious impediment to further growth. This was corrected by incorporating a street railway company on April 20, 1912,

Above: This is the only known photograph of the Venice Park Railroad's original car. Acquired from the Union Railway of New York, it is shown here at Ohio and Marmora avenues on September 7, 1910. Lacking a number, it was supplemented by Central Passenger Railway cars when through service was established in 1912. LeRoy O. King. Sr., LeRoy O. King, Jr. collection

CHAPTER FIVE | *A Decade of Turmoil*

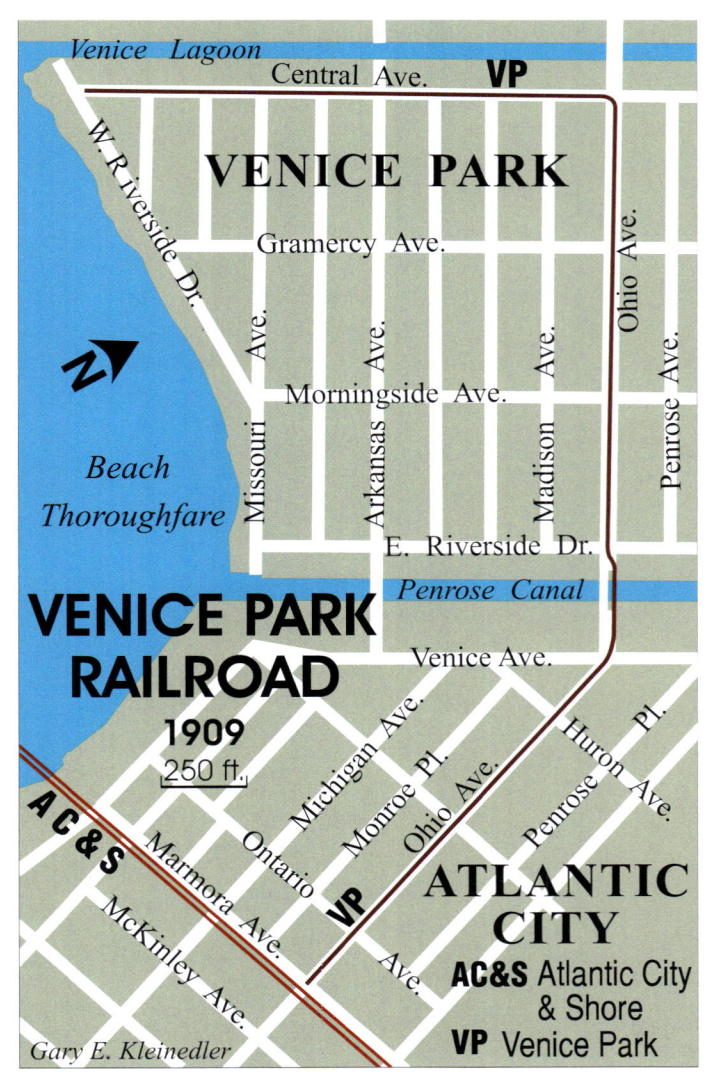

Above: Venice Park Railroad in 1909.

called the Venice Park Railway Company, with a capitalization of $20,000. It was controlled by Kuehnle and Joly.

From a connection with the original route at Ohio and Marmora avenues, a line was built easterly on Ohio Avenue to Hummock Avenue, where it turned onto Illinois Avenue for a short distance (one block) to Adriatic Avenue. It continued along Adriatic to South Carolina Avenue, connecting with the Central Passenger Railway's line on those streets, permitting the establishment of through service from the beach to Venice Park. The city council approved an ordinance in June 1912, granting a street railway franchise to the Venice Park Railway. At the same time, an agreement was made with the Central Passenger Railway authorizing through service, beginning on August 15, 1912. Both companies ran cars from the Boardwalk at South Carolina or Virginia avenues to Venice Park, a distance of 1.86 miles. A five-cent fare was charged, with the money going to whichever company operated the particular car a passenger boarded. However, the Central Passenger Railway operated the line.

Cars ran from Virginia Avenue and the Boardwalk to Venice Park every 30 minutes, leaving on the hour and half-hour. In 1916, no service was offered because of a dispute between Stern and Silverman and the Venice Park Railway. The Central Passenger Railway refused to renew its through service agreement. With the help of Mayor Harry Bacharach, cars again went to Venice Park, beginning on July 28, 1917. Most likely, traffic was light on the Venice Park portion of the route, as the development was not that large. The highest volume of fares came between the Boardwalk and Atlantic Avenue. Half-hourly service was offered on this short route.

A Hectic Decade

At this time, profound changes were taking place in the world, the nation, and locally. Woodrow Wilson was sworn into office in March 1913. His administration began developing a moderately progressive program, with laws reforming banking, the tariff, and business regulation.

Wilson tried to keep the country out of the conflict engulfing Europe, but continued provocations by German U-boats and other incidents caused the country to declare war on Germany in April 1917.

The war forced many changes in the American economy and way-of-life. A conscription law called almost five million men into the Army; two million being sent to the battlefields in France. Everything was subordinated to winning the war. Industry was disrupted; taxes were raised; prices increased rapidly as inflation took hold; federal agencies such as the War Industries Board, the United States Railroad Administration, and the Emergency Fleet Corporation wielded unprecedented powers, and labor became more militant. The 18th Amendment, ratified in January 1919, authorized national prohibition. Although Atlantic City was primarily a resort area, the war affected the Stern and Silverman properties there as well.

Steamboat Service Declines

The 1907 lease of the West Jersey and Seashore operations to the AC&S included the steamboat service connecting Longport and Ocean City. Five boats were available, running every half-hour, from about 5 A.M. to 6 P.M. from late June until mid-September. The 2.75-mile route took 30 minutes to traverse. The AC&S promoted the boat line as part of a through route to and from Ocean City. Travelers could use the boats in one direction and Shore Fast Line cars in the other.

The boats were moored and coaled at the 2nd Street wharf in Ocean City, where connections were made with the PRR trains from Stone Harbor and with Ocean City Electric Railway cars. Both routes crossed the Shore Fast Line tracks on 8th Street, providing an easy transfer. In Longport, the 16th Street pier was longer, with a restaurant and freight house. Convenient connections were made with the Atlantic Avenue trolleys. In the winter, the boats were maintained and stored at the Quigley and Dorp Shipyard on the Delaware River in Philadelphia.

The boats ran subject to storms, occasional engine failures, and tidal conditions, that could be quite strong at the entrance channel from the ocean to the bay. Steamboat service timetables warned passengers trips might be annulled during periods when the tides were too swift for the small boats. At such times, the vessels operated "pleasure trips" on the more placid waterways and coves along the western shore of the bay. Partly because of the unreliability of the service, patronage gradually declined. This was especially true after the Ocean City Automobile Bridge Company opened a 25-cent toll road on April 11, 1914, including four bridges, linking Somers Point with 9th Street in Ocean City. This span closely paralleled the Shore Fast Line trestles and it attracted former passengers of both the trolleys and the boat line. In an effort to gain more business, the AC&S hired musicians to play on selected boat trips in 1915, but the decline continued. After the 1918 season, the boat line was discontinued.

The PRR billed the AC&S for the loss it sustained in the anticipated sale of the boats. Originally valued at over $37,000, they realized only $10,000 in sales, a deficit of over $27,000. When the pier rentals and taxes for 1919, already paid for by the AC&S, were deducted, the trolley company paid the balance of $353 to the PRR in 1920.

Maintaining the Shore Fast Line

During these years, service on the interurban line remained good. In the summer season, cars ran between Atlantic City and Ocean City every 30 minutes, from 5:30 A.M. to midnight, supplemented by two weekday short-turn runs. In the winter headways were increased to one hour.

Maintaining the line was expensive and required constant attention. A 1912 state inspection noted the 80-pound rail was ballasted with cinders and gravel, while the bridges over the steam railroads in Atlantic City were "getting in poor condition," with many decaying ties. The trestles over the bay, constructed with creosoted timber and piling, were better. Maximum speed over them was 15 miles per hour, and only four miles per hour over the two drawbridges. In 1916, dredging near the Rainbow channel cost almost $1,600.

A 1914 state inspection revealed the Atlantic City bridges over the steam railroads had not been improved, and the earlier recommendations were repeated. The inspectors were concerned about the PRR running its class D-16 steam locomotives over the bay trestles and bridges and urged they be strengthened to reduce the stress. Locomotives were to be restricted to ten miles per hour. As a result, the PRR prohibited the steam locomotives from using the trestles. The 1915 inspection noted that all materials for renewing the bridges were at hand and repairs were underway.

Above: *The railroad steamer Somers Point is seen at the Longport pier in this postcard view. Operating only in the summer, the five-vessel fleet was expensive to maintain. As automobiles began to encroach on passenger loads, the service became uneconomical and was discontinued after the 1918 season.* James Kranefeld collection

CHAPTER FIVE | *A Decade of Turmoil*

About 100 feet of fill had been added at the Somers Point end of the trestle, and the bulkheads were renewed. The Atlantic City bridges were also being resurfaced.

Funeral Cars and Special Cars

In addition to its regular service, the Shore Fast Line ran special cars. Until about 1917, one of these was a funeral car, the Absequam. Late in the nineteenth century, before the development of paved roads and automobiles, a number of electric railways began to offer specially designed cars to carry the deceased and mourners from homes or churches to cemeteries located along their lines. Among the companies operating funeral cars early in the new century were those in Baltimore, Los Angeles, Chicago, St. Louis, Buffalo, Brooklyn, Wilkes-Barre, and Philadelphia.

The funeral cars generally contained a compartment in the front of the car, accessible from the outside, where the coffin was placed. Often a large glass window was above this compartment, for placement of flowers, visible from the street, and a bench was provided for the pallbearers. The rest of the car contained seats for the funeral party, and dark curtains and shades conveyed a somber impression befitting the occasion.

Although there is no direct evidence, it is likely that early in the century the bereaved used the Atlantic City and Shore to reach cemeteries, all of which were on the mainland. For this purpose, the company used one of its two combination cars, even though it was not modified for that purpose. In the spring of 1914, Stern and Silverman decided to convert one of the standard interurban coaches, car No. 100, to a funeral car. Although exact details are lacking, it is probable a compartment for the casket was installed; the regular seats were removed; and the car was refitted for its new service. Orders were placed with the prominent John Wanamaker Department Store in Philadelphia for 30 wicker armchairs, with dark green cushions and backs; green curtains, valances, and shades; and a dozen cushioned stools. The exterior was painted a dark green; the car number was replaced by a name, Absequam, which was painted in gold along the sides.

For the next three or possibly four years, the car carried mourners from Atlantic City to mainland cemeteries. One of these was Mount Calvary Cemetery, located on the PRR's Newfield Branch, two miles west of Pleasantville with a spur track into its grounds. The WJ&S charged 50 cents per mile, plus wages for a pilot, usually less than a dollar. These fees were included in the AC&S charge of $20, plus five dollars for the Adams Express Company for handling the casket. To promote the service, the company placed small ads in local papers, and noted the "Funeral Parlor Car seated 40 people."

Through 1916, the Absequam made one or two runs a month, but by 1917 demand for the car ceased as more convenient automobile hearses replaced it. The Absequam was removed from service and converted to a parlor car, retaining its name and wicker chairs, for runs between Atlantic City and Ocean City.

Other cars were run for special events. For example, in the summer of 1912, arrangements were made to run express cars from Ocean City to carry patrons to the Apollo and Savoy Theatres in Atlantic City. These cars left Ocean City at 7:30 P.M. and returning left the Atlantic City Boardwalk at midnight.

Above: No photographs of Shore Fast Line's funeral car have come to light, but this undated view shows the car on the left coupled to combine 119, probably in service as a parlor car. It was distinguished from its sisters by the stained glass in its upper sash windows. The rooftop bell has fallen out of its frame so a visit to the shop is in order. Robert Foley, Jeffrey Marinoff collection

Mail and Express Service

Since 1899, the WJ&S had operated railway post office cars on its Camden, Newfield, Pleasantville, Atlantic City line. When the route was electrified in 1906, multiple-unit cars were used. Mail was sent from Philadelphia and Camden and sorted into pouches for Linwood, Northfield, and Somers Point. These were transferred at Pleasantville to Shore Fast Line cars for distribution to the local post offices. The procedure was reversed for westbound trains. When the United States entered the World War in 1917, the postal cars were discontinued, but closed pouches were still carried for many years.

The AC&S also carried closed-pouch mail on the Atlantic Avenue-Longport line for a time. A train leaving Philadelphia at 4:30 A.M. carried mail to Atlantic City, where the pouches for Ocean City were placed on a trolley car and then carried to Longport. They were then transferred to a steamboat that arrived in Ocean City about 8:30 A.M.

AC&S provided a baggage and express service on Atlantic Avenue for much of the decade. Two combination passenger-baggage cars were used for this service. In 1914, eight trips were made daily, with the times listed in the public timetables. By 1916 and 1917, this had been reduced to only four daily trips. Later that year, the Adams Express Company took over this service using its own equipment. One of the combination cars continued carrying newspapers to Longport, and the other was put into service on the Venice Park line.

New Arrangements with the Ocean City Electric Railroad

Since entering Ocean City in 1907, the AC&S had arranged with the Ocean City Electric Railroad (OCER) to link the Shore Fast Line tracks on 8th Street with the boat line's pier at 2nd Street and Bay Avenue. The OCER line on Wesley Avenue crossed 8th Street and continued to 1st Street, then turned west to the bay and back to 2nd Street. Under the agreement, the OCER accepted AC&S tickets, receiving three cents in return, and remitted to the AC&S one penny for every five-cent cash fare collected between the two points. A switch at 8th Street and Wesley Avenue permitted the local Ocean City cars to turn east on 8th Street and use the AC&S rails to reach the Boardwalk.

By 1912, the OCER had built its own line to the Boardwalk down 9th Street. It also opened a new line on Atlantic Avenue to the north end of the island and the steamboat pier, discontinuing service on Wesley Avenue. Before the start of the 1913 steamer service, William C. Moore, president of the OCER, asked for a new arrangement with the AC&S. He proposed to use regular service cars, instead of the special cars that previously met the

Above: *An early postcard view at 8th Street and Central in Ocean City. The Shore Fast Line car has just departed from its Boardwalk terminal as it heads to Atlantic City.* James Kranefeld collection

Above: *This photo of new Nearside car 6801 at the Brill plant shows its wide front doors, arch roof, and maximum traction trucks. The narrow rear platform would later be lengthened and used as an entrance. These cars served Atlantic City until the arrival of the Brilliners in 1940. Historical Society of Pennsylvania, LeRoy O. King, Jr. collection*

steamers, and to run them on Atlantic Avenue to 9th Street and then on his tracks to the Boardwalk. Cars no longer used the AC&S's 8th Street tracks, but the OCER still accepted AC&S tickets for through riders to and from the steamboat pier, where they could change cars at 8th Street and Atlantic Avenue.

Leo Isenthal of Stern and Silverman agreed to drop any claim to a one-cent rebate on the normal cash fare of five cents, but he insisted the OCER accept three cents for each through ticket it collected, as they had under the original agreement. He requested that the switch from Wesley Avenue to 8th Street be kept in place, for possible use in the future. Moore agreed to this proposition, permitting the struggling OCER to cease running special connecting cars and to keep the full five-cent cash fares. This arrangement continued until the end of steamboat service in 1918.

Complaints and Minor Disruptions

Occasional complaints were leveled against the Shore Fast Line. In 1911, some frustrated passengers told the Public Utility Commission the car leaving Ocean City at 12:20 P.M. was severely overcrowded. In response, management claimed travel was "unusually heavy that day" due to "exceptional conditions" at the beach and they denied service was inadequate. The commission accepted this explanation.

In the same year, the Hotel Proprietors' Association of Ocean City lodged a protest with the PUC about a charge of 30 cents for a one-way fare when paid to the conductor, while 50-cent round-trip tickets could only be purchased from agents at the Boardwalk ticket office. They argued the Ocean City ticket office was inconveniently located, especially in the winter and that it should be moved several blocks to the center of town. The company responded with a vague statement about contacting the association and considering moving the ticket office, but it did not do so.

In 1916, a group of "working class" patrons from Pleasantville sent a petition to the PUC complaining of overcrowded cars in the early morning, with 127 people on a car seating 52, and 96 riders on another car. On that car, 21 men refused to pay their fares. They were met in Atlantic City by Shore Fast Line officials, with warrants. Five men were arrested.

In response to the PUC's demand for an explanation, the company conducted a survey for ten days and reported that a maximum number of 145 passengers were on a two-car train, meaning 21 patrons had to stand on each car for the 16-minute trip between Pleasantville and South Carolina Avenue. A second trip was assigned two cars, and only ten standees per car were on that run. Company officials added the irrelevant statement that the trains leaving Atlantic City were almost empty. This attitude did nothing to enhance the public's perception of the Shore Fast Line. Occasionally, other problems disrupted service. Winter ice storms caused long delays, as the buildup of ice on the third rail prevented the truck-mounted shoe from making contact with the electric rail. At other times, repairs necessitated detours as in 1919, when work on the Thorofare drawbridge required cars to terminate at the PRR Tennessee Avenue Electric Terminal on Atlantic Avenue rather than the Virginia Avenue Boardwalk station. Overall, however, service was good, despite the complaints.

New Cars for the Atlantic Avenue Line

In 1913, the Pennsylvania Railroad launched a two-part program to modernize its Atlantic City trolley line. The first step was taken when the company ordered 26 streetcars from the J. G. Brill Company of an innovative new design called the Nearside car. Unlike most cars of the day, with the doors at the front used for leaving the car and at the rear for entering it, the Nearside car had a large front platform, with wide double doors, to be used for both entering and exiting. On many properties, cars stopped on the far side of intersections, to save passengers a walk along a possibly muddy street next to the car, to reach the rear doors. As its name indicates, this car was designed to stop on the near side of each intersecting street to load or unload passengers, before crossing the intersection. Atlantic City already stopped cars on the near side of cross streets, so the new car fit the current traffic pattern.

PRR officials may have been impressed by the large number of new Nearside cars entering service in Philadelphia, where they were well received. The new cars were equally popular in Atlantic City and were numbered in open slots in the 6800- series used by the PRR for streetcars. They had glass panels in the doors, giving the motormen better visibility at car stops, and they were equipped with Ohmer fare registers. The conductor's booth was inside the car, directly behind the platform. It seated 51, in 14 cross seats on either side in the back half of the car, and on two longitudinal seats in the front half and the back end. As the Nearsides entered service in October 1913, a number of older cars were scrapped. By the end of the year, 69 streetcars, including four work cars, were leased to the AC&S.

At the same time, the WJ&S purchased six single-end, arch-roof open cars from the Southern Car Company. Three open trailers were scrapped. Several of the older cars were modified to a prepayment design. Three used cars, numbered 10, 11, and 12, were purchased from Newall, West Virginia, for the Central Passenger Railway.

The limitations of the Nearside design and the hazards of the open cars resulted in several experimental changes to existing cars. In 1915, two open cars were remodeled into center entrance, front exit cars while still retaining the popular open car features. One car had steel sheeting applied to the sides, from the floor

Above: The interior of the Nearside cars was plain with cane seats, but clean and bright. The windows could be raised into the roof making the car open to seashore breezes. A section of the conductor's booth is seen at the lower right. Nearside cars ran in Philadelphia until 1955. Historical Society of Pennsylvania, Robert L. Long collection

CHAPTER FIVE | *A Decade of Turmoil*

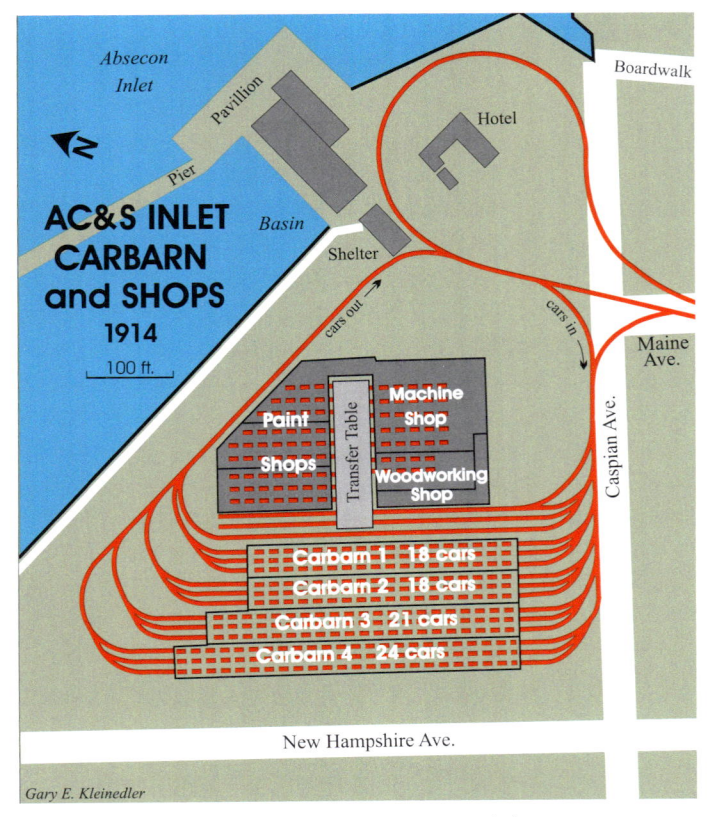

Above: *Track layout of the AC&S Inlet carbarn and shops in 1914.*

to a height of three feet, with screens above that to the roof. The other was enclosed entirely by screens. Cross seats on one side and a longitudinal bench on the other replaced the 12 cross-benches. These cars were safer and were designed for more ease in collecting fares, while they kept their open characteristics. General Superintendent George F. Faber made a number of mechanical improvements on some of the older cars. New lubricating boxes, bronze armature bearings instead of iron, and rebuilt motor frame housing improved performance and reduced car failures.

New Car House and Shops Are Built at the Inlet

As a second part of its improvement program, in 1914, the PRR constructed a modern carbarn, shops, and office building at the Absecon Inlet, the northern terminal of the Atlantic Avenue line. The complex was designed and constructed by Stern and Silverman, acting in their capacity as consulting engineers for the PRR's West Jersey and Seashore Railroad.

The facility, constructed at a cost $250,000, consisted of a 12-track car house, divided into four bays; a two-building shop structure, one containing the paint shop and the other the machine and wood shops, the boiler room and storage rooms; and a two-story office building. The shop buildings were opposite each other, 52 feet apart, and connected by a 36-foot-wide transfer table. The office building was erected at the head of the transfer table. On the first floor were a trainmen's room, lockers, a receiver's counter, and the dispatcher's office. Upstairs were offices for company officials and their staffs.

Pits were located under most tracks in the three buildings. The shops were equipped with the latest tools and several cranes, storage rooms, and locker rooms. Skylights, large windows, and incandescent lamps provided ample illumination; steam boilers provided heat, and special pipes and hoses gave fire protection. A large loop on the Inlet side was used to reverse the in-service cars. The company offices were moved from South Carolina Avenue in April, and the old carbarns on New Hampshire and Marmora avenues were demolished by September. Overall, the new barn and shops were "state of the art" facilities that were to serve the company well for the rest of its existence.

The Jitney Menace

Even as the AC&S was beginning to enjoy its modern shop and storage facilities, the line was confronted with a new threat that was so serious it would soon throw it into bankruptcy. On March 15, 1915, a young man named Frank Fairbairn, the proud owner of a Ford open-top touring car, decided to earn some money by running down Atlantic Avenue and picking up people who were waiting for a streetcar. He charged a nickel, popularly called a "jit" in the slang expression of the day. Soon he was joined by other car owners, anxious to make a few dollars. Within two months, over 400 of the automobiles, now called jitneys, roamed the avenue like a swarm of bees, carrying many people who would otherwise have paid their nickel to the AC&S. The phenomenon developed in many cities, where it was short-lived, but in Atlantic City it became a major problem.

Jitneys were a byproduct of the rapid growth in the ownership of automobiles. In 1900, the United States produced 4,000 automobiles; in 1908, Henry Ford introduced the Model T. Rugged and cheap, Ford sold 10,607 of them. By 1916, Ford alone sold 730,041 models.

The AC&S watched helplessly as thousands of potential riders were attracted to the novelty and seeming convenience of the jitneys. Partly this was a result of over-crowded streetcars, and the absence of free transfers from Atlantic Avenue cars to those on Virginia and South Carolina Avenues that reached the Boardwalk. The constant attacks by Progressive politicians against monopolies and big corporations created sympathy for the "little man," who was only trying to make a living battling the streetcar monopoly supported by the bankers and major hotels. The majority of the five-man board of city commissioners was also hostile to the traction company and its powerful ally, the Pennsylvania Railroad. In vain, President Isaac Silverman and Vice-President Charles Evans of the AC&S pleaded for the city to regulate the jitneys. The fact that the WJ&S had paid $150,000 to the city for paving Atlantic Avenue and $5,000 a year for maintenance of the road for ten years was forgotten.

The jitneymen, who were responsible to no one, formed an

association called the Automobile Service Association and took a defiant stand. They claimed to have a constitutional right to compete and said they offered superior service and convenience to the public. They threatened to appeal to Henry Ford to send 500 or 1,000 cars to Atlantic City, should the AC&S discontinue service. The jitneymen were supported by groups such as the Fourth Ward Business Men's Association, who criticized the slow service of the trolleys. Ventnor City officials supported the jitneys, blissfully asserting that if the AC&S ceased running, the Pennsylvania Railroad, the owner and former operator, would continue operations because of the valuable franchises. They urged the AC&S to sell cheaper strip tickets, to eliminate the three-cent transfer charge for Boardwalk cars, and to cut the Pleasantville-Atlantic City fare to five cents.

By November, matters came to a head. Silverman and Evans warned in vain the company had recorded a deficit of $80,000 during the year. They asked the jitneys be barred from running on Atlantic Avenue and that the drivers be bonded to protect the public. A bill to accomplish these aims was defeated in the city commission on November 11, despite support from business groups such as the Chamber of Commerce. The AC&S then gave up the fight and waited for the inevitable bankruptcy. The weakness of the jitneys was demonstrated on November 19 when a heavy storm kept most of them off the streets and forced riders to take the slower but reliable trolleys. On November 26, the company failed to pay a creditor's claim and admitted insolvency before Judge John Rellstab in the United States District Court in Trenton. Former Judge Clarence L. Cole of Atlantic City was appointed receiver and a hearing was scheduled for December 6.

The conflict reflected the over-simplified and one-sided view held by many Progressives, who could not understand that the heavy investment in facilities meant a regulated monopoly was a valid type of business structure.

Resolving the Jitney Problem

As the AC&S was battling the jitneys, Stern and Silverman hired a new superintendent to replace George Faber. Arthur J. Purinton was born in Massachusetts and received a degree in mechanical engineering from the Massachusetts Institute of Technology. He worked on several midwestern traction properties, including the Toledo and Chicago Interurban Railway and the St. Joseph Railway, Light, Heat, and Power Company. From July 1912 to May 1915, he was superintendent of the East St. Louis Suburban Railway Company, where he supervised over 190 miles of track.

Purinton was an able and forceful executive, who faithfully represented Stern and Silverman from his office at the Inlet. He rose rapidly, being elected to the board of directors of the AC&S in 1917, and he succeeded Judge Cole as receiver in 1919. On the death of Charles Evans in 1921, he was elected vice-president of the company. With the support of Cole, he implemented economies. Car crews were limited to working no more than nine hours a day, and many trips to Margate and Longport were turned instead at the Portland Avenue loop in Ventnor.

In Trenton, the legislature was under pressure from the railroads, banks, traction companies, and business organizations that feared the jitney idea might spread elsewhere in the state and undermine the financial stability of the traction companies

Above: View from Atlantic City's Boardwalk as a Shore Fast Line car departs from the terminal and heads down Virginia Avenue. Automobiles are beginning to appear in larger numbers. Fred W. Schneider, III collection

THOMAS E. MITTEN AND THE NEARSIDE CAR

Thomas E. Mitten, born in England in 1864, moved with his family to the United States in 1875 and settled in Indiana. Attracted to railroads, he secured several positions as a young man. In the 1890s, he became a manager for electric railways in Colorado and Milwaukee. In 1902, he was appointed general superintendent of the International Railway Company of Buffalo, New York; he was also president of the Chicago City Railway from 1905 to 1911. In that year, he moved to Philadelphia as chairman of the executive committee of the Philadelphia Rapid Transit Company. Mitten was innovative and well organized and greatly improved working conditions, winning the support of labor.

By 1911, city governments in Buffalo, Chicago, and Philadelphia passed ordinances requiring streetcars to stop on the near side of intersections to improve the boarding location for passengers. With the aid of Ralph T. Senter in Buffalo, Mitten developed a car expressly designed to be entered and exited at a large front platform with double doors. The conductor, who was usually stationed on the back platform in older cars, was relocated to a position on or next to the front platform. A small platform and single door were at the back of the car for emergency use.

The cars were single-end, which required turning loops to reverse direction, but they needed only one set of controls. They were 45 feet, 6 inches in length and 8 feet, 5 inches wide. Each car had steel underframes, wooden side panels covered by steel plates, and semi-convertible windows which rose into pockets in the arch roof. The cars were mounted on Brill No. 39-E "maximum traction" trucks, each of which had a 50-horsepower motor powering a set of 33-inch driving wheels plus a pair of 22-inch pony wheels, and air brakes.

Six cities purchased Nearside cars. Mitten's Philadelphia Rapid Transit Company acquired 1,500 of them, and much smaller numbers were ordered by properties in Buffalo; Chicago; Lincoln, Nebraska; Vancouver, British Columbia; and finally, Atlantic City.

The reign of the Nearside cars was brief. A major weakness of the design was the tendency of passengers to congregate in the front of the car, in order to exit at their stops. A much better arrangement was developed in 1914 by Peter Witt, street railway commissioner of Cleveland. He patented a car with double center doors, next to the conductor's booth, which were used by people leaving the car. This simple change greatly improved passenger flow and made the Nearside design obsolete.

Above: AC&S 6852, shown here at Longport on April 23, 1939, was one of 26 Nearside cars built by J.G. Brill and delivered to the AC&S in 1913. These cars served as the backbone of the Atlantic City trolley fleet until the arrival of the Brilliners in 1940. Electric City Trolley Museum collection

Mitten continued to manage the Philadelphia system, where he instituted many improvements, until his death in October 1929 in a boating accident at his country home in Pike County, in northeastern Pennsylvania.

and the investors and business groups who supported them. As a result, the legislature passed the Kates Act, effective June 1, 1916, allowing cities to license jitneys, requiring them to obtain insurance, and subjecting them to taxes or fees.

On Absecon Island, the down-island communities, angered at the reduced trolley service to their towns, complained loudly to the Atlantic City commissioners and demanded they act to regulate the jitneys. The city officials grudgingly took small steps, such as requiring the drivers to obtain mercantile licenses and to wear badges. In the spring of 1917, the city informed the AC&S that if it agreed to pay an annual license fee of $100 for each of its cars, instead of the normal $50, and if it took steps to resolve the free transfer dispute, the city was willing to prohibit the jitneys from operating on Atlantic Avenue. Isaac Silverman accepted these terms on April 4, 1917. One month later, the city passed an ordinance barring the jitneys and other "auto buses" from Atlantic Avenue. The jitneymen failed in their later attempts to force the commissioners to rescind the ordinance. The AC&S, in turn, abolished the three-cent charge for transfers to and from cars operating on Virginia and South Carolina avenues. [

Operating Modifications

During the decade, several changes were made in operating procedures and the right-of-way. In 1912, to the relief of the city, the PRR closed the Albany Avenue freight yard and sold the property for $125,200 to the city to be used as a park. A new switch was installed at Savannah Avenue in Margate in October 1916. A new system of fare collection was instituted on the Shore Fast Line, whereby passengers paid only once, to their destination, instead of paying in each zone, as had been the practice previously.

In 1917, with the United States participating in the Great War on the side of Britain and France, Atlantic City experienced a banner summer season, with an estimated 400,000 visitors. As prices rose rapidly because of wartime inflation, the AC&S was hard pressed to offer adequate service, but it did quite well. Cars were inspected and cleaned daily and washed frequently. Twice a week each car was fumigated. At regular intervals, the cars were overhauled, the seats removed and bleached, and the woodwork varnished. The former funeral car *Absequam* was rebuilt into a "luxuriously equipped parlor car" in April and made available for special groups. In July, a new service was instituted, with cars running from Savannah Avenue in Margate directly to the Steel Pier at Virginia Avenue. Running every 15 minutes in the afternoon and evening in the summer, the cars carried a green light to make them easy to identify.

The company's efforts were rewarded with an unusual complimentary editorial in the Atlantic City *Gazette-Review* in September. Declaring that it realized it was violating all previous critical comments about the trolley service, the journal congratulated the railway for its handling of the "enormous traffic demands" made upon it, and it especially commended the crews for their courtesy and consideration of their passengers.

Hoping for more frequent service, some local merchants proposed that a loop be constructed around the Soldiers and Sailors Monument at Providence Avenue, so some cars could be turned there instead of running to Portland Avenue in Ventnor. The monument was encircled by roadways and the loop could easily

Above: Car 110, seen here in 1934, had been modified somewhat from its original features with steel side plates and closed clerestory windows. No two interurban cars were exactly alike as they were updated individually as time and circumstances permitted. William Lichtenstern, LeRoy O. King, Jr. collection

Following Page: A photo from the same period shows AC&S 104 parked on a siding. William Lichtenstern, LeRoy O. King, Jr. collection

CHAPTER FIVE | *A Decade of Turmoil*

Above: This photo of the interior of interurban car 113 was taken around 1940 but it is essentially unchanged from its original configuration. The cars were modified in various ways including lights and seat coverings, but the sloping sides and clerestory designs betrayed their age. David H. Cope, Robert L. Long collection

be built. The AC&S referred the matter to the city commissioners, who never discussed it. A plea that the plan be submitted to a public referendum was also ignored. Despite support from some newspapers, the proposal eventually was dropped.

Better Public Relations

After falling into bankruptcy late in 1915, Stern and Silverman became more conscious of the need to improve the public image of the AC&S. One step was to publish a weekly, four-page, "take-one" pamphlet called "Trolley Talks," designed to enlighten the public about the railway's importance to the community. They presented the company's view on various issues and tried to offset the hostile position of the city's newspapers. The first was distributed in November 1916, and it continued to appear until July 1917. Among the topics covered were the company's stress on safety, the significant financial investment in the property (cited as three million dollars), and the ongoing expenses during the slow winter season, such as heating the cars and maintaining special snow-fighting equipment. There were snippets of factual information, interspersed with commendations of employees, humorous stories, and a few advertisements. The pamphlets were available in all the company's cars and offices.

Shore Fast Line timetables were also readily available, as were folders describing the frequent service, sights to be seen, the fares, and the combination trolley-boat pleasure trips the company offered. A longer, illustrated Guide Book noted the numerous attractions to be found along almost every mile of track, as well as ocean cruises, fishing sites, the natural beauty of the water and woods, schedules for the Ocean City and Longport divisions, and a map, with the heading, "Look at the map, see where we go." All these were easily obtained by those who wanted them. How much they affected revenues is impossible to say.

Another improvement was the creation of a public relations department that answered complaints and fostered better relations with patrons. The methods of outstanding motormen and conductors were held up as examples for other crewmen to emulate. While these efforts did not soften the hostility of the city government, most newspapers, or some of the public, they did improve the company's image.

Inflationary Pressures Hit the AC&S

Aside from its local problems, the AC&S was affected by a

CHAPTER FIVE | A Decade of Turmoil

wave of inflation that gripped the nation during the decade. The outbreak of the World War in August 1914, upset and dislocated the financial and commodity markets, as the European powers demanded American goods. The Wilson administration, while professing neutrality, supported the Allied cause, and new trading patterns were forged. These economic upheavals were exacerbated by American entrance into the conflict in April 1917.

One result was an intensification of inflation, as the country shifted to a wartime basis. The administration's financial policies, forged by Secretary of the Treasury William Gibbs McAdoo, stressed borrowing money at the lowest rates and using the new Federal Reserve System to create new money, thereby fostering an intense inflationary spiral. Between 1914 and 1920, the total supply of money grew by 75 percent, and the consumer price index leaped from 46.6 to 85.7. The overall cost of living index jumped from 100 in 1913 to 203.7 in 1920.

As severe as inflationary pressures were, even more threatening to the electric railway's future was the increasing number of automobiles. New Jersey motor vehicle registrations jumped from about 82,000 in 1915 to 142,000 in 1917, 191,000 in 1919, and 228,000 in 1920. In similar fashion, state highway expenditures increased from $1,306,000 in 1914 to $6,320,000 in 1919. The White Horse Pike from Camden was designated a state highway in 1917, and it was extended across the meadows from Absecon into Atlantic City by 1919; two years later it was completely paved. The AC&S found itself squeezed by regulation, taxes, rising costs, and more intense competition.

Fare Adjustments

Basic fares on the company's lines had not changed for many years. In Atlantic City the charge was five cents; to travel to Ventnor, Margate, or Longport, another zone fare of five cents was required. On the Shore Fast Line, zone fares were five cents each; the route from Atlantic City to Pleasantville was considered to be two zones, and ten cents was levied. A run to Ocean City cost 30 cents, although round trip tickets were 50 cents. The steamers charged 20 cents. Pressure mounted to raise these rates.

Above: AC&S timetables of the period were relatively small as this example issued on June 25, 1916, reveals. Both interurban and city service were listed as well as connections to both Pennsylvania and Philadelphia & Reading trains. The back cover shows a Shore Fast Line car somewhere on the Somers Point branch. Robert Wasche collection

In 1916, the company pointedly reminded its riders that costs were increasing for all commodities except for the basic five-cent car fare.

Effective on May 7, 1917, in keeping with its agreement with the city, the unpopular three cent charge to transfer to and from Boardwalk cars on Virginia and South Carolina avenues was abolished. While pleasing the public, this action did nothing to fill the company's depleted coffers. In the spring of 1918, the AC&S applied to the Public Utilities Commission for permission to increase zone fares from five to six cents and to charge 12 cents instead of ten cents for the Pleasantville-Atlantic City run. After a hearing, the PUC granted approval, and the new rates went into effect at once. Later in the year, the round-trip fare between Atlantic City and Ocean City was increased from 50 cents to 60 cents, or double the one-way rate. Still later in 1920, zone fares were raised to seven cents.

Collecting the fares was sometimes a challenge to the conductors, especially on the open cars. A peculiar culture had developed in Atlantic City where certain people played "the game" of trying to ride for free. This involved such techniques as staring straight ahead when the conductor came by, looking at him with expressions of surprise or disinterest, or talking with their companions, all to convey the impression they had already paid. A local psychologist explained that group cultural mores held "it was all right to beat the trolley company of its nickel." The conductor had to combine finesse with firmness to collect his fares.

Labor Troubles

Inflationary pressures hit the employees too, and they demanded higher pay, especially after the fares were raised. In an effort to placate the men, Superintendent A. J. Purinton granted an increase of two cents an hour in September, 1917. This set the wage scale on the city lines at 26, 27, and 29 cents an hour, and on the interurban line to 27, 29, and 31 cents.

This modest increase did not satisfy the workers, who joined the Amalgamated Association of Street and Electric Railway Employees. They continually agitated for a further increase in pay. As the summer of 1918 approached, the company quietly began to hire new men earlier than usual. After the crewmen's demand for another raise was rejected, they went on a brief strike beginning on May 23.

A hasty conference called by the receiver, Clarence Cole, produced an agreement early in June. A six-cent-an-hour boost in pay was given to the operating and shop employees, who agreed to a ten-hour day. Future disputes were to be settled by arbitration. The union withdrew a demand that six men who had not walked out be fired, since they were "old hands." The raise cost the company an additional $14,000 annually in wages.

Wages were not the only problem involving workers. In 1916, the AC&S was beset by a gang of unscrupulous swindlers who obtained work as conductors by writing false letters of recommendation for each other. They then stole whatever they could by withholding fares. Three of the miscreants were arrested, indicted, tried in the Atlantic County Court in Mays Landing, and received prison terms.

Financial Setbacks

The nickels stolen by dishonest conductors were a relatively minor nuisance compared to the major financial losses suffered by the AC&S at this time. The first years of the decade saw modest profits, but these changed to deficits from 1915 through 1919, largely as a result of the jitneys, automobile competition, and higher costs.

The companies controlled by Stern and Silverman were interrelated and heavily capitalized. Three owned small sections of track: the Central Passenger Railway, the Atlantic City and Ocean City Railroad, and the Atlantic City and Shore Railroad. Two were holding companies, incorporated in Delaware: the Atlantic City and Shore Company and the Atlantic City and Ocean City Company. Both held the securities of the other companies and issued stock and bonds themselves. The AC&S Railroad was the sole operating company. Collectively, these corporations had issued stock valued on paper at $2,725,000, and bonds whose face value was $1,800,000. This was a high sum indeed for a relatively small system that leased most of its trackage and facilities from the PRR. All were controlled by Stern and Silverman, Inc., as reflected by the officers of the companies who were also officials of the Philadelphia financial firm.

It was not surprising that the AC&S Railroad entered receivership in November 1915 as passenger revenues fell under the weight of the jitney onslaught. The West Jersey and Seashore noted glumly in its 1915 Annual Report that its income from leased property fell almost 49 percent because of the reduction in receipts from the AC&S. In January 1916, the PRR moved to grant relief to the beleaguered trolley company. The 1905 and 1908 lease terms were significantly modified. The WJ&S suspended rental payments for at least five years, from November 1, 1915, and possibly indefinitely thereafter. In its place, the AC&S was to pay interest at the annual rate of 4.5 percent on the value of the right-of-way, stations, and maintenance, but only to the proportion of its car mileage to the total mileage, passenger and freight, carried on the PRR-owned lines. With the aid of a benevolent PRR that recognized its interests were best served by assisting Stern and Silverman, the AC&S system was able to weather the wartime pressures and the postwar depression, returning to profitability in 1920. On June 21, 1921, Judge John Rellstab ruled the property be restored to private control and declared the receivership ended.

At the end of the decade, as prosperity returned, the AC&S group looked ahead to better times. The ever-growing number of automobiles challenged Stern and Silverman managers to develop innovative means to serve the seashore communities and still earn a profit.

Atlantic City & Shore Railroad: Selected Financial Data

Year	Operating Revenues	Operating Expenses	Railway Operating Income	Fixed Charges	Net Income	Operating Ratio
1914	$623,600	$421,500	$199,949	$183,000	$16,920	62.1%
1915	545,149	422,772	122,377	205,686	(78,285)	70.6%
1916	414,051	372,107	41,944	63,083	(17,485)	78.9%
1918	539,487	471,164	68,324	80,087	(25,652)	78.5%
1919	766,239	608,133	158,136	188,013	(30,871)	71.9%
1921	1,056,523	799,233	257,290	246,606	24,730	73.7%

Central Passenger Railway: Selected Financial Data

Year	Operating Revenues	Operating Expenses	Railway Operating Income	Fixed Charges	Net Income	Operating Ratio
1914	$29,900	$28,700	$1,280	$5,129	($3,898)	85.9%
1915	21,931	22,706	(775)	6,729	(6,504)	94.1%
1916	27,309	23,853	3,451	6,278	(2,827)	79.8%
1918	30,303	30,724	(421)	6,275	(6,617)	92.6%
1919	43,028	41,094	1,934	6,275	(4,322)	87.8%
1921	71,612	65,258	6,354	5,915	1,157	84.5%

Source: Public Utilities Commission of New Jersey

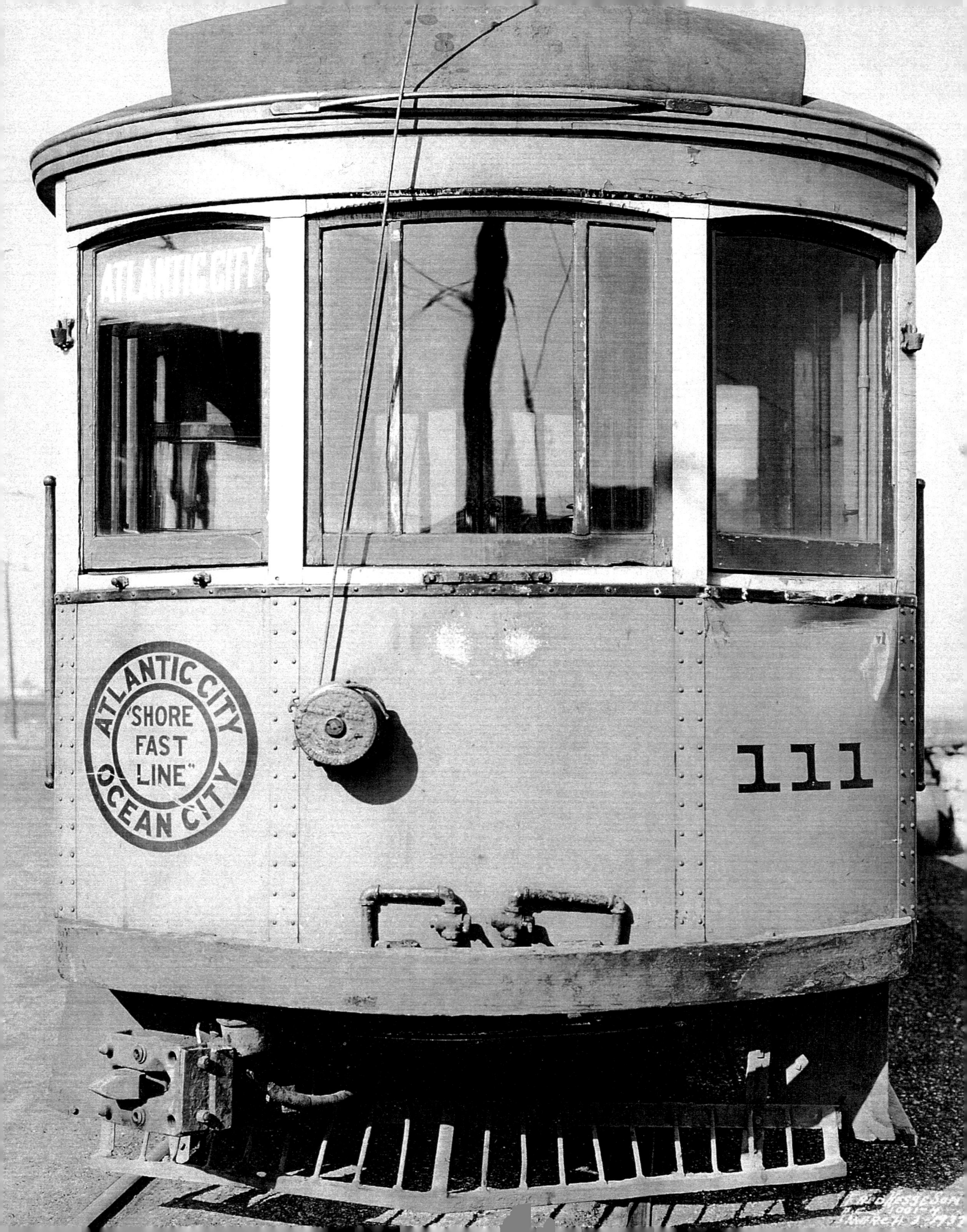
ATLANTIC CITY
ATLANTIC CITY
"SHORE FAST LINE"
OCEAN CITY
111

CHAPTER SIX

The Return of Prosperity

A Decade of Uneven Prosperity

The third decade of the century saw the return of an uneven prosperity and a decade of Republican control of the White House and the Congress. The public was tired of wartime privation, inflation, a postwar recession, and Democratic policies imposed during the Wilson years. Confronted by a series of uninspired Democratic office seekers, voters elected conservative Republican candidates, whose economic policies favored business and believed the Constitution gave limited powers to the federal government.

The prosperity of the decade was stimulated by the growth of new industries, such as the automobile, radio, sound motion pictures, and air travel, but it affected only parts of the population. A relative handful invested in the stock market, but by the end of the decade, speculators created a frenzy of buying that pushed prices far above realistic levels. Labor made only limited gains, and farmers, about 30 percent of the population, were largely untouched by the "good times."

Socially, national Prohibition sparked the rise of criminals and a defiance of the law by certain elements in the country. Old values were weakened and were partially replaced by a new stress on jazz, flappers, "bathtub gin," and relaxed standards of sexual behavior. By the end of the period, the market for new products was saturated; production began to fall, and unemployment rose. The collapse of the stock market in October 1929, ended the orgy of speculation and symbolized the end of the years of free spirits and easy living.

Atlantic City and its surrounding region basked in the glow of prosperous times, and so did the Atlantic City and Shore Railroad as it saw a return of profits after the losses of the war years. The population of the seashore towns continued to grow, as did the number of summer visitors. Atlantic City added about 15,500 people between 1920 and 1930, to claim a peak population of 66,200, a 30 percent increase. Even more impressive was the growth of the mainland towns of Northfield, Linwood, and Somers Point. They recorded increases of 2,804, 1,514, and 2,073 residents respectively, which were increases of 148 percent, 137 percent, and 146 percent. Pleasantville had 11,580 people in 1930, a gain of 97 percent, and Absecon grew by 207 percent to 2,158 in the same decade. Ocean City had an estimated 5,500 permanent residents in 1930.

On Absecon Island, the three towns south of Atlantic City all recorded impressive percentages of growth. In 1930, Ventnor claimed 6,674 residents, Margate 2,913, and Longport 223. In percentage terms, each community grew by 204, 1,000, and 128 percent respectively. These increases were to benefit the AC&S during the long off-season from the fall through the spring. The Shore Fast Line evolved into a commuter route from the mainland to Atlantic City. However, offsetting these gains to some extent was a rapid increase in automobile registrations.

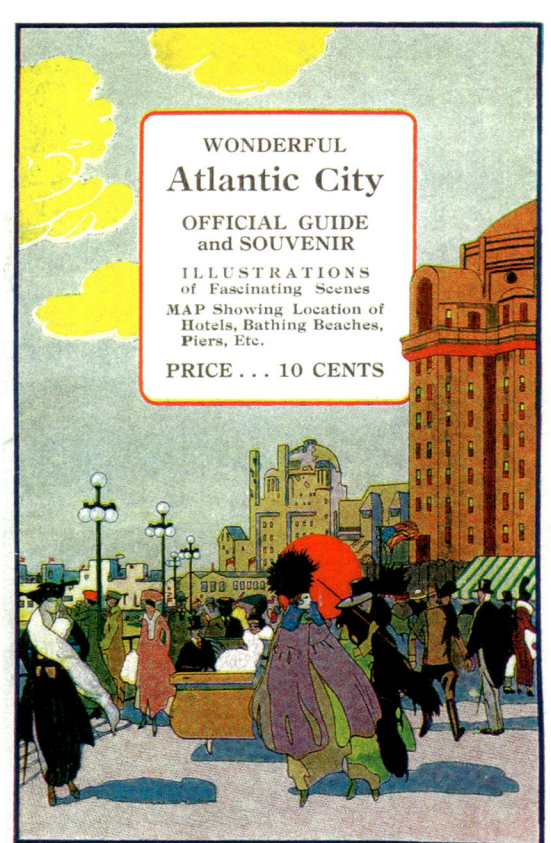

Facing Page: An end view of car 111 records its condition on March 3, 1931, when this photo was taken. By now the car has received steel sheathing, although three cars never received this upgrade. By now 111 is 25 years old and is beginning to look worn and tired. Yet this car and its sisters would soldier on for another 17 years. Jeffrey Marinoff collection

Above: *This color edition of the Atlantic City Official Guide depicts a fashionable, well-dressed crowd along the Boardwalk with a backdrop of some of the resort's hotels. The artist has rendered the city as it would like to be seen rather than as it actually was. LeRoy O. King, Jr. collection*

83

Road Improvements Increase Competition for the AC&S

Highway access from the west was eased by the construction of two roads which crossed the meadows. The first, and more northerly one, was Absecon Boulevard. Work began in 1916 in Absecon to build a road into the resort. It crossed the Thorofare and entered Atlantic City parallel to the Shore Fast Line right-of-way. The highway was improved by the city to accommodate increasing vehicular traffic. A gravel surface was applied in 1919 and paving with a bituminous compound was completed in 1925. This road, popularly called the White Horse Pike, was designated as United States Route 30. It extended from Atlantic City westward to Camden.

A short distance to the south, construction began on a parallel road, through Mays Landing and Pleasantville, and then to Atlantic City, which it entered along Albany Avenue. Progress was slow, but the finished paved highway, called the Black Horse Pike, finally opened in 1932. Route 40, extending from Pennsville, on the Delaware River opposite Wilmington, Delaware, joined it about 20 miles west of Atlantic City. It was designated United States Route 40-322 in the seashore resort.

On the mainland, the north-south Shore Road became a state highway in 1923; it was located a short distance east of the Shore Fast Line tracks. Soon a parallel through highway was constructed, slightly to the west of the rail line, called the New Road. In effect, a bypass route for the older Shore Road, it was designated United States Route 9. Both these roads offered automotive competition to the electric cars. In 1922, the state took over the Ocean City Automobile Bridge Company, a connection to the resort with Somers Point, and abolished the toll charge.

Access from Philadelphia by automobiles and buses was greatly improved in July 1926, by the opening of the Delaware River Bridge between that city and Camden. Two years later, a bridge opened spanning Risley's Channel at the south end of the Thorofare, and the Great Egg Harbor Inlet. It connected Longport with the northern end of Ocean City, duplicating the former steamboat link. It provided a more direct and shorter way to travel between the two resorts than the inland route of the Shore Fast Line.

Atlantic City in the 1920s

By 1930, Atlantic City had reached a state of maturity, when it recorded its peak population. The era of constructing ocean piers had ended, and only a few grand hotels were built or expanded. Visitors still flocked to the city, especially in the summer. Holidays, such as Easter, July 4, and Labor Day, saw 200,000 to 400,000 people enjoy the varied attractions.

Promoters staged events such as weddings under the sea, marathon dance contests, high-diving horses, and elephants bathing in the ocean. In 1926, 400 conventions met in the city. New and existing theatres offered vaudeville, legitimate plays,

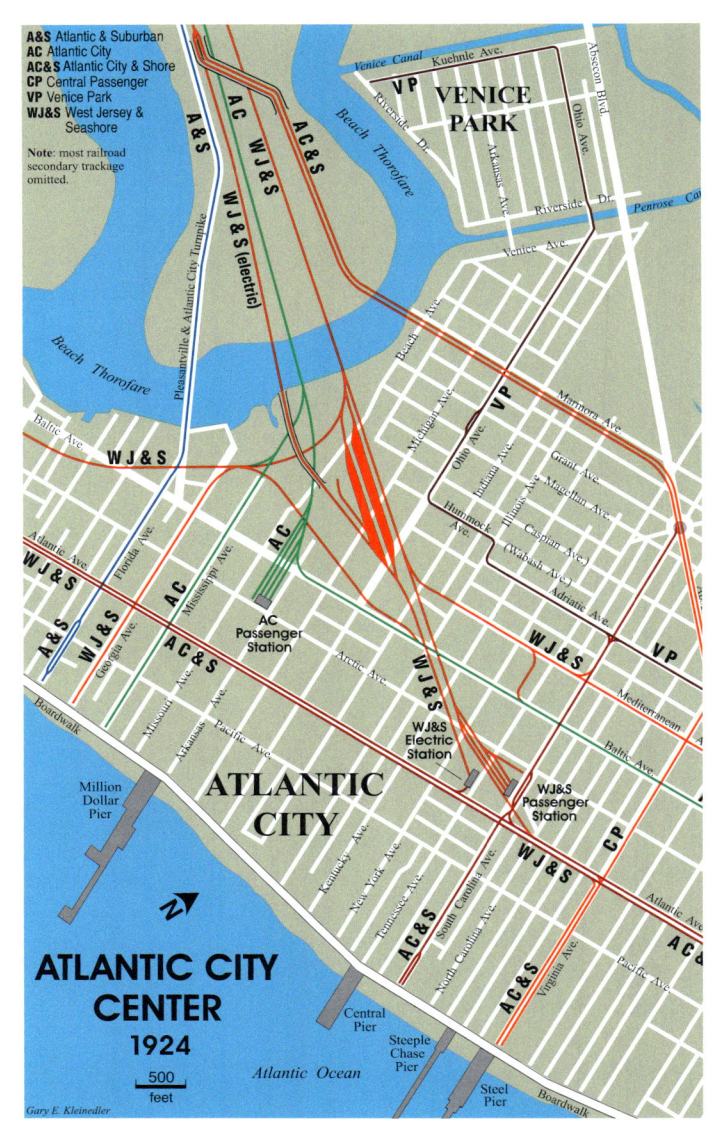

Above: Atlantic City center city trackage in 1924.

and motion pictures, including sound by the late 1920s. Night clubs featured a variety of entertainers, while illegal gambling flourished. Stately structures such as the War Memorial Monument, the Masonic Temple, and the huge Convention Hall offset to a degree the gaudy activities found in much of the town. The AC&S benefited from the influx of summer visitors, and a parade of trolleys, closed and open models, ran up and down Atlantic Avenue to serve them. Both Stern and Silverman and the PRR were pleased with the return of good times.

New Arrangements with the Pennsylvania Railroad

The end of the receivership in 1921 restored Stern and Silverman to a position of complete control under its lease provisions with the PRR. In April, 1923, Isaac Silverman wrote to Samuel Rea, the president of the PRR, pointing out that the lease of the Atlantic Avenue and Longport Division would expire in 1927. He noted that many issues, such as fares, betterments, maintenance, and the political scene, would involve the period after 1927. Consequently, he felt it would be wise to negotiate the terms of an extension.

Rea immediately referred the matter to Vice-president William W. Atterbury, commenting that the AC&S make decisions regarding upkeep and other matters based on the terminal date of its lease. He suggested an extension of about 20 years, but he also said the sale of the line might be considered. Atterbury told Elisha Lee, vice-president for the Eastern Region, to make a recommendation. Lee established an eleven-man committee of executives, which met on April 26. This group unanimously reported that the lease should be extended to 1945 (the date when the lease of the Somers Point Branch to the AC&S was set to expire) because it was more profitable to have the AC&S run the line than for the PRR to do it directly. The committee rejected the idea of selling the line, since "it may be desired for use . . . in the future development of Atlantic City."

By April 1924, an agreement was reached, extending the contract on the same terms until December 18, 1945, except that after January 1, 1925, the interest rate paid by the AC&S to the West Jersey and Seashore for all additions and betterments be the actual cost of the money expended by the railroad rather than the previous flat rate of six percent. Both the PRR and Stern and Silverman were satisfied with the new arrangements, although if they could have foreseen the hardships of the next decade, they might have been less optimistic.

Changes in the Car Fleet: The War Board Cars

While negotiations were underway, the PRR managers were busy acquiring used and new cars and rebuilding older ones for the Atlantic Avenue line. The Nearside cars provided most of the service on the route, supplemented by several older cars built in 1906, now well past their prime. An opportunity arose in 1923 to purchase newer cars when the Emergency Fleet Corporation offered to sell the group of 30 cars that had been built by Brill in 1918 for service to the Hog Island Shipyard in Philadelphia. With the closing of the yard after the end of the war, the cars were surplus.

The PRR purchased four of them in May 1923 and numbered them 6885-6888. They were arch-roof, double-end cars painted orange. They brought needed flexibility to the line, since during emergencies they could be reversed at crossover switches. So pleased was the management with these cars they ordered two new identical ones from the Brill factory, completed and delivered later in the year. They were joined by six similar cars in 1926, purchased from the Ocean Electric Railway of Long Island, New York. These twelve versatile cars supplemented the Nearsides and the summer season open cars, and they ran until the end of rail service in 1955.

Above: War Board car 6847, seen here at Inlet Barn in 1948, has changed very little since it was acquired by the AC&S from the Ocean Electric Railway of Rockaway, New York, in 1927. It was built by Brill in 1918 for service on the Hog Island Shipyard line in Philadelphia. AC&S has 12 of these Spartan but flexible cars which could reverse direction at the many crossover switches, something the single-end Nearside cars could not do. LeRoy O. King, Jr. collection

Rebuilding the Nearside Cars

The War Board cars were of the rear-entrance front-exit type, with the conductor stationed at the back-entrance doors, whereas the single-end Nearsides were front-entrance and exit cars, with the conductor near the front platform. Partly to make the fleet compatible and less confusing to riders, and partly because the cars were due for an updating, the AC&S shops rebuilt the Nearsides, by lengthening the rear platform and installing regular double doors in place of the small emergency door originally there. The conductor was moved to the back platform, now the entrance, and the front doors were used by exiting passengers. Orange paint and cream trim replaced the earlier yellow car bodies. This update gave the Atlantic Avenue line a standardized fleet of two similar types of cars and made it easier for passengers to know where to board them.

Improvements to the Shore Fast Line Cars

The interurban cars used on the Atlantic City-Ocean City route were also updated and modified during the decade. Mechanical improvements included the creation of a pneumatic sleet-cutter side, with control valves in the motorman's cab.

Another innovation of the Inlet shops was dipping and baking armatures and field coils three times in a liquid substance called Chinaluc, resulting in greatly reduced failures. Journal and armature bearings were heated slowly over a fire before they were rebuilt. A portable vacuum cleaner was purchased to clean the interiors of the cars, including the seats, window sills, and arm rests. Cars were cleaned on a regular basis, and it took from four to five hours to do the job. The rattan seats, now dirty and discolored, were stained green and then covered with a cane glaze that restored their appearance.

An extensive rebuilding of some of the Ocean City Division cars was undertaken by the Inlet shop force in 1927. The rattan seats were covered with felt, woven hair, cotton, and Pennsylvania Railroad plush; new green pantasote curtains were installed; the ceilings were painted white and gold and the cherry woodwork cleaned and polished. The window sash in the monitor roof was sealed and new ventilators were installed. A new composite flooring of a substance called Magnesite was laid, and the lighting was improved.

Exterior changes included replacing the original fixed wooden steps with steel drop steps, called Pullman steps by

Above: Nearside 6839 is stopped at a "safety zone" on Atlantic Avenue in this undated photograph. It has been rebuilt with a larger rear platform with double doors, although passengers entered and left via the front doors when the car was in one-man operation. William Lichtenstern, LeRoy O. King, Jr. collection

third rail shoe for use during winter ice storms. Hard steel blades with toothed edges were welded to the underside of a shoe; air pressure was used to hold it down on the third rail. When storms threatened, two of them were applied on each car, one on each the company, accessed by a movable steel platform or "trap," operated by a foot release. Sheet steel panels were placed over the wood sheathing on the car sides and the end dashers. New couplers replaced the original ones. The weight of each car was

Above: Shore Fast Line interurban 110 models the rebuilding and updating done at Inlet Shops. The clerestory windows have been sealed, steel plates cover the wooden sides, new doors and steps were provided, and interior changes made. All the interurban cars mounted an illuminated number board on the roof for the benefit of the operators at Meadows Tower. The truss rods with turnbuckles betray the car's original wood construction. William Lichtenstern, LeRoy O. King collection

increased by about 1,000 pounds. Modified cars 106, 110, 117, and 118 entered service in April, followed by 113, 108, and 116 in June.

Maintaining the appearance of the cars, both city and interurban, was difficult in the harsh seashore environment, where the moist salt air, often containing fine particles of sand, caused fading and potential corrosion. To combat this problem, the company repainted each car about every 20 months. In the six-man paint shop, old paint was burned off or sanded down, then a coat of primer paint was applied, followed by three successive coats of "Burning Bush Orange" color. Striping and numbering in black was done by hand, and black paint was also used on the trolley poles and bases, the bumpers, and the trucks. The final step was to apply three coats of varnish. Interiors were sanded, painted and varnished as well. Depending on the car's condition, it took seven to ten days to repaint it. With their bright orange paint and cream window posts, the cars presented an attractive and pleasing appearance.

The Central Passenger Railway received four used cars in 1924 for its Boardwalk-to-Venice Park service. Two were single-truck, ten-bench open cars, purchased from the Ocean City Electric Railway, and numbered 13 and 14. The others were single-truck, eight-window closed cars, acquired from the Warren Street Railway of Pennsylvania, and numbered 15 and 16.

Parlor Car Service

The former funeral car Absequam was converted into a parlor car circa 1918, retaining its name. It was placed in service as a chair car, operating between the Boardwalk at Virginia Avenue and Ocean City. In 1919, the car initially made four trips on Saturdays and Sundays, leaving Atlantic City at 10 A.M., 12 noon, 2 P.M. and 4 P.M., and returning from Ocean City one hour later. This was soon reduced to three weekend round trips. The service was promoted as a sightseeing car, and advertisements, with considerable exaggeration, described its wicker seats as having a "luxury and ease unequalled by any upholstered Pullman." An additional fare of 15 cents was charged, later increased to 25 cents.

On summer weekdays during the 1920s, the car operated on sightseeing trips from Virginia Avenue and the Boardwalk to Ventnor, Margate, and Longport, making three trips a day. A lecturer was on board to describe the passing scene. The round trip was scheduled for one hour and 45 minutes, and the fare was 50 cents.

By the fall of 1928, the car was in need of refurbishing. General Superintendent A. J. Purinton considered converting the car to a coach and sought estimates for 20 cross seats if this were done. Equipment suppliers and the J.G. Brill Company submitted estimates. Prices per seat ranged from $33 to almost $55, depending on whether the seats were rattan or plush.

Above: Stern & Silverman were passionate in updating equipment on their Central Passenger Railway. No. 16 was built by Kuhlman in 1911 for the Warren (Pennsylvania) Street Railway as part of a five-car order. Two of these homely vehicles were purchased in 1924 for the short runs on the Venice Park line which was converted to buses in 1927. LeRoy O. King collection

Armed with this information, in March 1929, Purinton wrote to Stern and Silverman noting that if the Absequam were to continue as a parlor car, it needed cleaning and varnishing, a new carpet or rubber aisle runner, and new steps, which would cost at least $527. To convert the car to a coach with rattan seats, new steps, a rubber runner, and new lighting would cost $1,310. If plush seats were installed, the cost would be $1,990. He recommended conversion to a coach, unless the parlor car service had an advertising value and it "... was a matter of company policy."

Isaac Silverman chose the cheapest option. He felt there were a sufficient number of coaches and he rejected the idea of spending the sizeable amounts to rebuild the car. Noting that the parlor operation generated roughly $2,000 in revenue in recent years, he decided to continue it in service, with a minimal expenditure of $77 for cleaning, repairs, and a rubber aisle runner.

Realigning the Absecon Boulevard Tracks

The route of the Shore Fast Line cars leaving or entering Atlantic City ran from Virginia and Adriatic Avenues on a diagonal line to the Thorofare Bridge. Originally open land, a roadway now paralleled the tracks and the extension of east-west streets created a number of grade crossings. In 1921, the city decided to widen and improve Absecon Boulevard, as it was now called, by creating roadways on both sides of the tracks, which were realigned to run in the median. Single steel line poles, with double cross-arms, replaced the old wooden ones. The city paid most of the expense of the changes, and it also relieved the company of a tax imposed on the right-of-way. When completed, the new road attracted considerable motor vehicle traffic, which, in conjunction with the grade crossings, slowed the electric cars and increased accidents.

Agreements with Ventnor, Margate and Longport

By the 1920s, the three towns on the south end of Absecon Island had developed sufficiently that they demanded formal agreements regulating the rights of the railway company within their boundaries. These agreements were between the West Jersey and Seashore Railroad, the legal owner, and the respective towns, and they were approved by the Public Utility Commission (PUC).

The 1911 compact with Ventnor City was updated in 1925, permitting the company to retain the Portland Avenue loop. Two years later, the WJ&S deeded to Margate City and the Borough of Longport all of its Atlantic Avenue property, except for a strip 24 feet, 3 inches wide in the middle of the street, which it kept as its "absolute property" for railway purposes. The towns promised not to permit any other company to offer competing transit services by any mode on Atlantic Avenue.

CHAPTER SIX | *The Return of Prosperity*

The Challenge of Maintaining the Tracks

The seashore climate and the varying requirements of the municipalities presented challenges to the track maintenance forces of the AC&S. The salt air, sandy surfaces, high ground water, and windy conditions, plus the occasional operation of steam railroad freight cars, contributed to corrosion and the need for careful maintenance practices.

Paved, rigid track construction was used on Atlantic Avenue in Atlantic City. Nine-inch, 140-pound grooved girder rail was the standard here, placed on tie plates resting on untreated yellow pine crossties. Rows of granite stones, called "block stretchers," were laid lengthwise along each side of the rail, with a three-inch layer of asphalt providing a smooth surface for street traffic. The subsurface structure consisted of a continuous slab of six-inch concrete, laid on sand, with a two-inch layer of broken stone under the ties.

In Ventnor, T-rail laid on treated ties placed on sand and gravel was used. A local ordinance required that a layer of broken stone cover the ties almost to the top of the rails. In Margate and Longport, the same method was used, except no broken stone covering the ties was required.

Corrosion was an ongoing problem. In 1924, sections of track in Atlantic City were rebuilt. In places, the base of the rail had been destroyed by rust from the spikes, which were replaced by screw spikes and cast-iron clips inserted in new holes drilled in the concrete. The ties laid in 1906 were still in good condition, as was most of the rail. Defective sections were replaced by new ten-foot lengths of rail, and new granite blocks were installed where needed. Corrugated rail surfaces were smoothed by grinding.

The open track in Ventnor fared less well. Salty seashore sand sifted into crevices between the broken stone, causing extensive deterioration of the base of the rail around the spike heads to such an extent that much of the track, laid in 1912, had to be replaced. In Margate and Longport, sand was also the enemy of the open track. Workers made continuous efforts to keep the sand at least one-inch below the tops of the ties, but on-going corrosion, especially of the tie plates, required their frequent replacement. The average life of the rail in these areas was only 16 years.

In the spring of 1925, workers replaced the double track on

Above: *Nearsides 6827 and 6808 pass on Atlantic Avenue over the 140-pound girder rail bordered by the "black stretcher" blocks seen here. A passenger waits in the safety zone—a painted line on the street—reflecting the city government's negative view of streetcars. The filigree supports for the cross arms supporting the overhead wires provided a touch of class.* Francis Goldsmith, Jr., Fred W. Schneider, III collection

Virginia Avenue between Atlantic Avenue and the Boardwalk with new seven-inch girder rail, in 62-foot lengths, laid on steel ties embedded in concrete. The joint plates were fastened by bolts and the rail ends were welded together to reduce bumps and noise. A seven-inch concrete slab was laid below the base of the rail, covering the ties, and two inches of asphalt paving provided a smooth surface for traffic. During the work, which lasted several weeks, Shore Fast Line cars ran down South Carolina Avenue to the Boardwalk. The cost of the repairs and paving was split, with the AC&S paying 40 percent, the PRR 37.5 percent, and the city the remainder.

In 1926, the 2,000 feet of single track on 8th Street in Ocean City, originally laid in 1908 with 85-pound T-rail, had deteriorated to such an extent that it had to be replaced with seven-inch, 128-pound grooved girder rail, in 66-foot sections. Again, the rails were placed on steel ties covered with concrete extending almost to the top of the rails. The joints and tie plates were welded. This rigid track structure proved to be durable and reduced noise.

In 1927, a great fire destroyed most of the Boardwalk area in the central part of Ocean City. The municipal leaders decided to move the new Boardwalk a half-block closer to the ocean, thus permitting them to sell what had been beaches at high prices. This move left the track on 8th Street about 400 feet short of the new Boardwalk. Consequently, in the spring of 1928, the company received approval to extend its track that distance, so it could still claim to run "Boardwalk-to-Boardwalk."

New Stations Constructed

The mainland communities of Pleasantville, Northfield, Linwood, and Somers Point experienced considerable development during the prosperity of the 1920s. To accommodate the new residents as well as the existing ones, the AC&S improved stations or built new ones. The Somers Point station was graced with trees and flowers and had a heated waiting room served by a ticket agent. In 1923, new stations were built at Launch Haven in Somers Point and at the Country Club in Linwood. The following year, a new station with a waiting room opened at Dolphin in Northfield. A local developer gave a 15-foot by 135-foot strip of land, a platform, and a new station to the WJ&S at Meyron Avenue, near Launch Haven, in 1925. He also built a grade crossing at that point and agreed to maintain it. In similar fashion, another developer in Northfield built a new station and platform near Bakersfield and presented it to the railroad in 1926. Finally, new stations with agents were built at Smith's Landing and Northfield in 1930.

Elsewhere, in 1923 a storm destroyed the Longport station and it was replaced by a new structure. In Ocean City a new ticket office and waiting room opened at Eighth Street and Atlantic Avenue. Tickets could also be purchased at the Boardwalk ticket office and at the PRR's Eighth Street station at West Avenue.

As automobile traffic increased on Atlantic Avenue, the hazard of boarding or leaving trolley cars in the middle of the wide street provoked complaints and concern. The AC&S appealed to the

Above: In this undated scene, a northbound car approaches Northfield where a few passengers wait. The structure appears to be the 1930 station. The line from Pleasantville to Somers Point was flat and mostly straight, permitting fast timings. But population increases and grade crossings gradually affected speeds. Presumably the roof bell is clanging as required by New Jersey state law. George Krambles collection

city in 1926 to construct safety islands at the car stops, pointing out that many drivers ignored the law requiring motor vehicles to stop eight feet behind a standing trolley, and endangering the 30,000 winter and 60,000 summer passengers. As a result, safety islands were constructed at a number of intersections.

Modifications in the Supply of Electric Power

From the beginning of its operations, the AC&S had purchased its power from the PRR. It was generated at the WJ&S power station in Westville for use by the Newfield Branch electric trains and the Atlantic Avenue trolley lines. This electricity was also fed to the Ocean City line through substations in Atlantic City and Somers Point. In 1924, the PRR determined it was cheaper to buy power from the Philadelphia Electric Company that was transmitted by a line over the Delaware River. The Westville plant was then shut down.

The power was carried on a pole line to substations along the Newfield Branch and was subjected to occasional interruptions. To maintain service at such times, a tie-line from the Atlantic City Electric Company was maintained to the PRR's New York Avenue station. However, in a reappraisal of its power system, the PRR discontinued this tie-line connection in 1924.

The use of power generated in Philadelphia in the territory served by the Atlantic City Electric Company aggravated officials of that firm and the holding company controlling it, the American Electric Power Company. In October 1924, C. S. Tingley of the holding company requested PRR vice-president C. H. Krick to arrange a conference to discuss the possibility of the Atlantic City Electric Company furnishing power to operate the Atlantic Avenue trolleys, something Isaac Silverman favored. Several meetings were held between a PRR committee and the general manager of the electric company, but no agreement could be reached.

The absence of a functioning tie-line to the Atlantic City Electric Company for use in an emergency was still a matter of concern to AC&S officials. The PRR committee recommended the railroad should make a new contract with the electric company, without any guarantee that the utility had to reserve energy for its use, thereby making it cheaper. However, PRR electrical engineers and the chief of motive power, J. T. Wallis, based in Altoona, Pennsylvania, felt such an emergency connection was unnecessary. Wallis wrote there was no need to insure "... against a failure which may not occur," and advised Krick to drop the matter. This made the AC&S entirely dependent on the stability of the transmission pole line running from Philadelphia to Atlantic City.

Service Frequencies

Service during the decade was good. On the Ocean City line, cars ran every half- hour from 5 A.M. until after midnight between the Boardwalk terminals, supplemented by rush hour cars to and from such points as Northfield, Linwood, and Somers Point. In the summer, 20-minute headways were offered, for a total of 106 daily trains. All cars stopped at Pleasantville, Linwood, and Somers Point, with the remaining stations designated as flag stops. Running time was 49 minutes, and the round-trip fare early in the decade was 50 cents. By 1930, the fare had increased to 85 cents, although excursion rates of 50 cents were offered periodically. Additional cars ran on holidays such as Easter, Memorial Day, Independence Day, and Labor Day. Two-car trains operated on some trips, with the second car cut off at one of the mainland points. The parlor car offered three trips on Saturdays and Sundays for an additional fare of 25 cents.

As the volume of commuter traffic grew from the mainland towns, additional runs were scheduled. In 1928, the AC&S announced that, beginning in June, it would offer 15-minute service to those points, with 75 trains, plus more rush hour service. This was in addition to the regular Ocean City trains.

On Absecon Island, Ventnor City residents and officials complained about the frequency of service and the double fare they had to pay to travel into Atlantic City. They petitioned the Board of Public Utility Commissioners in 1922 for relief. A series of meetings were held among Superintendent Purinton, Ventnor councilmen, and Atlantic City Commissioner Harry Bacharach to resolve the dispute. In August, an agreement was reached, whereby from May to October 15, all cars would run to Portland Avenue loop in Ventnor, with free transfers to those who wished to go to Savannah Avenue in Margate. During the morning and evening rush hours, all cars would run to Savannah Avenue loop. Most importantly, the double fare was eliminated, with a single seven-cent fare from the Inlet to Margate.

In the summer of 1923, extra cars were scheduled between the Boardwalk and Virginia Avenue and Cedar Grove Avenue in the lower end of Margate. The recently acquired War Board double-end cars were used for this run. They ran every 20 minutes from approximately 4 P.M. until midnight. This service ended in 1926 and was replaced by a single double-end car, referred to as a "transfer car," running on Virginia Avenue from the Boardwalk to Atlantic Avenue only.

Overall, service frequencies were good, especially in the summer, despite occasional complaints. From 5:30 A.M. until 8 P.M., a car left the Inlet for Longport every 15 minutes; a 20-minute headway was maintained until midnight. In the 1921 season, open cars ran from Virginia Avenue and the Boardwalk to Portland Avenue loop. During the following summer, two cars ran to the city boundary at Jackson Avenue. Thereafter, double-end open cars ran from the Inlet to Jackson Avenue, while single-end open cars operated through to Savannah Avenue loop in Margate, while every third car continued on to Longport. (In 1930, Savannah Avenue was renamed Douglas Avenue.) A night car left the Inlet every hour from 1 A.M. to 5 A.M. for Margate, an operation that continued until the end of rail service in 1955.

James N.J. Henwood

Above: *The motorman on open car 6830 had little room and no seat as seen in this July 1927 company photo. His car was among a group built between 1895 and 1899 and, like all cars, bore the name of the legal owner, the West Jersey & Seashore Railroad. No doubt crews were tired after a long day on the line in these cars.* Jeffrey Marinoff collection

The two-zone fare system of seven cents each zone, with the break at Savannah Avenue, continued until almost the end of the decade, much to the displeasure of residents. Fares had to be paid separately in each zone; there were no through fares. Conductors were instructed not to count passengers carried, and to turn in all moneys collected, regardless of fare register totals. The company expected errors to occur, and conductors could neither keep surplus money nor pay for any shortages. This cumbersome arrangement finally ended in April 1929, when the AC&S established a single, seven-cent fare on Atlantic Avenue streetcars, from the Inlet to Longport.

Occasionally, minor problems disrupted service. For example, a broken trolley wire at Connecticut Avenue caused delays on the Longport line on the afternoon of September 21, 1925. Power failed on a section of Adriatic and South Carolina Avenues in February 1927. The company rented a truck to pull a stalled car from the dead section and hired taxis to carry passengers to and from the Boardwalk. The second car of a train in the same area split a switch in March 1930, and three buses were used to ferry passengers to the terminal. Workers cleared the line in two hours.

The 1924 Strike

While service levels were good, relations between the management and some of the motormen and conductors were decidedly not. The AC&S did not recognize unions, but some of the workers had joined the amalgamated association, which was attempting to organize all the platform men and to negotiate a formal contract with the company. There was agitation for a wage increase and improvements in working conditions.

Superintendent A. J. Purinton, backed by Stern and Silverman, flatly rejected recognition of a union, especially since it represented only some of the men, and he stated the company could not afford a pay increase. Faced with this adamant stand, P. J. O'Brien, the national organizer for the union, dropped the demand for a closed shop and offered to submit the dispute to arbitration. Purinton rejected this proposal.

With no prior warning, at 2 A.M. on Saturday, June 21, 1924, at the start of the summer season, many of the motormen and conductors walked out, bringing trolley service to a halt. Atlantic City Mayor Edward L. Bader immediately ordered about 100 jitneys to move from Pacific Avenue to Atlantic Avenue to run from the Inlet to the city limits at Jackson Avenue. Riders would be charged a flat ten-cent fare. In addition, about 15 buses, normally used on sightseeing runs, were pressed into service. These measures, plus many automobile drivers who picked up stranded trolley riders, minimized the effects of the strike.

Purinton quickly hired substitute workers, described as strikebreakers, to restore service, on about five-minute headways, the next day. Shore Fast Line cars continued to run from Pleasantville to Ocean City on their normal schedules, and the Atlantic and Suburban, unaffected by the strike, carried passengers from the Boardwalk at Florida Avenue to Pleasantville, where they made convenient connections to the truncated Fast Line cars. Mounted police sent by Mayor Bader patrolled Atlantic Avenue to prevent acts of violence. The public, on the whole, supported the management and blamed the union for any inconvenience they suffered.

The company appealed to the courts and eventually secured an injunction prohibiting the union from interfering with its operations. Some frustrated union leaders were caught placing ties across the Shore Fast Line tracks in Somers Point and were promptly arrested. With the strike clearly a failure, the men returned to work on June 29, in what was a victory for the company. About 100 loyal men retained their seniority, but those who walked out were treated as new applicants, as Purinton had warned them they would lose their seniority rights if they struck.

The strike cost the company lost revenue and additional expenses and it embittered and angered some of the workers. The public was inconvenienced but still managed to reach their destinations.

Express Shipments are Discontinued

As an indication of changing conditions, in 1925 the AC&S decided it was no longer feasible to continue carrying express shipments to Linwood and Somers Point for the American Railway Express Company. This service had been provided since the beginning of the Shore Fast Line operations, but its use and the revenues received had been steadily declining. After discussing the matter with the express company, the AC&S announced it would discontinue carrying packages and other items by July 1.

The city of Somers Point complained to the AC&S, which maintained it was only an agent for the express company and that the service required special cars. Dissatisfied with this explanation, the Board of Solicitors for Somers Point filed a complaint with the Public Utility Commission; a hearing was scheduled on June 19 in Atlantic City. The AC&S attorneys testified that an average of only four items daily were shipped to Somers Point in 1924 and even fewer to Linwood. The company received only $439 in total revenues, as compared to over $1,227 in 1908, a decrease of 64 percent, yet it had to maintain facilities to carry express. American Railway Express said it could not increase the railroad's compensation for such a low volume of traffic and that other means were available to carry such shipments. The board concluded on August 10 that the railroad could not be forced to continue this costly operation.

The Venice Park Line is Abandoned

Since 1917, the Central Passenger Railway had operated the Venice Park Railway line for a five-cent fare, with free transfers to Atlantic Avenue cars. The route extended from Virginia Avenue and the Boardwalk to Adriatic Avenue and the connection with the original line to the bridge over the Penrose Canal and into the Venice Park section of the city. Returning, cars ran on South Carolina Avenue to the Boardwalk, where they changed ends and returned to Atlantic Avenue. They then ran to Virginia Avenue, and down that street to the Boardwalk. This routing covered all of the Central Passenger Railway trackage, but it offered more service than the traffic justified. Cars ran every 30 minutes.

In 1919, the bridge over the Penrose Canal was condemned, and service stopped at that point. In 1923, Stern and Silverman decided to simplify operations. The Central Passenger Railway purchased the franchise of the Venice Park Railway and returned it to the state. This was approved by the Board of Public Utility Commissioners in 1924. As of July 16, a new route was established. Two cars, on a 20-minute headway, ran on South Carolina Avenue to Adriatic Avenue, and then on the original line to the Penrose Bridge. A "transfer car" ran on Virginia Avenue from Atlantic Avenue to the Boardwalk in the summers.

The revised route, served by elderly cars, proved to be short-lived. The rails were worn out and in need of replacement, an investment the company did not want to make for a low-volume route. Instead, conversion to motor bus operation was seen as a better choice. Stern and Silverman already had limited experience with running buses that had replaced Atlantic and Suburban cars on the Pleasantville to Absecon branch in 1925.

By then, the motor bus had come of age. More commodious and comfortable vehicles began to appear on the routes of many traction companies, often serving as feeders to existing trolley lines or even replacing electric cars on short, low-volume routes. Eminently practical, they cost less, could be operated more cheaply, were more flexible in their routings, and eliminated the need to maintain tracks and overhead wire. They were an obvious choice to replace the antiquated Venice Park trolleys.

Stern and Silverman executives in 1926 proposed a tentative bus route serving Venice Park and another residential development north of Adriatic Avenue along Massachusetts Avenue and Gardiner's Basin called Bungalow Park. Trolley cars were to be retained on South Carolina Avenue, from the Boardwalk to Ohio Avenue, to provide service in that area. Superintendent A. J. Purinton objected to this plan. He pointed out the proposed route was too long and indirect for Venice Park residents going to Atlantic Avenue and would require keeping part of the Venice Park rail line. Instead, he proposed converting the Venice Park line to bus operation and extending it into Venice Park via another bridge. Two buses on a 20-minute headway could adequately serve the line. Purinton suggested a separate line be established to Bungalow Park, primarily along Massachusetts Avenue to the Gardiner's Basin area, with one bus providing service on a 20-minute headway. The superintendent noted electric cars cost 36 cents per car mile to operate, even with a one-man crew, while buses cost only 25 cents per mile. He wanted to retain the tracks on South Carolina and Adriatic avenues for emergency use.

Bus Service Begins in 1927

Isaac Silverman and his managers took the advice of Purinton and modified their proposed bus service in the manner he suggested. An Atlantic City ordinance passed on December 30, 1926, granting the Central Passenger Railway the right to operate buses to Venice Park and Bungalow Park, was approved by the PUC on February 28, 1927. Service began on May 16 from South Carolina Avenue and Commerce Drive, across the street from the PRR's Tennessee Avenue Electric Station on Atlantic Avenue, where a waiting room and ticket office were located.

The Venice Park buses generally followed the trolley route, except they used North Carolina Avenue, a wider route than South Carolina Avenue. In Venice Park, the line was extended a short distance along West Riverside Drive to the Lu Lu Yacht Club. The line was 2.2 miles long and the running time was 13 minutes. Bungalow Park buses left the South Carolina Avenue terminal and ran north on Arctic Avenue to Massachusetts Avenue, and on that street to Adriatic Avenue, a distance of 1.3 miles. The fare was ten cents, with free transfers to Atlantic Avenue cars and to Shore Fast Line cars within the city. Passengers transferring from electric cars to buses had to pay a ten-cent fare. At first, the buses were operated by the Central Coach Lines, a new entity created for the bus service. Thirty minute- headways were maintained on both lines, from 6:30 A.M. to late evenings.

In September, the company opened a third line, from a connection with the Atlantic Avenue trolleys at Albany Avenue, south on Ventnor Avenue to a new development called Ventnor Heights on the Thorofare side of the city, a distance of 1.75 miles. The route was operated by the AC&S, as were all subsequent routes, and the designation Central Coach Lines disappeared.
To operate these routes, the company had six Yellow Model X, 21-seat coaches, and one Model Z, 29-seat bus. The latter was used on the Ventnor Heights line. As of early 1928, the revenue per mile was 30 cents, while the cost of operation was 33 cents, but the management felt the routes fed passengers to its rail lines. The vehicles were maintained and stored in the Inlet car house by bus mechanics. The drivers were former motormen.

The Bus Service is Expanded

Once bus service started, it expanded rapidly. This was partly due to replacing discontinued trolley lines, to the opportunity to run on new highways, and to a desire to prevent competition from independent bus operators who were appearing in growing numbers in the region. The Stern and Silverman corporation was determined to maintain the transportation monopoly it had in the seashore region.

In August 1928, the PUC approved the establishment of a single bus line from Albany and Atlantic Avenues, along Albany Avenue to Chelsea Heights and West End Avenue. When a new bridge opened between Longport and Ocean City, the AC&S lost

CHAPTER SIX | *The Return of Prosperity*

no time in beginning a summer service between the Tennessee Avenue terminal and Ocean City, via Albany and Ventnor avenues. In Ocean City, the route followed West Atlantic Boulevard and Battersea Road in the Gardens section, to Ocean Avenue. It continued down the entire length of Ocean City, using Ocean Avenue, 15th Street, Asbury, and Central Avenues to 34th Street, with a few trips extended to 55th Street. No local passengers were carried in Ocean City and no stops were permitted in Margate. At first, buses ran every 30 minutes, but this was soon changed to a more realistic 60 minutes. The round-trip fare was 85 cents, but 20-trip family tickets, also good on the electric cars, were 35 cents each. Running time was 37 minutes to 8th Street in Ocean City.

Pleasantville and then the Shore Road. A few runs were extended to Ocean City via the 9th Street highway bridge, terminating at 8th Street and the Boardwalk. The Absecon-Pleasantville line was continued, and a few trips were extended to the border with Northfield. Headways were hourly on the Somers Point line, and 30 minutes on the Pleasantville–Absecon route, which connected with all Fast Line cars.

A final opportunity to add bus service came in 1930 when the Ocean City Electric Railway, surviving only with financial support from the city, decided to abandon its line at the end of 1929. The AC&S agreed to pay $17,000 for its franchise and rights, and it gained approval from the city and the PUC to operate a local

Above: A type X Yellow Coach bus rests in the Inlet Barn in 1932. This type of vehicle operated on the Venice Park line and the other routes established in the late 1920s. Whether is was an improvement over the electric cars was a matter of opinion. Motor Bus Society Library

This competed with the Shore Fast Line route, and it was faster and more direct. Stern and Silverman recognized the advantages of securing rights to this route rather than having an outside operator gain them.

The abandonment of the Atlantic and Suburban Railway in 1929 prompted the AC&S to secure PUC approval to run buses from the Tennessee Avenue terminal to Pleasantville, Northfield, Linwood, and Somers Point, using Albany Avenue Boulevard to

line on the island beginning in 1930. The PRR reimbursed Stern and Silverman $17,000 for the franchise. All the bus routes and equipment were considered part of the West Jersey and Seashore Railroad and covered by the 1907 lease of the Atlantic Avenue line to the AC&S. The Ocean City local line duplicated the former trolley route, from the Gardens section, south along Atlantic and Central avenues to 59th Street. This summer-only line operated every 30 minutes.

THE WAR BOARD CARS

With the onset of the Great War in August 1914, the European powers, especially Britain and France, greatly increased their purchases of American goods. This vast trade, combined with German submarine attacks, created a severe shortage of ships on the trans-Atlantic routes. The American merchant marine, very small at the time, was unable to meet the challenge.

By 1916, in response to the growing demands for more shipping, Congress passed the Federal Shipping Act, creating a new agency, the United States Shipping Board, composed of five members appointed by President Woodrow Wilson. With an initial appropriation of $50,000,000, the board was given regulatory powers over steamship lines and charged with the construction of more vessels to relieve the shortage of merchant ships.

After the United States entered the war in April, 1917, the Shipping Board created the Emergency Fleet Corporation, which initiated a ship-building program by coordinating existing yards and building new ones. The largest of the new shipyards was built in the extreme southwestern section of Philadelphia at a site with the unglamorous name of Hog Island. This massive yard, with 50 ways for assembling vessels, was a public-private enterprise, managed by the American International Corporation, a subsidiary of the Boston-based engineering firm of Stone & Webster.

To transport the 34,000 workers needed at the new yard, the Emergency Fleet Corporation acquired a fleet of streetcars leased to the two lines serving Hog Island. The smaller of these was the Philadelphia Railways, running from 3rd and Jackson Streets in South Philadelphia into lower Delaware County. A perennial money-loser, the company could not afford to buy new cars itself, so in 1918 the Emergency Fleet Corporation purchased a group of 30 cars under construction by the J. G. Brill Company for the American Cities Company, dubbed the "War Board" cars by Brill. They were sent to the Philadelphia Railways and the Philadelphia Rapid Transit Company for service on lines to Hog Island. Ownership remained with the federal agency.

The cars were double-ended, with doors at each end. They were 46', 9" long, 9', 1" wide, with Brill 77E trucks with 26-inch wheels, mounted four Westinghouse 514A motors of 35 horsepower each, and were equipped with K-35 controllers. They had longitudinal seating for 52 people and could move at about 30 miles-per-hour on level track.

After the end of the war in November 1918, construction at Hog Island gradually came to an end by January 1922 after building 110 ships. The War Board cars were offered to Philadelphia Railways, which had now reverted to Stern and Silverman control. The line could not afford them, so ownership remained with the Emergency Fleet Corporation, who put them on the market. In 1922, six of the cars were sold to the Ocean Electric Railway of Long Island, where they were numbered 136-141. In May 1923, the PRR purchased four cars (numbers 136, 140, 141, and 148) and renumbered them 6885-6888, and placed them in service on the Atlantic Avenue line.

CHAPTER SIX | *The Return of Prosperity*

Above: *This 1946 photograph shows the electric sign at the Virginia Avenue terminal of the Shore Fast Line, beckoning people to enjoy a ride to Ocean City. A similar sign was erected in that town advertising service to Atlantic City. Both resorts catered to tourists, some of whom might enjoy a ride through the seashore region. Stern & Silverman were well aware of the value of advertising.* Richard Allman collection

To service its routes, the railroad purchased additional buses, primarily Yellow Model X, 21-seat and Model Z, 29-seat coaches. In 1930, the AC&S operated 20 buses.

Advertising and Promotional Efforts

Whether people traveled by rail or bus, Stern and Silverman was keenly aware of the importance of advertising, especially in an area heavily dependent on tourists and visitors. Timetables, usually containing a map, were reissued regularly and were easily available. Bus timetables were printed when motor coach lines began. Separate folders promoted the parlor car service. Advertisements were placed in newspapers and guidebooks for holidays, special events, and excursions. The Miss America Pageant began in 1921 in an effort to extend the season into September. Part of the festivities was a parade down the Boardwalk, and the company contributed a float carrying a local beauty dubbed "Miss Shore Fast Line." The "Trolley Talks" folders were carried in all cars and buses and were available in stations.

A particularly successful long-running promotion from 1923 through 1929 was the "best gardens" contest conducted along the Pleasantville-Somers Point section of the Shore Fast Line. Cash prizes totaling $39 were awarded to six people each year. The contest gained considerable favorable publicity for the line.

Another promotion in 1930 was the distribution of free match books to passengers. Trainmen were asked to report to the Advertising Department how effective the free matches were in gaining riders. Since the program was not continued, one can assume that the response was minimal.

A more tangible project was the erection of two large electric signs at the Boardwalk terminals in 1922. The one at Virginia Avenue proclaimed in large, 12-inch letters, "Shore Fast Line to Ocean City." The 8th Street sign declared "Fast Line to Atlantic City." The signs, which cost $613, faced the Boardwalk, and they remained in place for many years.

All told, Stern and Silverman and its local managers recognized the importance of frequent advertising in an environment where large crowds of potential riders were available only for the summer season. The number of passengers carried in the 1920s vindicated the expense of the advertising budget.

Financial Results

The financial returns during the 1920s were much improved over those of the previous decade. They reached their peak in 1925 and then began a slow but steady decline, as paved highways lured more and more rubber-tired vehicles to the region. As was its practice, the secretive—and privately held--Stern and Silverman Corporation made no reports to the financial agencies, but the companies it controlled did.

The operating company, the Atlantic City and Shore Railroad, began the decade with a clouded record. During the period of its receivership, from December 1915 to December 1921, it had defaulted on interest payments on its $950,000 of outstanding bonds. From December 1921 to December 1922, the bondholders agreed to accept only one-half the interest due them. Thereafter, the company resumed regular payments. The firm reported a net income each year except for 1930, when it reported a deficit of $7,700.

The AC&S Railroad declared dividends in 1924, 1927, and 1929, most of which went to the Atlantic City and Shore Company, the majority owner of its stock. The holding company itself paid no dividends on its $995,000 in stock, but since its $591,000 in outstanding bonds had been secured by the stock and bonds of the Atlantic and Suburban, which were essentially worthless, presumably the dividends were used to bolster the bonds.

The Central Passenger Railway, which absorbed the Venice Park Railway, reported deficits in five years between 1922 and 1930, but it managed to declare a dividend in 1930. Its securities were owned entirely by the AC&S Company.

Financially, the decade ended on a sour note, similar to the conditions when it began. But much worse was to come, as the nation and its people were soon to struggle through the difficult years of the Great Depression.

Above: If one tired of the many restaurants, shops, and other amusements, there was always the beach. For many city dwellers a trip to Atlantic City to enjoy the salt air and sunshine was a restorative. This view dates from 1924, the beaches are crowded and business is booming. LeRoy O. King, Jr. collection

CHAPTER SIX | *The Return of Prosperity*

Atlantic City & Shore Railroad: Selected Financial Data

Year	Operating Revenues	Operating Expenses	Railway Operating Income	Fixed Charges	Net Income	Operating Ratio
1922	$1,194,854	$ 946,497	$ 248,357	$237,829	$30,479	73.7%
1924	1,285,707	1,030,138	205,509	213,019	14,300	77.9%
1926	1,366,159	1,117,644	248,495	235,272	39,332	76%
1928	1,222,663	1,007,609	215,054	190,471	55,244	76.9%
1929	1,145,680	990,880	154,800	168,106	19,243	80.4%
1930	1,004,765	899,515	105,250	153,634	(7,700)	82.6%

[1924: 12% dividend of $120,000 declared; 1927: 11% dividend of 110,000 declared; 1929: 10% dividend of $100,000 declared.]

Central Passenger Railway: Selected Financial Data

Year	Operating Revenues	Operating Expenses	Railway Operating Income	Fixed Charges	Net Income	Operating Ratio
1922	$82,077	$73,277	$ 8,799	$ 6,275	$ 3,156	81.6%
1924	88,506	95,587	(7,071)	6,278	(12,117)	99.2%
1926	98,269	71,035	27,234	5,180	22,523	63.5%
1928	28,495	17,844	10,652	2,000	9,001	46.9%
1929	27,705	17,421	10,283	2,000	8,335	50.9%
1930	18,370	16,858	1,462	2,000	(481)	77.9%

[1930: 6% dividend of $15,000 declared.]
Source: Public Utilities Commission of New Jersey

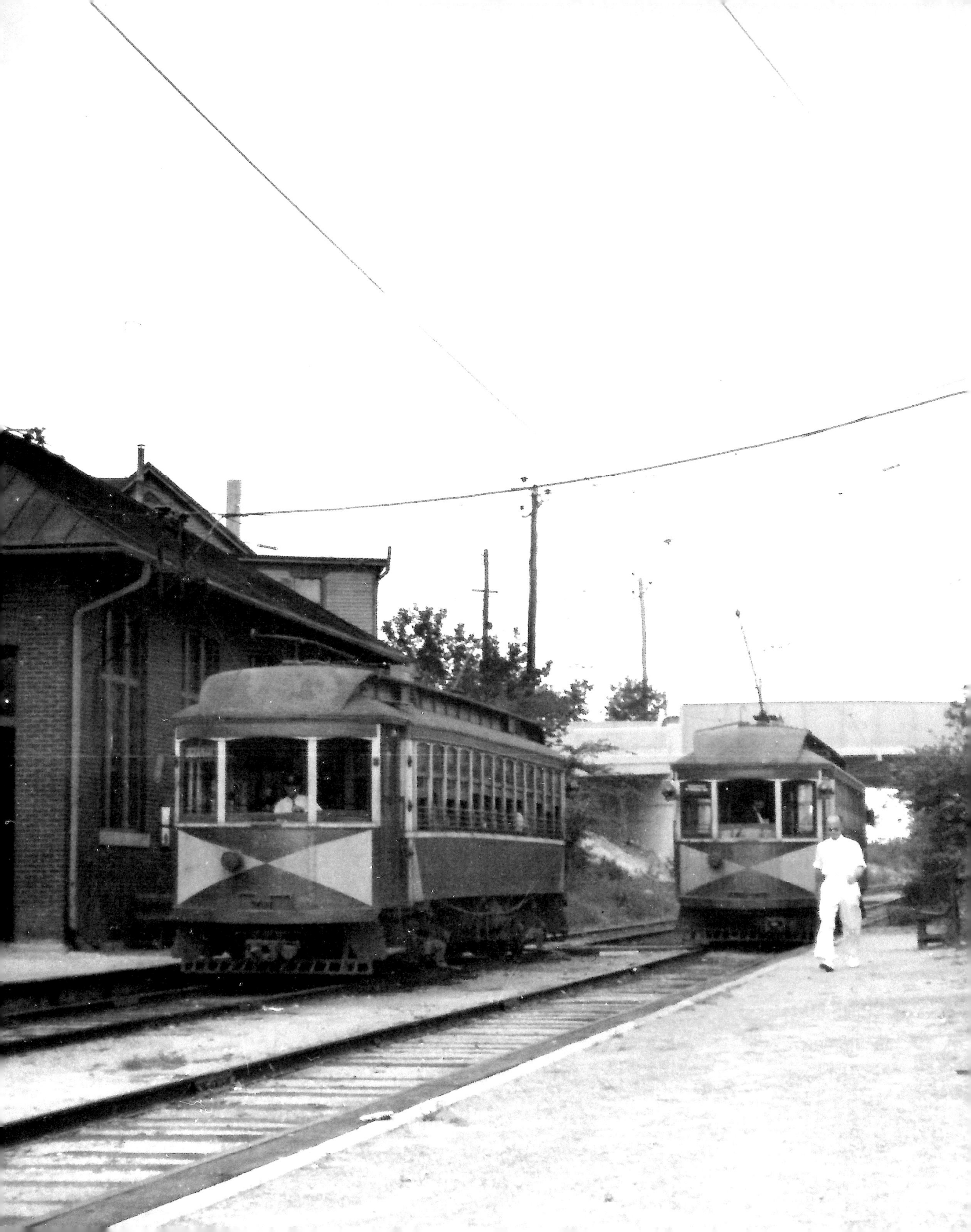

CHAPTER SEVEN

A Decade of Difficulties: the 1930s

The Great Depression

The decade of the 1930s developed in sharp contrast to the general prosperity of the 1920s. The economic shock of the stock market collapse touched off a contraction in business, bank failures, falling factory orders, cuts in wages and salaries, railroad bankruptcies, widespread unemployment, and devastation on the farms. An economic paralysis extended to virtually all aspects of American life. These dramatic and painful events would affect enterprises and cities large and small, including the Pennsylvania Railroad, the Atlantic City and Shore, and Atlantic City itself. Despite continuous efforts to alleviate the hardship, the Depression would not end until the outbreak of war in Europe in 1939 revitalized the American economy.

Governments struggled, at first fitfully and ineffectively, to deal with the crisis. The Hoover Administration preached the need for a restoration of confidence and increased spending for public works. It created the Reconstruction Finance Corporation to lend money to banks, railroads, and businesses threatened with collapse. But its efforts were hobbled by Hoover's view of federal powers as limited by the Constitution. He urged state and local governments, as well as private charities, to help, but when they exhausted their resources, he rejected direct relief to individuals.

In the 1932 elections, Hoover and the Republicans were soundly defeated by a resurgent Democratic Party, under the leadership of the charismatic Franklin Delano Roosevelt of New York. Born into a wealthy and privileged family, a distant cousin of Theodore Roosevelt, whom he admired and tried to emulate, FDR had held local offices, had served as assistant secretary of the Navy during the Wilson years, and he had run for vice-president in 1920. He was twice elected governor of New York, in 1928 and 1930. A natural politician, with a melodious voice that he projected over

Facing Page: Two Shore Fast Line cars meet at the Somers Point station. Normally a through station, several short-turn runs terminated at this point. Electric City Trolley Museum collection

Above: Many a journey to the seashore began here at the head house of the Pennsylvania Railroad's Delaware River ferries at the foot of Market Street in Philadelphia. Designated Market Street Wharf in the PRR timetable, the structure contained a large waiting room, several ticket windows, and several aprons with access to the ferry slips. The aprons could be raised or lowered, depending on the tides, by chains. The fare was five cents, but ticket holders were treated to a free ride. There was also a token issued by the company. One of the towers of the Delaware River Bridge (later called the Benjamin Franklin Bridge) rises at the left. Ed Birch photo

Above: The Pennsylvania Railroad ferry Millville is in mid-river heading for Market Street Wharf. The half-mile crossing took about five minutes as boys would congregate at the gates breathing in the pungent air of the murky Delaware. Once the boat had entered the slip and was safely secured, the gates were opened for passengers and vehicles to cross the head house to the street. The Camden headquarters of the Radio Corporation of America can be seen in the background. Ed Birch photo

the new medium of radio, he was toughened by an attack of what may have been Guillan-Barre syndrome, which left him crippled, a handicap he faced with courage and determination. A pragmatist, he was open to new ideas and methods, and he promised a New Deal for the American people.

The new administration launched a plethora of federal agencies and programs, aimed at reviving the banking system, relieve the farm crisis, create new regulations for Wall Street, strengthen labor, provide relief for the unemployed, encourage conservation, establish social security, and instill a new sense of confidence among the people. The Democrats greatly expanded federal powers, especially those of the executive branch.

But not all the New Deal reforms were successful and they did not end the Depression. Unemployment remained a major problem, involving 25 percent of the work force in 1933, and averaging 18.8 percent in the decade. A sharp recession in 1937 and 1938 showed the economy was still shaky. But the reforms did ease pain and suffering and increased public spirits. Roosevelt won a sweeping victory in 1936 and gained a second term.

The Pennsylvania-Reading Seashore Lines

Throughout the 1920s, the volume of passenger and freight traffic carried by southern New Jersey's two rival railroads experienced a steady decline, especially after the opening of the Delaware River Bridge in 1926. An increasing number of automobiles, trucks, and buses took advantage of the improved public highways and relatively short distances to provide stiff competition to the Pennsylvania's West Jersey and Seashore and the Reading's Atlantic City Railroad. The onset of the Great Depression exacerbated this situation. Burdened by miles of duplicate trackage and high fixed costs, the managements of the two Philadelphia-based carriers, although still intensely competitive, began to recognize that changes were necessary and probably inevitable.

Both railroads began to operate buses to seashore points to supplement their train services. But the Delaware River Bridge was already carrying heavy traffic to and from New Jersey, causing delays and complaints. The railroad ferries were an alternate, but they were slow and inconvenient to many.

CHAPTER SEVEN | *The 1930s*

Various public officials and civic leaders began to argue for a direct rail connection between Philadelphia and Camden, utilizing the new Delaware River Bridge where space had been provided for four tracks. In October 1929, New Jersey Governor Morgan Larson established the South Jersey Transit Commission to address the travel problems in the region. The commission made a number of recommendations in February 1930, one of which was a consolidation of the competing rail systems to reduce costs and promote efficiencies.

its lease of the West Jersey and Seashore to the new, jointly owned Atlantic City Railroad, which then changed its name to the more appropriate Pennsylvania-Reading Seashore Lines (PRSL). The Atlantic City stations were combined into a new terminal, built one block west of the Reading's former station, at Arkansas and Arctic avenues. State and federal regulatory agencies approved the new arrangement, and the PRSL officially began operation on June 25, 1933. The main offices were established in Camden under the supervision of General Manager John O. Hackenberg,

Above: As a replacement for its once busy electric M.U. cars between Camden and Atlantic City, the PRR substituted economical but noisy and uncomfortable gasoline-electric cars such as No. 400 seen here at the Atlantic City terminal. The cars ran to Pleasantville and Newfield where they connected with the electric cars that still ran between Millville, Newfield, and Camden. By the 1930s few people rode to Atlantic City on the route and the Shore Fast Line cars served mostly local passengers. This was because the PRR now had a direct route to Ocean City and no longer needed the Somers Point route for its passengers. David H. Cope photo, Collection of Railroad Photography, courtesy of the Hagley Museum and Library

A long period of discussion and negotiations ensued. The Reading, whose Atlantic City Railroad was a constant money-loser, supported the concept, but the Pennsylvania was reluctant, since the West Jersey and Seashore still generated profits, largely because of freight traffic. But the worsening economic conditions, pressure from the state Public Utility Commissioners and Atlantic City Mayor Harry Bacharach, and the obvious advantages of eliminating 79 miles of duplicate tracks led to an agreement to merge, which was announced on November 2, 1932. Under its terms, the Reading sold two-thirds of its stock in the Atlantic City Railroad to the Pennsylvania for one dollar, and the PRR assigned

a former PRR officer. Although the PRR was careful to consult the Reading in all significant matters, as the owner of two-thirds of the stock, the PRR effectively controlled the PRSL. From the viewpoint of the Atlantic City and Shore, the change made little real difference.

The PRSL did impose many economies; numerous grade crossings were eliminated with the abandonment of duplicate tracks, and train services were consolidated. The PRR had previously discontinued through electric train service between Camden, Newfield, and Atlantic City, effective on September 26, 1931. Gasoline-electric motor cars, on a limited schedule, replaced the multiple-unit electric cars between Newfield and Atlantic City. This reduced the connection with the Shore Fast Line cars at Pleasantville to insignificance, and with the new PRSL schedules and route, the PRR had a much better direct line to Ocean City. The third rail was removed between Newfield and Pleasantville, but it was kept between that point and Atlantic City for use by the Shore Fast Line. Also retained was the overhead transmission line

The Seashore Region in the Great Depression

Like towns across the nation, the seashore area suffered during the Depression years. Growth all but ceased. Atlantic City recorded its first population decline since its founding, a decrease of 2,100 residents or three percent. Absecon, Pleasantville, Linwood, and Somers Point also lost population, by about three percent. Ocean City reported 4,670 residents, a loss of 15 percent. Ventnor and Margate gained about 15 percent, and Longport 32 percent, but its population was only 300. On the mainland, only Northfield managed a slight gain of one percent, to 2,850 people.

If population figures were flat, motor vehicle registrations were not. New Jersey registered 1,100,000 vehicles in 1940, compared to 899,000 ten years earlier. Pennsylvania registrations jumped from 1,775,000 in 1930 to 2,100,000 in 1940. Even during hard times, many people considered having their own car a priority. Across the country, trolley lines were under attack; their mileage fell from 26,750 in 1935 to 19,600 in 1940. The push for buses would also be heard increasingly in Atlantic City during the period.

During the summer, Atlantic City continued to attract large crowds. A relative few were well-off citizens who stayed at the large hotels, but the majority were workers and their families, many spending only a day or two at the resort. They arrived by train, bus, and automobile. The ocean was the main attraction, but the city offered other diversions to help them briefly forget the hard times. The Boardwalk was lined with shops and amusements; fudge and taffy were available in abundance, and those who could afford it might spend an hour being pushed down the boards in a rolling chair. Some thirty theatres lined Atlantic Avenue and the Boardwalk, where the 4,200 seat Warner opened in 1929, just in time for the economic collapse. Also opening that year was the massive Convention Hall, the largest building in the world without pillars or roof supports, which contained the world's largest pipe organ.

On the ocean side of the Boardwalk were the great piers, the most notable of which was the Steel Pier, advertising itself as "The Showplace of the Nation." Containing three theatres, an opera house, the Marine Ballroom, and many amusements, it featured vaudeville, plays and the famous orchestras of the "big band" era, led by such notables as Benny Goodman, Tommy Dorsey, Paul Whiteman, Rudy Vallee, and others, all for one admission price. Off Arkansas Avenue, the Million Dollar Pier, operated by entrepreneur George Hamid, charged a lower admission price. It also featured the top orchestras in the Ballroom of the States. Other entertainment was offered in the pier's Hippodrome Theatre, with the added enticement of lockers and a bath house for those seeking the beach. All told, people could find entertainment venues of their choice at relatively low prices. Special excursion fares offered by the PRSL made access to the city from the population centers of Philadelphia and New York quick, convenient, and cheap.

During the decade, the AC&S faced significant challenges, but it continued to carry residents and visitors alike, albeit in fewer numbers. Red ink appeared in the ledgers in 1930, and bankruptcy was a real threat, but by the decade's end the company would have a fleet of handsome, new streamlined cars for its Atlantic Avenue Line courtesy of the Pennsylvania Railroad. Through it all, the same managers, both in Philadelphia and in Atlantic City, continued to direct the company's affairs.

The Pennsylvania Railroad Reduces Rental Payments

As the Depression deepened and losses mounted, the AC&S looked for ways to reduce its expenses. The interurban line to Ocean City had never lived up to expectations and was a likely candidate for change. In January 1932, Isaac Silverman wrote to PRR Vice-president of Operations Martin W. Clement, noting that the AC&S was bearing a larger proportion of the maintenance expenses and taxes on the Newfield and Somers Point branches that the Shore Fast Line cars used. Under earlier agreements, these charges were assessed on a mileage basis, but the PRR had drastically reduced its mileage after the discontinuance of its electric train service between Camden and Atlantic City. Silverman said the AC&S share of expenses had increased from $20,000 in 1916 to $43,000 in 1931, and that it was paying an estimated 58 percent of the Newfield Branch and 90 percent of the Somers Point Branch charges. He suggested the mileage arrangement be replaced by the flat rental rate of $20,000 per year.

Clement understood that treating heavy railroad trains as the equal of much lighter electric cars was inequitable, and that because the PRR's business was diminishing, a greater burden was being placed on the AC&S. He agreed with Silverman's view and told PRR Eastern Region Vice-president C. S. Krick that a new arrangement should be made. In his letter, he said the PRR might abandon the Somers Point line at some point in the future, as the AC&S might find it more profitable to run buses on the public roads. In that case, the right-of-way could be sold to the state or county as the route for a "high speed highway."

Krick agreed, and in its usual fashion, a PRR committee negotiated a new agreement by July, 1932, where the AC&S was to pay a flat fee of 7.75 cents per car mile for its trackage rights over the PRR lines and continue to maintain its stations and the electrical facilities. The document noted that the AC&S had lost over $21,000 on the route in 1931 alone. It estimated the new system would cost the electric line about $20,000 per year to operate its Shore Fast Line cars over the route.

CHAPTER SEVEN | The 1930s

Route Changes on the Ocean City Division

Within the space of four years, two changes were made on the Shore Fast Line interurban route in Atlantic City. The first of these was temporary, but the second was a permanent change.

On September 2, 1931, a fire of undetermined origin destroyed part of the high trestle carrying the interurban cars over the tracks of the Reading Railroad in the Meadows, immediately to the west of the Thorofare drawbridge. About 1,000 feet of the wooden structure was burned. An alternate route was quickly established under which the trolleys entered the city on the PRR's electrified Newfield Line and terminated at the Tennessee Avenue Electric Station. The PRR trains had already been curtailed and would cease running entirely on September 27, so the line could easily accommodate the additional traffic. As the PRR route was more direct and on private right-of-way, the running time between Atlantic City and Ocean City was reduced from 52 minutes to 37 minutes.

During the disruption, a shuttle car operated from Tennessee and Atlantic Avenues to Virginia Avenue and the Boardwalk. A second shuttle car covered the original route from the Boardwalk to Adriatic Avenue and then Absecon Boulevard and Marmora Avenue, to the eastern end of the Thorofare drawbridge.

In rebuilding the trestle, fill from the Meadows was used to shorten the bridge structure. By December 6, 1931, work had progressed to the point that service was restored on the original route, except for four inbound commuter runs and five outbound runs, which continued to use the Tennessee Avenue Station until January 3, 1932, when all cars returned to their normal route.

A second route change occurred on July 14, 1935, when Ocean City cars turned from Virginia Avenue onto Atlantic Avenue and continued through the business district, past the new PRSL station at Arkansas Avenue, to Mississippi Avenue. The PRR strung trolley wire over this former Reading track, used by the interurbans to reach the former PRR electric line tracks over the Thorofare drawbridge. After crossing this bridge, they joined their regular route at Penred Tower (formerly called Meadows Tower). Inbound cars used Georgia Avenue, a former PRR line, from the bridge area to Atlantic Avenue. They proceeded up that artery to Virginia Avenue and then to the Boardwalk.

There were several advantages to the new route. All the Shore Fast Line cars now ran through the resort's business district on its prime street, pleasing many riders, especially shoppers. An easy connection was made with PRSL trains at the new station. Street-running on South Carolina and Virginia Avenues was eliminated west of Atlantic Avenue, as was trackage in the median of Absecon Boulevard and Marmora Avenue, the scene of many minor grade crossing accidents. The AC&S Thorofare drawbridge and the expensive-to-maintain trestles over the former Pennsylvania and Reading tracks were removed. State and city officials were pleased by the reduction in the number of hazardous grade crossings. Running times were essentially the same.

Above: Shore Fast Line 104 is seen in May 1947 crossing the bridge over the Black Horse Pike in Pleasantville, erected in 1935 to eliminate a busy grade crossing. The car might have been a special movement as the portable headlight was rarely hung in daylight hours. The car is heading south to Somers Point. A string of boxcars occupies a siding on the PRSL Newfield line in the background. LeRoy O. King, Jr. collection

Right-of-Way Improvements on the Shore Fast Line Route

A number of less dramatic but necessary improvements were made along the Ocean City line. The state was improving the Black Horse Pike, part of which involved erecting a concrete overhead bridge in Pleasantville for the interurban cars to pass over the highway. The bridge was completed in 1935, and the AC&S assumed responsibility
for its maintenance. At the other end of the branch, the bridge carrying Shore Road over the railroad was rebuilt in 1938, with the state, county, and the railroad sharing the cost of maintenance. Old road bridges at Braddock Avenue and George Street were removed.

design were installed over the third rail between Pleasantville and Atlantic City.

The Interurban Car Fleet

Just as the right-of-way needed attention, so did the interurban cars, now well past their prime, and whose design reflected the ideas of a previous generation. Ideally, they should have been replaced, but there was no money for such an undertaking. Each car had individual elements that distinguished it from its sisters. Cars were modified as time, circumstances, and money permitted. A few of these differences are noted below.

Some cars had rattan seats while others had either imitation

Above: A Boardwalk-bound car stops at the 8th Street crossing of the PRSL's branch in Ocean City which ran on Haven Avenue to the north end of the island at the Gardens. This was a former Reading Railroad line; the ex-PRR route along West Avenue had been removed after the formation of the Pennsylvania-Reading Seashore Lines in 1933. The branch was later cut back from the Gardens to 10th Street. Today the scene is unrecognizable as it has been fully developed and both rail lines have disappeared from Ocean City. David H. Cope photo, Richard Allman collection

New or improved crossing warning signals were installed at the Smith's Landing stop in Pleasantville, and at Zion Road and Mount Vernon Avenues in Northfield between 1937 and 1939, and a new crossover was added at Florida Avenue. Lineside signals on the drawbridges over the Great Egg Harbor Bay were updated. In Ocean City, the old ticket office at the Boardwalk had fallen into disrepair and it was removed in December 1936, by the city's building inspectors. The derail at the PRR's West Avenue tracks were removed, as the PRSL concentrated its Ocean City trains on the ex-Reading Haven Avenue line. New wood covers of a better

leather or green plush seats. By 1940, only car 104 retained the original rattan seats. A few cars still had wood floors, while other cars had concrete flooring, covered by an aisle mat. Interiors were of mahogany or oak, with some cars having dark green ceilings, while others were repainted white. The clerestory windows varied greatly; except for two cars, most had metal sheeting and ventilators installed to reduce leaking. Most cars had eight fixtures in the center of the ceiling, while two cars had lights over the seats and only three fixtures over the center aisle.

Exteriors were also distinctive. Gradually, most of the cars had

CHAPTER SEVEN | *The 1930s*

Above: *Still wearing its orange and cream paint, refurbished car 106 poses for its picture outside the Inlet Barn in the bright sunlight of May 21, 1932. One must admire the work of the skilled artisans in the shops who modernized and maintained the wood car fleet so capably. The nation was in the grip of the worst year of the Great Depression but standards were still upheld by Stern & Silverman. LeRoy O. King collection.*

Below: *By the date of this October 1938 photograph, combine 119 showed advance signs of deterioration. No longer in service, it would soon be demoted to a storage shed behind the car barn. There was no longer a need for a combination baggage-passenger car by the 1930s, so Isaac Silverman felt it was wasteful to refurbish the car during the lean times of the Depression. By the time of the wartime resurgence of traffic, the car was too far gone to rehabilitate. Francis J. Goldsmith, Jr., Fred W. Schneider, III collection*

their wood sides and ends covered with sheet metal, but these improvements were made on an individual basis rather that in an orderly, coherent fashion. The standard orange-and-cream livery was modified by adding cream "bow ties" on the end panels, beginning in 1936.

Occasionally, rebuilding was the result of accidents. In October 1936, car 105 caught fire in the paint shop at the Inlet barn; damage was confined to one end, and the car was rebuilt with a new roof. Evidently a smoldering spark from a torch used in removing old paint was the cause. Four years later in March 1940, car 104 caught fire late in the evening while stored overnight on the siding at Dolphin. Damage was minimal.

Combination car 118 was converted to a straight coach in 1925. The remaining combine, 119, retained its original design, with longitudinal benches in the baggage section. The clerestory windows were defective and the car leaked heavily in rain storms. Unpopular with passengers and crews, it was removed from regular service in 1936; in 1941, it was converted to a storage shed behind the barn and used as a parts supply for the other cars. The parlor car remained in storage, with occasional thought given to upgrading it as a coach.

By 1940, three cars, 103, 107, and 116, had deteriorated to the point that they were scrapped. The fleet then numbered 15 cars, plus the parlor car, now considered sufficient for the passenger volume at that time. World War II would increase patronage, but the remaining cars had to carry the load as best they could.

Maintenance on the Atlantic Avenue Line

Although busy with trolleys, this route saw very limited and rare freight service. There was only one customer, a lumber yard at Illinois Avenue, which received an occasional car. At Longport, a spur track ran from the loop along the bay, which was used primarily for storing the few cars consigned to that station, usually tank cars for the towns and, rarely, flat cars of stone used to reinforce the ocean jetties. At most, only two or three freight movements a year took place.

With money scarce, track repairs were made only when absolutely necessary or in response to complaints. For example, in April 1935, a resident wrote to the PRR about excessive noise as cars passed over a rough section of track. Vice-president John F. Deasy referred the matter to J. O. Hackenberg, general manager of the PRSL, who inspected the track and in turn queried Isaac Silverman. The offending rails were smoothed by grinding, although Hackenberg noted the track was laid on a concrete slab, covered by bituminous, which had "a sounding board effect," exaggerating the noise. Rail grinding was the only way to minimize the problem.

The federal Works Progress Administration (WPA), a New Deal relief agency, repaved Atlantic Avenue in 1936 and 1937, as part of a program to provide jobs to the unemployed. By the end of July 1937, the avenue had been repaved with asphalt its entire length in Atlantic City, from Maine to Jackson Avenues. The WPA paid the labor costs; the city paid for the materials, and the AC&S reimbursed the city for the section between the trolley tracks.

The municipal government, ever hostile to the trolleys, took advantage of the WPA project to have the safety islands at most intersections removed. The city regarded them as an impediment to traffic and an obstruction to visiting organizations who conducted parades along the avenue during their conventions. By the end of 1936, the islands were gone. This made boarding and alighting from the trolleys more hazardous to passengers, but it also strengthened the city's argument that buses were safer and superior to rail cars, since they could load at the curbs.

As the PRR and the AC&S continued rail service, complaints mounted. In November 1937, the city authorized the establishment of safety zones at certain intersections. These consisted of yellow lines painted on the road surface next to the tracks, protected by weighted portable stanchions marking the area where passengers could wait. While not as desirable as the concrete islands, they did provide some relief to passengers.

Peculiar to Atlantic City was a procedure giving fire engines absolute superiority when going to a fire. At the sounding of an alarm, all the traffic lights in the city would flash yellow for two or three minutes, while all traffic, including trolleys, stopped. This disrupted schedules, but it eliminated the unlikely danger of collisions when fire trucks raced to a probable blaze.

A major project in 1937 was the resurfacing of the tracks in Margate from Fredericksburg to Douglas Avenues. The PRSL delivered 12 carloads of crushed stone, complete with a device that unloaded the rocks, and a man to operate the machine. The PRR provided the material; the only expense incurred by the AC&S was for its track crew to distribute the ballast. Three years later, the company purchased 300 used creosoted ties from the Trenton Transit Company for the price of $120, or 40 cents per tie. An unexpected expense was repairing the Longport pier after two mysterious fires broke out there in October and December 1940.

The Power Problem Resolved

From the beginning of its operations, the AC&S had purchased power from the Pennsylvania Railroad, initially generated at the railroad's Westville power plant and later purchased from the Philadelphia Electric Company. The current was carried over the Delaware River on the Delair railroad bridge and then sent down the high-tension transmission line paralleling the Newfield Branch. This arrangement was increasingly unpopular with Stern and Silverman and the local Atlantic City Electric Company. But even after the PRR discontinued its electric train service between Newfield and Atlantic City, it insisted on providing the power for its Atlantic City Line, which was fed into the railroad's New York Avenue substation and the AC&S's Somers Point substation. Several failures in the transmission line and the subsequent

Above: Atlantic City welcomed male organizations and fraternal orders that had their annual conventions in the city; some of them staged parades. Here a procession of Shriners march down Atlantic Avenue in the mid-1930s, disrupting traffic and attracting the attention of the sidewalk crowds. A Nearside car heading for the Inlet passes the colorful procession. The city government removed permanent safety islands to accommodate parades, forcing trolley passengers to stand in the middle of the streets, protected by only painted pavement and a few removable stanchions. This strengthened the argument of those demanding that buses replace the electric cars. Jeffrey Marinoff collection

shutdown of trolley service were to force changes.

In January, 1935, a severe storm blew down 60 poles carrying the high-tension lines over the Meadows, disrupting trolley service for over a day. The company placed advertisements in the newspapers apologizing for the interruption, claiming ". . . it was through no fault of ours." The PRSL assembled a large crew of workers to restore service.

Less serious, but still annoying to passengers, was a power failure during the morning rush hour on October 9, 1935, when a large crane loaded on a flat car in the Chelsea Yard tipped over and falling across the adjacent feeder line. An alternate line was quickly activated, and power was restored in less than an hour.

A major failure took place between February 14 and 16, 1936. An ice storm in Philadelphia caused the high-tension transmission line to break and to fall into the Delaware River, cutting electric power to the AC&S for almost three days. Superintendent A. J. Purinton quickly chartered buses from several operators to supplement the railroad's own small bus fleet, but service was spotty at best, and it did little to quiet the hue and cry from the public and city officials, who cited the disruption as another example of the Philadelphia-based managers' incompetence. The inconvenience increased the demands from various quarters that the trolleys be replaced by modern buses.

Partly because of these failures and the criticism they aroused, and partly because the railroad managers recognized that their 25-cycle power was becoming obsolete, the PRR installed new equipment in its substation to receive 60-cycle power. More importantly, the railroad finally acceded to Stern and Silverman's plea that power should be purchased locally. On July 15, 1938, the Atlantic City Electric Company began feeding current from its Baltic Avenue station to the PRR's New York Avenue station. In September, the railroad began dismantling its transmission line from Pleasantville to Newfield. The AC&S updated its Somers Point station with new converters in April 1939, permitting it to be fully automatic. The transmission line between Pleasantville and Somers Point was also improved.

Advertising and Promotions

Stern and Silverman had always recognized the importance of advertising in a resort area such as Atlantic City. Despite the Depression and falling revenues, they continued to promote their service, especially on the Shore Fast Line, which might appeal to visitors. The company used newspaper advertisements, flyers, handouts, timetables, and especially its "Take-One" folders, placed in all its cars and buses. It appeared under varying titles, including "Trolley Talks," "Transit Topics," and "Shore Fast Line Talks."

sat an attractive young woman. Over her head, a sign proclaimed "Shore Fast Line – famous Scenic Route to Ocean City." Fifteen thousand "Take-One" folders promoting the 75 cent excursions were ordered and distributed in 1938.

Electric signs were used to attract riders to the Shore Fast Line in Atlantic City. One was a large billboard mounted on the roof of the Virginia Theatre, next to the trolley terminal. Placed at a 45-degree angle, a simple message appeared: "Take Shore Fast Line Cars Here," with an arrow pointing downward. Another sign was on the Boardwalk at South Carolina Avenue, directing would-be passengers to walk another two blocks to Virginia Avenue.

Above: Typical of the advertising effort used by the company was this ink blotter which was widely distributed. Often the ads promoted the Shore Fast Line, as seen here, which was regularly operating in the red. No doubt the frequent promotions did attract some riders, but they were insufficient to remove the red ink on the ledgers during the decade of the Depression. Ronald DeGraw collection

For the 1930 season, the company extolled a "Delightful Sightseeing Ride for Visitors," who could choose from five options: by rail car or bus between Atlantic City and Ocean City for 85 cents round-trip, or by parlor car for $1.35, or to Longport for seven cents on regular cars, or for 50 cents on the parlor car, including a lecture. As the Depression deepened, round-trip fares were cut to 60 cents in 1932. The next year the AC&S advertised a "Circle Tour" for 85 cents by cars or buses, as ". . . the only way to see the natural beauty of the shore district."

By the 1934 and 1935 seasons, special one-day round-trips were offered for 75 cents, ten cents less than the regular fare. Slogans such as "Avoid Parking and Traffic Worries" and "Use the car you do not have to park. Trolley and bus transportation give you more for less" were advertised. Special events such as the Horse Show in the Convention Hall were featured. The line continued to take advantage of the Miss America Pageant in September by entering a float consisting of a replica of an interurban car, behind which

The purpose of this sign, which had to be manually illuminated at night by the dispatcher, was to avoid confusion among tourists, who might think the unused electrified track on South Carolina Avenue was the Shore Fast Line terminal. Partially offsetting advertising expenses was revenue received from the Post Office for carrying mail pouches and money paid by the Jersey Railways Advertising Company for the right to place advertising cards inside the cars and buses.

Probably the most successful promotion developed by the AC&S was hiring five attractive young ladies to serve as hostesses on Shore Fast Line cars beginning in the 1940 summer season. Outfitted with uniforms and jaunty caps, they greeted riders, lent them copies of newspapers or magazines, and in general provided a friendly and pleasant presence. An elaborate schedule called for a hostess on each hourly departure from Atlantic City. The ladies worked an eight-hour day, and if their last trip arrived early, they were expected to stand outside the cars until their full working day was over. For this, they were paid $60 a month.

While the stunt probably did not attract many additional riders, it gained much favorable publicity for the company, both locally and nationally. In 1941 the hostesses received a three-dollar raise, but the experiment was terminated at the end of the 1942 summer season, as wartime pressures and austerity mounted.

Operations during the Depression Decade

While advertising was important in attracting riders, modifications in operating practices were implemented in an effort to maximize revenue and minimize expenses during this time of great economic distress. Both rail and bus lines, on and off Absecon Island, were involved in these experimental efforts, but none were a panacea for the company's mounting financial problems.

One-day round-trip excursions were offered on the Shore Fast Line each year during the spring and summer seasons. Fares ranged from 50 cents in 1930 to 75 cents by the end of the decade. Shoppers and school ticket books were sold, offering trips at reduced rates. Schedule headways were fairly constant: hourly during most of the year and half-hourly during the summer. Local runs varied somewhat, but they usually offered 30-minute service to and from Linwood, Northfield, and Pleasantville, on what were essentially commuter runs. Cars were parked overnight on mainland sidings, at places such as Pleasantville, Dolphin, Floral Avenue, Northfield, Linwood, or Somers Point, as close to the residences of assigned crews as possible. The one-way running time of 53 minutes was constant, giving crews a seven-minute break at the terminals, if their runs were on time.

Some experiments were unsuccessful, such as express trains in 1930, which offered a 35-minute one-way running time. In 1932, the parlor car, no longer scheduled, was operated in place of a regular car on Sundays at the regular fare. The opportunity to ride what was regarded as a luxury car without paying extra in the depths of the Depression attracted so many people that it became overcrowded. This led to many complaints from those who had to stand. The experiment was quickly ended and the car was placed in storage.

During the school year, the AC&S earned additional revenue by running a special car for pupils at Pleasantville High School. The car was stored overnight at Linwood and was attached to the 8 A.M. train from Ocean City. A second regular car was also added at that point, making a three-car train from there to Pleasantville. The school car was uncoupled there, and after unloading its passengers, it was stored during the day on a nearby siding. In the afternoon, the process was reversed.

Pleasantville, once an important connecting point for passengers on the PRR's electric trains, no longer fulfilled that role after the creation of the Pennsylvania-Reading Seashore Lines in 1933. With the opening of the new Atlantic City Station in 1934 and the rerouting of Shore Fast Line cars down Atlantic Avenue the following year, the timetables noted that connections for steam trains to Philadelphia and New York could be made at the Arkansas Avenue station.

Above: Seen here is the small station at Pleasantville located on the Newfield Branch line, which replaced the original station on the Somers Point branch. In this undated view, car 113 loads more passengers on its way to Atlantic City. All Shore Fast Line cars had to follow PRR rules, which required two oil markers on the rear of the car. Barely seen in the street behind the station is the connecting bus from Absecon. George Krambles collection

The original Shore Fast Line station at Pleasantville, located beyond the junction on the Somers Point Branch, was closed with the cessation of PRR electric train service in 1931. The track arrangement was simplified, and a new, small wooden shelter was built on the Newfield line, slightly east of the PRSL station. This structure served until the abandonment of the line in 1948.

As an economy move throughout the decade during the 39-week winter season, cars from Atlantic City arriving in Linwood after 9 P.M. ended their runs at that point. The few passengers were asked to transfer to a waiting bus to carry them to Somers Point and Ocean City. This saved the company the wages of the two drawbridge tenders on the bay bridges and the expenses of the Somers Point substation, which was closed at that hour. No mention of this transfer was made in the timetables, but the handful of passengers affected accepted it as a necessity in the dismal economic conditions of the day. Even during the twelve-week summer season, the Somers Point substation closed at midnight, despite the presence of one or two late cars on the lower end of the line. The reduced power resulted in slow speeds and dim lights until the cars drew closer to the Pleasantville substation.

Storms periodically battered the region and disrupted operations. Ice was a problem on the third rail section of the line, although the PRSL sprayed it with a chemical solution designed to retard the freezing process. In heavy snow, the railroad ran one of its heavy multiple-unit cars down the line to clear the tracks for the lighter interurban cars. The more powerful motors and larger wheels usually were sufficient to maintain some service. In a few instances, the PRSL ran steam-powered trains down the branch to Somers Point, where a connecting bus would carry any passengers to Ocean City. In November 1935, a severe "northeaster" hit the region causing extensive flooding, covering the tracks and the third rail in places and forcing the cancellation of service over the bay trestles and bridges. Interurban cars ran only between Pleasantville and Somers Point, with bus connections at both ends until the storm abated.

Considering the volume of service, the many grade crossings, and the long bay trestles, the line was quite safe, with no major accidents, reflecting well on the crews and management. An exception was a collision between a northbound Shore Fast Line car and a seven-car PRSL freight train near Somers Point in May 1936. The crew of the freight train was reversing direction, with the locomotive on the north end of the train, preparing to return to Pleasantville. The conductor failed to assign a flagman to protect his train. The interurban car motorman saw the freight train backing to a crossover and had stopped his car, but the slow-moving freight struck the car before he could reverse it, doing only minor damage. Only three passengers were on board, and no one was hurt. A subsequent hearing assigned blame to the PRSL crew. Two months later, an inattentive motorman whose car was approaching the Thorofare drawbridge, open for water traffic, waited too long to apply the brakes at the stop signal. The car slid past the lowered smashboard at the signal, breaking it and seven windows, before safely stopping. Thereafter, the drawbridge was made a mandatory stop, regardless of the signal indication.

All crews on the Shore Fast Line had to pass a Pennsylvania Railroad Rule Book examination before they could be qualified to

Above: The days of the open cars were numbered when this unidentified model rolled down Atlantic Avenue in Margate. On the ocean side of the road, the large wooden elephant affectionately named "Lucy" gazes at the incoming waves. Erected in 1881 as part of a real estate promotion, the iconic pachyderm still stands, a symbol of the Jersey shore. At various times it served as a house, a restaurant, a tavern, and now as a tourist attraction. The last of the open cars ran only one day in 1939. William D. Hamilton photo, Fred W. Schneider, III collection

Above: War Board car 6889 sits at the Virginia Avenue Boardwalk terminal on July 10, 1932. In shuttle service, the double-end car would run the two blocks to Atlantic Avenue, change ends and return to the Boardwalk. Free transfers for the Atlantic Avenue cars were issued and accepted, but many passengers paid the seven-cent fare to avoid the long walk between the avenue and the Boardwalk. Known as a "transfer car," it ran more frequently than the Shore Fast Line interurban which also carried local passengers. Francis J. Goldsmith, Jr., Fred W. Schneider, III collection

work the line, and they were subject to periodic re-examination. All trains had to have two oil marker lamps attached to the rear of the car. Conductors needed red and white hand lamps, and they were required to walk back 500 feet if their car stopped in the Meadows. A New Jersey law required the roof-mounted bell to be sounded at all grade crossings, which were frequent on the Pleasantville-Somers Point section. Some motormen let the bell ring continuously between those points, much to the annoyance of some of the passengers. The lighted number boxes on the roofs of the cars were kept in service, even after they were no longer needed, with the 1931 termination of the PRR electric train service.

Presiding over the day-to-day operations was the dispatcher stationed at the Virginia Avenue terminal. He was responsible for seeing cars left on time, for making up trains, and generally seeing that operations were conducted smoothly. A ticket agent assisted him as necessary. On summer weekends he was very busy. As a representative of management, he was not popular with some of the crews, who still nursed resentment over the loss of seniority after the failed 1923 strike.

The Atlantic Avenue Line during the Depression

Unlike the faltering interurban route, the Atlantic Avenue and Longport Division was the company's economic salvation. To be sure, passenger loads declined, especially during the winter, but the hot summers still brought large crowds to the resort, many arriving by train or bus. While the Shore Fast Line promised a relaxing ride through the mainland communities and a visit to a sister resort, the high fare and running time deterred those of limited means. For only fourteen cents, one could have a round-trip journey through pleasant suburban communities, close to the ocean, to the southern tip of the island. Nonetheless, economies were imposed here also.

An obvious source of potential savings would be elimination of the two-man crews required by the city. The normal practice was to have two men on all cars running from the Inlet to Albany Avenue. At this point, the motorman left the car and the conductor took the controls and operated the car to its destination. The motorman waited for the next northbound car, which he ran back to the Inlet.

Under pressure from the financially distressed management, the city permitted one-man cars for most of 1936, from January 1 to December 1. The city then withdrew its permission and two-man crews were reinstated.

Service frequencies were good, especially in the summer. On busy weekends, cars left the Inlet about every two minutes; two of the cars turned back at Douglas Avenue in Margate, while every third car ran through to Longport. In the winter, headways were about ten minutes, and half-hourly to Longport, where loads were very light.

During the summer, the big open cars ran in ever-decreasing numbers. Although popular with the public, they were expensive to operate, requiring a two-man crew. They were more hazardous, with a greater potential for injuries if passengers boarded or alighted before the car stopped. By 1937, they operated only on weekends. The following year, only July 4 and one weekend in August saw them leave the barn. Their last appearance was on July 4, 1939. Twenty-four of the cars were scrapped in September 1938 and the remaining cars were gone by December 1939.

Another summer weekend service was a "transfer car," which shuttled along Virginia Avenue, from the Boardwalk to Atlantic Avenue and back again. Free transfers to and from Atlantic Avenue cars were issued and accepted; others paid the usual seven- cent fare. The blocks were long in this part of the city, and many people, especially the elderly, found it convenient to ride between the business district and the ocean. One of the double-ended War Board cars was assigned to this run.

Storms occasionally disrupted service. For example, a November 1935 tempest flooded the Inlet section and deposited up to two feet of sand on the loop and adjacent tracks. No cars could run to the Inlet for over 30 hours. In Longport, sand also buried the rails, forcing cars to terminate at Douglas Avenue, with a bus substituting for three days. These natural events were used by trolley opponents to strengthen their arguments that buses should replace the electric cars.

Bus Service

The AC&S bus lines continued unchanged. Operated as feeders to the rail lines, they were also a deterrent to any potential outside competitor. The level of service varied greatly, depending on the season.

The two north side lines, Venice Park, a 4.5-mile round-trip route, and Bungalow Park, a round trip of 2.7 miles, provided basic local service, with transfers to the Atlantic Avenue cars. The Pleasantville-Absecon route, of 5.6 miles, offered the most frequent year-round service, with 30-minute headways connecting with every Shore Fast Line car.

Above: *Shore Fast Line bus No. 72 rests outside Inlet Barn in the late 1930s. Acquired from the Worcester, Massachusetts, system in 1933, the vehicle was built by Yellow Coach and replaced older buses on the AC&S. Critics of the trolleys argued that buses such as this one were more superior, more comfortable, more flexible, and more popular than the old cars running on the AC&S. Owner PRR felt otherwise. Motor Bus Society Library*

An Atlantic City-Ocean City direct route, via Ventnor, Margate, and the Longport-Ocean City bridge, offered hourly departures from 7:30 A.M. to 9:30 P.M. in the summer, with the buses running the length of Ocean City to 59th Street, with a 55- minute running time. In the off-season, this schedule was reduced to only one morning trip. In similar fashion, an Atlantic City-Albany Avenue-Pleasantville route provided approximately 60-minute summer headways, with two trips extended to Somers Point and one to Ocean City. In the winter, four trips were scheduled, with one going to Somers Point. An Atlantic City-Ventnor-Margate line had 30-minute summer service but just seven weekday rush hour runs in the off-season. The Ocean City local lines operated only during the summer season, basically duplicating the two former routes of the Ocean City Electric Railway, with headways of 30 and 60 minutes respectively. The Stern and Silverman management regarded the bus lines as feeders to the trolley lines and ran them to protect the company from competition.

A number of old buses were scrapped in 1935. Five new Ford buses arrived the same year, and five Yellow coaches were added to the roster in 1937, permitting the scrapping of two older models.

Overall, the bus lines were a minor part of the AC&S operations although they had a good safety record. Perhaps the best indication of the relative importance of buses in the general transportation picture is shown in a memo written by Arthur J. Purinton in 1935. The local PRSL freight agent called and asked how many buses could be furnished to the company ". . . in case the railroad broke down." The AC&S superintendent said they could ". . . probably, during the middle part of the day, furnish two, 29-passenger buses . . ." to the railroad.

Disappointing Financial Results

Like many business enterprises, the AC&S struggled through the Great Depression. Gross earnings fell drastically and the operating ratio reached dangerous levels. Economies were instituted wherever possible, and wages and salaries were cut ten percent in 1931 an additional ten percent in 1932. For trainmen, this amounted to a considerable reduction from their 1920s wages.

Facing severe financial embarrassment, Isaac Silverman was forced to appeal to PRR Vice-President Elisha Lee in October 1932, begging the railroad to defer payment of $50,000 of the rental due for the Atlantic Avenue and Longport Line. This was about one-half of the total rental obligations for that line and it was essential to cover the deficit that year. Silverman claimed the AC&S had paid the PRR about $2,000,000 in rentals, plus $1,500,000 as half of the profits, since it began operating the line in 1907. During the same period, he said, the company had paid $750,000 in taxes. These figures excluded the rentals for the Shore Fast Line route.

Silverman noted the Atlantic Avenue Line profits had been used to meet the deficits of the interurban line, to pay for the losses of the former Atlantic and Suburban Railway, whose ownership was essential to eliminate competition, and to retire bonds. He complained about losses incurred from the bus service, deemed necessary to avoid competition, and about an annual expense of $40,000 to maintain the tracks in Ventnor to that city's satisfaction. He reminded Lee that the PRR had provided financial relief from 1915 through 1917 during the jitney wars.

As Lee was aware, Silverman's arguments were technically irrelevant, since the AC&S was under legal obligation to pay the charges. After consulting with other officers, Lee told Silverman the PRR would reduce its charges for electric power by $18,000, and he suggested the AC&S president negotiate with Ventnor to secure reductions in the amount paid to that town. Lee concluded by hinting at the possibility of further concessions, provided the PRR could audit the AC&S books. After more consultation, the railroad agreed to defer the payment of $35,000 of the Atlantic Avenue Line rental due for 1932.

But financial pressures continued. In 1933 and again in 1935, the AC&S failed to make its full rental payments to the railroad. Passengers carried declined from almost 12,000,000 in 1931 to only 8,200,000 in 1938, and deficits were reported every year except 1936, when a small profit was achieved. The trolley company was also remiss in repaying the PRR the $17,000 it had borrowed in 1930 to purchase the Ocean City Electric Railway. It was carried on the books as an ongoing charge, and the company paid six percent annual interest through the end of the decade. PRR executives were frustrated and unhappy, but they recognized that instituting legal action or terminating the lease was self-defeating. Both companies were struggling to survive during the Depression decade. However, a subtle change slowly began to develop toward Stern and Silverman; the old cordial relationship started to erode, and the railroad officers began to wonder about the value of their Atlantic City trolley line. They decided to commission a study to examine their property and to consider the alternatives for possible changes.

Atlantic City & Shore Railroad: Selected Financial Data

Year	Operating Revenues	Operating Expenses	Railway Operating Income	Fixed Charges	Net Income	Operating Ratio
1931	$932,000	$821,870	$110,000	$165,000	($17,600)	81.3%
1933	668,000	549,930	118,578	151,525	(20,360)	75.1%
1935	681,000	569,030	111,579	141,420	(22,272)	77.7%
1937	710,450	592,969	117,490	129,497	(1,860)	77.1%
1939	685,077	632,298	52,779	102,230	(8,969)	92.2%

Central Passenger Railway: Selected Financial Data

Year	Operating Revenues	Operating Expenses	Railway Operating Income	Fixed Charges	Net Income	Operating Ratio
1931	$15,979	$13,631	$2,349	$2,000	$378	72.7%
1933	12,708	10,117	2,590	2,648	13	67.9%
1935	11,526	8,428	3,098	2,000	1,098	60.3%
1937	10,059	7,021	3,068	2,000	1,068	56.0%
1939	5,772	6,443	(671)	2,000	(2,671)	

Source: Public Utilities Commission of New Jersey; Moody's Manual

CHAPTER SEVEN | *The 1930s*

Above: *Views representative of how the Shore Fast Line cars appeared in the 1930s. In the top view cars 112 and 104 pose for a company photo. No. 112 has received steel sheathing. No. 104 posed again at the Atlantic City Boardwalk terminal with sister car 116 which has also been steel sheathed. Alas, 104's turn in the shop never came about. It was one of four of the Shore Fast Line interurbans that retained their exterior wood finish to the end. Both photos from* Electric City Trolley Museum collection

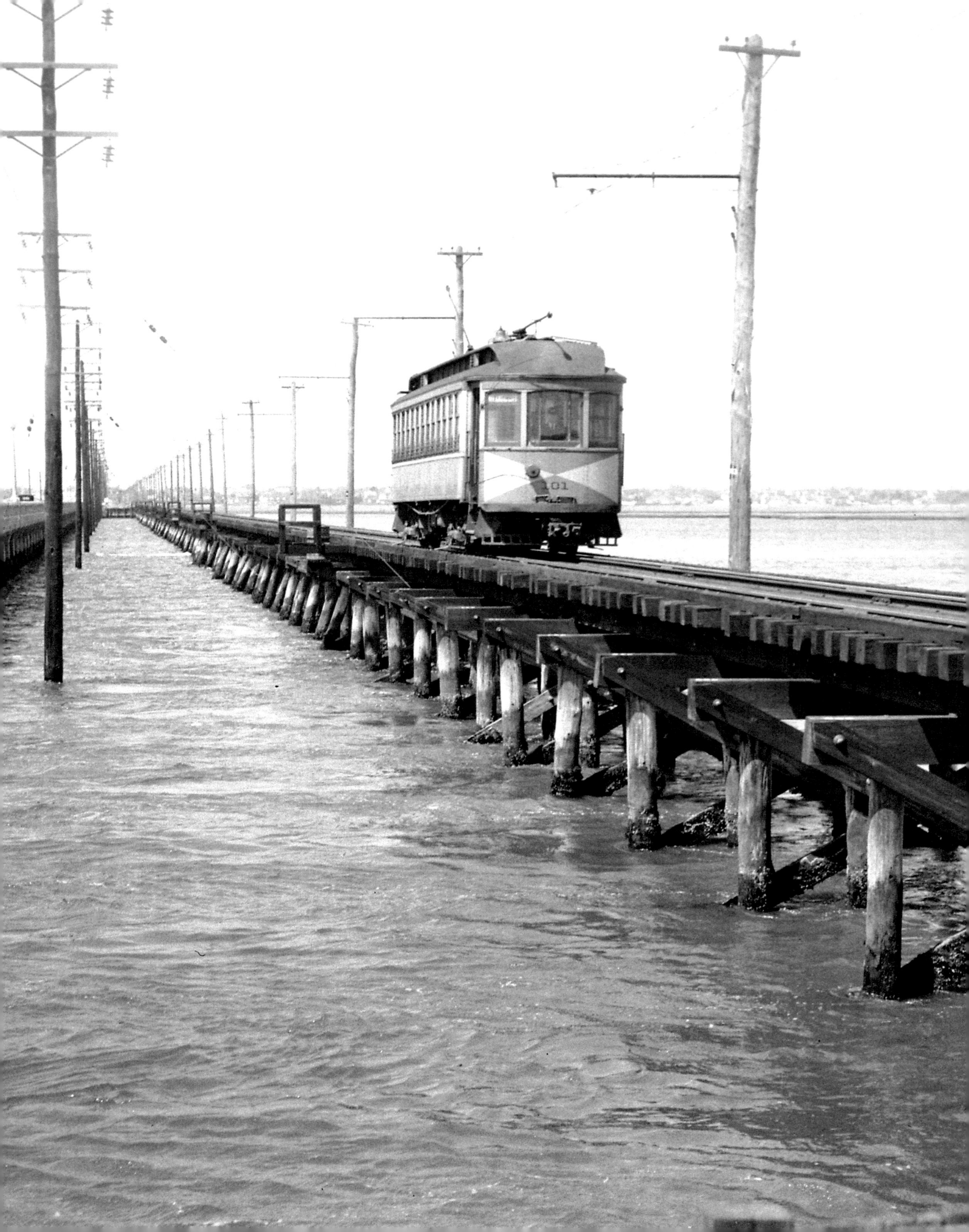

CHAPTER EIGHT

Trolley or Bus?
The Pennsylvania Railroad Decides

The Conway Report

In 1935, Pennsylvania Railroad executives decided to appraise and evaluate their Atlantic City properties to determine the future status of their trolley line. Should changes and improvements be made or should the line be converted to buses or even sold? They were motivated in part by the difficult economic conditions as the Depression wore on with no end in sight despite the efforts of the Roosevelt Administration. They were also concerned about the condition of their lessee, the Atlantic City and Shore Railroad, and the attitude of its owners, the firm of Stern and Silverman. There were frequent complaints voiced by city politicians and the press about the quality of service offered by the AC&S and growing demands for the conversion of the Atlantic Avenue and Longport Line to bus operation.

Across the nation many trolley lines, especially in small or medium-size cities, were being abandoned with replacement buses being touted as modern, attractive, more versatile and cheaper to run than rail cars. The current fleet of Nearside cars was well past its prime and the dozen War Board cars, while newer, reflected a previous generation's acceptance of spartan accommodations, in contrast to the perception that buses were more comfortable and appealing to the public.

To help determine the best course of future policies, Vice-President for Operations John F. Deasy decided to have a consultant study the Atlantic City properties and to make recommendations. Reflecting uncertainties about the competence of the operating company, Deasy did not inform Stern and Silverman in Philadelphia or the local management in Atlantic City of the

Facing Page: A Shore Fast Line interurban has left Somers Point behind and heads towards its ultimate destination of Ocean City. David H. Cope photo, Robert Long collection *Above:* Interurban 104 readies for a run to Ocean City while a War Board car 6845, assigned to the Atlantic Avenue shuttle, lays over at the Shore Fast Line Atlantic City terminal. No. 104 would never see the steel sheathing applied to most of its sister cars. View dates to August 29, 1935. Electric City Trolley Museum collection

study. To undertake the project, the PRR hired the well-known transit expert, Thomas Conway, Jr., who had a national reputation as one of the leaders of the industry. Since 1924, he had operated a consulting firm, the Conway Corporation, located in an office building near the PRR's Broad Street Station.

Never one to waste time, Conway promptly got to work, hiring agents and checkers to examine every aspect of the PRR's Atlantic City properties and their prospects. In September 1935, he submitted a voluminous report of over 120 pages, complete with maps, charts, an analysis of the physical and financial details of the AC&S, and with recommendations for action.

Conway painted a grim picture of the financial condition of the AC&S, with declining revenues and deficits, especially on the Ocean City Division. The bus operations he described as minor, recording deficits and using mostly obsolete vehicles operated primarily to prevent competition.

For the Atlantic Avenue and Longport Line, Conway argued rebuilding the track and acquiring new cars would be too costly and not likely to increase revenues substantially. He noted that trolley buses, while desirable in many respects, would require a complete rebuilding of the overhead wire structure in order to enable them to load and drop off passengers at the curb.

The ideal solution, Conway felt, was motor buses, which were flexible and mobile. They could stop at curbs, provide express service, and permit removal of the tracks, poles, and overhead wires, thereby improving the appearance and traffic flow on Atlantic Avenue. For the peak summer months of July and August, he recommended the purchase of 16 rebuilt tractor-trailer buses, seating 50, once operated by Greyhound at the 1933 Century of Progress Exposition in Chicago. Conway urged the PRR to expand bus service to Pacific Avenue. He claimed "intense competition" by buses could drive the jitneys out of business. This unrealistic proposal ignored the difficulty of securing city approval and the likely bitter opposition of the jitney owners and much of the public.

The Shore Fast Line, Conway declared, was essentially a money-loser that had outlived its usefulness. Only four percent of its riders went the full distance between Atlantic City and Ocean City; most were commuters from the mainland towns who traveled in and out of Atlantic City. Modern buses, he stated, could turn this obsolete rail line into a profitable operation.

Above: Atlantic City & Shore right-of-way at Dolphin Avenue in Northfield looking south on December 3, 1935. Heavy rail and tangents such as this made this line a raceway for Shore Fast Line trains. Jeffrey Marinoff collection

CHAPTER EIGHT | *Trolley or Bus?*

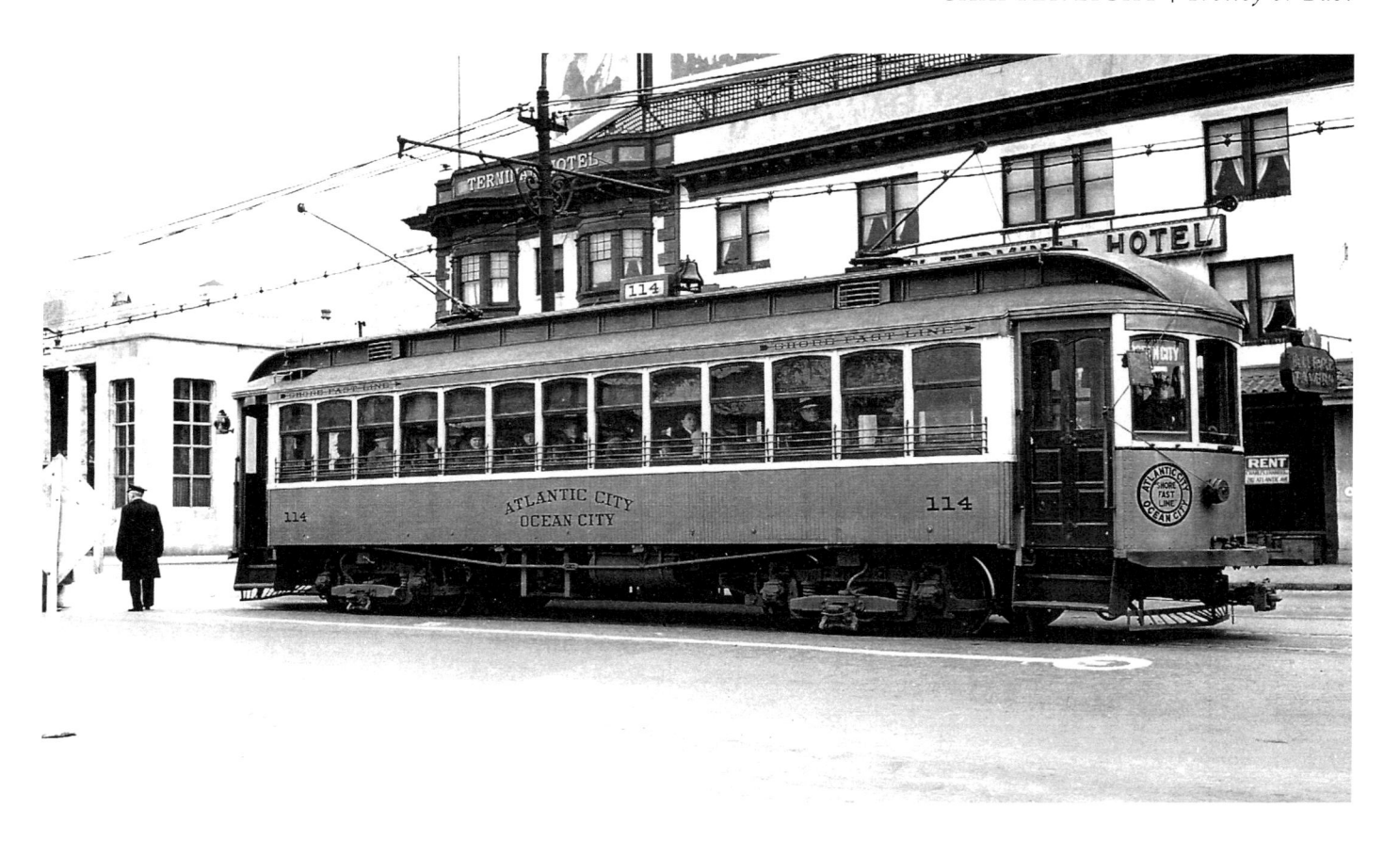

Top: *Bound for Ocean City, Shore Fast Line car 114 passes a typical car stop in front of the Terminal Hotel. Only a painted line in the street protects waiting passengers from automobiles. No. 114 carries a decent load of passengers, but there were never enough to make the line profitable. The car has been updated, but its wood sides are lacking the steel sheathing that was being applied to most of the cars. This car eventually received this treatment as well. William Lichtenstern, LeRoy O. King, Jr. collection* ***Above:*** *A two-car train of newly refurbished equipment has just left street running in Atlantic City behind and begins a fast run over PRSL track to Pleasantville. Current collection was by third rail on PRSL with a changeover to overhead trolley wire at Pleasantville. William Lichtenstern, LeRoy O. King, Jr. collection*

Conway estimated a new investment of about $474,000 could produce net income of over $300,000 versus the 1934 income of only $4,000. He said the PRR should secure monopoly rights for transit service from the several municipalities, an unlikely possibility. He felt the railroad's absolute ownership of the Atlantic Avenue right-of-way gave it a strong advantage in dealing with the Absecon Island towns. The municipalities would be given the right-of-way for road purposes in exchange for monopoly rights, with a proviso that the PRR could reclaim its property and reinstitute rail service should its exclusive transit rights be abridged or diminished. This proposal greatly underestimated the difficulty and likelihood of such an arrangement being accepted. Conway admitted the Shore Fast Line could continue as a rail operation, even if the Atlantic Avenue Line was converted to buses, by utilizing its original route into Atlantic City via the trestles and Absecon Boulevard. Access to the Inlet carbarn could be maintained by electrifying the PRSL's Mediterranean Avenue freight track and building a connection at Maine Avenue. However, he argued bus service would be cheaper and more profitable and he urged motorization of this route as well.

The Conway Report gave PRR managers much food for thought. His recommendation that buses should be substituted for rail cars promised increased financial returns and perhaps better relations with city officials and civic groups, but they felt there were several flaws in the report.

The railroad officials believed Conway had underestimated the number and size of replacement buses, and conversion would cost more than he estimated. They rejected his idea of buying used tractor-trailer buses for the summer season, a plan the city was unlikely to accept. They had doubts about the prospects of replacing jitneys on Pacific Avenue with railroad-owned buses. Also problematic was Conway's plan to vacate the Atlantic Avenue right-of-way and to permit the towns to occupy it, with the hope the PRR could reclaim the property and restore rail service if so desired. They recognized that the PRR operated its trolleys without the need for franchises by virtue of its absolute ownership of the Atlantic Avenue right-of-way; such would not be the case with buses. Nor did Conway seem to recognize that the AC&S management owned the interurban cars and electrical facilities along the Shore Fast Line, and these were protected until 1945 under its agreements with the PRR. Any changes on that route would be subject to negotiations with Stern and Silverman, who had not even been informed of the Conway study. Nonetheless, the PRR executives recognized that the question was not settled and would have to be addressed in the future.

The Pennsylvania Railroad Considers Bus Service on Atlantic Avenue

In 1936, Mayor Charles White and the city commissioners pressed the PRR to replace the trolley line with buses. White wrote to Martin W. Clement, president of the PRR, urging this step be taken as soon as possible. As a result, E. W. Scheer, president of the PRSL, J. O. Hackenberg, general manager of the PRSL, and John F. Deasy met Mayor White and City Commissioner Ott on August 28, where the mayor again asked for buses to replace the streetcars. The PRR officials were noncommittal, saying they

Above: While the crew takes a break, Nearside 6817 waits at Longport before its return to Atlantic City. Although well maintained, cars such as this were regarded as unappealing and old fashioned by hostile city officials. Nonetheless, they could handle heavy summer loads far better modern buses could. PRR officials recognized their Atlantic City trolleys must be updated or replaced by buses, but there were many factors to consider in reaching a decision. William Lichtenstern, LeRoy O. King, Jr. collection

CHAPTER EIGHT | Trolley or Bus?

Above: A blindside view of the Nearside 6814 at Longport. There was even a plug for the Atlantic City-Ocean City service painted on the side.
William Lichtenstern, LeRoy O. King, Jr. collection

would give the matter consideration and confer with them later.

Vice-President Deasy appointed a three-man committee to update the Conway Report and to make a recommendation. In a month, the committee reported that buses were the best option, primarily because net profits would be higher. They stated the investment in buses would be cheaper than upgrading the rail line, and the change would give the city a "…a modern transportation system," in keeping with national trends.

Deasy referred the question to Hackenberg, the PRSL general manager, and officer most directly involved in Atlantic City affairs. In December, he responded, expressing concern about the continuing agitation for buses, but fully endorsing the committee's recommendation. Hackenberg noted how important Atlantic City was to the Seashore Lines and the PRR. He stressed that the railroad should keep all its facilities and property since they enabled the line "to wield a strong influence" in molding Atlantic City's future. He concluded by urging the Philadelphia officers to develop a policy so the question could be settled.

The Pennsylvania Railroad
Considers its Options: Buses or Trolleys

The pot continued to boil into 1937, and the question increasingly involved legal opinions. The PRR managers had two contradictory aims: to convert the line to buses to earn higher profits, and to preserve its fundamental right to control Atlantic Avenue transportation by virtue of its ownership of the railroad line from the Inlet to Longport.

President Martin W. Clement asked Deasy to explain his position regarding the Conway Report. The vice-president took issue with Conway's estimate of the number of replacement buses needed. Instead of 36 buses on Atlantic Avenue and ten buses on the mainland route, as Conway suggested, Deasy said the company would need to buy 54 and 28 buses respectively, thereby reducing potential profits. He assured Clement the railroad could secure perpetual franchises for bus service.

By the spring of 1937, Deasy decided to consult with Stern and Silverman. In May, he told Isaac Silverman, now chairman of the board, that a "material improvement" could be made in the net profits of the Atlantic Avenue Line if 40-seat buses replaced the cars. He claimed a maximum of 40 buses would be needed, plus ten more for the interurban line.

Silverman was not convinced, flatly stating that "the substitution is not justified" at the present time. He pointed out that as a resort, Atlantic City was unique, since it had to accommodate large numbers of summer visitors. He predicted the PRR could expect to receive the same net profits and rentals it had received in 1936 for the next five years. He also enclosed a copy of a long letter from the AC&S attorney, George A. Bourgeois, on the implications of the conversion plan. The lawyer undertook to answer several questions.

Buses would require securing permits from each of the towns and the approval of the Public Utility Commissioners. The railroad could not expect an exclusive franchise for bus service, only an approval to operate on a specific street. Bouregois stressed the PRR had an absolute right to operate rail cars on its right-of-way on the island, which was at the most 425 feet from the ocean at any point, and that this exclusive property could only increase in importance in the future as the population increased. He stated the railroad could not expect any compensation from the towns if it relinquished its right-of-way. Nor could the PRR expect a monopoly of transportation, only the right to run buses on indicated streets.

The Pennsylvania Railroad Decides to Keep Its Trolley Line

This dash of cold water caused the PRR managers to hesitate in their bus plans. An internal memo to John Deasy in July 1937 recapitulated the situation. The railroad's committee favored buses because they would produce higher profits, involve the smallest capital expenditure, and provide the public with modern transportation. On the other hand, the AC&S arguments were weighty indeed; the right-of-way, which had value only as a transit artery, would be lost if rail service ceased. Also lost would be the perpetual right to operate rail cars on it. What had seemed relatively simple and desirable for economic reasons now looked far more complex and potentially damaging to the railroad's long-

Above: Demonstrating its flexibility, War Board car 6849 has changed ends and is ready for a return to Atlantic City without the need of the loop at Douglas Avenue in Margate. Isaac Silverman recognized the large capacity of electric cars compared to buses, which were important in the short but profitable summer season. Although only seventeen years old when the photo was taken on August 29, 1935, its wood seats and drab interior lacked the appeal of modern buses. Francis J. Goldsmith, Jr., Fred W. Schneider III collection

Furthermore, if the line were abandoned, the railroad could not expect to keep its value as part of its rate base. Finally, because the Atlantic City situation was unique, only an act of the legislature could answer all the issues involved in abandoning the line.

In short, the PRR enjoyed a perpetual right to operate its cars on Atlantic Avenue, but if it removed them it would lose its right-of-way and should expect its replacement buses to be subject to local and the Public Utility Commissioners' control. Not stated but strongly implied was that the PRR would be well advised to retain its trolley service.

term interests in Atlantic City.

Late in July, as the PRR was considering its options, the impatient city officials and some of the press declared "war" on the trolleys. Mayor Charles White and the city commissioners were "disgusted with the stalling" of the AC&S officials and appealed to the Public Utilities Commissioners for relief. If this were not forthcoming, then the city would permit jitneys to run on Atlantic Avenue in direct competition with the "rumbling antiquities." Mayor White dismissed the protests of AC&S employees who feared losing their jobs, since they claimed they would be unable

Above: A War Board car works its way along Atlantic Avenue in a 1930s scene. The car was presumably bound for Longport, but could be short-turned at any crossover on the line. David H. Cope photo, Richard Allman collection

to drive the buses. White pointed to New York and other cities where motormen and conductors had made the transition to drivers. An editorial in the Atlantic City News fully backed the mayor, blaming the trolleys for traffic congestion, noise, and endangering passengers by forcing them to board and leave cars in the middle of busy Atlantic Avenue.

Unstated but underlying the aggressive anti-trolley campaign was Atlantic City's perception of itself as the premier seashore resort. Civic pride demanded that only the newest and best vehicles were suitable for the city's image of itself as modern and up-to-date. Probably another factor was a tone of resentment against the power and influence of the two operators, the Pennsylvania Railroad and the Atlantic City and Shore Railroad, both headquartered in Philadelphia. Some thought these out-of-state corporations did not have the best interests of Atlantic City in mind. But if city officials thought their public attacks would force the railroad to accede to their wishes, they were to be disappointed. The Pennsylvania Railroad had to consider its own interests, and it began to weigh the possibility of retaining the rail service. If it did so, it would have to equip the line with modern, streamlined cars that were beginning to enter service elsewhere.

The Pennsylvania Railroad Searches for a Modern Streetcar

Once the PRR officials realized that converting the Atlantic Avenue line to buses would mean the loss of its permanent right-of-way on Absecon Island, it lost interest in abandoning trolley service despite the stream of complaints from city officials. Railroads were primarily territorial by their nature. Land was fundamental to their operations, and the PRR managers were unwilling to relinquish the strip of land along the main avenue of the island which circumstances in the previous century had given them. Not knowing the future, but basing their decision on their previous experiences, they believed the right-of-way could be immensely valuable as the island developed. Therefore, converting the line to buses was rejected, and the search for a demonstration model of a modern streetcar began.

J. O. Hackenberg held a series of meetings late in 1937 among PRR motive power officials, representatives of the AC&S, and the J. G. Brill Company. A list of general specifications was developed. The new car was to be as noiseless as possible; be the equal of automobiles in acceleration, deceleration, and speed; be easy to enter and exit; seat at least 50 passengers; be modern in appearance, and suitable for one- or two-man operation.

Leo J. Isenthal, president of the AC&S, suggested that 35 horsepower motors instead of standard 50 horsepower ones would be suitable as there were no grades on the line and intersections were frequent and closely-spaced. The lower horsepower motors would reduce power consumption but still provide sufficient speed. Isenthal stated the car's maximum length should be 47 feet, due to the space between the buildings linked by the transfer table at the Inlet car house. The wheels should have a three-inch tread and a three-fourth inch flange to accommodate the standard railroad tracks and switches. Finally, the AC&S chief requested the installation of supports for an electric Ohmer fare register, with provision for either the motorman or a conductor to operate it. The center door treadle machines should be controlled by the operator.

The PCC Car and the Transit Research Corporation

Events began to move rapidly. On February 14, 1938, Brill vice-president Charles Guernsey sent F. W. Hankins, PRR chief of motive power, a formal proposal to build the demonstration car for $17,000. He noted that "certain features" of the car were covered by patents held by the Transit Research Corporation (TRC), and that the PRR should make arrangements with them

Above: Often described as one of the few successful projects developed by a committee, the Presidents' Conference Committee or PCC car, met the demand for a modern, comfortable, quiet, fast car which could compete with the automobile and bus. Although the PRR considered purchasing them for Atlantic City, it was deterred due to demands of the car's patents owner, the Transit Research Corporation. Seen here is an example of what the committee had wrought. Philadelphia Transportation Company's 2026 at the Parkside loop on September 14, 1941, assigned for Sunday service on Route 43, Spring Garden Street. Many observers were of the opinion the PCC was more attractive than PRR's choice: the Brilliner. Edward S. Miller photo, Fred W. Schneider, III collection

The participants agreed a car of the standard PCC design, as developed by the Electric Railway Presidents' Conference Committee of the American Transit Association, would meet most of the specifications. About 500 PCC cars, as they were called, were in service on the lines of several companies, all of whom were pleased with them, as were the respective public service commissions.

Hackenberg consulted with two officials of the Brill Company, C. O. Guernsey and W. J. Beatty, who said Brill could develop a car to meet all the specifications, except that it would have a riveted body instead of a welded one. With a few other modifications, it would sell for the same approximate price as the PCC: $17,000. The car could be ready in about five months. Hackenberg had no objections to riveting and the few other changes, and he submitted a detailed memo to John Deasy and other PRR officials.

for a license covering their use. Hankins promptly informed Hackenberg and suggested he form a committee consisting of Leo Isenthal, Guernsey, PRR mechanical engineer W. R Elsey, and electrical engineer H. C. Griffith to go over the details so an order could be placed as soon as money was authorized.

On February 16, Hackenberg conducted a meeting with AC&S officials Leo Isenthal, Superintendent A. J. Purinton, and Assistant Superintendent J. H. Cain. Also present were Guernsey, two Brill Company officials, and the PRR engineers. The specifications for the demonstration car were slightly modified and approved by all.

Hankins then wrote to the Transit Research Corporation asking for a license to build one experimental car of the PCC type. Charles Gordon, secretary of the TRC, quoted a royalty fee of $375 for one car. He also sent a detailed, seven-page "Patent License Agreement" for the PRR to sign.

The TRC wanted to protect its patents and to control the construction of its standard modern PCC car; therefore, the license agreement was specific, rigid, and demanding. Among other items, the licensee had to agree to transfer to the TRC without payment any patents it currently held which might pertain to the car. Any improvements the railroad's employees might make after the purchase that were in any way related to the car also had to be assigned to the TRC, nor could the railroad challenge any of the licensor's patents.

Hankins was taken aback by the stipulations of the TRC license agreement, and a flurry of correspondence among the PRR officers followed. Hankins consulted the railroad's patent attorneys, the firm of Paul and Paul, whose offices were nearby on Broad Street. Henry N. Paul, one of the partners, called the TRC document "unusually stringent and one-sided" in that the license was non-exclusive and it limited the purchase of the car to one made by a licensed manufacturer. He particularly criticized the clause that required the railroad to assign all existing patents and possible new ones that might improve or modify the TRC patents. He advised the PRR not to sign the contract.

The PRR managers and employees were always working on improvements to equipment, and they felt some of their patents for certain items having nothing to do with streetcars might have to be given to the TRC if there was a similarity or overlap. For example, PRR mechanical engineer Walter F. Kiesel had submitted a patent application for improvements he made with inside bearings on a railroad truck, or wheel-set. This had been challenged by E. H. Piron of the Transit Research Corporation, who claimed it violated one of the PCC car patents he had submitted. The matter was pending, subject to a resolution of the interference charges by Piron. Under the proposed TRC license agreement, the PRR would have to turn over any such patents for items affecting their railroad cars to the TRC, without compensation, if the licensor claimed they related to their PCC patents.

At this point, the Brill Company submitted a bid to build a modern, noiseless streetcar meeting the specifications desired by the PRR. Brill required no license agreement or royalty fee and agreed it would defend the railroad and hold it harmless against any charge of patent infringement by the TRC on all parts specified by the builder. In similar fashion, should the PRR specify certain items beyond those recommended by Brill, the railroad would defend the builder against any charges of infringement. In view of the complications and limitations imposed by the TRC, Hankins and his fellow executives decided to buy the Brill demonstration car, promised by the builder to be just as good as a PCC car-- and it came with no restrictions or patent obligations. On March 26, Hankins informed the TRC that the PRR "would not avail itself" of its license offer.

The Brilliner

Having made the decision to purchase the Brill "single-end, front entrance, center exit, double-truck electric motor car," Hankins moved rapidly to implement it. The actual order

Above: The first Brilliner, 6891, is seen at the Inlet Barn about 1939. Attractively painted in shades of green with gold stripes, it had a mostly flat front which had been Brill's standard since the late 1920s. In most respects it was similar to the PCC, but some found its blunt, squarish design less appealing than the PCC. Nonetheless, it performed quite well and was popular with the riding public. The PRR was pleased enough to order 24 additional cars from Brill in 1940. David H. Cope, Robert Long collection

James N.J. Henwood

Above: The interior of the Brilliner was bright and attractive. Only the original car had window shades and lift sash windows. Seats were upholstered in leather and stanchions replaced the standee straps found in older cars. The contrast with the old cars was dramatic. The wider aisle and higher ceiling made the new car more commodious than any bus. J.G. Brill Historical Society of Pennsylvania, Fred W. Schneider, III collection

was placed by the Pennsylvania-Reading Seashore Lines. J. O. Hackenberg, the general manager of the PRSL, received the approval of E. W. Scheer, president of the Reading Company and of the PRSL, and J. F. Deasy, PRR vice-president, for an appropriation of $20,000 to purchase the noiseless, modern car. Hackenberg consulted officials of the AC&S and Atlantic City Mayor Charles White and the city commissioners, who were forced to end their anti-trolley crusade. Even the hostile Atlantic City News, in a sarcastic editorial, admitted defeat in its ten-year fight to rid the city of trolleys, although it still considered buses superior to the electric cars.

Brill then modified its specifications for the new car by removing all references to PCC patents and substituting its own design trucks for the standard PCC trucks. The patents clause was retained, whereby Brill assumed responsibility for all its parts in the car, except those which might be demanded by the PRR. The order was placed on April 6 and delivery was promised for August. Since the PRSL did not have an engineering staff to inspect the construction of the car and to help solve any problems, the PRR agreed to do so.

As Brill began building the car, dubbed the Brilliner, Hankins asked Raymond Loewy, the prominent industrial designer, to visit the Brill factory and to offer suggestions to improve its style and design. Loewy, who was on retainer by the railroad, had already displayed his ability by his modifications to the design and appearance of the line's new GG-1 electric locomotives, the streamlining of several steam locomotives, the style of new passenger cars, and other projects. Loewy designed the interior and exterior color schemes of the Brilliner, replaced square glass windows in the doors with port-hole style ones, selected the floor materials, the seat fabrics, and the metal finishes. He redesigned the ventilating system, replacing the original grills with ducts. All

CHAPTER EIGHT | *Trolley or Bus?*

told, he helped Brill produce a handsome, modern, streamlined car that had great public appeal.

As built, the Brilliner met all its expectations and was similar to the PCC in most respects. The seating, heating and ventilation systems, interior lighting, the body structure and light weight were the equal of the PCC. It was equipped with Brill model 97-ER-1 trucks which mounted four, 55 horsepower motors, giving it a running speed of 42 miles per hour. Rubber springs and wheel inserts provided a smooth, noiseless operation, while three types of brakes, dynamic, magnetic, and air, insured a quick, smooth stop. With a length of 45 feet, four inches, it seated 52 passengers on leather-covered seats. The outside was painted in attractive aluminum and shades of green, separated by gold stripes.

By mid-August, work on the new car was nearing completion, and Brill invited PRR and Stern & Silverman officials to inspect the car on August 25. One week later, on September 2, the car arrived in Atlantic City, and it made its inaugural run on September 7, carrying invited dignitaries from the PRR, Brill, and the city. Pronounced a success, the car entered regular service on September 12.

As with any new equipment, a few minor problems arose, but they were quickly corrected. Noisy gears were replaced by a new design, and a burned-out field coil in the motor-generator set was quickly replaced. The public liked the stylish car, and some people let older cars pass so they could ride it.

More Brilliners for Atlantic City

After several months experience with the new car, railroad and AC&S managers were pleased with its performance. It met all expectations and it was considered a worthy replacement for the antiquated Nearsides. Consequently, PRR officials decided in the summer of 1939 to reequip the Atlantic Avenue line with a fleet of the new cars.

In the period between September 30, 1939, and July 1940, when the new cars began to arrive in Atlantic City, a great deal of time was spent in deciding the details of the new fleet. Many groups were involved in this effort.

On the Pennsylvania Railroad, overall supervision and approval was in the hands of the vice-president of operations, J. F. Deasy, but the bulk of the work was done by F. W. Hankins, the assistant vice-president and chief of motive power, who coordinated the work of engineers and various committees. The Reading Railroad was consulted on all major decisions as was J. O. Hackenberg, general manager of the Pennsylvania-Reading Seashore Lines, the PRR's operating arm in Atlantic City. Raymond Loewy was again employed in designing the appearance of the cars. Actively involved with suggestions and some decisions were Isaac Silverman and Leo J. Isenthal of Stern and Silverman, and their manager in Atlantic City, Superintendent A. J. Purinton and his assistant, J. H. Cain. The mayor and city commissioners

Above: The first Brilliner awaits its departure time in the Longport loop in 1939. The anti-climber would be lengthened across the full width of the car in the 1940 models and the letterboard would be changed to list the four Absecon Island towns. Raymond Loewy designed a new paint scheme that was applied to all the Atlantic City Brilliners. William P. Hamilton, III, Fred W. Schneider, III collection

were consulted, and the J. G. Brill division of the American Car and Foundry Company did the actual work.

To justify the expenditure of funds for the new fleet, Hackenberg noted the obsolete condition of the 26 Nearside cars. He stated the trolley line made money and would earn greater profits with modern cars, so there would be "a reasonable return on the investment."

No consideration was given to buying PCC cars because of Company and the Capital Transit Company of Washington to learn their views of the PCC car. The two companies were pleased with the cars and reported reduced maintenance costs. Both the PCCs and the Brilliners used identical electrical and control equipment, which was available only from the General Electric Company and the Westinghouse Electric and Manufacturing Company. Aside from a few differences, the Brilliner was the same as the PCC and it performed equally well in the seashore resort.

Above: Photographs of AC&S officials are difficult to find, but this advertisement for a 1936 convention shows the trio of A.J. Purinton, his assistant A.J. Cain, and secretary John M. Campbell. They managed the affairs of the AC&S for many years. Photographs of the Stern & Silverman officials in Philadelphia, William Stern, Isaac Silverman, and Leo Isenthal have not come to light. John Nieveen collection

the licensing and patent requirements involved. Initially, the PRR planned to buy 30 new cars, but Isaac Silverman wanted only 24, a number acceptable to Hankins. In Atlantic City, J. O. Hackenberg was able to get municipal approval for one-man operation of the new cars, which would reduce appreciably operating expenses. Brill was anxious to receive the order, and it quoted a price of $17,700 per car. Hankins and Deasy rounded this off at $18,000 each, to cover incidentals, which required a total appropriation of $432,000.

To further its position that the Brilliner was the equal of the rival PCC car, PRR electrical engineers contacted the Baltimore Transit

The engineering committee concluded the Brill car was "in no way inferior" to the PCC car.

Meetings and discussions among the interested parties resolved a number of issues. The electrical equipment was divided equally, with half the cars receiving General Electric motors and control and the other half receiving Westinghouse equipment. The two sets of equipment were not interchangeable, except for very short periods of less than a day during an emergency. This prompted Leo Isenthal of the AC&S to ask the PRR to buy spare motor equipment from both Westinghouse and General Electric

CHAPTER EIGHT | *Trolley or Bus?*

Right: With the arrival of the 24 new Brilliners, the AC&S placed large advertisements in local newspapers describing the streamliners and inviting the public to a celebration at the Inlet where the cars were officially christened and welcomed to their new home. The stylish and attractive cars only briefly quelled the criticism of city officials and the press of AC&S operations.
Fred W. Schneider, III collection

in the event of breakdowns. Hankins rejected this idea, pointing out the demonstration car had been running for 18 months with no problems and that the manufacturers could quickly make repairs. PRR electrical engineer W. R. Elsey thought the AC&S was simply trying to get two spare trucks. Minor modifications included a slight rearrangement of platform stanchions, a full-width anti-climber (or bumper), and the installation of a box to support the drawbars under the car ends.

Much discussion revolved around the Ohmer fare registers to be installed in the cars. Until 1940, the AC&S had rented Ohmer machines, but at that point a new model, designated number 90, was developed. It was slightly more expensive but superior to the older machines. Leo Isenthal prevailed upon the PRR to purchase them and Brill fashioned brackets and stanchions to install them.

Raymond Loewy worked out a striking new color scheme for the cars, black and yellow (also described as cream) with silver trim. His work enhanced the appearance of the fleet, and they carried the basic pattern for the remainder of their service lives. While the color scheme was being determined, the city commissioners asked that the word "Inlet," which was on the letterboards of all the older cars, be replaced by "Atlantic City." Hackenberg suggested that the names of the three other Absecon Island towns, Ventnor, Margate, and Longport, be painted on the letterboards too. This sensible suggestion was approved by all.

At the suggestion of the AC&S, the cars were numbered consecutively, which varied from the normal PRR practice in Atlantic City. The demonstration car, 6891, was renumbered 6901, and the new cars were numbered 6902 to 6925. All Atlantic City streetcars had the initials of the legal owner, the West Jersey and Seashore Railroad, stenciled on their interior, usually in the front. After some debate, the railroad decided to paint W.J.& S. R.R. in the front vestibule on the right-hand side of the destination sign door, in one-inch high letters.

Unlike the PCCs, the Brilliners had no shroud around the base of the trolley pole on the roof. This facilitated reversing the pole in the event the cars had to be operated from their rear backup controls due to flooding or other emergencies. In November 1942, trolley shoes replaced the small wheels at the top of the poles as a means of collecting power from the overhead wire.

Brill met its promised delivery dates, with car 6902 arriving on July 3, 1940, and 6925 was received on September 4. A. J. Purinton, general superintendent of the AC&S, invited the participants in the purchasing committees and various local dignitaries to attend a "short, informal celebration" on Friday afternoon, July 19, at the Inlet car barn. Mayor Thomas D. Taggart presided over the ceremony, after which the group participated in the inaugural run of the new cars. The 26 Nearsides and five older cars were then scrapped.

The Brilliners were well received and fulfilled their promise of modernizing the Atlantic Avenue and Longport line. The most significant weakness was with the gearbox and bearings; these lasted only about one year, partly because of the harsh, sandy seashore environment. Brill defended its car against charges of patent infringement brought by the Transit Research Corporation, although ultimately it was found guilty of one charge of patent infringement.

According to some sources, Brill engineers proposed building a double-end version of the Brilliner for use on the Shore Fast Line route, in need of new equipment even more than the Atlantic Avenue line. Nothing came of this effort, probably because of the weak financial condition of the AC&S.

Changes in Management

An era ended on May 12, 1941, when Isaac Silverman, the surviving founding partner, died. Active in the affairs of the company until shortly before the end of his life, Silverman had guided the Atlantic City and Shore Railroad, from its birth in 1906, through prosperous and difficult times, until its partial

Above: *A bottle of champagne is smashed across the anti-climber of one of the new cars at a ceremony at the Inlet on Friday afternoon, July 19, 1940. Mayor Thomas Taggart does the honors while to his right AC&S superintendent of operations Raymond Stark looks on. The Loewy-designed paint scheme shows a silver stripe above and below the windows, an embellishment that did not survive the first painting. The basic style, however, would last the life of the cars.* Jeffrey Marinoff collection

CHAPTER EIGHT | *Trolley or Bus?*

Above: Stern & Silverman could not accept Brill's offer to build a fleet of double-end cars to replace the antiquated interurban cars on the Shore Fast Line route to Ocean City. If they had, the cars would probably have looked similar to Philadelphia Suburban Transportation Company's No. 6 (in this 1960s view) heading west on Garrett Road just outside the 69th Street terminal in Upper Darby. Red Arrow Lines, as PSTC was called, ordered ten of these Brilliner cars in 1940 and they ran successfully until their replacement by new cars in 1982. This line, now operated by the Southeastern Pennsylvania Transportation Authority (SEPTA), is still in operation. Dave Biles photo

rehabilitation by the PRR in 1940. Polite and competent, and always concerned about expenditures, he served as president and more recently as chairman of the board. He was succeeded by his long-time associate, Leo J. Isenthal.

The long-serving staff in the Land Title Building was aging, as was the AC&S manager in Atlantic City, A. J. Purinton, who had been superintendent since 1915. The majority of the work force of trainmen, shop and maintenance employees, and office help had also been on the job for many years. These employees, of whatever level, were the heart of the Atlantic City trolley lines. They and the PRR managers would soon be confronted with another great challenge: guiding the fortunes of the enterprise through the difficult and tense days of another world conflict.

See Ocean City

A delightful 50-minute ride on high-speed electric cars to Atlantic City's sister-resort, Ocean City. Board cars at Virginia Ave. and Boardwalk or any street on Atlantic Ave. bet. Virginia and Mississippi Aves. Cars leave at 6.00, 6.55 (7.25 Exc. Sun.), 7.55, 9.00 A.M. And every hour on the hour until 8.00 P.M. Then 10.00 and 11.30 P.M.

VIA THE SCENIC ROUTE

133

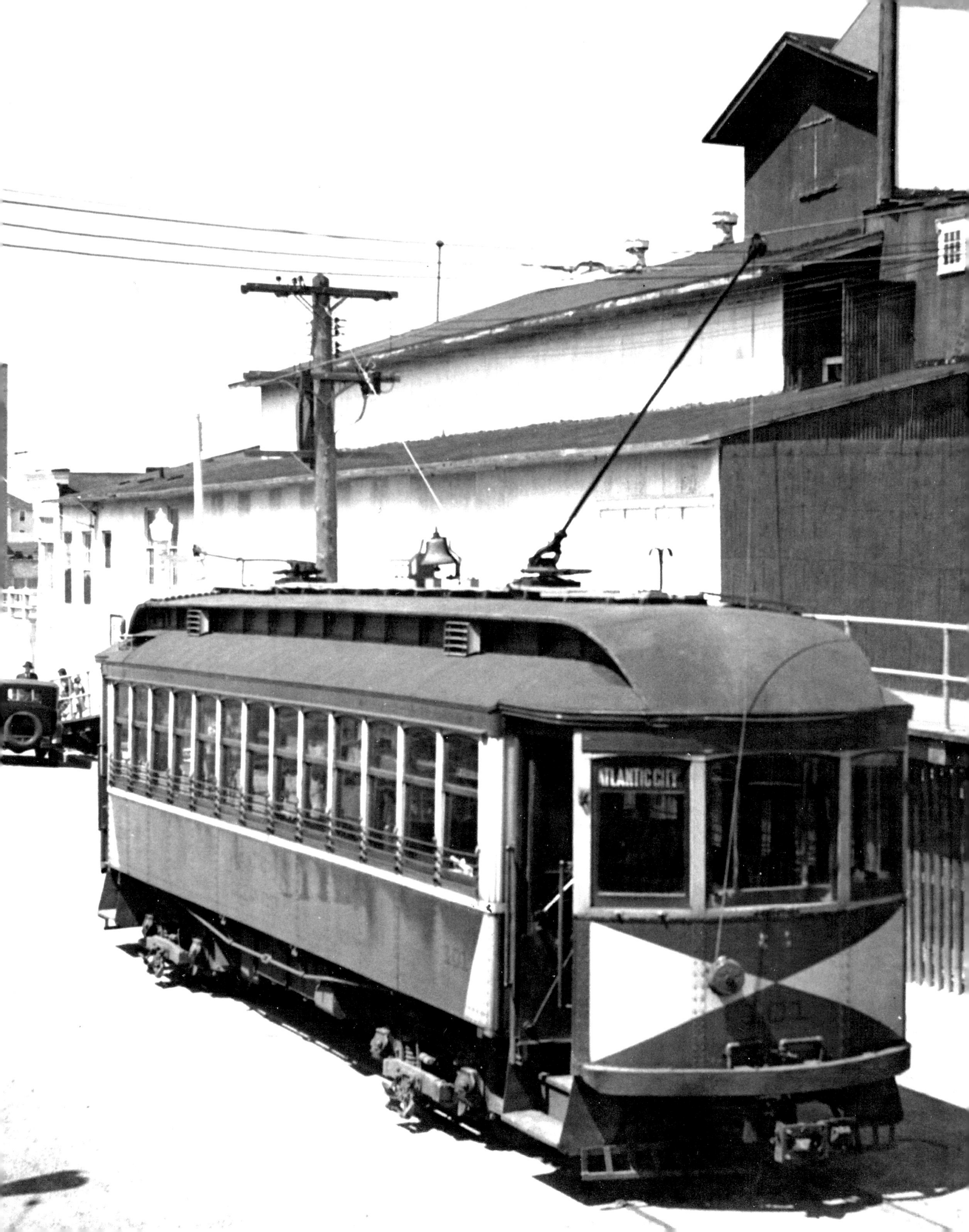
ATLANTIC CITY

CHAPTER NINE

Wartime Challenges

The World Again Plunges into War

While the Atlantic City and Shore, the Pennsylvania Railroad, and the entire country were struggling to overcome the economic problems of the 1930s, events were transpiring in Europe and Asia that would have profound effects on the nation in the following decade.

In 1922, a former socialist and journalist, Benito Mussolini, seized power in Rome as the head of a fascist movement. The dictator proclaimed the interests of the state were paramount and could override individual rights and freedom. In the next decade, a fascist government would take over Germany, under the leadership of Adolph Hitler. Both dictators launched a policy of expansion, with Mussolini invading Ethiopia in 1936, and Hitler, by far the more dangerous of the two, annexing Austria in 1938 and taking Czechoslovakia in 1939. When Germany invaded Poland in September 1939 with the support of the Soviet Union, Britain and France declared war. Poland was quickly overrun and in May 1940, German forces swept through Norway, the Low Countries, and northern France, driving the British armies from the continent, as France surrendered.

The American people were shocked by Hitler's conquest of most of western Europe but they did not want to get involved in another war. President Franklin D. Roosevelt, who won an unprecedented third term in the 1940 elections, favored intervention but he was deterred by public opinion. America settled for helping beleaguered Britain with aid short of war. In June 1941, Britain received further relief when Hitler invaded his former ally, the Soviet Union.

In the Far East, the Empire of Japan fell under the control of militarist factions. In 1932, Japan occupied Manchuria, nominally a province of China and already weakened by internal divisions. Japan invaded China proper in 1937 and soon extended its control down the entire coast, driving the Nationalist government far into the interior. By the end of the decade, Japan extended its domination to French Indo-China. The United States, long friendly with China, opposed Japanese expansion, and by 1941 it resorted to economic pressure, restricting Japanese trade and limiting the sale of petroleum and metals as well as closing its markets to Japanese goods. Confronted with American demands to leave China or face economic ruin, the Japanese responded by attacking the American fleet at Pearl Harbor,

Facing Page: Shore Fast Line's 101 at the line's Ocean City terminal on Eight Street and Boardwalk. The poles have been changed and the car is ready to return to Atlantic City. David H. Cope photo, Richard Allman collection

Above: Although the photo of Brilliner 6913 was taken by the company photographer to record damage to the doors from a minor accident, it also shows the black paint on the top half of the headlight to dim its beam. This was to lessen the chance of the light being spotted by an enemy plane or submarine. The date of the photo is October 25, 1942, the U.S. is at war and blackouts are in effect along the Atlantic coast. The Loewy paint scheme softened the Brilliner's flat front and the wings around the headlight emphasized speed. Jeffrey Marinoff collection

in the territory of Hawaii, on December 7, 1941. Germany and Italy quickly declared war, and the United States joined Britain and the Soviet Union in what was now a second World War.

The War Comes to Atlantic City

The eruption of another world war finally ended the economic depression that had gripped the country for a decade, and which the Roosevelt administration had tried vainly to end. At first, the resorts along the Atlantic seaboard ignored the blatant attacks by German submarines on Allied ships, many of them tankers carrying petroleum from the southern oil fields to northern markets. The ships, silhouetted against the bright lights of the coastal towns, made easy targets for the rampaging U-boats. Almost 200 merchant ships were sunk in these waters between January and April, 1942. Not until April 18 were the seaside towns ordered to extinguish signs and waterfront lights and not until May were "dimouts" enforced. Illuminations in store windows were reduced, and later all outside lighting was shielded to reduce glare. The top halves of the headlights of the Brilliners were painted black for the same reason. Shades, awnings, and blackout curtains became commonplace.

Like Americans everywhere, shore residents had to adjust to shortages and rules promulgated by a plethora of new federal agencies. The War Production Board allocated scarce resources, and the Office of Price Administration established price controls on most commodities and imposed rationing on gasoline, tires, sugar, coffee, butter, meat, shoes, and other items. Labor shortages developed as millions of young men were called into military service. The Office of Defense Transportation restricted train service, suspending one-day excursions from Philadelphia, over the protests of Atlantic City businessmen.

Atlantic City itself was transformed by the conflict. Although throngs of tired war workers and families crowded into the city

Above: *Although taken in 1954, this view of an eastbound PRSL train on the double-track speedway linking Philadelphia, Camden, and Atlantic City typifies the heavy loads carried by the railroad during the war years. Headed by PRR K-4, No. 5022, the train of P70 coaches is seen at Lindenwold on August 27, 1954. In pre-air conditioning days, passengers often arrived with cinders on their clothes and bodies. Despite such problems, nothing could equal the railroad for carrying huge volumes of riders to their destinations. Some of the passengers will no doubt board AC&S streetcars on arrival.* Robert L. Long collection

CHAPTER NINE | *Wartime Challenges*

during the season, they were often outnumbered by the thousands of military personnel sent to the resort for basic training. Large hotels such as the Brighton, Traymore, and Denis, as well as dozens of smaller ones, were converted into barracks to house the troops. The army leased Convention Hall whose huge auditorium and offices were utilized for training purposes. Still more servicemen arrived after August 1943, when the Chalfont-Haddon Hall hotels were converted into the England General Hospital to care for wounded soldiers. The sight of troops exercising on the beaches and marching on the Boardwalk became common. The use of cameras and binoculars along the ocean front was forbidden for the duration.

Nonetheless, life went on. Theatres were crowded; the Steel Pier and the Million Dollar Pier continued their big band and entertainment programs, and bars and night clubs prospered. In 1943, the Claridge and St. Charles hotels were reopened to the public, and the ocean waves and breezes attracted visitors as they always had.

The Atlantic City and Shore Struggles to Meet Wartime Challenges.

The wartime period proved to be a profitable but difficult one for the AC&S. As Atlantic City became an active army base, the population grew with these temporary residents, who could ride the company's cars and at the same time contribute to overcrowding. Local businesses and commercial establishments also gained from wartime demands. With gasoline rationing and a shortage of rubber tires, and the cessation of the production of automobiles, people out of necessity returned to public transportation. The crowded conditions and general discomforts that resulted would produce a growing chorus of complaints that the PRR as owner and the AC&S as operator were forced to address.

The war curtailed long-distance travel, and during the summer season large numbers of visitors, many from Pennsylvania, New Jersey, and New York descended on the resort, seeking rest, relaxation, and entertainment. This influx was so great that in 1943 the Pennsylvania-Reading Seashore Lines recorded its first-- and only--profitable year. At the same time, the Office of Defense Transportation ordered the suspension of weekend seashore trains leaving Philadelphia by way of the Delair Bridge over the Delaware River. This forced the heavy Saturday and Sunday crowds to use the railroad ferries from the Market Street Wharf to the Federal Street Station in Camden, where all seashore trains originated and terminated. When the trains, often carrying over 1,000 people, arrived at the Arkansas Avenue terminal, large groups rushed to Atlantic Avenue where they tried to board the overloaded streetcars, disrupting schedules and generating complaints about the erratic and poor service.

Above: The only new station constructed by the Pennsylvania-Reading Seashore Lines was the classic structure at Arctic and Arkansas avenues in Atlantic City. Although shown here in 1952, it was a beehive of activity during the war years as large crowds entered and left daily. Many people walked the long block back to Atlantic Avenue to board streetcars, which were almost overwhelmed near train time. The failure of the AC&S to assign starters and fare collectors at this point would later be the cause of harsh criticism from the Board of Public Utility Commissioners. Ed Birch collection

Above: Former parlor car 120 rests in the Inlet Barn in the late 1930s where it had been stored for most of the decade. With traffic increasing, the car was reactivated and returned to service as a coach. Its service life was brief, however, as it was destroyed by fire during the 1944 hurricane. The shop force must be credited with keeping 120 and her elderly sisters available and in service during the hectic wartime years. John Nieveen collection

The number of passengers carried by the company increased rapidly. In 1940, the two rail lines and the small bus routes carried over 8.5 million people. By 1943, this increased to 14.5 million riders, and in 1945 over 16.3 million fares were collected. The peak came the following year when 17 million riders were accommodated.

Equipment Limitations Hamper the AC&S

To handle this mass of humanity, the company had a limited number of vehicles, with few prospects of adding to the fleet. On the very busy Atlantic Avenue and Longport line, only the 25 Brilliners and the dozen War Board cars were on hand. The Virginia Avenue "transfer car" was abolished and more cars were turned at Douglas Avenue, but delays and uneven schedules were common. Often standing passengers congregated in the front half of the cars and refused to move to the rear, despite pleas from the motorman. This angered those who could not get on, when they saw cars passing them with ample room in the back of the car.

On the Ocean City Division, the 15 serviceable cars were barely adequate. Their advanced age led the company in 1943 to lengthen the running time between the terminals from 53 to 67 minutes. Two-car trains were common, but the standard hourly headways in the off-season and 30-minute headways in the summer were maintained.

The Parlor Car is Converted to a Coach

To ease slightly the pressure on the Shore Fast Line fleet, Superintendent A. J. Purinton turned to the parlor car then in storage in the Inlet barn. In 1937, Purinton had asked Master Mechanic J. W. Gordon to estimate the cost of reactivating the car. Gordon reported the sum of $105, but no action was taken. In 1939, the superintendent considered converting the car into a coach, but again nothing was done.

By 1941, with traffic increasing on the line, Purinton decided to reactivate the car as a coach. Gordon said the job could be done for $550. Rebuilt and reupholstered seats from retired cars, rewiring, installing new heaters, and painting the exterior and interior would make the car available for service. The proposal was sent to Philadelphia, where Leo Isenthal gave his approval. Only a few days later, the United States was drawn into the war. Renumbered as 120, the car joined the fleet in 1942.

Other Proposals to Strengthen Shore Fast Line Service

Aware of the pressure on the limited number of interurban cars, Purinton weighed other options. In 1939, two of the War Board cars, numbers 6845 and 6850, were equipped with third rail shoes and tested on the Ocean City route. With 40 horsepower motors versus the 60 horsepower motors on the interurban cars,

CHAPTER NINE | *Wartime Challenges*

they were judged too slow and their small wheels and low floors did not mix well with the larger and heavier interurban cars.

Also considered was using a few of the wood MU cars of the Pennsylvania-Reading Seashore Lines, which had opened the Camden-Newfield-Atlantic City electric line in 1906 and were still operating between Camden, Newfield, and Millville. Although these large cars had run successfully between Atlantic City, Pleasantville, Somers Point and Ocean City on occasion and were used to keep the line open during heavy snow storms, they were not suitable for the street trackage on Atlantic Avenue and they could not negotiate the curves at Virginia and Atlantic avenues. As a result, the 16 active interurban cars struggled as best they could to carry the wartime loads.

on hand of the type needed to operate the turntable and the drawbridge over the Thorofare. Checking an inventory equipment list, he discovered two such motors, Westinghouse number 12A types, were on the AC&S sprinkler car. General manager J. O. Hackenberg then asked the AC&S if they could send them to the railroad, which would slightly reduce the annual rental paid by the traction company.

The request caused confusion in Philadelphia and Atlantic City, where the records were not up-to-date, and no one knew the origins of the car. After investigating, Arthur Purinton found the motors mounted on a Brill 21E single truck supporting the small flat car and water tank, numbered B-99. With Isenthal's approval, he had the motors removed and sent to the PRSL. The car was

Above: *This view of the line's sprinkler car was taken early in its existence when it was used for reducing dust along the Atlantic Avenue tracks. After the avenue was paved, the car was withdrawn from service and stored, probably in a dark corner of the car barn where it was forgotten. The sprinkler was scrapped in 1941 with its motors given to Seashore Lines for use on the Thorofare moveable bridge. LeRoy O. King, Sr. photo, LeRoy O. King, Jr. collection*

The Mysterious Sprinkler Car

Among the odd pieces of equipment on the roster was a sprinkler car, essentially a water tank mounted on a flat car that was used to hold down dust in the days before streets were paved. It had not been used for many years.

In March 1941, the PRSL engine house foreman in Atlantic City became concerned because there were no backup motors

scrapped. Hackenberg and Isenthal agreed the motors were valued at $951 and the rental rate was reduced by that amount.

The Brilliners at Work

During the war, the rail car fleet carried immense numbers of people, although not without problems. The speedy Brilliners were the mainstay of the company's operations. Generally, they

Above: Brilliner 6907 glides up Atlantic Avenue at Georgia Avenue in 1941 headed for the Inlet. With their full skirting covering the trucks, the Brilliners appeared to be floating over the rails, although they would gently rock after coming to a stop. Despite a few flaws they performed well over the course of their lifetime. They were only fifteen years old when trolley service ended in 1955. Sadly, all were scrapped at Bordentown, New Jersey, along with the one remaining PTC Brilliner No. 2023. William C. Janssen photo, Fred W. Schneider, III collection

performed well, and it is unlikely the old Nearsides could have handled the loads. Nonetheless, there were several issues peculiar to them.

The cars were not only fast but they also had a rapid acceleration rate. This caused some impatient motorists to misjudge how quickly they could start or approach a crossing. Consequently, there were a number of "fender-bender" accidents that required time in the shops for repairs of dents, broken doors, and other problems. Fortunately, the company had a group of skilled and competent shop workers, who kept the Brilliners as well as the War Board cars and the ancient wood interurbans in working order, able to meet the challenge of mushrooming loads.

Characteristic of the Brilliners was their swaying and rocking, which some passengers found unsettling. Even when the cars came to a stop, they would continue to gently bounce for 30 seconds or more. Evidently nothing could be done to correct this tendency, as the cars continued to roll their entire active lives.

A more serious weakness of the Brilliners was the problem of worn motor bearings, which disabled the cars. The bearings were mounted in a gearbox, where a "cage" held them in place, supporting the gears powered by the motors. When the bearings failed, the "cage" soon disintegrated, and particles of metal within the gearbox locked the wheels attached to the axle, immobilizing the car. When this happened out on the line, the car had to be pushed back to the Inlet carbarn, with the locked wheels sliding along the rails. Consequently, the affected wheels became flat on the contact side. The truck then had to be dismantled and the damaged parts repaired or replaced, at an average cost of $200 plus lost time. The cause of these failures was attributed to the damp air and blowing sand of the seashore environment. Bearings lasted only an average of 15,000 miles instead of a more normal 100,000 miles. So common was the problem that for the first ten months of 1945, there were 144 bearing failures, and for the entire year there were 172 failures.

Another problem with the Brilliners was the front doors; these opened out and were susceptible to damage in accidents. None of the frames for the doors were exactly alike on the 25 cars. Consequently, each replacement door had to be hand-crafted and fitted, which took about seven days and involved considerable labor. Aside from the expense, the lost time removed cars from

CHAPTER NINE | Wartime Challenges

service where they were desperately needed. It remained for the successor company to solve the problem.

Track Repairs Cause a Dispute between the AC&S and the PRR

Having struggled through the Depression years, Leo R. Isenthal, president of Stern and Silverman and the Atlantic City and Shore, was anxious to reduce expenses. As a first step, in December 1939, he asked the railroad to reduce the rate paid as rental on the value of additions and betterments made to the property. After consulting with comptroller F. J. Fell, PRR vice-president John Deasy agreed to reduce the rate paid by the AC&S from six percent to five percent, effective January 1, 1940.

More significant was the poor condition of the track and ties by 1940 and the question of who should pay for necessary renewals.

Under the terms of the 1907 lease, the AC&S was responsible for maintaining the property in good condition. It if failed to do so, the railroad could make repairs and charge the cost to the AC&S.

However, maintenance of the line had been erratic and conducted in a piecemeal manner for many years. Most of the line was laid with 85-pound rail and the only major replacements were made in the 1920s, when girder rail was laid in Atlantic Avenue within the city and new 127-pound rail was installed in the open track from Massachusetts Avenue to the Inlet. South of the city, the track was open, except in Ventnor, where it was covered by a loose layer of sand, gravel, and stone. Small sections of track had been replaced where the web and base of the rail was eaten out because of salt water and electrolysis. During the Depression, the barest minimum work was done by the AC&S.

In 1940, with the advent of the Brilliners, the PRR became concerned about the maintenance of the line. An inspector from

Above: A view of the right-of-way looking south in Longport dated October 6, 1941, shows the difficulty encountered in maintaining the track. The damp atmosphere and the wind-blown sand combined with indifferent maintenance caused corrosion and rotting ties. The open lots and virtually empty street reflects the small population of Longport during the off-season. Headways were 30 minutes between cars at this time of year. Jeffrey Marinoff collection

James N.J. Henwood

Top Photo: *The photographer was standing in the back of car 108 as it rolled westward towards Somers Point on Saturday, September 27, 1941. It had just crossed one of two moveable bridges on the long trestle connecting Ocean City, seen in the background, and the mainland at Somers Point. The cost of maintaining the trestle and operating the bridges partly accounted for the poor financial status of the Shore Fast Line route. There were no catwalks on the trestle nor end doors on the cars. Speed was limited to fifteen miles per hour.* John Brinckmann photo

Bottom Photo: *The bay trestle was broken by using the Rainbow islands, which also provided room for a rarely-used passing siding as seen from car 108 as it approaches Somers Point drawbridge and the mainland. Traffic is light on the parallel causeway which entered the island town at Ninth street. The highway is still there, but there is no indication that a trolley line ever existed.* John Brinckmann photo

the Engineering Department noted the joints between the T-rails were loose and in poor condition, resulting in noise from passing streetcars and complaints from the public. The worst track was in Ventnor and Margate, between Jackson and Douglas Avenues.

Both the PRR and the AC&S agreed on the need for track renewals, and the railroad developed a program to begin improvements. As a first step, in January, 1941, the PRR proposed to Superintendent A. J. Purinton that metal shims should be inserted in rail joints to improve riding conditions, which the AC&S promptly rejected. In April, the PRR ordered 600 tons of 85-pound rail to renew the tracks in Ventnor, between Jackson and Portland Avenues, 300 tons of which was immediately sent. Leo Isenthal agreed to perform this work, insisting at the same time that the railroad pay the cost through its accrued depreciation accounts. Vice-President John Deasy firmly rejected this argument. At the same time, Superintendent Purinton requested three carloads of ties to replace some of the defective ones which a joint PRR-AC&S inspection had revealed. The PRR promptly sent the ties. Isenthal was forced to recognize the clear terms of the 1907 lease requiring the AC&S to pay the cost of maintenance.

Because of the onset of the war, only 300 tons of new rail were laid, although 600 tons were on hand. Over 1,500 feet of track was replaced between October 1 and November 15, 1941. Repairs to the 8th Street tracks in Ocean City were made in June and July. For the duration of the war, the company kept a welder and his helper working constantly on the deteriorating track.

As a result of the track maintenance disputes, the PRR began to reconsider its ownership of the troublesome trolley line. The officers resented the manner in which Leo Isenthal and the AC&S tried to escape their lease obligations. Assistant General Counsel W. F. Cousins believed the PRSL had been too lenient in its dealings with the electric line and that there was a "good deal of deferred maintenance to be made up by the Atlantic City and Shore" before the expiration of the lease on December 18, 1945. The affair further soured relations with Stern and Silverman and contributed to a slowly developing view that the property might be sold should an opportunity present itself.

As an indication of the diminishing role of the PRR in the affairs of Atlantic City, the PRSL began to gradually abandon sections of the Baltic Avenue branch, beginning in 1943. Originally opened in 1887 by the Atlantic City Railroad, it had at one time carried passengers as well as freight traffic. Despite the war, by 1942 the five industries located on the line provided only 441 carloads of traffic, most of which could be served by the nearby Mediterranean Avenue branch. Some 152 tons of relay girder rail were salvaged and annual savings of almost $8,000 in rental, taxes, and maintenance were realized. The retreat of the railroad from its prime seashore resort had begun, and it would intensify in subsequent years.

Above: The colors and graphics used in Shore Fast Line timetables were both attractive and attention-getting. This issue emphasized fun on the Jersey shore made possible by the convenient service offered by Shore Fast Line trolleys and buses. Lew Hoy collection

Ongoing Maintenance and Repair Issues Continue

The increased wartime traffic carried by the Atlantic Avenue cars by 1942 prompted the city to place additional safety standards at some of the car stops along the avenue. These portable signs created safety islands next to the tracks, in both directions, at intersections from Pennsylvania Avenue as far south as Brighton Avenue. They could be removed for parades with little difficulty. About the same time, the connection between the old Chelsea branch and the Atlantic Avenue line was removed; it had not been used for many years.

In Margate, where short-turn cars had to cross the southbound lanes of Atlantic Avenue to enter the Douglas Avenue loop, a warning signal of two red lights was mounted on a pole, clearly visible to automobile drivers. Activated by a contactor installed on the trolley wire, the lights would flash whenever a car turned from the median to enter the loop. This lessened a long-standing hazard at this point. The following year the Douglas Avenue station

James N.J. Henwood

Right: *Bus Routes in the Atlantic City area, 1942.*

burned down, but a new station promptly replaced it.

Shore Fast Line Issues

On the Ocean City Division, the deteriorated Linwood station was removed in December 1938. The shelter at Franklin Avenue suffered damage from vandals, probably high school students, who kicked out some of the boards in 1942. PRSL crews quickly made repairs. The following year a small fire damaged part of the roof at the Pleasantville station; it, too, was quickly repaired. The crossing gates at Main Street in Pleasantville, the responsibility of the PRSL, periodically caused problems. Crews were extra-cautious at such times, and no accidents were recorded at this busy crossing.

More expensive was the demolition in 1942 of the trestle approaches to the old drawbridge over the Thorofare at Missouri Avenue. Two years later, the AC&S dredged the Rainbow channel, under the Great Egg Harbor Bay trestle, which had become clogged with mud, impeding the passage of boats. Between October and December, 1944, extensive repairs, including new pilings and supports, were made to the trestles. A bus replaced rail cars between Somers Point and Ocean City during this period.

An echo from the past was heard in 1942 when the federal Works Progress Administration removed some 1,200 tons of old rail from the Shore Road, starting in Absecon. This track had been laid by the Atlantic and Suburban Railway, abandoned in 1929. Subsequently, it was paved over and largely forgotten until wartime necessity led to its removal. The program was launched with an elaborate ceremony, attended by federal and local officials and by Leo Isenthal, president of Stern and Silverman.

Advertising Efforts

The AC&S continued to advertise frequently during the war. Aside from the illuminated permanent signs along its tracks and on nearby buildings, ads were placed in the local newspapers, the weekly "Amusements" guide, and in the "Trolley Talks" folders readily available in all cars, buses, and stations. Old themes were repeated, directed at visitors, stressing attractions and sightseeing along the lines. The attractive streamliners were often mentioned for their comfort and speed. One ad showed a man leaving a Brilliner, saying "Pick me up at 5:15." The copy read, "Now more than ever, your streamliner is ready to meet your transportation needs. Use safe, fast, and comfortable streamliners." Another ad promoted walking for health benefits, but if distance or time required it, then "Take the Trolley! It's safe, swift, convenient, economical."

America's entry into the war made only slight changes in ads. Shore Fast Line timetables noted that workers traveled during morning and evening rush periods and urged "shoppers and others" to ride between 9 A.M. and 3 P.M. and after 6 P.M. The public was encouraged to buy war bonds. USO service centers and clubs were often listed. Frequent ads were placed in the newspapers. A November 1942 notice proclaimed "Watch out in the Dim-Out,"

CHAPTER NINE | *Wartime Challenges*

Left: *Examples of a few of the advertisements placed in local newspapers encouraging the public to ride the trolleys.* John Nieveen collection

urging passengers and motorists to be especially cautious by keeping alert and driving slowly. Other ads with illustrations of the Brilliners asked riders to have exact change, to move to the rear, and to keep the exits clear. These pleas seemed to have little effect on the public, who persisted in crowding the front half of the cars when there was ample room in the rear.

Labor Issues Trouble the AC&S

During its existence, the AC&S had successfully resisted sporadic attempts by operating employees to organize a union. But times were changing, and there was little Stern and Silverman or Superintendent Arthur Purinton could do about it. In 1935, the Democratically-controlled Congress had passed the National Labor Relations Act, creating a National Labor Relations Board (NLRB). Among other things, this legislation upheld the right of employees to join unions and to bargain collectively through representatives they chose. The NLRB was empowered to supervise elections to create a union, with which employers were required to negotiate.

It took some time, but by 1944 union organizers had signed up enough men to justify an election to determine if the workers wanted a union. On May 6, by a vote of 132 to 14, the men agreed to affiliate with the American Federation of Labor's Amalgamated Association of Street, Electric Railway, and Motor Coach Employees, forming Local Division No. 1358.

Union representatives met with Purinton, Secretary John W. Campbell, and company attorney Thomas Hyndman of Philadelphia. The union's demands included a wage increase from 63 cents to 93 cents an hour, a 40-hour week, the end of the system of requiring workers to wait at the barn to see if they were needed, and a closed shop. Negotiations were difficult, with Stern and Silverman reluctantly making concessions. To pressure the company, the workers staged a brief strike in the early morning of Saturday, June 24, refusing to operate the hourly night car to Margate. Would-be passengers, including soldiers due back in their barracks, were left stranded. Taxis were mobilized to pick up them up.

The union denied they were on strike, claiming the men were engaged in an all-night session to discuss proposed contract demands. Purinton also denied there was a strike, saying the stoppage was due to "a misunderstanding in operating orders." An official of the NLRB urged the men to return to work, which they did in time for the morning rush hour.

The company was forced to grant the union a stunning victory in a contract signed on July 3. The workers received a 13 percent wage increase, sick benefits, free life insurance, a uniform allowance, overtime pay, pensions at age 65 after

20 years service, a closed shop and dues check-off, an arbitration clause, paid travel time, and seniority rights. After union members overwhelmingly ratified the contract, the NLRB approved the pay increase. The workers were pleased, but the contract would add appreciably to operating costs, and ultimately it was the public who would pay them.

carried almost 11,000 riders. On the same date one year later, the equivalent figures were 54,000 and 10,500.

Even in the off-season, heavy loads were accommodated. On November 1, the Atlantic Avenue line loaded 32,052 passengers and the Shore Fast Line route accommodated 5,905 riders. One year later the numbers were slightly larger.

Above: Although old and noisy and none too comfortable, the company was glad to have the dozen War Board cars to help carry the heavy loads during Word War II. Car 6887 is southbound on Atlantic Avenue at South Caroline Avenue in 1941, before the huge influx of passengers brought about by the war. Despite criticism leveled at them by hotels, politicians, and newspapers, these cars served well and kept the public moving. The fact they were double-end cars gave them great operational flexibility. William C. Janssen photo, Fred W. Schneider, III collection

Increasing Wartime Crowds and Restrictions Challenge AC&S Service

During the war, and especially in 1944 and 1945, the city hosted large numbers of visitors. The month of July 1944, was the best in the city's history, with bank deposits up 63 percent over 1942, and virtually every hotel room sold every day, an unprecedented event. Restaurants and stores were often crowded and the Boardwalk had constant parades of people walking the promenade. The AC&S carried 2,423,646 passengers, double the number carried in 1942; an average of 78,172 persons rode the trolleys each day. For example, on July 1, 1944, 60,883 people rode the Atlantic Avenue trolleys and the Ocean City Division

But with more riders came more complaints. In February, the Press predicted that trolley travel would be "as irregular, sardine-like, and unsatisfactory" as it had been in 1943. An editorial urged eliminating some car stops as a way of speeding service. A letter writer complained about the poor condition of the grade crossings in the Inlet section, while another claimed five cars passed him without stopping, noting they were packed in the front but empty in the back. *The Daily World* took the company to task for tolerating certain motormen who routinely passed car stops when there was still room in their cars for more passengers. The War Board cars were described as "contemporary to stage coaches," with flat wheels creating loud noise, while the tracks needed repair. In an editorial a month later, the paper called on the AC&S to scrap the "Toonerville

CHAPTER NINE | Wartime Challenges

cars" as soon as possible, replacing them with streamliners.

Normal breakdowns and accidents added to the company's woes. In May 1944, a short-circuit on an interurban car at Pleasantville caused a small fire and disrupted service. A broken overhead wire on Mississippi Avenue stopped the cars soon thereafter. A lightning strike in June disabled the Somers Point substation for half a day, halting service south of Linwood. The next month a War Board car hit the rear of a Brilliner when its brakes failed. Damage was slight and only one passenger was injured. A Brilliner breakdown at New York Avenue in August caused a long line of trolleys to back up behind it, until it could be pushed to the barn.

The company tried to carry on as best it could. An official said all cars were in service and 120 men were at work, but it was difficult to find additional workers. Nonetheless, the company had chartered a car for the duration to the Kiwanis Club to carry members to their weekly luncheon meeting and return them after their gathering ended. In what was probably an unwise move, the firm raised the ire of city politicians by canceling passes to all city workers, except for police and firemen. The state legislature complicated life by outlawing smoking in all public transit vehicles. Warning signs were posted in the cars and buses but they had no effect. The smokers congregated in the rear and simply ignored operators who asked them to stop. Disgruntled passengers complained in person and by letter, but nothing was done.

The 1944 Hurricane

Even nature seemed to be against the AC&S. On the afternoon of Thursday, September 14, 1944, a severe storm swept up the New Jersey coast, hitting the city about 3 P.M. Heavy rain, winds over 70 miles per hour with higher gusts, and devastating floods as ocean waves covered much of the island, especially in the Inlet section and along the beaches, causing extensive damage. Roofs were blown off; trees were downed; signs were destroyed; countless windows were broken and basements flooded. Half of the Boardwalk was destroyed and other sections were buckled and damaged. The Heinz Pier was so battered that it was torn down the following year; other piers suffered minor damage. Telephone service failed, and electric power was out from about 6:20 P.M. until midnight when it was partially restored. All area physicians were called to duty to care for the many people injured by flying

Above: On May 3, 1943, when this picture was taken, the tracks approaching Maine Avenue appear safe, but the waters of the Absecon Inlet are immediately to the right. Hackney's Seafood Restaurant and the stretch of Boardwalk behind it suffered heavy damage during the 1944 hurricane as did many of the lodging houses. The flooding of this section of the line disrupted trolley service and led to demands for a loop closer to Atlantic Avenue. The track to the left is PRSL's Madison Avenue line which was called Mediterranean Avenue in the city south of the Inlet section. A loop was built here after the war. Jeffrey Marinoff collection

147

Above: Brilliner 6904 lays over at the Inlet loop on September 5, 1945, ready for another trip to Margate. The 25 Brilliners proved their worth during the busy war years carrying prodigious numbers of people. Their accomplishments were not appreciated by the ever critical press, politicians, and much of the public, who refused to be satisfied with anything the AC&S did. John Brinckmann collection

debris and falls. Parts of the city remained under several feet of water during the high tide periods.

Damage was particularly heavy in the Inlet section. Hackney's Restaurant was partially destroyed, and Captain Starn's Restaurant near the trolley loop suffered as well. Great waves washed over Maine Avenue, breaking the doors of houses and covering the area with several feet of water until after midnight. Train service into and out of the city was disrupted as dozens of telegraph poles paralleling the tracks were blown down.

The AC&S kept its trolleys on the streets in the midst of the tempest until the power failed. Consequently, many of the cars were damaged by the rising waters. One Brilliner was washed off the rails on the long curve at Maine and Adriatic Avenues. On the meadows, an outbound two-car Shore Fast Line train stalled when a wire fell across the tracks and set fire to the rear car, former parlor car 120. The crew moved the passengers into the front car and uncoupled 120, which was destroyed. The passengers were stranded about four hours, but no one was hurt.

The next day, recovery efforts began. Buses resumed operating and filled in for the trolleys. Sporadic trolley service was restored between Massachusetts and Portland avenues in the morning. The serviceable Brilliners were run in reverse as necessary, an awkward and cumbersome procedure. During the next two days, crews cleared debris and parts of the Boardwalk from the tracks between Portland and Douglas avenues. It took two days for workers, aided by a bulldozer, to dig out the Maine Avenue tracks from the tons of seaweed, sand, and debris that covered them and to restore service to the Inlet loop. Damage in Longport was severe and considerable repairs were needed, as the ocean had covered the tracks during the storm. Not until September 26 did trolleys once again reach Longport.

Ocean City, too, suffered heavy damage. The island was partially flooded; the Boardwalk was torn apart; roofs were blown off; residents south of 34th Street were cut off, and the streets were filled with wreckage.

All told, the storm caused losses of over $4,500,000 and considerable time to make repairs. On October 29, the AC&S published an advertisement in the local papers thanking the public for their help and understanding. The ads said the storm damaged the right-of-way, the tracks, and the cars, which suffered especially from the corrosive effects of salt water on the motors. Half of the Brilliners and several War Board cars were disabled. The shortage of skilled labor and parts made repairs difficult, and not until four months passed were all cars returned to service. The remains of car 120, still on the meadows, were loaded onto a PRSL work train in December and hauled to the Inlet where it was scrapped.

Some criticized the AC&S for not withdrawing its cars as the storm approached, but management justified its decision to keep them on the streets until power failed by its sense of duty and its determination to serve the public. Attempting to improve its image after all the problems of 1944, the company placed a large notice in the newspapers early in 1945, headed, "A Report from your Transportation Company," below which in large type was the statement, "It Was Tough Going in 1944….but You Were Swell!" A slightly smaller statement proclaimed, "War Shortages, Hurricane, Nor'easters, Crowds, Rationed Gasoline, Manpower Problems, Priorities. It was a super-human effort to meet abnormal demands in the face of terrific odds…." Five following paragraphs referred to delays and disruptions of service, justified the company's handling of the hurricane, noted the abnormally large crowds and the manpower shortage, praised the Brilliners and the company's safety record, and thanked the public for their patience and understanding. In the conclusion, A. J. Purinton vaguely alluded to recommendations that would "enhance and speed" transportation in 1945. No doubt the half-page ad was an attempt to counter the wave of criticism besetting the company, but it did little to ward off the most vocal of the critics.

The great storm of September 1944, was only one of the difficulties facing the company that year. The other problems confronting it were caused by men, not nature, and Stern and Silverman would find them more difficult to solve.

Operational Problems Continue to Beset the AC&S

The 1944 hurricane caused the most extensive interruption of AC&S operations, but other lesser difficulties confronted the company in 1945. Many of these were of the type that affected most transit systems, but in Atlantic City they seemed to produce unrelenting criticism, encouraged by the hostile municipal government, aided by most of the press, which seized every opportunity to denounce the trolleys and to seek a panacea in bus service.

For example, an electrical storm in March caused a short circuit in the substation at the peak of the morning rush hour, stopping all trolley service. Although the outage lasted only 20 minutes, hundreds were delayed. A car leaving the Portland Avenue loop in July derailed in the evening rush hour, blocking both tracks, causing a traffic jam, and stopping all service for 90 minutes. In September, the wire over the long unused track on Virginia Avenue at Arctic Avenue fell as a result of high winds. Service was unaffected, but the incident reflected poorly on the AC&S.

Even worse were fatalities involving the trolleys. In January, a car derailed on Maine Avenue near the Inlet, swerving across the street, and striking a pedestrian, who died the following day. Service was delayed for over an hour; the cause was attributed to sand on the track. A couple crossing the tracks in Ventnor was struck by a streetcar in July; the woman was killed and the man severely injured. A similar incident occurred in November in Ventnor where a car struck and instantly killed an elderly gentleman crossing the tracks. Rain and poor visibility were blamed for the tragedy. In all cases, the motorman was arrested on a charge of technical manslaughter.

These unfortunate events provoked critical editorials and demands that the police control "the excessive speed" of the

Above: Drawing power from the third rail, a Shore Fast Line car on the Newfield branch nears Pleasantville station in the distance. It will then turn left onto the Somers Point branch heading for Ocean City under trolley wire. The line carried many school pupils, some of whom caused problems with their unruly behavior. David H. Cope photo, Richard Allman collection

trolleys. The towns were critical too because, except in Atlantic City, there were no illuminated safety islands and no traffic lights south of Albany Avenue, which encouraged speeding.

While not as serious, the company was plagued with a spate of vandalism, perpetrated mostly by unruly high school students. The miscreants threw hats around; made marks on seats; tore down advertising posters; used abusive language; insulted, threatened, and shoved passengers, and caused general disturbances. The company received numerous complaints about the disorderly youths. It was finally provoked into placing advertisements offering a $100 reward for information leading to the conviction of anyone damaging company property. The police did occasionally respond, arresting small groups of people, but the problem was never completely eliminated.

A minor change was an agreement on April 8, 1944, between the WJ&S and Clarence Starn for the sale of a section of land at the Inlet, occupied by part of the loop tracks. Captain Starn was the owner of a large, popular seafood restaurant and pier on Absecon Inlet who wanted to enlarge his parking lot. The transaction involved relocating and reducing the size of the trolley loop. The work was done in 1946, and it had no effect on trolley service.

Personnel Changes

As the public eagerly awaited the end of the war, the AC&S suffered a personal loss on March 5, 1945, when long-time Superintendent and General Manager Arthur J. Purinton died. He had been in declining health for some time, and the weakening of his strong hand had contributed to the company's problems. Since 1915, he had supervised the operations of the two rail lines with dedication and ability and always under the direction of the Stern and Silverman officials in Philadelphia.

The PRSL also experienced managerial changes in this period. J. O. Hackenberg, general manager of the PRSL, took a leave-of-absence in February 1944 because of ill health. He returned the following year in a new position.

Hackenberg's replacement at the helm of the Seashore Lines was Harry Babcock. Like his predecessor, he was a long-time employee of the PRR. Born in Egg Harbor Township, he began his career in 1903 as a clerk for the West Jersey and Seashore Railroad. He rose rapidly through the ranks, becoming the passenger trainmaster on the Maryland Division and later superintendent of the Washington Terminal Company. He soon found it necessary to devote a considerable amount of time to the affairs of the AC&S.

Above: A view on the Somers Point branch in 1939 as Shore Fast Line 109 approaches Pleasantville and the run over PRSL track where the changeover will be made to third rail current collection. James P. Shuman photo. Electric City Trolley Museum collection

Above: Car 105 bound for Ocean City is about to enter the Somers point branch while the connecting bus is ready to depart from the Pleasantville station for Absecon. This was the busiest of the AC&S bus routes. The small AC&S station is overshadowed by the more attractive PRSL Pleasantville station, which served only a few trains daily. These consisted of a single gas-electric car running between Atlantic City and Newfield where it connected with the Millville-Camden M.U. cars. This once busy line now sees minimal service. David H. Cope photo, Richard Allman collection

Bus Service is Restricted

The bus lines had always produced deficits and were run in order to protect the rail lines from outside competition. This situation did not change during the war years. There were six routes, none of which earned a profit. Two short routes, Bungalow Park and Venice Park, served neighborhoods north and west of Atlantic Avenue and required a maximum of only three buses. The Atlantic City to Ocean City via Longport line offered only one round trip most of the year and six trips in the summer. The Atlantic City-Ventnor line and its extension to Margate had a maximum of eight trips, while the Atlantic City to Ocean City via Pleasantville and Somers Point ran only one trip. The busiest route was the two-mile Pleasantville-Absecon line, carding 34 round trips but it lost the most money. A local line in Ocean City provided mostly seasonal runs. School trips were also provided.

In May 1943, the Office of Defense Transportation ordered the Margate route to be discontinued and restricted the Pleasantville-Somers Point line to summer only operation. The Bungalow Park, Venice Park, and Absecon-Pleasantville lines offered regular service with headways of 30 minutes. The other lines were essentially franchise runs with as few as one trip daily. Since many of the routes paralleled the rail lines, they were regarded as expendable during the war emergency. The Ocean City line, running the length of the island, scheduled half-hourly summer service but very limited operations were conducted in the off-season.

Most bus runs originated at Tennessee Avenue at the former electric station, converted to a bus terminal after the electric trains were discontinued. On Absecon Island, buses ran primarily on Arctic and Ventnor Avenues and on Shore Road on the mainland.

To service these lines, the company had a fleet of 13 buses. Ten of them, Ford and Yellow model coaches, were purchased new in 1936 and 1937; they were supplemented by three second-hand vehicles added in 1942. Until 1940, the buses were painted orange and cream; after the Brilliners arrived, they were painted black and yellow, similar to the rail cars. The bus routes seemed to escape the criticisms that were directed at the trolley lines, probably because they were a relatively small part of the company's system and because some people regarded them more highly than the trolleys.

The Samuel Backer Attacks

Above: A Shore Fast Line bus is preparing to reverse direction on 8th Street near the Ocean City Boardwalk. In this wartime view, headlights are partially covered by black paint. The bus was running on the Ocean City local lines which spanned the length of the island, but which proved to be unprofitable—as were all AC&S bus routes. Motor Bus Society Library

While officials in Philadelphia and employees in Atlantic City struggled to provide service, they were forced to deal with a major attack on the company and its trolley lines by a former city solicitor, Samuel Backer. Acting as a private citizen, although he was a law partner of Atlantic City Mayor Joseph Altman and part of the city's political establishment, he filed a complaint with the Board of Public Utility Commissioners, charging the AC&S provided "woefully inadequate service" and created traffic hazards. He demanded restoration of the five-cent fare (instead of seven cents) and claimed the line was making huge profits. He urged abandonment of rail service at the end of the war that would permit removal of tracks, poles, and overhead wire, thereby beautifying Atlantic Avenue and increasing property values.

Other groups immediately supported Backer. The president of the Real Estate Board asserted that everyone wanted buses; "they are the modern thing." His view was echoed by the head of the Restaurant Association, who said that buses "would be a good thing." The Board of Commerce demanded the AC&S hire conductors or "conductorettes," while others suggested eliminating some of the traffic lights and instituting "skip-stop" service.

In an unusual dissent, the Press pointed out service was also inadequate for restaurants, hotels, cabs, trains, and most organizations dealing with the public. The paper pointed out that the bus supporters had not foreseen the war, and if they had been successful earlier, people would be biking and walking instead of protesting the "incomparably superior sardine existence of overcrowded trolleys."

In August, the Board of Public Utility Commissioners announced it would make "a detailed analysis of the . . . operation and financial affairs" of the trolley company. It sent staff members to check on conditions on the line and followed this with a letter on August 11 making four "recommendations." The board stated there should be on-street supervisors at the Inlet loop, Arkansas Avenue where the PRSL station was located, and the Douglas Avenue loop from 6 A.M. to 1 A.M. daily; that signs should be posted urging the use of center or rear doors; that fare collectors be assigned to points of heavy loading, and that the company eliminate at once the practice of cars passing waiting passengers at corners without stopping. The AC&S was directed to make an immediate reply to the board, which it did, but it was slow to act.

Additional PUC Recommendations

Dissatisfied with the seeming inaction by the AC&S, the PUC conducted a traffic survey on both the Atlantic Avenue and Ocean City Divisions between August 6 and September 4, 1944. They concluded, in a letter to Purinton on October 9, that if supervisory and operating forces were not expanded and training improved, the quality of service to be offered in the summer of 1945 would be as poor as that of the previous summer. The board added eight

CHAPTER NINE | *Wartime Challenges*

additional recommendations the company should meet, and a reply was expected by the end of the month.

In order to maintain service when the Inlet area tracks were flooded, the board wanted a wye-track installed at Virginia and Atlantic avenues, by adding a switch connecting the outbound Virginia Avenue track with the northbound Atlantic Avenue rails so the single-end Brilliners could be reversed at that point. To improve loading cars at busy intersections, the board ordered the Brilliners be modified by giving the operator control of the center doors, as well as retaining the current method of exiting passengers stepping on a treadle. The brakes should be adjusted to apply automatically whenever the side doors were opened. In a similar manner, rear door controls and interlocking brakes should be installed on the War Board cars. The Shore Fast Line interurban cars were to have their doors closed whenever they were in motion, instead of the usual practice of keeping them open on Atlantic Avenue to speed loading and unloading.

In addition, the PUC recommended the installation of an electric switch leading into the Douglas Avenue loop from Atlantic Avenue instead of the manual switch then in place, which required the operator to leave the car to throw it. Finally, the company was ordered to submit its program for training and increasing its supervisory and operating personnel.

Leo Isenthal sent copies of the PUC demands to Harry Babcock, general manager of the PRSL, and J. F. Deasy, PRR vice-president, with a strong hint that the PRR should pay for these changes. The railroad executives were less than pleased by this latest evidence of problems on its trolley line. The matter was referred to H. W. Jones, the chief of motive power, who called a meeting in Atlantic City on October 24, attended by Leo Isenthal, Arthur Purinton, auditor J. M. Campbell, and Master Mechanic J. W. Gordon of the AC&S, while D. Hengstler, the foreman of car inspectors for the PRSL, represented the railroad. They estimated it would cost $3,100 to make the changes in the door valves and brakes on the cars.

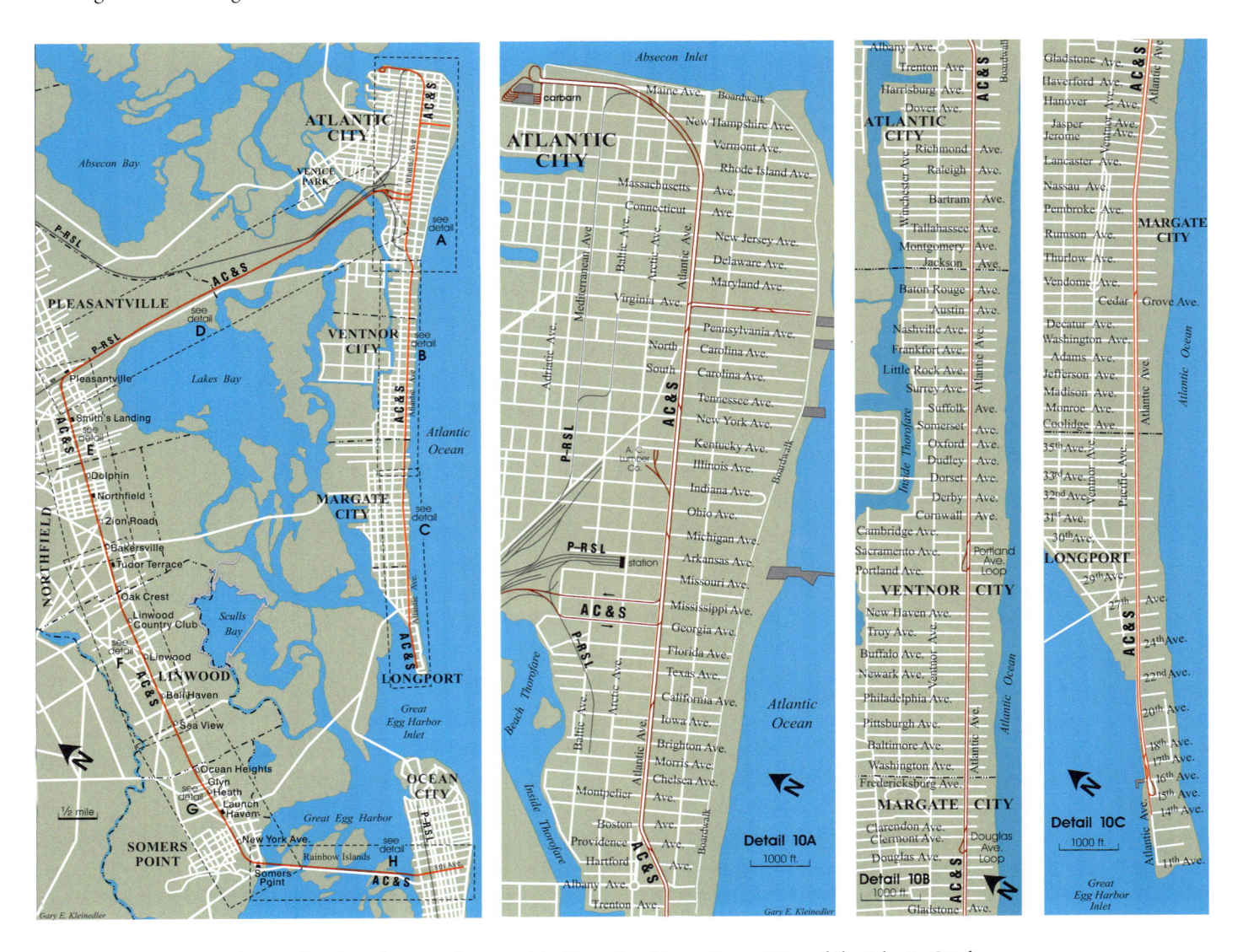

Above: *Atlantic City & Shore Railroad as of 1944 with maps of the Shore Fast Line to Ocean City and the Atlantic City lines.*

The AC&S Responds to the PUC

Armed with this information, Leo Isenthal replied to the PUC on October 28. He reported the training program consisted of 54 hours of instruction by experienced operators followed by a trial run over the line. He promised to try to increase the number of operators for the summer but he warned the manpower shortage was acute. He agreed to make the changes on door controls and to apply interlocking brakes, but he hoped activating just the front half of the Brilliner side doors would be sufficient. Doors on the interurban cars would be closed, except on Atlantic Avenue, where the stops were close together. He agreed to install an electric switch at Douglas Avenue, but he rejected the wye track at Virginia Avenue because of its hazards and traffic congestion. Instead, he suggested the construction of an off-street loop on railroad property between Madison and Melrose Avenues, in an area that very rarely flooded. This would permit the Brilliners to reverse and maintain service on most of the line. He estimated it would take four months to complete this work. Harry Babcock informed John F. Deasy of this reply.

The PUC accepted the response, except it insisted that both side doors of the Brilliners be controlled by the operator. The board also stressed, once more, the importance of training sufficient supervisory and operating personnel to meet the service demands of the coming summer.

Samuel Backer dismissed the AC&S letter as insufficient and he resumed his attacks, demanding two-man cars and lower fares. The Chamber of Commerce pronounced the trolley situation as "hopeless," and the city commissioners added the poor condition of the track to their complaints. In this instance, however, the PUC rejected the demand for two-man crews, citing the manpower situation, and it stated the fare question would be considered later separately.

The PRR Tries to Settle the Dispute

Well aware of the growing criticism and disturbed by the seeming inability of AC&S management to deal with it, PRR officials called a meeting on January 31, 1945. Attending were Leo Isenthal and AC&S Attorney Thomas Hyndman; Harry Babcock, general manager of the PRSL; a Reading Company and a PRR attorney, and four other PRR officials.

Isenthal spoke at length and said he would do anything the PRSL wanted. As the time was rapidly approaching when the PUC expected a reply, he urged a lengthy detailed response be made, explaining why the AC&S had failed to modify its cars. The group decided that Hyndman should draft the reply, subject to the approval of the railroad attorneys.

A few days later, Isenthal told PRR officers he had been severely criticized by PUC officials at a private meeting because no improvements had been made, all of which had to be funded

Above: Ex-Atlantic & Suburban car 10 now renumbered as WJ&S 499200, rolls up Atlantic Avenue at Indiana Avenue passing the Earle Theater. It had been converted into a rail grinder equipped with moveable abrasive stones used to smooth rough spots on the rail heads. It was the only survivor of Suburban's fleet of Brill cars. William P. Hamilton, III photo, Fred W. Schneider, III collection

by the PRR. At the same time, Ventnor, Margate, and Longport joined Atlantic City in complaining about poor service, although not about reducing the fare.

In its formal response later in February, the AC&S maintained that its fares were "fair and reasonable" and it ignored demands for two-man cars. It claimed the company had only one profitable year in the decade between 1930 and 1940, and that although revenue had recently increased, due to the "abnormal conditions," so had expenses, especially wages. It flatly denied that its cars were packed and that thousands of people were left standing on corners. It added that it had procured most of the parts needed to modify its cars, but stated it could not make the changes until all the items were on hand. Only one car had been modified. Neither Backer nor the PUC were satisfied with this statement, and the agency scheduled a formal hearing in April to deal with the issues.

The AC&S then went on the offensive against the continuous public assaults made by Backer. It hired an advertising agency and appointed its head as director of public relations. The new official said Backer never used the trolleys, which were "in his way in driving his own car," and that he "just doesn't like public transportation." While a step in the right direction, it did not silence the former city solicitor.

The PUC Hearings

On April 13, 1945, the Board of Public Utility Commissioners formally convened a hearing in the City Hall of the resort town to determine if it should issue a formal order to the trolley company. Only two witnesses testified, both members of the PUC staff.

James A. Judge, superintendent of the street transportation division, said the Atlantic Avenue line was "very poorly managed." He criticized the company for not assigning loaders at Arkansas Avenue and for failing to modify its cars so the side and rear doors could be used. He noted the automatic switch at Douglas Avenue had not been installed, nor had the company assigned supervisors at key points or adequately trained its personnel. He had checked car frequencies on several days and said they often tended to run in bunches, eight or ten minutes apart, instead of every two or three minutes. Judge concluded by saying that instead of every fourth car going to Longport, at times only one in nine did. He blamed traffic lights, automobiles, and fire alarms for the delays.

The second witness was James Leonard, the principal engineer for the PUC, who examined the track. He declared it was "decrepit and far below standard. To express it frankly, I would call it lousy." He concluded by saying the track should be rebuilt as soon as possible. The hearing was then adjourned, to reconvene two weeks later.

At the second session on April 25, a prominent local attorney, Thomas H. Munyan, was granted permission to testify. He said he represented prospective new owners who were negotiating with the PRR to purchase the Atlantic Avenue line. He promised they would carry out any PUC recommendations still not completed when they took over, except they would not accept two-man cars until it was determined they were necessary. Upon hearing this testimony, Backer and the other complainants withdrew their charges in order to give the new group the opportunity to improve service. The hearing was then closed.

The AC&S drafted a response to the PUC charges. It argued there was no need for supervisors at the Inlet, as the dispatcher was located there. It agreed to assign supervisors at Arkansas and Douglas avenues during the summer season as ordered, but for the remainder of the year they would be on hand only when trains were arriving and departing. Fare collectors would be at Arkansas Avenue at train times, but not continuously. The cars were to be modified as soon as all the parts needed were received. The automatic switch at Douglas Avenue would be installed as soon as it was obtained, and work on the Madison Avenue loop was almost finished. Even as this response was made, work on the loop was completed, and the first car, a Brilliner, was operated around it on May 5.

Not satisfied, the board issued a formal reprimand to the AC&S for its failure to implement its recommendations, saying the company had not shown good faith. It charged the line with offering inadequate service and failing to maintain its equipment. The board then ordered the company to carry out the recommendations it had earlier proposed and to improve the condition of its tracks as soon as materials were available. Thomas Munyan, speaking for the prospective new owners, promised to carry out any of the PUC orders that the AC&S failed to do, and the complaints were formally withdrawn on June 4, 1945.

There is no question that some of the charges directed at the AC&S were justified. The company should have addressed earlier the bottleneck at Arkansas Avenue when trains were arriving and departing. While Stern and Silverman was determined to avoid the restoration of two-man crews at all costs, it should have stationed supervisors and fare collectors there earlier and modified its equipment so side and end doors could be used. Better training and overall supervision could have lessened some of the complaints of poor and irregular service.

Part of the problem was the weakening of leadership at the top. Arthur Purinton was in declining health by 1943 and he was no longer able to exercise the firm control he had practiced in earlier years. In Philadelphia, Leo Isenthal and the reclusive staff at Stern and Silverman were also elderly, lacking sufficient energy and ability to address the mounting problems brought on by the war.

Munyan's announcement that new owners were planning to take control of the Atlantic Avenue line lessened but did not end the barrage of criticism directed at the AC&S. The company continued to operate the line through most of the year, while negotiations were conducted with the PRR and the new owners; the status of the Shore Fast Line route was determined.

The PRR managers had also become disillusioned about the merits of its trolley line, and in 1944 they had begun to take steps to end their long-time control of local transportation on Absecon Island, thereby opening the door for new people to quell the criticism and to point the trolley lines in a new direction.

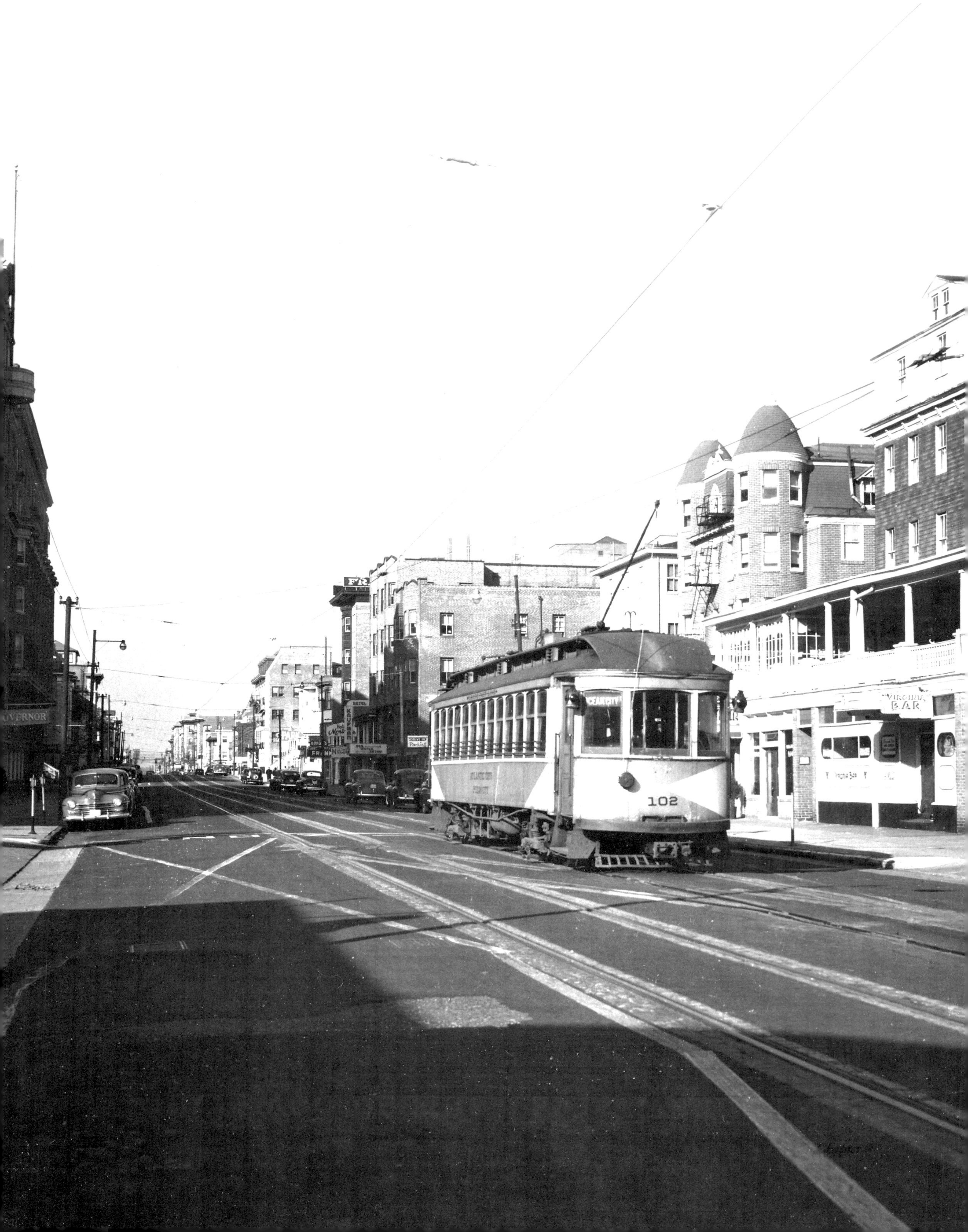
OVERNOR
CEAN CITY
102
VIRGINIA BAR

CHAPTER TEN

The Pennsylvania Railroad Bows Out

The Pennsylvania Railroad Reappraises the Future of its Atlantic City Trolley Line

On January 21, 1944, Leo Isenthal, president of the Atlantic City and Shore Railroad, met John F. Deasy, vice-president of the Pennsylvania Railroad, concerning the upcoming expiration of the lease of the Atlantic Avenue and Longport Line and the trackage rights agreement over the Newfield and Somers Point branches used by the Shore Fast Line. Both these arrangements were to terminate on December 18, 1945, and Isenthal was anxious to renew them well before that date, while hoping for more favorable terms for the AC&S.

Four days later, Isenthal wrote a follow-up letter to Deasy with additional information. He stated that from 1908 through 1942, the AC&S had paid all operating expenses for the Atlantic Avenue line as well as $5,000,000 in rentals and profits to the PRR. From 1932 through 1942, the company had paid over $250,000 for trackage rights over the Newfield and Somers Point branches. Claiming that the AC&S was considering a simplification of its corporate structure, he desired an early renewal of the arrangements with the railroad. In response, Deasy said the subject was being examined and he would give a more detailed answer later.

In characteristic fashion, Deasy then formed a committee, headed by F. C. Wilkinson of the Chief Engineer's Office, to make an extensive analysis of the AC&S operations and problems during the forty years of its control and to make recommendations concerning the advisability of renewing the arrangements or of considering other options.

The 1944 Report

By September 1944, the committee completed its work and produced a comprehensive report on the Atlantic Avenue and Ocean City lines, replete with maps, graphics, and detailed

Facing Page: There is very little traffic on Virginia Avenue as Shore Fast Line 102 departs from the Boardwalk terminal for a quick run to Ocean City, circa 1947. Electric City Trolley Museum collection

Above: Car 115 leads a two-car interurban train as it moves briskly along on PRSL third rail trackage near Pleasantville in 1947. The Shore Fast Line cars continued to make their regular runs between Atlantic City and Ocean City as they always had seemingly unaware that their days were numbered. Electric City Trolley Museum collection

financial information. It included a description of the property and a history of its operations; agreements made with the towns; details of the lease and trackage rights agreements with the AC&S and the rental payments made under their terms; the bus lines; a financial analysis from 1927 through 1943, and recommendations.

The report stated the operations of the AC&S were "remunerative" to the railroad. During the 1927-1943 period, the average annual return from the Atlantic Avenue line was $145,000 before depreciation; the bus lines incurred an average deficit of $942 per year. The AC&S realized an estimated average annual income of $44,000 during the same period.

The Shore Fast Line route, operated under a trackage rights agreement, realized an average annual payment to the railroad for the seventeen year period of $21,000, while the AC&S incurred an estimated deficit of almost $30,000 per year during the same period. Combined, the PRSL received annually an average payment of $121,800, and the AC&S earned an estimated average of $14,500 each year. The report noted the wage increase granted to AC&S workers in 1944 would increase annual expenses by almost $80,000.

In view of the profits received, the committee concluded the railroad should extend its agreements with the AC&S, with a few minor modifications. It suggested the Pleasantville-Atlantic City section of the Shore Fast Line should be changed to a single-track operation, with overhead trolley wire replacing the third rail. The number of bus routes should be reduced to only those necessary to protect the Atlantic Avenue line from possible competition.

In a separate analysis, PRR Treasurer H. W. Schotter determined the railroad could lawfully sell its property and the buyer would be responsible for obtaining franchises and permissions from public officials to operate the service. The sale would not affect the Pennsylvania-Reading Seashore Lines or the PRR regarding income taxes, but the West Jersey and Seashore might realize a savings of about $57,000. The proceeds from a sale could be used to reduce the bonded indebtedness of the WJ&S; these bonds were held by the PRR and the Reading. The treasurer suggested a sale price of $1,000,000, based on the average annual earnings of the property, under which a buyer could realize a yearly return of about nine percent on his investment.

Schotter concluded by stating the sale would require the approval of the Board of Public Utility Commissioners, the WJ&S stockholders and trustee of its mortgage bonds, and the board of directors of the PRSL. No approval was needed from the Interstate Commerce Commission or the PRSL stockholders. The buyer would have to obtain approval of the towns to operate the line. Albert Ward, general attorney for the PRR, and R. C. Miller, the comptroller, concurred with Schotter's recommendations.

Potential Buyers of the Atlantic Avenue and Longport Line Appear

The possible sale of the AA&L line could not be kept secret and rumors of such a transaction spread. At the same time, two prominent Philadelphia building contractors emerged. They were part-time residents of Atlantic City and were looking for opportunities to invest some of their wartime profits in the resort.

Above: A view of activity at Inlet Loop in the late 1940s with two Brilliners in the loop while a former Ft. Wayne car, purchased in 1946, awaits a call to duty. Ridership was still heavy immediately after the war. Electric City Trolley Museum collection

CHAPTER TEN | *The Pennsylvania Railroad Bows Out*

Above: Bound for Linwood, Shore Fast Line car 101 turns from Virginia Avenue onto Atlantic Avenue in the mid-1940s. Burdened by obsolete equipment coupled with high rental and maintenance costs, the interurban line was unprofitable and the possible sale of the property posed a major problem for Leo Isenthal. Without the profits from the Atlantic Avenue line, the AC&S faced financial collapse. David H. Cope photo, Richard Allman collection

They were John McShain and Matthew McCloskey, who had already jointly purchased the Claridge Hotel. The prospect of selling the property when wartime traffic was at its peak appealed to the PRR officers, and they decided to open negotiations with McShain's and McCloskey's representative, Atlantic City attorney Thomas H. Munyan.

In preparation, Vice-President John Deasy asked Harry Babcock, general manager of the PRSL, to review the entire question and to offer his opinions. On September 18, 1944, Munyan called the railroad offices to arrange an appointment with Deasy to discuss a possible purchase.

Leo Isenthal Is Confronted with a Major Problem

On October 20, Deasy called Leo Isenthal and informed him that prospective buyers were interested in the Atlantic Avenue line and the railroad was inclined to sell it if it could get the proper price. Isenthal immediately expressed concerns about the Ocean City Division which although then profitable, could be expected to revert to its normal money-losing status at the end of the war. He asked if the buyers might not purchase the Shore Fast Line as well. Deasy promised to inform them of the possibility. He added that he had tried on several occasions to persuade Isaac Silverman to buy the property, but without success. Isenthal asked if the buyers wanted the AC&S to continue operating the line. Deasy replied this was a possibility, and he would bring it up in the negotiations. He added he would keep Isenthal informed of the progress of the talks.

In a follow-up letter the same day, Deasy noted the bus lines were to be part of the sale and that he expected the franchises for them, held by the AC&S, would be turned over to the new owners. Isenthal sent an evasive reply on October 31, saying he would have to consult his board of directors, and discuss the issue at a later date.

Soon thereafter, Munyan requested detailed information about the Atlantic Avenue line, including finances, franchises, the AC&S, and the price. Deasy arranged a meeting with Isenthal, noting in a memo that the PRSL's only obligations to the AC&S were in the 1907 lease agreement.

On November 1, Deasy, his assistant, W. W. Patchell, and General Attorney Albert Ward met Isenthal and AC&S attorney Thomas Hyndman. Deasy explained negotiations were underway and he had no objection to Isenthal speaking with the prospective buyers. Isenthal had two questions: Could the AC&S continue to operate the trolley line, and would the new owners take over the Ocean City Division? Deasy had no answer to either question, but he promised to keep him informed. Isenthal responded by saying that if the buyers did not purchase the Shore Fast Line, he would be forced to discontinue operations, making the PRR responsible for the service and answerable to the PUC. He was still not ready to discuss the bus franchises. With that, the meeting ended.

Deasy informed Revelle W. Brown, president of the Reading Company, of the negotiations and asked him to appoint a representative at future discussions with the buyers. In a sharp contrast with the PRR's position only a few years earlier, he said the trolley operation was "more or less a foreign business" for the railroad, which had thought "for a number of years it might be a good thing to sell it."

Isenthal remained uncooperative on the issue of the bus franchises. When contacted, he said his board of directors had not arrived at any conclusion but they planned to meet again. He was apparently using them as a bargaining chip to force the PRR to include the Ocean City Division in any sales agreement.

Deasy and McShain Reach a Tentative Agreement

On November 8, John McShain and Thomas Munyan met with Deasy in his Broad Street Station office. McShain tentatively accepted the railroad's price of $1,000,000 for the Atlantic Avenue and Longport Line. He maintained "an open mind" on the question of how the line was to be operated, and they agreed to meet again.

Deasy's office prepared a succinct version of the September 1944 report for circulation among railroad officials, most of whom knew very little of the history and lease arrangements governing the trolley line. It stressed the financial aspects of the deal, justifying the price and stating the proceeds would be used to retire WJ&S bonds. Included were basic aspects of the transaction and maps of the rail and bus lines.

Perhaps because of Isenthal's foot-dragging, Deasy did not inform him of the tentative agreement of sale. In mid-December, the AC&S president wrote to Deasy, saying a reporter had called to tell him the Press had heard the company had been sold and asking for confirmation. Isenthal had denied any knowledge of a sale, and asked the railroad executive to keep him informed. Deasy promptly told Isenthal the line had not been sold and he would let him know when it was. Obviously, relations between the two men were strained.

The PRR Defines Terms for a Sale Agreement

By early 1945, the PRR officers had developed certain stipulations regarding a sale. The buyer would have to grant trackage rights on Atlantic Avenue so the Shore Fast Line cars could reach Virginia Avenue from Georgia Avenue. The Absecon Island bus lines were included, but not those off the island. The two Atlantic City-Ocean City bus routes, via Longport and via Pleasantville and Somers Point, essentially summer operations, were to be split at the points where they left the island, unless the PUC decreed otherwise. In effect, the Atlantic City and Shore was to continue operating these routes, as well as the Pleasantville-Absecon and the Ocean City bus lines. If their buses entered Absecon Island, they would not be permitted to carry people locally. These conditions were essentially what McShain and McCloskey wanted: the Atlantic Avenue trolley line and only the local bus routes that were part of the system. The result would be two transit systems serving the region rather than one.

Above: Revelle W. Brown was president of the Reading Company from 1944 until 1951. He approved of the proposed sale of the trolley line to the new buyers. As the senior partner in the Pennsylvania-Reading Seashore Lines, the PRR determined the company's policies but it always sought the approval of the Reading, which was forthcoming. Reading Company photo file, Hagley Museum and Library

Deasy sent a memo to PRR president Martin W. Clement and Reading Company president Revelle W. Brown describing the Atlantic City operations and the reasons for making the proposed sale. Among them was the expectation that the AC&S was unwilling to pay even the current rental fees if the lease were

CHAPTER TEN | *The Pennsylvania Railroad Bows Out*

THE NEW OWNERS

JOHN MCSHAIN

Born on December 21, 1898, in Philadelphia to Irish immigrant parents, John McShain was educated in Catholic secondary schools and St. Joseph's Preparatory School. After graduating in 1918, he attended Georgetown University, but he withdrew after one year when his father died. He took over his father's construction business, studied drafting and bookkeeping, and soon established himself as a successful builder, specializing in constructing Catholic schools, convents, and rectories. [Insert Fig. 10.5—John McShain photo]

In 1927, he married Mary Horstman, the daughter of a clothing manufacturer and a Union League Republican. They had one child, Pauline, who entered the convent of the Sisters of the Holy Child Jesus; she was assigned to Rosemont College in suburban Philadelphia staffed by the sisters of the order.

McShain excelled as a building contractor, and his firm erected many well-known structures. Of particular note are the Board of Education Building in Philadelphia and over one hundred buildings in the Washington area. Among them are the Jefferson Memorial, the Library of Congress annex, the National Shrine of the Immaculate Conception, the Veterans Hospital, the Columbia Plaza Complex, the Pentagon, and the John F. Kennedy Center for the Performing Arts. He also built the Franklin D. Roosevelt Library in Hyde Park, New York.

As his business prospered, he looked for opportunities for investments, concentrating in Philadelphia and Atlantic City, where he was a frequent visitor. In the former city, he purchased the Barclay Hotel on Rittenhouse Square, and in the resort city, he invested in the Ambassador, the Traymore, and the 24-story Claridge Hotel at Park Place, which he had built in 1930. His search for investments led him to form a partnership with Matthew McCloskey in 1944 in order to purchase the Atlantic Avenue trolley line. An avid racing fan, he established his own stable in 1952 and enjoyed considerable success. In 1959, he purchased a 20,000-acre estate in Killarney, Ireland, where he and Mary spent much time. Although he was a Republican and interested in Philadelphia politics, he maintained business and social relationships with Democratic politicians.

McShain was a very generous man who donated sums to many causes and institutions, especially to Catholic colleges and schools, as well as to Philadelphia cultural institutions. He served on the boards of directors of a number of banks, corporations, and schools. He stipulated that after his and Mary's deaths, Killarney would be given to the Irish government. He retired in 1976 and died on September 9, 1989. Mary followed him in 1998.

MATTHEW M. MCCLOSKEY

Matthew McCloskey was born on February 26, 1893, in Wheeling, West Virginia, the grandson of Irish immigrants. Two years later, the family moved to Philadelphia, which became his home. He left school at the age of 15 and entered the building trade. In 1911, he established his first construction company in partnership with others, and in 1919 he chartered M. M. McCloskey Jr., Inc. The venture was not successful and he filed for bankruptcy in 1923. In six months, the case was discharged and McCloskey later paid all the creditors. He was soon back in business, and by 1930, he had organized McCloskey and Company with headquarters in Philadelphia.

Like McShain, McCloskey soon became a major building contractor. Among his many structures were the Philadelphia Convention Hall, the Sheraton Hotel, Veterans Stadium, the Spectrum, and apartment buildings on Rittenhouse Square. In Washington, he built the District of Columbia Stadium (later named after Robert Kennedy), a new front on the Capitol, and the gigantic House Office Building. He joined McShain investing in the Claridge and other Atlantic City hotels and in buying the Atlantic City transit lines.

Unlike McShain, McCloskey was actively involved in politics. An avid Democrat, in the 1930s he worked to build the Democratic Party in Philadelphia, raising money by sponsoring a $100 a plate dinner, an innovation he said he created. He was a delegate at the party conventions from 1936 through 1948.

In 1954, he was appointed treasurer of the Democratic National Committee, raising an estimated $20,000,000 during his seven-year term. He became a good friend of John F. Kennedy, who appointed him ambassador to Ireland in 1962. He was involved in political scandals in Washington concerning his contract to build the District of Columbia Stadium and was forced to resign as ambassador in June, 1964. The Democrats, who controlled Congress, eventually let the matter drop. He spent his last years quietly in Philadelphia, where he died on April 26, 1973.

extended; the AC&S management "had grown old in office," and had poor public relations; the Ocean City line was unprofitable; and the railroad, as a matter of policy, should not be in the city transportation business. The buyers had adequate finances and could be expected to improve service. The proceeds could be used to retire some West Jersey and Seashore bonds, saving the PRR and the Reading about $35,000 annually in interest payments. Both presidents gave their approval of a sale, and the PRR board concurred at the end of February.

Negotiations with the Probable Buyers

By February 20, 1945, the PRR was ready to make a commitment to sell its trolley line. On that day, John Deasy met John McShain and his attorney, Thomas Munyan, in his office. They agreed that the PRR sell the Atlantic Avenue line to McShain's group for $1,000,000, subject to approval by the controlling railroads. The lease with the AC&S, due to expire on December 18, was to remain in effect until that date. The PRR attorneys would draw up a formal agreement of sale.

While the lawyers were at work, Munyan asked if the final settlement, probably to be made later in the year, could be back-dated to the time of the agreement, so that any profits would accrue to the McShain group rather than the PRSL. Deasy rejected this request. He also insisted that Munyan start talking to Leo Isenthal so he could make plans about the future operations of the AC&S.

A Dispute over the Summer Receipts of the Atlantic Avenue and Longport Line

Thomas Munyan's request that payments made by the AC&S should be given to the buyers, retroactive to March, touched off a dispute between the seller and buyers. Such an understanding meant the McShain group rather than the railroad would receive the lucrative summer receipts. Munyan argued the retroactive payment was justified because the PRR could not settle without the prior approval of the PUC, and he claimed Deasy had agreed to this in a telephone conversation.

Albert Ward, the PRR general attorney, pointed out the McShain group was then making only a down payment, and was not scheduled to pay in full until settlement sometime later. Munyan countered that McShain was willing to pay the railroad two percent interest on the unpaid balance, but this would amount only to a fraction of the heavy summer receipts.

On March 13, Munyan called Deasy on the phone to resolve the dispute. The vice-president emphatically stated he had not agreed to any retroactive payment of AC&S rentals. He expected the McShain group to make a deposit of $5,000 on the date of signing

Above: Although it looks stately as it rolls down Atlantic Avenue, the Shore Fast Line train headed by car 113 was a money-loser. John McShain did not want the line but was forced by the Board of Public Utility Commissioners to buy it in order to preserve the regional transportation system operated by the AC&S. Abandoning this line was high on the agenda of the new owners. David H. Cope photo, Richard Allman collection

the agreement of sale, and the balance on the later settlement date. In the interim, the PRSL would continue to receive the monthly AC&S payments. He was willing to speak to McShain as soon as the sale agreement was completed.

The Agreement of Sale is Signed

By mid-March, shortly after the above conversation, the attorneys completed the sale agreement, signed on March 15. Under its terms, the sellers (the WJ&S and the PRSL) conveyed all properties and lands, including the trolley line, the carbarn, shops, and office building at the Inlet; equipment; licenses and Absecon Island bus franchises, to the buyers for $1,000,000. The settlement was to take place in Philadelphia on a date to be determined later.

The new owners agreed to honor the lease held by the AC&S until its December 18 termination date. They granted the PRSL trackage rights on Atlantic Avenue between Ohio and Georgia Avenues so the railroad could serve the one freight customer on the line, the Atlantic City Lumber Company, for a fee of one dollar per loaded car. The right of the Ocean City cars to use Atlantic Avenue between Georgia and Virginia avenues was guaranteed. Munyan made a down payment of $5,000, and he and Deasy signed the document. The WJ&S board approved it a week later.

The sale of the Atlantic Avenue line did not remain secret for long. On March 19, the newspapers reported the buyers were a group of Philadelphia area financiers and named specifically John McShain and Matthew McCloskey, represented by Thomas Munyan, who refused to provide details.

The Public Utilities Commissioners Urge Modifications to the Agreement

On April 6, 1945, the PRR sent an application for approval of the sale to the Board of Public Utility Commissioners. The board had reservations. It wanted more information about the buyers and their financial arrangements. It was particularly concerned about maintaining through service between Absecon Island and the other communities, which could be shattered by breaking the regional transit system currently existing under the AC&S control. The PRR assured the board it was willing to continue the trackage rights agreement for the Shore Fast Line cars, and the buyers asserted they were willing to allow the AC&S to continue its service from Atlantic City to the mainland towns and to Ocean City. They also stated they were forming a new company, to be called the Atlantic City Transportation Company (ACTC), to operate the Absecon Island trolley and bus lines.

In May, McShain and McCloskey hired J. O. Hackenberg, the former general manager of the Pennsylvania-Reading Seashore Lines, who had retired the previous year, to be general manager of the ACTC. At the same time, Raymond Stark, a 21-year employee of the AC&S, who was then chief inspector, was appointed assistant superintendent of the Atlantic Avenue line. A local man, who lived in Ventnor, he was praised in the local papers as an experienced, friendly, competent man, who understood "the human equation."

In the same month, the buyers decided to ensure they would receive the summer rentals and profits from the trolley line. Consequently, they paid the balance of $995,000 to the PRR. This strengthened the Munyan argument that the AC&S receipts should be turned over to the ACTC as of May.

The Buyers Are Welcomed by the Business Community

By this time, since everyone knew the line was changing hands, the local business community hosted a "sumptuous banquet" in the Claridge Hotel attended by 78 people to welcome John McShain and Matthew McCloskey to their ranks. The waiters and orchestra members were dressed as motormen and conductors. A miniature trolley was pulled along the banquet table as the gathering sang "The Trolley Song." McShain and McCloskey voiced their appreciation and promised to make improvements but offered no specifics.

The AC&S Lease is Modified

In Philadelphia, Leo Isenthal was trying to salvage as much as possible from the impending change of ownership. He had met Munyan in March, who had not shown much interest in having the AC&S continue to operate the line. Recognizing his weak position, Isenthal now concentrated on selling the Ocean City Division to the new owners for as much as he could get.

In June, Deasy and Munyan made an agreement to modify the AC&S lease of the Atlantic Avenue and Longport Line, effective July 1. From that date until December 18, the AC&S was to continue to operate the line, but as an agent of, and for the account of, the PRSL. Isenthal accepted this change. The net revenue was to be turned over to the PRSL each month as usual. This agreement was approved by the PUC at the end of July.

McShain and McCloskey Are Forced to Buy More Than They Wanted

A series of meetings and agreements took place in the second half of 1945 which resulted in the McShain group taking over all the AC&S operations, however reluctantly. Early in June, the PUC invited all the interested parties to a meeting in their Newark office. The commissioners did not favor a divided transportation system in the Atlantic City region and they strongly intimated the new transportation company should acquire all of the AC&S properties, including the Shore Fast Line, the two Atlantic City-Ocean City bus lines, the Ocean City local route, and the Pleasantville-Absecon line. Leo Isenthal was completely in favor of this view, and the McShain group was forced to agree.

The PRR and the new ACTC modified their revenue

Above: An unwanted stepchild included in the purchase of the AC&S by the McShain-McCloskey group, the Shore Fast Line interurban was running on borrowed time. Cars 112 and 119 prepare to depart from Pleasantville on their way to Atlantic City. Karel Liebenauer photo, LeRoy O. King, Jr. collection

agreement. Rental payments for the Atlantic Avenue line received after May 1, and profits received after July 1, were to be transmitted directly to the ACTC. That company, in turn, was to divide the funds equally between John McShain, Inc., and a McCloskey corporation. The buyers also agreed to be responsible for all claims and liabilities on the properties after July 1. The PUC approved these arrangements on June 26, with the added reminder that the PRR was still responsible for making the operational changes it had ordered as a result of its earlier hearing on the Samuel Backer complaints.

Accepting the fact that the ACTC would have to buy the AC&S lines, the McShain group negotiated with the PRR for trackage rights to operate the Shore Fast Line. The PRR executives imposed stiff terms, even though they knew the line was unprofitable. The ACTC would have to pay 7¾ cents per car mile on the Newfield and Somers Point Branches, pay all maintenance costs based on their usage of these lines, and assume the salaries of the operators of the Thorofare drawbridge. The railroad reserved the right to convert the Newfield Branch to single track and remove the third rail, with the ACTC responsible for erecting trolley wire.

John McShain was not satisfied with these terms, and in August he met with John Deasy and argued the 7¾ cents mileage charge was too high. He must have been persuasive, because Deasy lowered the rate to 4 cents per mile, retroactive to July 1. This reduced the annual mileage fee from approximately $29,300 to $15,100. The ACTC filed a petition with the PUC asking for approval of the acquisition.

Negotiations with Stern and Silverman

McShain and McCloskey also began negotiations with Leo Isenthal for the purchase of AC&S rail and bus equipment, the bus franchises, and their tracks in Atlantic City, Ocean City, and across the Great Egg Harbor Bay. Isenthal was concerned about certain capital expenditures he had made, which were normally the responsibility of the PRSL. They included a $500 deposit on new buses and $1,000 for a new welding machine. McShain assured him that he would personally guarantee to reimburse Isenthal

CHAPTER TEN | *The Pennsylvania Railroad Bows Out*

should the PUC not approve the purchase. For the AC&S and its related companies, Isenthal was forced to accept McShain's top offer of $162,000, for assets that on paper were valued at well over $1,000,000. To pay for these acquisitions, the ACTC proposed to execute a mortgage of $500,000, secured by bonds, and to issue preferred and class A and B common stock valued at $672,000.

A New Manager is Installed

As negotiations continued, McShain had to select a new general manager to handle the daily operations of the transit system, a task neither he nor Matthew McCloskey wanted. On September 21, J. O. Hackenberg, who had been appointed general manager in May, announced he was retiring but would continue in "an advisory capacity." Munyan said had "rendered a very valuable service" to the public and the company.

To replace him, the McShain group hired an experienced transportation executive, Tallmadge Conover. A graduate of Harvard in 1920, he spent seven years with the engineering firm of Stone and Webster. He then became a superintendent with the St. Louis Public Service Company and with the Peoples Motor Bus Company of St. Louis. Later he became a superintendent of the Southern Pennsylvania Bus Company, which he left in 1943 to serve in various posts with the Office of Defense Transportation, including the Highway Transport Department. Probably his extensive experience with buses appealed to McShain and McCloskey, who expected eventually to convert the rail lines to highway vehicles.

Evidently Conover was not impressed with the work of Assistant Superintendent Raymond Stark, who had been

Above: Among the property of the newly-formed Atlantic City Transportation Company, were the 24 Brilliners. Only five years old, they were still in very good condition even after their recent exertions handling the deluge of wartime riders. This view is inside the Inlet Barn in 1947. Ed Birch photo, Electric City Trolley Museum collection

promoted from chief inspector in May. He was dismissed on December 1 but allowed to return to his former position. No reason was given by Conover for the demotion.

The New Atlantic City Transportation Company Takes Over

Applications for approval of these transactions were submitted to the PUC on November 9, with hearings conducted in Newark on November 27. The next day, the agency issued certificates granting approval of all the changes. Conveyed to the ACTC were the Atlantic Avenue trolley line; the Shore Fast Line; the Atlantic City and Ocean City line across the Great Egg Harbor Bay and on 8th Street in Ocean City; the Central Passenger Railway tracks on Virginia Avenue, and the long unused ones on South Carolina and Adriatic Avenues; the original AC&S tracks, still in place, along Absecon Boulevard and paralleling Marmora Avenue; all overhead wire; the Somers Point substation building; municipal consents for all the bus lines; all electric cars and buses, and all structures and lands previously owned by the sellers. On December 18, 1945, a smooth transition from the AC&S to the ACTC took place, with no visible changes, and service continued undisturbed.

For the first time, the transit routes in the Atlantic City region passed from the hands of the Pennsylvania Railroad companies and the Stern and Silverman organization.
McShain and McCloskey, who bought more than they originally intended, were to find their expectations of a profitable investment was to be tempered by the harsh realities of public transportation in the postwar world.

In Philadelphia, Leo Isenthal and his small staff began to dismantle the complex corporate structure that Stern and Silverman had erected. How the remaining assets were distributed among the stock and bond holders is unknown. Nor is it possible to indicate to what extent, if any, profits were earned. The various companies under the Stern and Silverman banner were intertwined and closely held by a small group of people.

By February 1946, the distribution was complete, and the officers of Stern and Silverman submitted a certificate of election to the Pennsylvania Department of State, certifying that all the stockholders had agreed to dissolve the corporation. Listed as officers were Edwin H. Silverman, president; Leo R. Isenthal, treasurer, and A. Hilton, secretary. The directors were Silverman, Isenthal, and Beatrice Winlein. The Department of State approved the petition, and on July 11, 1946, the firm of Stern and Silverman formally sent articles of dissolution to Harrisburg, certifying that all debts had been paid, property distributed to the stockholders, and no suits pending. On August 9, the Department of State issued a formal certificate of dissolution, signed by the secretary of the commonwealth. Thus, did the firm of Stern and Silverman, originally chartered in February 1907 for a term of 99 years, come quietly to an end. The related corporations, in New Jersey, were also dissolved. It remained to be seen how the new management would meet the challenges facing it in operating a transportation enterprise in the seashore region.

Selected Financial Data: Atlantic City & Shore Railroad, Central Passenger Railway, Atlantic City Transportation Company

Year	Company	Operating Revenues	Operating Expenses	Gross Operating Income	Fixed Charges	Net Income	Operating Ratio
1941	AC&S	$712,263	$543,666	$168,597			70.7%
1941	C. P. Ry	5,885	6,493	(608)			87.9%
1943	AC&S	1,164,483	757,897	406,596	335,058	111,462	53.4%
1943	C.P. Ry	4,803	5,637	(834)	2,000	(2,834)	
1945	AC&S	1,253,582	786,587	466,995	414,198	69,138	58.1%
1945	ACTC	84,865	85,633	(768)	80	688	97.2%
1946	ACTC	1,357,061	1,147,392	209,669	48,073	161,596	
1948	ACTC	1,559,171	1,447,071	112,100	85,947	26,220	84.3%

Source: Public Utilities Commission Reports

CHAPTER TEN | *The Pennsylvania Railroad Bows Out*

Above: *A southbound Brilliner on Atlantic Avenue skirts around the Civil War Soldiers and Sailors Monument at Providence Avenue. The work was dedicated in 1916; the sculptor remains unknown. Anthony F. Krisak photo, Richard Krisak collection*

167

VENTNOR-MARGATE
DOUGLAS AVE ONLY.
FRONT ENTRANCE
FARE READY PLEASE
PLACE 10¢ IN BOX
218

CHAPTER ELEVEN

The Atlantic City Transportation Company

Atlantic City in Decline

The postwar years saw population increases in the region but not in Atlantic City. Compared to 1940, Pennsylvania had 10,488,000 residents in 1950 and 11,319,000 in 1960, increases of six and seven percent, while New Jersey's population grew from 4,835,000 in 1950 to 6,067,000 in 1960, increases of 16 and 25 percent respectively. Philadelphia reached its peak in 1950, with 2,071,600 people, but it had lost 69,000 by 1960, the beginning of a long trend of decline. On Absecon Island, Ventnor, Margate, and Longport gained residents, with 8,150, 4,715, and 618 people respectively in 1950. Atlantic City, however, lost 2,400 people between 1940 and 1950 and another 2,100 by 1960, or over seven percent, giving it a population of 59,544 in 1960. On the mainland, all the communities grew, with 1950 populations of 2,344 in Absecon, 11,938 in Pleasantville, 3,498 in Northfield, 1,925 in Linwood, and 2,480 in Somers Point. Ocean City grew by 1,368 from 1940 to 6,040 residents in 1950. None of these was large enough to provide a strong base for a public transit system.

The population decline in Atlantic City boded ill for the new Atlantic City Transportation Company (ACTC). The Atlantic Avenue line had always been the financial mainstay of the transit system, and the falling city population could not be offset by the gains elsewhere.

Facing Page: : There's activity at Inlet Loop at Brilliner 218 is set to begin a short-turn run to Douglas Avenue while two sister cars wait in the wings. Even into the 1950s, the Brilliners were still clean, well-maintained, and attractive in appearance. Although this was to be the only one of two groups of Brilliners to operate (the other was on Red Arrow Lines), the cars acquitted themselves well. Anthony F. Krisak photo, Richard Krisak collection

Above: Now operated by the Atlantic City Transportation Company, Brilliner 214 stops on Atlantic Avenue at Kentucky Avenue on a southbound run to Longport in 1950. John Stern photo, Fred W. Schneider, III collection

Above: An indication of the poor condition of the track is in this October 1941 view looking south at Atlantic and Coolidge avenues, the border between Margate and Longport. It was no better five years later when the line was examined by the Gilman Company engineers. The necessary rebuilding would be expensive and the new owners did not intend to make such an investment. Jeffrey Marinoff collection

Even more alarming for the prospects of the ACTC was the increase in motor vehicle registrations. New Jersey's vehicle count increased to 1,579,000 in 1950 and 2,400,000 ten years later. Pennsylvania's figures followed the same pattern, jumping to 3,010,000 in 1950 and 4,287,000 in 1960. While many of these drivers never or rarely went to the Jersey shore, the significant fact was that more people had more motor vehicles than ever before and chose their automobiles over public transit. [slight rewording]

Another statistic that should have been disturbing to the managers of the ACTC was the growing disparity in net property valuations in the seashore region. While Atlantic City, with its commercial and entertainment centers, had the highest valuations by far, the value per capita was higher in Ocean City and Longport, while Margate and Ventnor were not far behind. Relatively speaking, Atlantic City had a less affluent population than its neighboring towns, and consequently most of the region was less dependent on public transportation.

Atlantic City was far from alone in experiencing declining ridership in the postwar era. Nationally, in the period between 1945 and 1956, revenue transit passengers carried by rail fell from 12,124,000 to 2,756,000 and bus passengers dropped from 9,886,000 to 7,043,000. This decline was a harbinger of the end of privately-owned transit systems and their replacement by publicly-owned, heavily-subsidized authorities. The plain fact was that automobiles, operating on highways and streets built and maintained by all taxpayers, were too mobile, numerous, and popular for mass transit to compete effectively in the area.

Changing Public Perceptions

Contributing to Atlantic City's decline were changes in public tastes and perceptions in the postwar period. Atlantic City was seen as somewhat dated and worn, and too urban when more people were attracted to suburban living and less crowded communities. Other seashore resorts, easily reached by automobiles, increased in popularity. Ocean City, claiming to be the greatest family resort, attracted numerous visitors, in spite of (or perhaps because of) retaining its prohibition on the public sale and consumption of alcoholic beverages. Sea Isle City, Avalon, and Stone Harbor became more appealing; Wildwood, with its wide beaches and many Boardwalk amusements, catered to a younger crowd, while Cape May, the oldest of the resorts, marketed its Victorian architecture and myriad shops. Collectively, these resorts slowly eclipsed Atlantic City's claim to be "the Showplace of the Nation."

With improvements in highways and the expansion of air travel, people could seek rest and relaxation as well as new experiences in distant places, here and abroad. The ease of travel, coupled with economic prosperity and the proliferation of automobiles, made the idea of a trip to Atlantic City less attractive than it had been.

The opening of the Atlantic City Race Course in 1946 in nearby McKee City did stimulate, at least periodically, passenger loads as special buses were operated to the track. For a time, movies and theatres still enjoyed good patronage, but the new medium of television by 1949 kept many people at home and thereby reduced transit riding. Inflation, higher fares, and increased labor costs presented new challenges to management.

The piers and Boardwalk amusements continued to draw visitors, but in declining numbers. Gimmicks, such as weddings under the sea in the Steel Pier diving bell, generated publicity but not crowds, and a 1949 fire damaged much of the Million Dollar Pier. Night life remained popular, and many restaurants offered a variety of food, but similar establishments could be found elsewhere.

Atlantic City became a fading resort, beset by a corrupt municipal government, a growing number of poor residents, a falling population, outdated amusements, and Boardwalk establishments that satisfied past generations but could not appeal to postwar Americans. Collectively, these trends meant the ACTC faced a difficult future.

The Atlantic City Transportation Company Takes Control

As the new organization assumed responsibility for conducting transportation in the resort area, John McShain hired the New York engineering firm of W. C. Gilman & Company to study the property and make recommendations for its operations. Gilman engineers inspected all facilities and operations, spoke with supervisors, and reviewed operating and maintenance practices. Their report, submitted in December 1946, made grim reading for

Above: *Not all days in Atlantic City were warm, sunny, and bright. On a cold rainy day War Board car No. 6889 rolls down Atlantic Avenue. No doubt passengers welcomed the dry interior and warmth provided by the electric heaters. Despite their age and the disdain in which they were held by the press and city, The cars gave good service for many years and reflected the quality of the work done by its builder, the J.G. Brill Company.* LeRoy O. King, Jr. collection

McShain and Matthew McCloskey.

Gilman found the Ocean City Division obsolete, with "antiquated" cars, and track, bridges, and overhead wire "in need of extensive rehabilitation." Because of the high cost of such improvements, and the financial losses on the route, the report suggested bus substitution should be considered. The same conclusion was drawn for the Atlantic Avenue line, which, despite its modern cars, suffered from "very poor" track and overhead conditions. The engineers estimated a cost of $650,000 to rehabilitate the line and suggested a study to determine if buses were a better option.

To meet jitney competition, the firm recommended establishing a bus line on Pacific Avenue with a potential of up to $250,000 in annual revenues. Like Thomas Conway before them, the engineers ignored the difficulty of dealing with the jitney operators and the municipal government.

A more useful proposal was to institute the sale of tokens, to install fare boxes, and to introduce promotional or seasonal fares to stimulate riding. Another recommendation was to revise the outdated reporting forms in order to give a clearer picture of financial returns.

Presuming rail service continued, the Gilman Company urged a study to determine whether to install new rail or to continue the current practice of replacing only short sections of worn rail with thermit-weld joints. In either case, portable crossovers should be used to better maintain service when repairs were underway; more mechanical equipment should be acquired, and work be done at night, something not likely to please nearby residents.

The engineers found preventive maintenance practices on equipment were weak and needed improvements. The shop machinery was described as "old and antiquated," and they urged that the current overhead shaft and pulley system should be replaced with individual motor drives on the machines. The automotive shop was particularly wanting and needed new machine tools.

The Gilman agents reported service could be improved by more short-turn runs and the supplemental use of buses. Supervisors needed training to improve their efficiency, and they suggested the use of aptitude tests to improve the quality of the motormen. More frequent changes of schedules could eliminate unnecessary services and reduce expenses. An aggressive campaign to improve relations with the public and city officials, utilizing extensive advertising needed to be undertaken. Also missing were means of controlling expenses and a process of planning for future changes. Labor costs needed to be more carefully controlled, as the terms of current labor agreements were "rather drastic for a small property."

The engineers stated the company's facilities could support a much larger system, and they recommended the firm expand its operations over a greater geographic area to enhance its prospects. The current management lacked "a general overall knowledge of good transit operations," but this could be improved by proper training and education. Overall, they recommended more and better planning and policies to improve the company's operations and prospects.

Above: *On an unknown date a Brilliner speeds south on Atlantic Avenue in Margate. The full skirting and Loewy paint scheme give the car its streamlined appearance and it rode well over the rough open track.* Lester K. Wismer photo, Richard Allman collection

CHAPTER ELEVEN | *The Atlantic City Transportation Company*

The immediate reaction of McShain and McCloskey is not known, but the weaknesses and recommendations in the report could not have been a complete surprise after a year's experience in running the company. While business was fairly good at the moment, it was already showing signs of decline as automobiles proliferated and changes in public tastes took hold. Neither owner was committed to rail service, and they intended to abandon the Shore Fast Line as soon as possible. They were sufficiently impressed with Gilman's work that they signed a contract for an additional year of advice, studies, and recommendations from the New York firm.

hard worker, he had many interests besides the Transportation Company; nonetheless, he kept a sharp eye on its affairs. He was always courteous and polite with his managers in Atlantic City, but sometimes he would display impatience at a slow response to an inquiry or shock at the deterioration of the financial condition of the company. Overall, he had good relations with his employees.

Above: Ford Transit buses were used on the Atlantic City local lines. In this December 3, 1950 view, buses 309 and 304 are at the Atlantic City terminal at Tennessee Avenue awaiting their departure times. These short lines were unprofitable but they were maintained to forestall competition. Motor Bus Society Library

Managing the Atlantic City Transportation Company

Most of the stock in the new company was held by McShain and McCloskey, with a small amount held by Attorney Thomas Munyan. Both the primary owners took a direct interest in the property, posing questions and making recommendations and decisions on a number of matters. Generally, they seemed to get along well, although they were competitors in their major profession as building contractors. Neither had any interest in continuing rail service, but the substitution of buses for trolleys could take longer than they had expected.

Although they collaborated closely, McShain seemed to take a more active role than McCloskey, possibly because of his experience with the Trenton Transit Company. Always a

McShain's main office and his residence were in Philadelphia, and he maintained additional offices in Trenton, Baltimore, and Washington. He liked Atlantic City and he was a frequent visitor. He was also close to attorney Thomas Munyan and often sought his advice. He and McShain often consulted and they remained life-long friends.

Matthew McCloskey also took a direct interest in the company, and he and McShain consulted on major questions. In time, as he became more involved in politics, his interest waned, and in 1954 he withdrew from the company.

Tallmadge Conover, who was on-hand when McShain and McCloskey took over, was a transitional manager. He was replaced in 1946 with a more dynamic and energetic manager, Thomas E. Whitehead. With an engineering and mechanical background, he was skilled at making analyses and improving conditions, but ending the downward spiral of passenger loads was beyond his abilities. After nearly a decade of labor, he left the company.

Joseph Hamilton, who remained with the firm for many years, succeeded him. He had been an auditor in the Claridge Hotel, owned by McShain. Impressed by his skills, McShain brought him

173

to the ACTC and made him general manager after Whitehead left. He was knowledgeable and capable, although sometimes irritable, and some felt he was too abrupt and demanding with his subordinates. Nonetheless, he was kind to some people, such as a motorman who was prone to go on occasional drunken binges, but Hamilton kept him on the payroll. A boy in the neighborhood liked to visit the carbarn, and Hamilton was always nice to him. McShain liked Hamilton and appreciated his efforts, giving him bonuses at Christmas time, but he also expected him to handle problems in Trenton and real estate issues too. Eventually, Hamilton took over the company from McShain.

Public Criticism Continues

Although the management was new, complaints from the public continued. An editorial in the Sunday Press in January 1946, criticized crowded cars and overworked operators and again called for two-man crews. In the same month, a disgruntled passenger wrote that he waited in the "cold, cramped unheated, smelly" station at Douglas Avenue for a Longport car that finally arrived after five Margate cars came. To make matters worse, the Longport car was an orange "back-breaker."

Nor were the buses immune to criticism. In October 1945, a

Abandonment of the Madison Avenue Loop

As noted earlier, an emergency loop had been constructed at Madison and Maine avenues in 1945 on order of the Board of Public Utility Commissioners to provide an alternate loop for the Atlantic Avenue cars when the regular loop at the Inlet was flooded during storms and abnormally high tides. Ironically, the loop had never been used, since at the end of the war the city constructed a seawall and a bulkhead along Absecon Inlet, effectively stopping the street flooding. At the same time, the ACTC shortened the Inlet loop and moved it 200 feet inland in order to sell land to Captain Starn's Restaurant for parking. The grade of the new loop was raised nine inches, providing further protection. Several storms in 1946 and 1947 demonstrated the new seawall was effective and no flooding occurred. Consequently, the company appealed to the Public Utility Commissioners to permit the removal of the Madison Avenue loop. In March 1948 the PUC approved the request. The work was done by the PRSL at a cost of $878.

Serving the Atlantic City Race Course

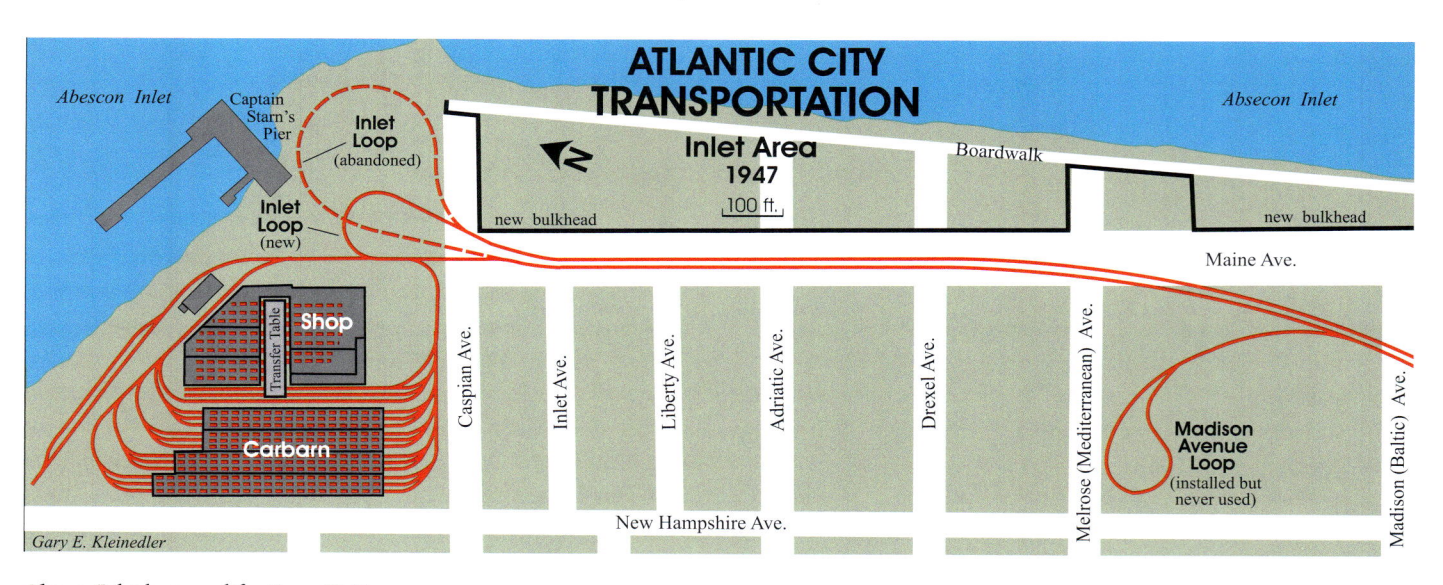

Above: *Inlet loop modifications, 1947.*

patron of the Bungalow Park Line complained of the "extremely poor service" on that route. A 7:10 A.M. bus was filled by students, and there were no buses between 8:40 A.M. and 1:30 P.M. The writer asked for larger buses and more frequent schedules. In reply, Tallmadge Conover noted that ten new buses were on order and expected soon. He pointed out the vehicles on the line seated 21, and the usual load was 25 to 30; he did not regard this as overcrowding. He promised the company would analyze the service when the new buses were on hand and make the necessary adjustments.

The end of the war stimulated renewed economic activities in the region. A major project was the construction of a new race track off the Black Horse Pike near Mays Landing, about 14 miles from Atlantic City. Among the backers were Philadelphia building contractor John B. Kelly and several wealthy businessmen, plus a number of Hollywood personalities. Matthew McCloskey won the contract to build the facility, and the total cost was over $3,000,000. The track opened on July 22, 1946, to a large crowd of racing fans.

Interest was such that the Pennsylvania-Reading Seashore

CHAPTER ELEVEN | *The Atlantic City Transportation Company*

Above: Former Indiana Service Corporation car now ACTC 296 is on a charter run for the National Railway Historical Society. It is seen near the end of the line in Longport on May 11, 1947. The car looked attractive in its modified Loewy black and cream livery, but its riding quality left something to be desired. The former Ft. Wayne cars were hastily purchased to relieve the pressure of the immediate postwar period when riding remained heavy. Soon ridership went into its inevitable decline and the cars were made surplus, seeing only limited service in later years. M.D. McCarter photo, Fred W. Schneider, III collection

Lines constructed a spur to the track and ran race trains from Philadelphia. The ACTC hastened to establish bus links to the new attraction. Management scrambled to buy enough buses to serve the routes. New buses were not yet available, so the company purchased 31 used vehicles from various sources. All were old, pre-war models, mostly White and Yellow coaches built between 1929 and 1935. The service was advertised extensively, including banners attached to the sides of the Brilliners.

The main route began at Albany and Atlantic Avenues and ran on Albany Avenue Boulevard and Black Horse Pike to the track. Fares ranged from 15 cents to 60 cents, depending on the distance traveled. The line operated only during the racing season and carried only passengers going to and from the track. Additional routes ran from Ocean City and Pomona. The PUC approved 16 "consents" for the main route, nine for Ocean City and twelve for the Pomona service.

The race track lines were moderately successful. For example, on July 31, 1946, the buses carried 29 passengers from Ocean City, 416 from Pomona, and 1,124 from Atlantic City, earning revenues of $30, $146, and $737 respectively, or a total of $913.

Additional Cars are Purchased

The AC&S had struggled through the war years with only 37 city cars and it had been subjected to intense criticism for its service. The new owners were anxious to improve operations quickly, and since a number of cars were out-of-service for repairs, they decided to purchase additional ones. As with the buses, only older cars were available, and the company selected six, well-worn cars from the Indiana Service Corporation of Fort Wayne, Indiana. Built by the St. Louis Car Company in 1924 and 1925, they were one-man, lightweight, double-end models, with 26-inch wheels. Powered by four, 25-horsepower motors, they seated 44 passengers on rattan, reversible seats. Five interior lamps in the center of the ceiling provided illumination. The cars were numbered 294 to 299 and painted black and cream.

They entered service on June 22, 1946, and soon revealed their limitations. Only marginally better than the older War Board cars, they were slow and much nosier, with their motors emitting a loud, high-pitched whine. As traffic fell in the postwar years, they saw limited use.

Modifying the Rail Car Fleet

The ACTC made few changes to the elderly War Board cars. No. 6845 was renumbered 245 and painted black and cream. In time, sisters 6846-6850 were also repainted and renumbered to 246-250. The other six cars retained their orange paint until the end. No changes were made to the dreary interior of these cars, with their dark brown paint, bare light bulbs, worn celluloid standee straps, and rattan seats.

The Brilliners were renumbered 201-225. As they were repainted, the silver trim was omitted, but they retained their basic black and cream Raymond Loewy design. Interiors were bright and well maintained. More fundamental changes were made by T. E. Whitehead, who designed new doors that could be built in quantity, with spares kept in stock for quick replacement. The upper windows were enlarged and changed to a rectangular style providing improved visibility. Whitehead also extended the life of the car wheels by correcting an imperfection that the manufacturers of the wheels had overlooked.

Whitehead's most significant improvement was solving the motor bearing problem, a cause of frequent failures and locked wheels, immobilizing the cars. He estimated that such failures in 1945 alone had cost the AC&S $35,000 in repair costs. The number of disabled cars was a contributing factor in the decision to purchase the six cars from Fort Wayne. Determined to solve the problem, Whitehead contacted the Brill Company and was told the problem was sand penetrating the gearboxes. The SKF Ball Bearing Company of Philadelphia, manufacturer the bearings, supported Brill's explanation. While riding a car, Whitehead noticed "an abnormal humming noise in the trucks." He had the car returned to the shop, where an inspection of the bearings showed "that the cage had become loose and was about to disintegrate," a possible cause of the failures plaguing the cars. An examination of the bearings and oil convinced him that both Brill and SKF were giving the company "the run-around." He concluded the bearing failures were due to "an improper design" by the Brill Company.

Whitehead consulted the chief engineer of the Marlin Rockwell Company who agreed with his views. He provided drawings for a new type of bearing without charge. When installed, the bearing failures were greatly reduced. In two weeks, there were only seven failures, and five of them were in cars where the older bearings were still in place. The new type served for over 100,000 miles, in contrast to 15,000 miles for the original bearings. Whitehead claimed his modifications saved the company $25,000 annually.

Other minor changes to the Brilliners included replacing the names of the Absecon Island towns on the letterboard with the

Above: In its new black and cream paint scheme, War Board car No. 246 navigates the Douglas Avenue loop in Margate. Only half of the twelve War Board cars were repainted in this livery; the others retained their traditional orange and cream colors. Unfortunately, nothing was done to brighten the drab interiors. Lester K. Wismer photo, Richard Allman collection

phrase "The Miss America Fleet." Advertising panels were installed on the front of the car, over the headlight, and on each side of the center doors. The cars continued to roll, in their attractive paint scheme, until the end of service.

Changes in Management Policies and Practices

As was to be expected, a number of changes were made as the new officers took over, especially Thomas E. Whitehead. An early decision was to change the percentage of overhead costs charged to the Shore Fast Line. The AC&S had charged only nine percent to that division, probably to reduce its operating losses. Whitehead maintained that was unrealistic and he increased the charge to 25 percent, the percentage of the total car miles run by the Ocean City cars. This change in accounting was certain to increase the losses and strengthen the company's effort to abandon the line.

In November 1948, the general manager did a month-by-month analysis of the number of passengers carried on the Atlantic Avenue trolleys. He found they fell from 14,827,000 in 1946, to 13,794,000 in 1947, and to 9,868,000 for the ten months of 1948. Every month showed a decline, the most severe being in the summer. In percentage terms, June passengers fell 30 percent, and July and August loads fell 26 percent in each month.

Whitehead instituted a program of reducing the work force, partly because of lower traffic loads and partly by introducing more efficient practices. The number of supervisory personnel was cut from 27 in 1946 to 18 in 1950, who did the same work for less money. Payroll costs fell from $8,000 to $6,000 monthly. The

Above: A photo from the roof of the Inlet Barn affords one a view of the new and smaller loop at the Inlet. Land occupied by the original loop was sold to Captain Starn's restaurant for parking. The first loop circled the outer edge of the property and the covered shed used to protect waiting passengers is still in place on the left. Also depicted is the new seawall installed by the city adjoining Maine Avenue which ended the flooding in this location. The Boardwalk is over the waters of the Absecon Inlet. The view also shows the flat roofs of the three Brilliners on the lead track. No shrouds were at the bases of the trolley poles which could be turned if the cars had to run in reverse during an emergency. No trace of this scene exists today. Jeffrey Marinoff collection

general manager noted total payrolls in 1950 were lower than in 1947, despite a wage increase of 39 cents per hour granted to union employees. This was accomplished by a 27 percent reduction in man-hours.

Salaries paid to managers were gradually increased. Whitehead's salary rose from $480 monthly in 1946 to $600 four years later. Joseph Hamilton earned $350 a month in 1947 and $450 in 1950. Overall, lower rank managers earned about $300 monthly in 1950. As union workers gained wage increases, it was necessary to increase managers' pay proportionally.

Whitehead changed insurance practices. The AC&S was self-insured, setting aside two percent of gross revenues to cover liability claims. The ACTC, however, had a policy with an insurance company whose basic rate was 3.49 percent of gross revenues. In addition, each employee was given a $500 life insurance policy whose premiums were paid by the ACTC.

To improve the company's image, Whitehead urged the hiring of a public relations firm to handle publicity for an annual fee of $10,000. McShain supported the idea but McCloskey did not. McShain admitted it was something of a gamble but he felt it would benefit the company. He urged Whitehead to see McCloskey and promised to accept whatever decision they made.

The company continued the advertising practices of its predecessor by placing frequent, small, double-column ads in the local newspapers, promoting services such as streamlined trolleys, race track buses, and explaining such innovations as new fare boxes and the sale of tokens. A new practice was converting individual War Board cars into rolling billboards by painting them white or similar colors and then using darker colors for promoting attractions such as pageants, Steel Pier acts, the Miss America contest, and certain films, such as 1951's A Streetcar Named Desire. These cars might run only a week or two and then they had to be repainted for another promotion or back into their regular colors. The revenue from these mobile advertisements was sufficient to cover the time and expense of the modification.

Another means of increasing revenues was the sale of small lots and properties acquired with the purchase of the AC&S. A total of 32 parcels were identified. One lot was adjacent to the Longport loop, including the old steamboat pier and riparian rights. Another was the right-of-way of the Shore Fast Line between Somers Point and Ocean City over the three islands in Great Egg Harbor Bay. Other lots were on Marmora Avenue along the original route of the Shore Fast Line from Atlantic City. Most of these had frontage on Marmora Avenue, but they were narrow in depth from the street. For example, the site of the old carbarns had a street frontage of 412 feet but a depth of only 94 feet. Some lots were of odd shapes suitable only for transportation purposes.

The most obvious method of increasing revenues was to raise fares, and this was done several times, with disappointing results. The PUC was slow to approve the increases and sometimes reduced the amount requested. In February, 1948, the company asked for an increase from seven to ten cents for basic fares. While this was granted, tokens were sold at a slightly reduced rate, although only 20 percent of the riders used them. Because the

Above: *Not long out of Inlet Loop, Brilliner 217 leaves a jitney in its wake as it passes Hackney's Seafood Restaurant on a short-turn run to Douglas Avenue in Margate. Hackney's was a block long and could accommodate over 3,200 diners at one time. Note the modified door glass and addition of an advertising rack to the front of the car. The scene is from April 17, 1954, and business owners were looking forward to the approaching summer season.* John Brinckmann photo

number of passengers carried declined, the expected $270,000 in increased revenues was only about $150,000.

In 1952, the company applied for a further increase, and the right to eliminate all reduced fare tickets and school fares with the intent of increasing annual revenues by an estimated $110,000. After a delay, the PUC approved the increase but denied permission to eliminate the reduced rates. As other transit companies learned, increased revenues were offset by declines in ridership, making the earning of profits increasingly difficult.

Fire on the Great Egg Harbor Trestle

In September 1946, a fire of undetermined origin damaged a section of the trestle over the Great Egg Harbor Bay. No effort was made to repair the trestle, since McShain and McCloskey had already decided to abandon the Shore Fast Line. One car was temporarily isolated in Ocean City, but it was started, and with no one on board, it slowly rolled over the trestle and safely reached the mainland in Somers Point.

carry passengers to Ocean City, a shuttle bus ran over the nearby 9th Street causeway linking Somers Point with the seaside resort.

The ACTC Proposes to Abandon the Shore Fast Line

From the beginning, the new owners agreed that the Shore Fast Line, forced on them by the PUC, should be converted to buses. Early in 1947, they informally advised the Pennsylvania-Reading Seashore Lines they were seeking the approval of the various towns served by the line to substitute buses for the trolleys. The cars were old and worn out, and the Pleasantville-Somers Point tracks needed extensive repairs, the responsibility of the ACTC. The transit company wanted the PRSL to join them in their forthcoming application to the PUC. From an economic point of view, abandoning the trolley service was a sensible and logical step, but it also posed some questions for the owner of the property, the Pennsylvania Railroad.

Harry Babcock, general manager of the PRSL, informed

Above: A War Board car painted as an advertising billboard pauses at the Longport loop on July 4, 1952. The ACTC found it profitable to paint these cars to showcase different events. The painting was always professionally done and could not help but attract attention as it rolled by. The advertising cars were used mostly during the summer months. Robert L. Long photo

Thereafter, cars went a short distance on to the trestle, where the crew changed ends, and then returned to the shore, switching to the inbound track. Cluster lights were installed on a pole to facilitate the process. The two drawbridges were left open for maritime traffic. To

John Deasy, PRR vice-president, and Revelle W. Brown, Reading Company president, at that time president and vice-president respectively of the PRSL, of the impending abandonment. He sought their advice on whether the PRSL should join the ACTC in the application to the state agency. Noting the possibility of some opposition to ending rail service, Babcock feared if the ACTC gained approval, the PUC might force the PRSL to establish substitute rail service on the line. At best, the Somers Point Branch was marginal to the railroad. By then PRR was following a policy of abandoning unprofitable branches in order to reduce the line's annual losses. He suggested it might be best for the PRSL to apply separately to the PUC to abandon all service on the line "to avoid any complications that might arise in being forced to maintain some semblance of passenger service on the branch."

In response to Babcock's questions, Brown pointed out to Deasy that when the PRSL made an agreement with the ACTC in November 1945, granting them the right to continue rail service on the Shore Fast Line for a minimum of two years, both parties expected that buses would replace the trolleys. Fearing the PUC might order the PRSL to operate passenger service on the branch, he concluded it would be best not to join the ACTC in its application but simply to lie low, since no steam passenger trains had run on the line for forty years. Should any party seek to force the railroad to provide such service, the PRSL should threaten to abandon the line entirely. The PRR executives, including President Walter Franklin, agreed with Brown and the PRSL took no part in the abandonment proceedings.

The ACTC Applies to Substitute Buses for Rail Cars on the Shore Fast Line

On April 8, 1947, the ACTC formally applied to the Board of Public Utility Commissioners for permission to substitute buses for trolleys on the Shore Fast Line. The bus route was to be 16.4 miles long and the running time one hour. The petition noted all the towns involved had agreed to the change, except the City of Linwood, where there were strong objections. The company asked for authority to use Linwood's streets, with doors closed, but this was denied. Attachments contained maps, schedules, fares, and other information. The company argued that public convenience and necessity would be better served by buses than by trolleys.

The buses followed essentially the same route as the trolleys. Beginning at Virginia Avenue and the Boardwalk, they were to run on Atlantic Avenue to Albany Avenue, and by that road and the Atlantic City-Pleasantville Boulevard to Pleasantville, and then south on the Shore Road to Somers Point, and over the highway causeway to 9th Street in Ocean City, then over West Avenue to 8th Street, to the Boardwalk. Some short-turn trips would use streets in Northfield to serve local neighborhoods and to reverse directions to return to Atlantic City.

Except for Linwood, the other towns approved the bus conversion, although not without some objections. In each case, however, there were more who favored the change than opposed it.

Above: *On an unknown date a Shore Fast Line car is about to cross the swing bridge over the channel nears Somers point. The expense of operating the two bridges and maintaining the long wood trestle made the decision to end service to Ocean City an easy one for ACTC management, especially after the September 1946 bridge fire.* Charles Wagner photo, Fred W. Schneider, III collection

CHAPTER ELEVEN | *The Atlantic City Transportation Company*

Above: In a scene recorded after the bridge fire, Shore Fast Line car 108 has arrived at the Somers Point station (seen in background) while a connecting bus for Ocean City waits. From September 1946 until the final abandonment of the line in January 1948, Somers Point was the terminal for Shore Fast Line trains. Lester K. Wismer photo, Richard Allman collection

The Linwood Objections

In Linwood, a group of individuals known as The Mainland Citizens League, were joined by the local government in objecting to the change and to the operation of the buses through their town, even though the Atlantic City and Shore had done so for many years. This group hired an attorney to represent them.

At public meetings and in polls and petitions circulated through the town, a majority of respondents indicated they preferred the trolleys, although they did not say they rode them. Consequently, the opponents submitted a 20-page brief to the PUC containing their objections. Essentially, the protestors charged the ACTC with planning to keep the profitable Atlantic Avenue line but deliberately refusing to maintain and modernize the Ocean City Division. Their attorney presented a one-sided argument against the changes, accusing the ACTC of presenting a misleading and distorted application.

Linwood claimed the removal of the trolleys could result in lower property values and result in higher taxes. The town stated the Shore Road was too narrow and hazardous to support buses, even though they currently operated on it. Their attorney complained some people would have to walk greater distances, despite the every-corner bus stops planned by the company; that there were no shelters to protect the public; that the buses would likely be unable to meet their schedules, and that school children would be inconvenienced. Attorney Thomas Munyan rebutted these arguments in a memorandum, rejected by Linwood. Nonetheless, on October 23, the PUC approved the abandonment.

The End of the Shore Fast Line

After receiving permission to convert the line, the company set the date of Sunday, January 18, 1948, for the last day of rail service. Beginning at 2 P.M. that day, the first of the new buses entered service, while car 105 made the final run from Somers Point. The Press, never a friend of trolleys, published a photograph of a two-car train, with the phrase "Farewell, Old Rattletraps" above it. In a sarcastic caption, the paper said "the loveable old specimens will no longer leak rainwater on people's heads, stall in the meadows, or zip through the offshore communities at a breathless ten miles per hour." The cars were stored at the Inlet for about a year and then scrapped. They had served a commendable 42 years.

James N.J. Henwood

Top View: Car 101 has stopped at the ticket office and waiting room on Virginia Avenue near Atlantic Avenue circa 1947. Signs abound advertising cigars, cigarettes, and salt water taffy as well as the trolley service. The car will turn left onto Atlantic Avenue on its way to Linwood. The rails of the original route out of Virginia Avenue to Absecon Boulevard and Marmora Avenue are still in place although unused since 1936. David H. Cope photo, Richard Allman collection **Above:** In this view from the highway bridge, an Ocean City-bound car has stopped at the Somers Point station beyond which lies the long trestle over the Great Egg Harbor Bay. Double track ended at this point. Substituting buses would permit the company to eliminate the expense of maintaining the trestle and two bridges. Bus access to Ocean City would be over the publicly-maintained highway bridge paralleling the Shore Fast Line trestle. Such economic realities helped to end rail service, however attractive it still appeared to some. M.D. McCarter photo, LeRoy O. King, Jr. collection

Dismantling the Shore Fast Line

Following the cessation of trolley service, the PRSL began the process of converting its lines to diesel freight operation. The effort was not easy, as it involved the modification of the power supply and signal systems for the Thoroughfare drawbridges and the engine facilities and station in Atlantic City. The Atlantic City, or Meadows, substation was closed and replaced by a new facility, near Atlantic Tower, served by the Atlantic City Electric Company. One track and all electric traction facilities between Pleasantville and Atlantic Avenue were removed.

On the Somers Point Branch, the ACTC removed the overhead wire and line poles, while the railroad retired one track and the passenger stations. Flashing light signals at highway crossings were removed. The small number of freight customers slowly diminished, and the line was gradually cut back, from south to north. As early as 1950, the PRR considered abandoning the line entirely. Without the trolleys, the Somers Point Branch slowly withered and ultimately disappeared.

The biggest project in the dismantling process was removing the trestle and two drawbridges linking Somers Point and Ocean City, being the responsibility of the ACTC. The wooden trestle was relatively easy to remove, and the piles supporting it were pulled out or cut down to the minimum 2.2-foot level. Also, relatively easy was dismantling the steel drawbridges. A major challenge was removing the concrete piers on which the two bridges sat. Examination showed the piers, whose tops were five feet above the water line, rested 24 feet below the water line on 34 piles. Each pier was surrounded by a timber and pile fender. A Philadelphia contractor noted the timber fenders and supporting piles could be removed by a floating crane, and the concrete piers could be shattered into little pieces by small charges of explosives. Any remaining pilings could be driven deeper, cut off, or pulled out. The work was done in 1948 and 1949. Thus, one of Stern and Silverman's impressive achievements disappeared from the landscape.

General Manager Whitehead supervised the project and was pleased with the result. To replace the cars, the company purchased 25 model 41-S Twin Coach buses between 1947 and 1949, supplemented by five additional model 45-S vehicles in 1951. He also felt the conversion of the rail line to buses, something he had advocated since 1946, had greatly reduced the man-hours required to operate the line. This reduction offset wage increases won by the workers. Whitehead concluded that the substitution "had resulted in a much cheaper operation than could have been carried on with the trolleys and the rehabilitation that would have been necessary." Even with the buses, however, the line was a poor performer, and neither McShain nor McCloskey were happy with it.

A smaller project was waterproofing the Inlet carbarn and modifying it for buses. Water was seeping through the south wall and flooding some of the repair pits. A Philadelphia contractor was hired to do the work and to repair some defective downspouts as well.

Top: A few years earlier Jim Shuman was responsible for this classic shot of southbound Shore Fast Line 101 approaching Linwood on April 23, 1939. James P. Shuman photo, Electric City Trolley Museum collection

James N.J. Henwood

Top View: *Shore Fast Line car 109 sits on the siding at Linwood while car 104 passes by on a special run on June 16, 1947. Note that the special sports a portable headlight, a feature not found on most daytime SFL trains. James P. Shuman photo, LeRoy O. King Collection* ***Above:*** *In a scene welcomed by many, but mourned by friends of the trolleys, No. 105—the last car—arrives at the Virginia Avenue terminal on January 18, 1948. As was common in those days the car sides have been crudely painted with "last car" and "rest in peace," A sign on the dash proclaims "I made it. Next stop: scrap pile." The new replacement buses are ready to enter service, but they did not increase patronage and they lacked the inherent appeal of the electric cars. The Stephenson-built cars, the only ones that ran on the line, would soon be scrapped, but they had served long and well. David H. Cope photo, Richard Allman collection*

CHAPTER ELEVEN | *The Atlantic City Transportation Company*

The Pennsylvania Railroad was no longer involved in local transportation in the seashore resort area, but the Atlantic City Transportation Company continued to struggle to provide service in the face of declining ridership, higher costs, and increased competition from private automobiles. Although beyond the scope of this history, a final chapter will briefly examine the remaining years until private ownership was no longer possible.

Top: New replacement Twin Coach buses line up outside the Inlet Barn, now partly converted to a garage. Former motormen and conductors are now bus drivers; only one man was needed on the motor coaches. A banner on the side proclaims "Brand New for You." The buses took about the same time to cover the route as the electric cars and they were cheaper to operate, but traffic on the line continued to decline. ACTC photo, Jeffrey Marinoff collection

185

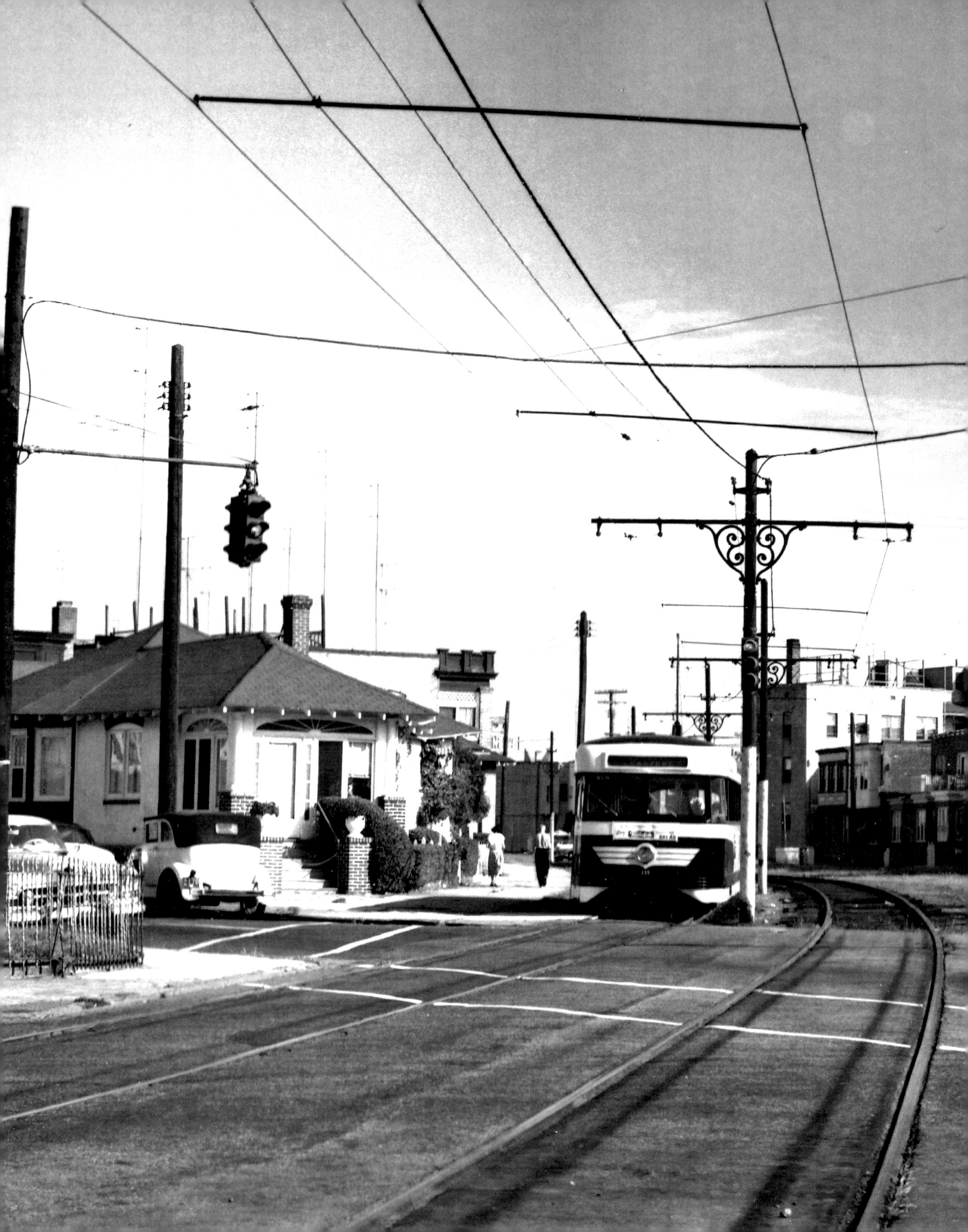

CHAPTER TWELVE

The Final Years of Rail Service

Changes at the Top: John McShain Takes Over

Although detailed coverage of the history of local transportation in the region ended with the abandonment of the Shore Fast Line, this chapter will briefly describe the subsequent years, including the abandonment of the Atlantic Avenue and Longport Line.

In the early 1950s, the company was only marginally profitable. After a loss of $54,000 in 1952, profits of $14,000, $69,000, and $72,000 were recorded for 1953, 1954, and 1955. By 1954, the joint ownership of the property by McShain and McCloskey was coming to an end. The only question was who was to be the remaining owner, as both men were willing to sell their shares to the other. To ensure a fair price, McShain suggested that McCloskey set a price for purchasing McShain's stock on condition that if McShain considered the stock was worth more, he then had the option of buying McCloskey's stock at that price. In either case, the corporation was to be the purchaser. Ultimately, McCloskey decided to sell his holdings. At the same time, Attorney Thomas Munyan, who drew up the agreement, decided to sell his minority shares for the same price McCloskey received. Both he and McCloskey resigned as officers and board members. At the conclusion of these transactions on August 14, John McShain was the sole owner of the ACTC.

Negotiating to Sell the Atlantic Avenue Right-of-Way

One of the motives of McShain and McCloskey in buying the property from the Pennsylvania Railroad was to gain control of the narrow strip of land containing the trolley right-of-way extending down Atlantic Avenue the entire length of Absecon Island. Neither owner was enamored with trolleys, which they regarded as obsolete. The sale of the right-of-way could partially repay them for the money they had spent in acquiring the property. As with most things they planned, the process took longer than they had expected.

Negotiations with the four island municipalities began in 1950. Although Atlantic City had demanded the elimination of trolleys since the mid-1930s, the talks soon bogged down. The main issues were the price the company set for the property and who would pay for the cost of paving the track area. After much haggling and bickering among the parties, by 1953 a tentative price

Facing Page: The stillness of a Saturday morning is broken as Longport-bound Brilliner 225 leaves the private right-of-way and enters street running at Baden and New Hampshire avenues. The car had departed from Inlet Loop only minutes earlier on this early September day in 1953. Edward S. Miller photo, Richard Allman collection

Above: Atlantic City trackage in the final years of operation.

James N.J. Henwood

Top View: *A former Capital Transit Mack Model CT, now ACTC No. 350, loads a few passengers at the 8th Street station in Ocean City. The bus is running on the Ocean City local lines, which ran the length of the island from the Garden section to 59th Street. This money-losing service ended in 1959. Motor Bus Society Library* **Above:** *Former Fort Wayne No. 299 makes a rare appearance outside the Inlet barn in 1953. The presence of a snow sweeper behind hints that this is probably a railfan event. As the days of rail service were coming to an end, various groups visited the city to ride the cars while they still could. Regardless of their age, the ACTC cars were clean and well maintained. The Indiana cars were used sparingly. Ed Birch photo*

CHAPTER TWELVE | *The Final Years of Rail Service*

Above: *This photograph is the first of several showing the line in its final years. Brilliner 215 is ready to leave the ready track at the Inlet on Saturday, September 5, 1953, at 7:40 a.m. to begin its day's work, carded for Longport.* Edward S. Miller photo, Richard Allman collection

of $625,000 was reached, which seemed to satisfy no one. While the towns argued about how much each would pay, McShain told the board of directors in 1954 that this was the minimum sum they would accept.

At the same time, in August, McCloskey, who was preparing to leave the company, gained the impression that his partner was lukewarm to the idea of substituting buses for trolleys. McShain assured him he was "just as anxious to have the changeover take place as you and Tom [Munyan]." He added, "I am not so unwise as to believe that trolleys have not outlived their time." McCloskey complained about the "unlimited delay" in making the conversion. McShain said the towns had not yet reached agreement among themselves on the price to be paid, but once they did, he would "strive with all my power to have the conversion effected [sic] as soon as possible." He promised McCloskey that if he could not reach a reasonable agreement with the towns, the company was to be turned over to him.

Although no longer officially involved with the ACTC, McCloskey kept a close watch on the negotiations. Impatient and anxious for an agreement, in January 1955, he unilaterally announced the company would sell its land for $475,000. A surprised McShain wrote, "I am at a loss to understand why our cost two years ago could have been in excess of $600,000 and, now, dropped to $475,000." He recognized that the $625,000 price was subject to modification, but he was embarrassed because he had earlier committed himself to it. But Munyan, Thomas Whitehead, and Joseph Hamilton all believed the lower price was "sufficient to justify the conversion," so McShain accepted it, but he was "not happy with the situation."

Agreement is Reached on the Sale of the Atlantic Avenue Property

Contentious negotiations among the four towns and between them and the Transportation Company dragged on into 1955. Atlantic City, as was to be expected, was the most difficult to deal with. The ACTC wanted to route some buses to Ventnor Avenue south of Albany Avenue and hoped to secure a waiver of the interest the city demanded on unpaid taxes, as well as a higher price than the city was willing to pay. In June, McShain wrote a restrained letter to Major William F. Casey, one of the city commissioners, asking his cooperation in settling the dispute. In his reply, Casey noted the "absolute necessity of having the changeover to buses" as soon as possible. He concluded with a vague warning that unless the issues were settled in "a friendly manner," the city had "no other alternative but to proceed under the authority according to law."

Finally, the two major issues were resolved. On the question of how much the ACTC was to receive for its right-of-way, the agreement determined that Atlantic City pay $325,000, Ventnor $46,500, Margate $46,500, and Longport $20,000, or a total of $438,000. The issue of paying the cost of paving the right-of-way was divided among the parties. Atlantic City agreed to assume the entire

James N.J. Henwood

Top View: *Brilliners 205 and 217 pause on the long curved private right-of-way at Bader and New Hampshire avenues, view to the northeast. This section between Atlantic Avenue and Maine Avenue retained the character of the original Camden & Atlantic Railroad, which constructed the line in the 1850s. Photo was snapped on the same day as the previous one—September 5, 1953. Edward S. Miller photo, Richard Allman collection*
Above: *Brilliner 203 leaves Atlantic Avenue at Massachusetts Avenue to enter the long, gentle curve leading to Maine Avenue and its destination at Absecon Inlet on the same morning. A safety zone for southbound passengers is behind the car, protected only by moveable stanchions. Edward S. Miller photo, Richard Allman collection*

cost within its borders. The ACTC agreed to pay to pave the center strip in Ventnor, but be reimbursed by the city from franchise taxes it had collected from the company. Margate avoided the argument by agreeing to pay the paving charge itself; and in Longport the cost was divided, with the borough paying to pave the section from the Margate border to 22nd Street, and the ACTC assuming 5, 1954, a step finally approved by the PUC on August 31, 1955. Shuttle buses replaced the cars between Margate and Longport.

When agreement on the conversion to buses was finally reached, the company applied to the PUC for approval, granted on November 9. The last day of rail service was scheduled for December 28, 1955.

Above: On the same day as the previous photos, Brilliner 225 is nearing the end of its southbound journey as it approaches the Longport loop. This last section of the line was the most picturesque as the tracks abutted a section of Great Egg Harbor Bay. However, the island here was at its narrowest with the ocean and the bay only one block apart making the trolley line susceptible to damage from storms. Service between Margate and Longport ended a year prior to the final abandonment of the line. Edward S. Miller photo, Richard Allman collection

responsibility for the rest of the line. With these understandings, it was now possible to abandon the Atlantic Avenue trolley line.

The Last Months of Trolley Service on Absecon Island

While John McShain was negotiating with the island towns, rail service continued on Atlantic Avenue. The Brilliners provided most runs, but the War Board cars and occasionally the Fort Wayne cars also appeared. Summer visitors continued to crowd aboard, but in decreasing numbers. Only necessary maintenance was undertaken.

The south end of the line in Longport, where the island was narrowest, suffered from severe storms which periodically battered the area. A November 1950 tempest so damaged the line that service was curtailed at the Douglas Avenue loop in Margate for several months. In the fall of 1954, another storm further damaged the line in Longport. The tracks were in such poor condition by then that it was dangerous to operate over them. Rail service was discontinued south of Douglas Avenue on Sunday, December

The end of trolley service was regarded as cause for celebration rather than a sad occasion, a not uncommon attitude at the time. The Press hailed it as "the triumphant conclusion of a campaign to replace old-style transportation with the modern." In an advertisement, the company pledged "more frequent, faster, more flexible service for Atlantic City, Ventnor, Margate, and Longport."

The focus of the "last day" events was a parade of 20 cars, twelve Brilliners and eight War Board types, starting at Douglas Avenue at 3:30 P.M. and running to the Inlet. The first car, a War Board model, was reserved for local dignitaries, politicians, and company officials, including John McShain and Joseph Hamilton. The next two cars carried the marching bands of the Atlantic City High School and Holy Spirit High School. A number of cars chartered for $100 each by various groups, such as the Kiwanis Club, the Rotary Club, local businesses and banks, followed. Last in the parade were cars for the general public, who rode for two dollars. Brilliners and War Board models made up the parade. All proceeds were donated to the Atlantic City Hospital Building Fund.

When the cars reached center city, crowds lined the curbs and

James N.J. Henwood

Above: Heading south, Brilliner 211 waits patiently at Georgia Avenue for a short freight train pushed by a PRR switcher crossing Atlantic Avenue. The Illinois Central boxcar is headed for Convention Hall at the Boardwalk and probably contains material for a scheduled event at that large building. Until 1948 Georgia Avenue was also used by Shore Fast Line interurban cars to enter Atlantic Avenue enroute to their destination at Virginia Avenue and the Boardwalk. It must be a hot day—all the windows are open. Robert Wasche photo

traffic was snarled. Most people interviewed by reporters were pleased the trolleys were disappearing. A luncheon for officials was provided before the parade at the Claridge Hotel, and a buffet and a cocktail party were offered to invited guests at Hackney's Restaurant following the last runs. Cars were chartered by four groups after the parade and ran up and down Atlantic Avenue into the nighttime hours. One of these cars was stripped of everything removable. A final trip was made in February 1956, on a War Board car chartered by the North Jersey Chapter of the National Railway Historical Society. The overhead wire, line poles, and rails were removed and the center strip paved in time for the summer season.

The company scrapped most of the older cars and hoped to sell the Brilliners, but no buyers could be found. Seoul, South Korea, was interested, but the narrow-gauge track there precluded a sale. The company contacted firms in Europe, South America, Mexico, and Cuba, but none were interested. After about a year, they too were scrapped.

To replace the cars, the company substituted 24 General Motors TDH 4512 diesel transit buses. Route variations included runs on Ventnor Avenue as well as Atlantic Avenue. Minor modifications were made over the years, but the principal routes from Atlantic City to Longport and the "off-shore" line along Shore Road from Absecon to Somers Point and Ocean City provided most of the service. The money-losing, summer only, local service in Ocean City ended in 1959.

Afterward

Buses proved to be no panacea for the problems facing public transportation companies, in Atlantic City or elsewhere. For the next thirty years, until 1985, the ACTC struggled to survive against the effects of declining ridership and rising costs.

The company's bus lines were marginal and eventually they lost money, but the firm survived for a time from rental income

CHAPTER TWELVE | *The Final Years of Rail Service*

Top View: *This was the scene at Douglas Avenue on December 28, 1955, the last day of trolley service in Atlantic City. On the extreme left bus 3201 is on shuttle service to Longport. Heading a line of new buses purchased to replace the trolleys is No. 3909, a GMC TDH-4512 model. Some of the Brilliners and War Board cars form a parade of cars readying for their final trip on the last surface streetcar line in New Jersey. Robert Wasche photo*
Above: *Northbound Brilliner 2132 is about to cross Jackson Avenue, the border between Ventnor City and Atlantic City. From this point south to Longport, a center median was reserved for the trolleys. Ventnor insisted the tracks be covered by loose gravel, but in Margate and Longport they were open and unpaved. The sign on the pole warn motorists to keep to the right of the private right-of-way. Date is September 5, 1953. Edward S. Miller photo, Richard Allman collection*

James N.J. Henwood

Top Photo: *Nearing the end of its run, Brilliner 219 approaches the Longport loop next to Atlantic Avenue at 19th Avenue on September 5, 1953. Edward S. Miller photo, Electric City Trolley Museum collection* ***Above:*** *Brilliner 209 enters the Douglas Avenue loop at the southern end of Margate to make its return trip to the Inlet. The general pattern was for every third southbound trip to turn back at this point as Longport had the smallest population of the four Absecon Island communities. The warning red flashing signal on the pole in front of the shelter was installed in 1945 at the insistence of the Board of Public Utility Commissioners. This view also dates to September 5, 1953. Edward S. Miller photo, Richard Allman collection*

CHAPTER TWELVE | *The Final Years of Rail Service*

and the sale of property. In 1957, for example, the firm reported operating revenues of over $1,170,000, but operating income, after expenses, was only $11,000. In 1966, revenues were $1,420,000, but operating income after expenses amounted to $14,400. Other income produced total net income of $43,000, but as the report indicated, the operating ratio was a frightening 98.9 percent.

McShain remained president of the company until 1972. Despite his other investments and interests, McShain continued to follow the financial affairs of the firm. His relationship with Joseph Hamilton, the vice-president and general manager who actually ran the company, was generally positive, but there were periods of disagreement and suspicions, particularly on the sale of non-operating property. In 1972, Hamilton and several associates

was reached with New Jersey Transit Corporation, a state-owned operator, to take over the faltering line. The era of private ownership, extending back to the nineteenth century, had come to an end.

The story of Atlantic City transportation lines reveals the rise and fall of privately owned, taxpaying enterprises that performed an important public service. Even with the dominance of the automobile, there were those who needed and relied on transit lines and most cities could not afford to do without them, even Atlantic City, where jitneys still run.

Today, the railroad has only a tiny toehold on Absecon Island, next to the Beach Thorofare, and few are aware of what an important role it played in the growth and development of the seashore resorts. Nor are many conscious of the numerous rail lines that girded the

Above: Elevated view of the open track in Margate as No. 213 moves briskly along with a group of passengers out for a trolley ride on this Memorial Day in 1954. George E. Votava photo, LeRoy King, Jr. collection

purchased the company from McShain, but as the latter held a mortgage, little real change occurred.

Earnings fell or were nonexistent by the 1960s, despite charter and school bus revenues, fare increases, and property sales. Expenses also rose, including labor costs and benefits, and periodically new buses were purchased to replace older worn-out models. The line suffered a strike in 1969, ended by granting a significant wage increase.

Subsidies from local and state agencies began in the 1960s and increased regularly. By 1982, these amounted to $2,000,000, but they were not enough to cover the losses. A number of efforts were made to sell the property to local and county public authorities were discussed but never implemented. Finally, in 1985, agreement

island and linked the communities on it and the off-shore towns into a common whole. Despite their weaknesses and problems, overall, the people involved in building and operating the transit lines deserve our recognition and thanks for helping to make the seashore towns the viable communities they are today.

This Page: *Shore fast Line trains brought their passengers directly to the Boardwalk where the line maintained a terminal on Virginia Avenue. In this 1947 view, a two-car train has taken the crossover out of the terminal and will continue on to Ocean City. The line had months to live with operations ending the following January. Electric City Trolley Museum collection*

CHAPTER THIRTEEN

Scenes from the Atlantic City & Shore

The Shore Fast Line was a 16.2-mile interurban that ran from its Atlantic City terminal at Virginia Avenue and the Boardwalk to a more modest terminal at 8th Street and Boardwalk in Ocean City employing a combination of overhead wire and third rail pickup. Service ended on the line on January 18, 1948.

Top View: The Inlet Barn served both the Shore Fast Line and Atlantic Avenue trolley line. Equipment was stored and maintained here and Atlantic Avenue cars initiated their runs to Longport from a nearby loop. Car 113 poses for its picture at the Inlet car house on a sunny November 30, 1946. This car would deadhead the short distance to the Virginia Avenue and Boardwalk terminal to go into service for the day. David H. Cope photo, Krambles-Peterson Archive

Right: Looking down from the Boardwalk, two Shore fast Line trains await departure from the Atlantic City terminal in this view from the mid-1940s. The twenty cars built by the John Stephenson Company in 1906 served the Shore Fast Line for the length of its existence the line. Brill proposed building an order of double-ended Brilliners around 1940, but the AC&S was no longer inclined to make any sort of heavy investment in its interurban line. Craig Knox collection courtesy of Electric City Trolley Museum

James N.J. Henwood

Top View: *Shore Fast Line 115 rolls down Atlantic Avenue to Mississippi Avenue where it will turn off for a fast run over the PRSL tracks to Pleasantville. This is a short-turn car that will terminate at Linwood. View dates from the mid-1940s. Charles Houser, Sr. photo, Jeffrey Marinoff collection* **Bottom:** *Outbound cars to Ocean City turned off of Atlantic Avenue at Mississippi Avenue to connect to PRSL. Inbound cars arrived on Georgia Avenue where car 101 is turning off of that thoroughfare and onto Atlantic Avenue where it will continue to its terminal at Virginia Avenue and the Boardwalk. Eugene Van Dusen photo, William D. Volmer collection*

CHAPTER THRITEEN | *Scenes from the Atlantic City & Shore*

Above: *Shore Fast Line cars 105 and 108 have just entered onto PRSL track where the train will run on third rail power to Pleasantville where a changeover to overhead trolley wire will be made. Photo circa 1947. Electric City Trolley Museum collection*

Above: *Jim Shuman recorded this view of car 101 on third rail trackage near Pleasantville on April 23, 1939. AC&S trains had to comply with standard railroad operating rules, such as displaying marker lights on the ends of its trains. James P. Shuman photo*

James N.J. Henwood

Top View: Shore Fast Line has left its modest Pleasantville depot behind and will continue on to Ocean City under overhead wire. The more substantial station in the background belonged to Pennsylvania-Reading Seashore Lines. The bus seen in the distant background is the AC&S connecting bus to Absecon. Photo circa 1940. Electric City Trolley Museum collection **Above:** Ocean City-bound 114 has just left Pleasantville and takes a curve as it hurries along to Ocean City. View looks north from the Verona Avenue overpass. Electric City Trolley Museum collection

CHAPTER THRITEEN | *Scenes from the Atlantic City & Shore*

Top View: *Shore Fast Line car 106 breaks the quiet of a hot August day in 1941 as it sprints over a grade crossing on its way to Ocean City. Electric City Trolley Museum collection* ***Above:*** *A post card view from the "red car" era shows a two-car train passing the Northfield station. Like many interurbans AC&S was keen to promote recreational activities along its route whether it be golf or the pleasures of the Boardwalk and the Jersey shore at either of its end points. Electric City Trolley Museum collection*

201

James N.J. Henwood

Top View: Shore Fast Line provided sidings at several locations along its route for short-turn trips. A common end point on may of these short-turn runs was Linwood. Car 114 maintains its schedule on the mainline while a short-turn car lays over in the siding awaiting its next assignment. Electric City Trolley Museum collection **Above:** Somers Point was the last mainland stop before it crossed over Great Egg Harbor Bay on a long trestle to its ultimate destination in Ocean City. When part of the trestle to Ocean City was destroyed by fire in September 1946, all Shore Fast Line trains terminated at this point and passengers were shuttled via bus over to Atlantic City. Car 108 makes it stop at Somers Point in this wintery 1946 view. Electric City Trolley Museum collection

CHAPTER THIRTEEN | *Scenes from the Atlantic City & Shore*

Above: Shore Fast Line 112 lays over at Somers Point in 1947. By this time all runs terminated at this point to meet an Ocean City shuttle bus. This car received a partial rebuilding by the AC&S shop crew receiving metal sheathing on the front dash while the sides retained their original wood finish. Lee Rogers collection **Below:** *This undated photo shows AC&S 113 approaching Somers Point after a run over the long trestle that connected the line to Ocean City. The winter months were a fallow period for many of the tourist-oriented Atlantic City businesses and the residents eagerly anticipated the return of warm weather. David H. Cope photo, Richard Allman collection*

203

James N.J. Henwood

Top View: *Another view in the same area as car 118 approaches Somers Point on its run to Atlantic City. Jeffrey Marinoff collection* **Above:** *Once the cars had crossed the trestle the cars operated over single track leading into 8th Street where the runs terminated at the Ocean City Boardwalk. This two-car train was in Ocean City in a photo from the mid-'40s. Jeffrey Marinoff collection*

CHAPTER THRITEEN | *Scenes from the Atlantic City & Shore*

Above: *Trains ended their runs in Ocean City at 8th Street and the Boardwalk where there was a modest two-track terminal. Passengers are alighting from the car in this 1945 scene while a trainman prepares to raise the rear trolley pole for the return trip to Atlantic City.* David H. Cope photo, Krambles-Peterson Archive

Above: *Supplementing the Brilliners in later years were twelve cars which were among 100 originally built by Brill at the behest of the Emergency Fleet Corporation for service to the shipbuilding facility at Hog Island in Philadelphia, and an additional 30 for the U.S. Housing Corporation. These cars were purchased after the war for Atlantic City service and numbered 6845-6850 and 6885-6890. No. 6887 retained its traditional orange and cream livery as it basked in the sun outside the Inlet Barn on June 8, 1952.* Randolph Kulp collection

This Page: Brilliner 219 is at 19th Avenue slows at it approaches Longport Loop and the end of the line. This was the narrowest portion of Absecon Island with only a blockwide strip of land separating Great Egg Harbor Bay from the Atlantic Ocean making the line susceptible to the elements. It was this factor among others that led to the cutback to the Douglas Avenue loop in Margate in December 1954. Trolley service on the remainder of the line ended a year later. *Edward S. Miller photo, Richard Allman collection*

CHAPTER THRITEEN | *Scenes from the Atlantic City & Shore*

Atlantic City & Shore's Atlantic Avenue trolley line ran the length of Absecon Island from its originating terminal at the Absecon Inlet for 8.25 miles down to the island's very tip in Longport. The line saw heavy use and for years turned profits for its parent company, the Pennsylvania Railroad. The line, with its original Frank Sprague-supplied bracket arm line poles, survived until December 28, 1955. A farewell trip was operated the following February to close out the electric traction era in Atlantic City.

Top View: *The Brilliner demonstrator arrived in Atlantic City in September 1938. Brill brought in designer Raymond Loewy to add several design features including the arresting paint scheme seen here from a Brill promotional flyer. Officials of the controlling PRR were satisfied enough to order an additional 24 Brilliners in the summer of 1939 which would go into service on the Atlantic Avenue line. Electric City Trolley Museum collection*

Above: *A Brilliner is seen here at the Inlet terminal in June 1952 showing a few modifications made over the years. The door window glass was rebuilt and the Lowey-designed paint scheme was simplified from the original but held to the original design. Where the names of the principal communities along the Atlantic Avenue line were featured above the windows, new lettering appeared naming the cars "The Miss America Fleet." The Brilliners served well and reliably in their fifteen years of service in Atlantic City. Randolph Kulp Collection*

James N.J. Henwood

Top Photo: Trips to Longport and intermediate points along Atlantic Avenue originated from the Inlet Loop on the north end of Absecon Island. Brilliner 208 awaited passengers for a southbound run on August 3, 1954. Krambles-Peterson Archive *Right:* Bound for its Inlet terminal, ACTC Brilliner 225 has left street running behind and rolls over the short private right-of-way at Bader and Madison avenues on September 5, 1953. Edward S. Miller photo, Richard Allman collection *Right Bottom:* A view just south where car 212 entered street running at Massachusetts and Atlantic avenues on the same day as the previous photo. Edward S. Miller photo, Richard Allman collection

CHAPTER THRITEEN | *Scenes from the Atlantic City & Shore*

Top Photo: Further south on Atlantic Avenue at Albany Avenue, Ray DeGroote caught two Hog Island cars passing each other on June 8, 1953. One car 286, had been renumbered and received the more modern black and cream livery while car 6880 retained its original number and earlier paint scheme. Raymond DeGroote, Jr. photo **Bottom:** *A Brilliner on Atlantic Avenue glides around the Civil War Soldiers and Sailors Monument at Providence Avenue. The only significant curves along the line were encountered (westbound) at Boston and Albany avenues. Edward S. Miller photo, Richard Allman collection*

209

James N.J. Henwood

Top Photo: Atlantic City Transportation Co. 247 heads east on Atlantic Avenue near Raleigh Avenue in lower Chelsea. (That part of Atlantic Avenue below Albany Avenue is commonly called lower Chelsea.) The time is mid-winter 1954 and there had been a snowstorm the night before. No. 246 (formerly no. 6847 under AC&S) sported the Brilliner-inspired livery and in fact was replacing a Brilliner on this run as the newer cars did not run well in snow. This car was one of six purchased from the Ocean Electric Railroad in Rockaway, N.Y. in 1927 by AC&S. As the cars had been purchased by Ocean Electric from PRT, they were Hog Island cars by way of New York. Robert Wasche photo   ***Above:*** A profile of the blind side of Brilliner 219 running westbound on Atlantic Avenue around 1954. ACTC pursued every possible revenue source and increased advertising was noted on the cars. Robert Wasche photo

CHAPTER THRITEEN | *Scenes from the Atlantic City & Shore*

Top Photo: *Former Fort Wayne car 295 runs westbound on a special in Ventnor. Lucy the Elephant, an Atlantic City landmark, can be seen to the right. Purchased in 1946 to handle heavy postwar ridership, the Fort Wayne cars were soon relegated to the car barn owing to their poor riding qualities. That the car is running on a special is probably the only reason it was out on the line that day. Photo was from June 8, 1952. Randolph Kulp collection*

Right: *Another War Board car, no. 6887, is also seen in Ventnor on the same day. These cars had greater service flexibility than the Brilliners. Being double-ended, they could be brought just past a crossover, change poles, and return on a short-turn trip. This photo is from the same day as the previous one. Randolph Kulp collection*

Bottom Right: *Atlantic City played host to many fraternal organizations over the years. The Shriners were in town on this summer day in 1953 as War Board no. 6887 worked its way around the Portland Avenue Loop. Bernard Rossbach photo*

James N.J. Henwood

Top Right: War Board car 6890, running on a fantrip, passes a regular service Brilliner at the Douglas Avenue loop in Margate. Edward S. Miller photo, Electric City Trolley Museum collection

Middle Photo: Fantrip car 6890 poses at the Douglas Avenue Loop the same day. Service was cut back to this loop in December 1954 owing to worsening condition of the track in Longport. A shuttle bus was instituted to take passengers to the end of the line. ACTC bus 3202, a GMC 3103 purchased new in 1953, was gas-powered and finding itself out of place on a growing diesel fleet. The bus was finally sold in 1961. Robert Wasche photo

Bottom Photo: Brilliners 223 and 205 meet at the Douglas Avenue loop in Margate on September 5, 1953. Loops were available at both Portland and Douglas avenues in the event the Brilliners needed to be short-turned to meet ridership conditions. Edward S. Miller photo, Richard Allman collection

212

Top Photo: *ACTC Brilliner 207 is at Atlantic Avenue at 18th Avenue in Longport. The car is running along the bay on its way to the loop between 15th and 16th avenues. At this point the width of the island is only one block from the bay to the ocean. In the background is a drawbridge for a road to Somers Point. It has since been replaced by a high bridge.* Robert Wasche photo ***Above:*** *Brilliner 211 passes a fishing pier as it approaches Longport Loop on June 8, 1952.* Randolph Kulp collection

James N.J. Henwood

Top: *A couple of examples of the electric cars that best represented Atlantic City's interurban and city trolley lines. Above: Shore fast Line 110 lays over at Linwood after completing a short-turn run. Over the years the sides were completely sheathed in steel, a steel pilot replaced the older wooden one and the car sports one of SFL's finer paint schemes. Other features of the car were the roof-mounted bell, the illuminated run board on the roof, and third rail shoes and trolley poles for current collection. View dates to April 23, 1939. James P. Shuman photo*

Below: *On the very same day, photographer Shuman was at Inlet Loop at the tip of Absecon Island to catch a look at Brilliner 6891, the demonstration car Brill built as an answer to the PCC car. Atlantic City was pleased enough with the overall operation to purchase an additional 24 cars which arrived in 1940 and ran in daily service until the end of trolley operation in 1955. James P. Shuman photo*

CHAPTER FOURTEEN

Atlantic City & Shore Railroad
Atlantic City Transportation Corporation

A Select Roster of Equipment

Car Number	Builder	Built	Trucks	Motors	Control	Seats	Length	Width	Notes
AC&S "Shore Fast Line" Interurbans									
101-117	John Stephenson Co.	1906	Brill 27-E1	4-GE 87 @ 60 h.p.	GE Type M multiple unit	52	47'-1"	8'-8"	Double-end coach
118-119	John Stephenson Co.	1906	Brill 27-E1	4-GE 87 @ 60 h.p.	GE Type M multiple unit	36	47'-1"	8'-8"	Double-end combination baggage-passenger. 118 converted to coach (1924); 119 used as tool shed (burned 1953).
Absequam	John Stephenson Co.	1906	Brill 27-E1	4-GE 87 @ 60 h.p.	GE Type M multiple unit	28	47'-1"	8'-8"	Double-end funeral car, converted to parlor car 1920; converted to coach no. 120 in 1942. Burned in 1944.
AC&S Nearsides									
6801, 6804-05, 6808-19, 6825, 6827-28, 6331-32, 6836-39, 6852, 6858	J.G. Brill Co.	1913	Brill 39-E	2-GE 201P @ 50 h.p.	K-36-J	54	46'-6"	8'-5"	26 cars; retired with arrival of Brilliners in 1940.
AC&S War Board / Hog Island Cars									
6885-6888	J.G. Brill Co.	1918	Brill 77-E	4-WH 514A @ 35 h.p.	K-35	52	46'-9"	9'-1"	Purchased May 1923 by PRR. Former Ocean Electric Railway Nos. 136, 140, 141, 148.
6889-6890	J.G. Brill Co.	1918	Brill 77-E	4-WH 514A @ 35 h.p.	K-35	52	46'-9"	9'-1"	Purchased 1923
6845-6850	J.G. Brill Co.	1918	Brill 77-E	4-WH 514A @ 35 h.p.	K-35	52	46'-9"	9'-1"	Purchased 1927 from Ocean Electric Railway (Long Island). OE Nos. were 144-147; 149-150.
ACTC Indiana Service Corporation (Fort Wayne, Ind.)									
297-298	St. Louis Car Co.	1924	St. Louis	4-GE 264A	K-35-J	44	39'-11"	8'-7"	Acquired 1946 by ACTC. Former ISC 527 & 537
294-296; 299	St. Louis Car Co.	1925	St. Louis	4-GE 264A	K-35-J	44	39'-11'	8'-7"	Acquired 1946 by ACTC. Former ISC 540, 546, 550, 552
Brilliner Demonstration Car									
6891	J.G. Brill Co.	1938	Brill 97-4-R-1	4-GE 11986 @ 55 h.p.	GE Automatic	53	45'-4 1/8"	8'-4 7/8"	Renumbered to 6901 in 1940
AC&S/ACTC Brilliners									
6902-6925	J.G. Brill Co.	1940	Brill 97-4-R-1	4-GE 11986 @ 55 h.p.	GE Automatic	53	45'-4 1/8"	8'-4 7/8'	Retired 12-28-55; all cars scrapped.

James N.J. Henwood

Top: *Builder's photo of Atlantic City & Shore 111 posing on the transfer table at the John Stephenson Company plant in 1906. The builder delivered an excellent product as the cars ran reliably for over 40 years. LeRoy O. King, Jr. collection* ***Bottom:*** *Thirty-eight years later car 102 rests at the Inlet Barn in February 1944. Over the years the AC&S's shop forces constantly maintained and improved the cars when time and finances permitted. Note the portable headlight which seemed to be found on the front of the cars whenever a special was operated. Electric City Trolley Museum collection*

216

CHAPTER FOURTEEN | *A Select Roster of Equipment*

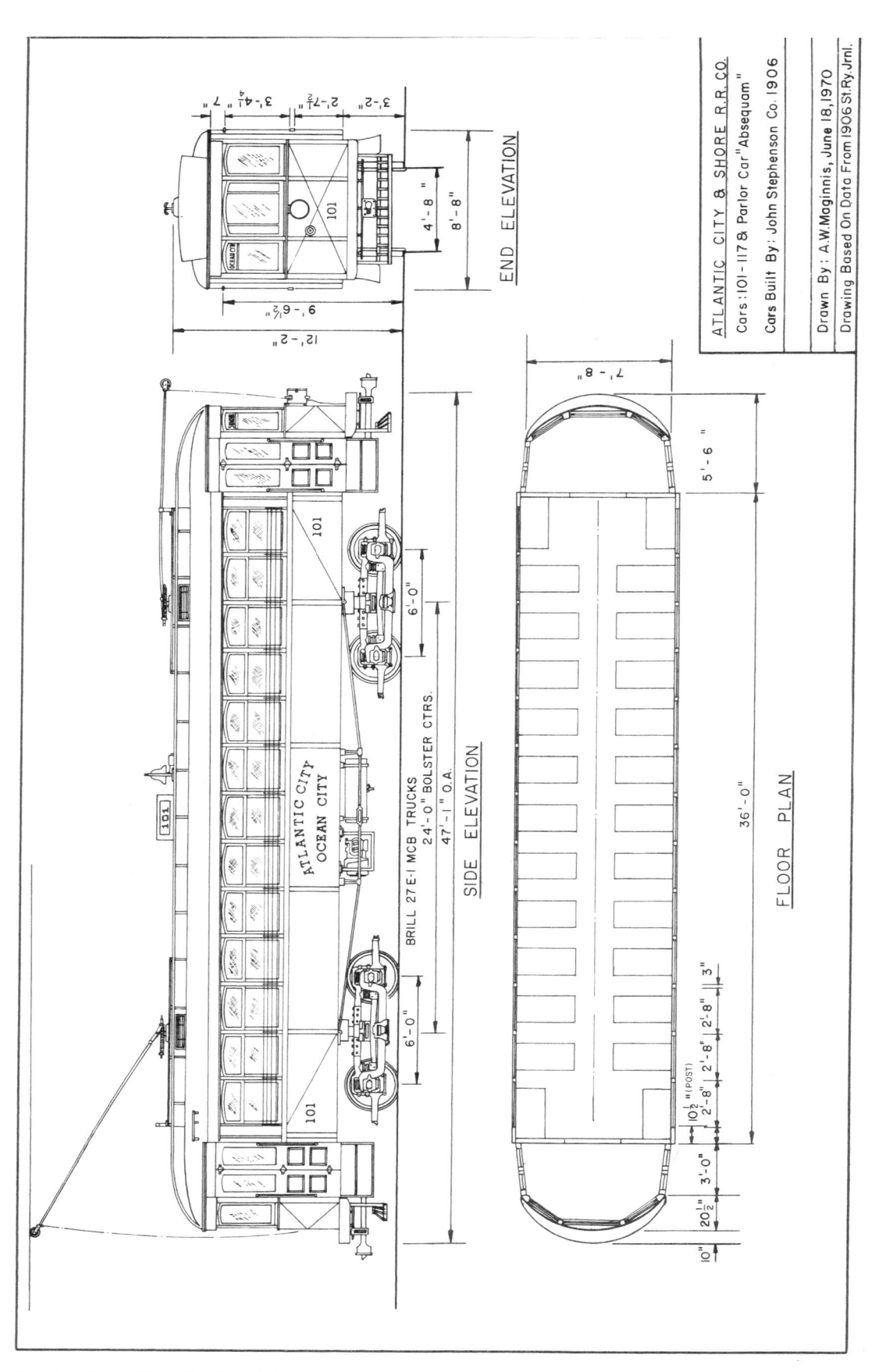

Car Drawing— Shore Fast Line interurban

217

James N.J. Henwood

Top: Two combination baggage-passenger cars were included in the 1906 order and were used in express service. By the 1930s the line's short run and increasing truck competition resulted in the discontinuance of express service. As early as 1924 one of the combines, no. 118, was converted to a coach. Combine 119 was still in service when photographed in the 1930s. William P. Hamilton, III. Fred W. Schneider, III collection

Middle: Shore Fast Line's parlor car was delivered to the railroad as a funeral car: Absequaim. Funeral service ended in 1920 and the Absequaim was converted to a parlor car and equipped with wicker chairs. Service was cut back to weekends only and the car saw additional weekday use in sightseeing service in Atlantic City. Electric City Trolley Museum collection

Bottom: This view shows the car stored inside the Inlet Barn in the late '30s. Because of the increase of traffic during World War II, the parlor car was converted to coach 120 in 1942. Its service length proved to be short-lived as the car was lost when struck by a fallen live wire during the infamous 1944 hurricane. James Richards photo

CHAPTER FOURTEEN | *A Select Roster of Equipment*

Top: *The paint on AC&S 104 fairly glistens as it turns off of Atlantic Avenue onto Virginia Avenue on August 29, 1935. The train has only two more blocks before arriving at its Boardwalk terminal. By 1935, most interurbans had been abandoned or were making preparations. The Shore Fast Line continued to soldier on through the '30s and the war years. Electric City Trolley Museum collection.* ***Bottom:*** *No. 118 pulls into the Inlet Barn in the late 1930s. Despite the hard economic times, the interurban car is in good condition, a testimony to the shop crew's maintenance standards. This car has received the steel sheathing on the end dash panels, but the sides remain "as built."* James Richards photo

219

This Page: Nearside 6816 went before the company photographer so the extent of some minor damage to its front could be viewed and assessed. This was a familiar sight to many an Atlantic City trolley rider waiting for the front doors to fold open and the step to flop down before boarding the car. As of this September 1931 date, the Nearsides still had many more years to run. Jeffrey Marinoff collection

Facing Page Top: An interior view of the front platform of Nearside 6801. The car was a "muzzle loader" with passengers boarding in the front and paying their fare to the conductor whose station was immediately behind the motorman. The Atlantic City Nearsides were rebuilt with a large rear platform, a feature that improved passenger flow. Historical Society of Pennsylvania, LeRoy O. King, Jr. collection

Facing Page Bottom: The larger rear platform of Nearside 6828 is evident as the trolley stops for passengers at Atlantic and Douglas avenues in August 1935. Electric City Trolley Museum collection

CHAPTER FOURTEEN | *A Select Roster of Equipment*

James N.J. Henwood

Top: Nearing the end of its service life, Nearside 6813 is at Inlet Loop, both sets of doors open, as it awaits departure for a short-turn trip to Douglas Avenue. In spite of this late date in its operational life, the car appears to be well cared for. M.D. McCarter photo, Fred W. Schneider, III collection

Bottom: We're afforded a view of the blind side of a Nearside car as no. 6819 works its way along Atlantic Avenue in September 1935. Alfred Seibel photo, LeRoy O. King, Jr. collection

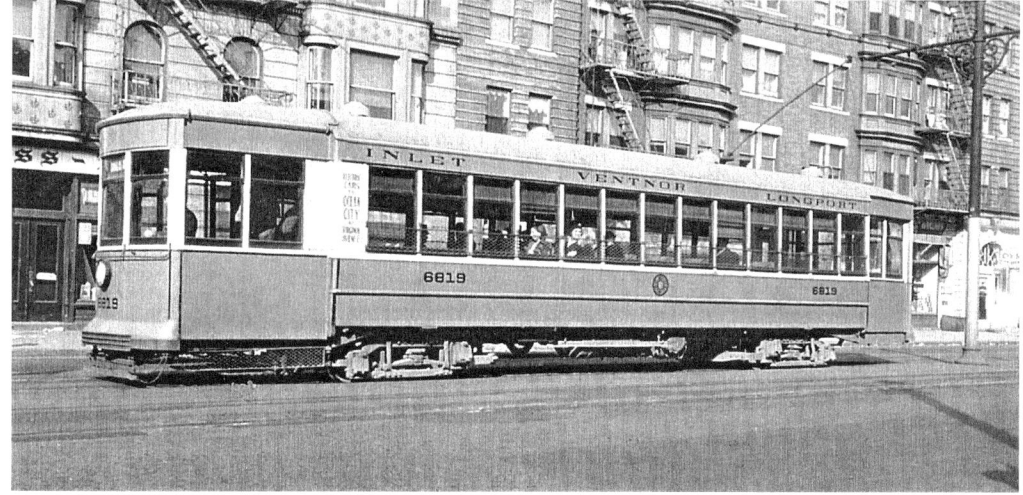

CHAPTER FOURTEEN | *A Select Roster of Equipment*

Top: *No. 6887, one of the first of the War Board car acquisitions, basks in the sun in front of Inlet Barn in the early 1950s. Unloved by Atlantic City politicians and the press, these cars nevertheless performed yeoman service for both AC&S and ACTC. When weather conditions, such as snow, caused problems for the new Brilliners, the War Board cars always got through. Anthony F. Krisak photo, Richard Krisak collection* ***Bottom:*** *Half of the War Board cars received an updated Loewy-inspired black and cream paint job. To the casual rider, the new livery improved the looks of the car if not the performance. Scene is at the Douglas Avenue loop. Lester K. Wismer photo, Richard Allman collection*

James N.J. Henwood

Top: The new exterior paint on six of the War Board cars did nothing for the "plain-Jane-vanilla" interior. It was 1950s on the outside, 1920s on the inside. This view is of the interior of no. 246. Dave Biles photo

Middle: As a means of additional revenue for the company, ACTC began painting several of the War Board cars for advertising purposes. One of the cars lays over at the Longport loop, an advertisement for the upcoming Miss New Jersey Pageant emblazoned on its sides. Lester K. Wismer photo, Richard Allman collection

Bottom: War Board car 6847 turns off of Atlantic Avenue and into the Douglas Avenue loop. This car was dedicated to advertising the ever-changing attractions at the Steel Pier. The fact that Billy May and his band and Frances Langford (aka Mrs. John Bickerson) were the attractions at the time might date this photo a few years. Electric City Trolley Museum collection

224

CHAPTER FOURTEEN | *A Select Roster of Equipment*

Top: *Ridership on the ACTC Atlantic Avenue line held up surprisingly well immediately after the war, motivating the company to seek additional cars to augment the fleet. Ultimately, six cars from the Interstate Public Service Fort Wayne, Indiana, streetcar operation were found. Unfortunately, ridership soon tapered off and the cars saw little use in later years even though they stayed around to the end. In later years if one saw an ex-Fort Wayne car out on the line, it was assumed it was running on a special. The cars' poor riding qualities were a major mark against them. Bushnell-Krisak Photo Archive*
Bottom: *ACTC 296 in what was to become its natural habitat for most of its Atlantic City tour of duty—the inside on the Inlet car barn. In this view the car actually has a pole on the wire, so perhaps an assignment is in the offing. James Richards photo*

225

James N.J. Henwood

Top: *A car that for its time had "modern" written all over it. Atlantic City's first Brilliner, 6891, is posed in front of Inlet Barn shortly after its arrival. The two-tone green with gold striping did indeed make for a striking appearance. Anthony F. Krisak, Richard Krisak collection* ***Bottom:*** *The interior of Brilliner 6093 presents quite a contrast to the earlier interior view of a War Board car. This view says "bright, spacious, and comfortable." View recorded on June 28, 1940. Electric City Trolley Museum collection*

CHAPTER FOURTEEN | *A Select Roster of Equipment*

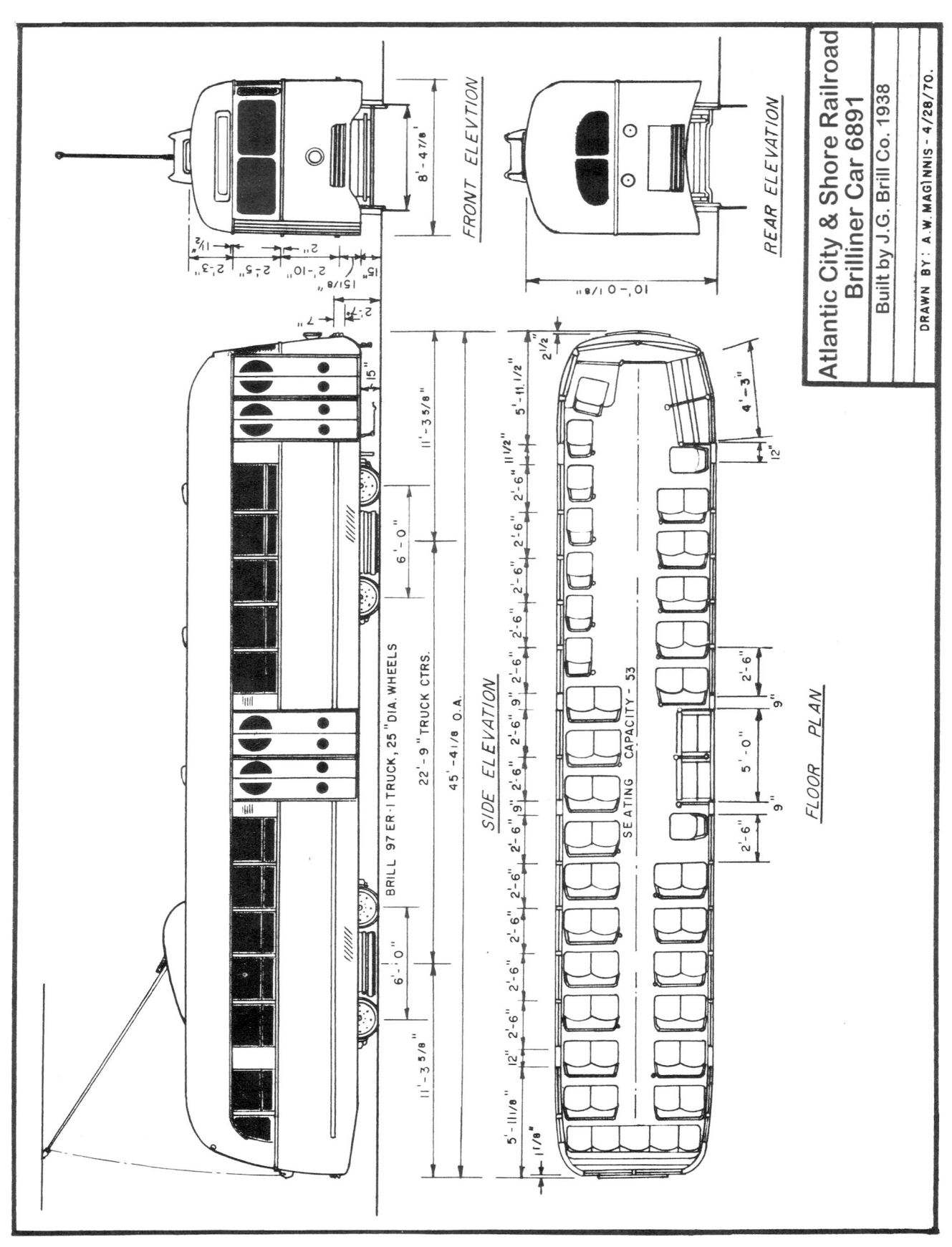

Brilliner drawing

James N.J. Henwood

A few photos of Atlantic City open cars.

Top: It's August 1934, a time of year when the open cars were revenue generators. No. 6806, an 11-bench open car carries a modest load of riders on a warm Atlantic City summer day. Jim Richards photo

Middle: No. 6840, a 15-bench open car seen in the Inlet car house on April 23, 1939, appears to be ready for service, but 1939 was to be an abbreviated season for the open cars as they only ran for one day and that was to be their last one. James P. Shuman photo

Bottom: An unusual open car is West Jersey & Seashore 6869, a 1900 Brill product. Robert Long

CHAPTER FOURTEEN | *A Select Roster of Equipment*

Top: *It's not always sunny and mild in Atlantic City. Sweeper 491182 (Brill 1897) and snow plow 498181 (Brill 1902) bide their time at the Inlet car house awaiting the arrival of winter weather. James Richards photo*

Middle: *Line car 498183 was built by Brill in 1896 originally for the Somers Point steam dummy line on the West Jersey and Seashore Railroad. The car was electrified in 1903 and ran on Atlantic Avenue to Longport. In 1917 it was transferred to the Venice Park Railway and after abandonment of that line, it was converted into a line car. It's seen here at Pleasantville on April 23, 1939. James P. Shuman photo*

Bottom: *No. 499200 was a combination salt car and rail grinder. Built by Brill in 1902, it began life in service on the Atlantic City & Suburban. Upon that line's demise in 1929, it was purchased by the AC&S and converted into work service, the last surviving Suburban trolley. It reportedly carried the highest number of any trolley in all of North America. James Richards photo*

Bibliography

ARCHIVAL COLLECTIONS

Atlantic City Files. New Jersey Archives, Trenton.

McShain, John, Papers. Hagley Museum & Library, Greenville, Delaware.

Pennsylvania Railroad Files. Railroad Museum of Pennsylvania, Strasburg.

Pennsylvania Railroad Collection. Hagley Museum & Library.

Pennsylvania Railroad Collection. Pennsylvania Archives, Harrisburg.

Reading Company Collection. Hagley Museum & Library.

STATISTICS AND REPORTS

American Street Railway Investments. New York: McGraw Publishing Co., 1907.

Conway, Thomas. *Report to the Pennsylvania Railroad Company on the Atlantic City & Shore Railroad Company, 1935.* Philadelphia: The Conway Corporation, 1935.

Lurie, Maxine E. and Mappen, Mark, eds. *Encyclopedia of New Jersey.* New Brunswick: Rutgers University Press, 2004.

McGraw Electric Railway Directory, 1924. New York: McGraw-Hill Co., Inc.: 1924.

Moody, John. *Moody's Analyses of Investments,* Part I: Steam Railroads. New York: Analyses Publishing Co., 1912-1938.

Moody's Analyses of Investments. Part II: Public Utilities and Industrials. New York: Moody's Investors Service, 1914-1919.

Moody's Analysis of Investments. Part III: Public Utilities. New York: Moody's Investors Service, 1920-1941.

Morris, Richard B. and Commager, Henry Steele. *Encyclopedia of American History.* New York: Harper & Row, 1965.

New Jersey. Board of Public Utility Commissioners for the State of New Jersey. *Annual Reports.* 1911-1945.

Pennsylvania. Department of State, Corporation Bureau. Stern & Silverman File.

Pennsylvania-Reading Seashore Lines. *Annual Reports.* 1937-1946.

Poor's Manual of Public Utilities. New York: Poor's Publishing Company, 1915-1941.

U.S. Department of Commerce, Bureau of the Census. *Historical Statistics of the United States, Colonial Times to 1957.* Washington: Government Printing Office, 1960.

U.S. Department of Commerce & Labor, Bureau of the Census. *Street and Electric Railways, 1902.* Washington: Government Printing Office, 1905.

U.S. Department of Commerce & Labor, Bureau of the Census. *Street and Electric Railways, 1907.* Washington: Government Printing Office, 1910.

U.S. Department of Commerce, Bureau of the Census. *Central Electric Light and Power Stations and Street and Electric Railways, 1912.* Washington: Government Printing Office, 1914.

U.S. Department of Commerce, Bureau of the Census. *Census of Electrical Industries, 1917: Electric Railways.* Washington: Government Printing Office, 1920.

U.S. Department of Commerce, Bureau of the Census. *Census of Electrical Industries, 1922: Electric Railways.* Washington: Government Printing Office, 1925.

U.S. Department of Commerce, Bureau of the Census. *Census of Electrical Industries, 1927: Electric Railways and Affiliated Motor Bus Lines.* Washington: Government Printing Office, 1931.

U.S. Department of Commerce, Bureau of Foreign and Domestic Commerce. *Statistical Abstract of the United States, 1921, 1928, 1930, 1940, 1962.* Washington: Government Printing, 1922, 1928, 1931, 1943, 1962.

SECONDARY SOURCES

Books

Andrew, Russell M. *Railroading in Atlantic County, New Jersey.* Somers Point: Atlantic County Historical Society, 1981.

Arburn, Robert W. and Foster, Alice M. *Pleasantville's Early Days, 1888-1988.* Privately printed. n.d.

Arnold, Ian, *Locomotive, Trolley, and Rail Car Builders: An All-Time Directory.* Los Angeles: Trans-Anglo Books, 1965.

Bezilla, Michael. *Electric Traction on the Pennsylvania Railroad, 1895-1968.* University Park: Pennsylvania State University Press, 1980.

Blum, John et al. *The National Experience: A History of the United States.* Sixth Edition. 2 vols. New York: Harcourt Brace Jovanovich, 1985.

Borgnis, Mervin E. *The Nearside Car and the Legacy of Thomas E. Mitten.* Privately printed, *1994.*

Bradley, George K. *Fort Wayne Trolleys.* Chicago: Owen Davies, Publisher, 1963.

Brill, Debra. *History of the J. G. Brill Company.* Bloomington: Indiana University Press, 2001.

Brough, Lawrence A. and Graebner, James H. *From Small Town to Downtown: A History of the Jewett Car Company, 1893-1919.* Bloomington: Indiana University Press, 2004.

Brush, John E. *The Population of New Jersey.* New Brunswick: Rutgers University Press, 1956.

Bullard, Thomas R. *Street, Interurban and Rapid Transit Railways of the United States: A Selective Historical Bibliography.* Forty-Fort, Pa.: Harold E. Cox, 1984.

Butler, Frank. *Book of the Boardwalk.* Atlantic City: Haines & Co., 1952.

Carson, Stephen P. and Schneider III, Fred W. *PCC: The Car That Fought Back.* Glendale: Interurban Press, 1980.

Cook, W. George and Coxey, William J. *Atlantic City Railroad: The Royal Route to the Sea.* Oaklyn: West Jersey Chapter, National Railway Historical Society, 1980.

Cox, Harold E. *The Birney Car.* Wilkes-Barre: Harold E. Cox, n.d.

Cox, Harold E. *Surface Cars of Philadelphia, 1911-1965.* Forty-Fort: Harold E. C ox, 1965.

Cox, Harold E. *Utility Cars of Philadelphia, 1892-1971.* Forty-Fort: Harold E. Cox, 1971.

Coxey, William J. and Kranefeld, James E. *The Reading Seashore Lines: A Pictorial Documentary of the Atlantic City Railroad.* Palmyra: The West Jersey Chapter, National Railway Historical Society, 2007.

Cunningham, John T. *The New Jersey Shore.* New Brunswick: Rutgers University Press, 1958.

Davis, Ed. *Atlantic City Diary: A Century of Memories, 1880-1985.* McKee City: Atlantic Sunrise Publishing Co., 1986.

DeGraw, Ronald. *Pig & Whistle: The Story of the Philadelphia & Western Railway.* Chicago: Central Electric Railfans Association, 2007.

Dictionary of American Naval Fighting Ships. 8 vols. Washington: Department of the Navy, 1959-1981.

Dunbar, Charles S. *Buses, Trolleys & Trams.* London: Paul Hamlyn, Ltd., 1967.

Eid, Joseph E. Jr. and Gummere, Barker. *Streetcars of New Jersey.* Privately printed, 2005.

English, A. L. *History of Atlantic City.* Philadelphia: Dickson & Galling, 1884.

Flanagan, Thomas F. *Scranton Railway Company.* West Chester: Ben Rohrbeck Traction Publications, 1979.

Funnell, Charles E. *By the Beautiful Sea: The Rise and High Times of That Great American Resort: Atlantic City.* New Brunswick: Rutgers University Press, 1983.

Gannon, Michael. *Operation Drumbeat: The Dramatic True Story of Germany's First U-Boat Attacks Along the American Coast in World War II.* Annapolis: Naval Institute Press, 2008.

Gladulich, Richard. *By Rail to the Boardwalk.* Glendale: Trans-Angelo Books, 1986.

Goldberg, Mark H. *The "Hog Islanders": The Story of 122 American Ships.* Kings Point, N.Y.: The American Merchant Marine Museum, 1991.

Giangreco, D. M. *Hell to Pay: Operation Downfall and the Invasion of Japan: 1945-1947.* Annapolis: Naval Institute Press, 2009.

Hall, John F. *The Daily Union History of Atlantic City and County.* Atlantic City: Daily Union Printing Co., 1900.

Heston, Alfred M. *Absegami: Annals of Eyren Haven and Atlantic City.* 2 vols. privately printed: 1904.

Heston, A. M. *Clippings: Trolley and Jitney Wars of Atlantic City, 1888-1889, 1915-1916.* Atlantic City Public Library.

Heston, A. M. *Heston's Handbook of Atlantic City.* Atlantic City: A. M. Heston, n.d.

Heston, A. M. ed. *South Jersey: A History, 1664-1923.* 4 vols. New York: Lewis Historical Publishing Company, 1924.

Hilton, George W. and Due, John F. *The Electric Interurban Railways in America.* Stanford: Stanford University Press, 1960.

Kestenbaum, Herbert, ed. *The Inquirer Regional Almanac.* Philadelphia: Philadelphia Newspapers, Inc., 1993.

Keenan, Jack. *Cincinnati & Lake Erie Railroad: Ohio's Great Interurban System.* San Marino: Golden West Books, 1974.

Kennedy, David M. *Freedom from Fear: The American People in Depression and War, 1929-1945.* New York: Oxford University Press, 1999.

Kennedy, David M. *Over Here: The First World War and American Society.* New York: Oxford University Press, 1980.

Kramer, Frederick A. *Pennsylvania-Reading Seashore Lines.* Ambler: Crusader Press, 1980.

Lane, Wheaton K. *From Indian Trail to Iron Horse: Travel and Transportation in New Jersey, 1620-1860.* Princeton: Princeton University Press, 1960.

Lee, Harold. *A History of Ocean City, New Jersey.* Ocean City: The Friends of the Ocean City Historical Museum, 1965.

Lee, Harold. *"Steamboats to Longport": Ocean City Memories.* Ocean City: Centennial Commission of Ocean City, New Jersey, 1979.

McKenney, Carlton Norris. *Rails in Richmond.* Glendale: Interurban Press, 1986.

McMahon, William. *So Young, So Gay.* Atlantic City: Atlantic City Press, 1970.

McMahon, William. *South Jersey Towns: History and Legend.* New Brunswick: Rutgers University Press, 1973.

Middleton, William D. *The Time of the Trolley.* Milwaukee: Kalmbach Publishing Company, 1967.

Middleton, William D. *Traction Classics: The Interurbans.* 3 vols. San Marino: Golden West Books, 1983.

Middleton, William D. *When the Steam Railroads Electrified.* 2nd edition. Bloomington; Indiana University Press, 2001.

Miller, Edward S. *Bankrupting the Enemy: The U.S. Financial Siege of Japan Before Pearl Harbor.* Annapolis: Naval Institute Press, 2007.

Morison, Samuel Eliot, Commager, Henry Steele, and Leuchtenburg, William E. *The Growth of the American Republic.* 2 vols. Sixth Edition. New York: Oxford University Press, 1969.

Nelson, William, ed. *The New Jersey Coast in Three Centuries.* 2 vols. New York: Lewis Publishing Company, 1902.

New Jersey Almanac and Travel Guide, 1966-1967. Second Edition. Cedar Grove: New Jersey Almanac, Inc., 1966.

New Jersey History Commission. *Outline History of New Jersey.* New Brunswick: Rutgers University Press, 1950.

De La Pedraja, Rene. *The Rise and Decline of United States Merchant Shipping in the Twentieth Century.* New York: Twayne Publishers, 1992.

Paulson, Martin. *The Social Anxieties of Progressive Reforms: Atlantic City, 1854-1920.* New York: New York University Press, 1994.

Rich, Bennett, M. *The Government and Administration of New Jersey.* New York: Thomas Crowell Co., 1957.

Robertson, Ross M. and Walton, Gary M. *History of the American Economy.* Fourth Edition. New York: Harcourt Brace Jovanovich, Inc., 1979.

Rogers, Elizabeth, complier. *A Nation in Motion: Historic American Transportation Sites.* Washington: Department of Transportation, 1976,

Rowsome, Frank. *Trolley Car Treasury.* New York: McGraw-Hill Book Co., Inc., 1956.

Schieck, Paul and Cox, Harold E. *Trolleys of Lower Delaware Valley, Pennsylvania.* Forty-Fort: Harold E. Cox, 1970.

Schneider III, Fred W. and Carlson, Stephen P. *PCC From Coast to Coast.* Glendale: Interurban Press, 1983.

Sebree, Mac and Ward, Paul. *Transit's Stepchild: The Trolley Coach.* Cerritos: Interurbans, 1973.

Sebree, Mac and Ward, Paul. *The Trolley Coach in America.* Cerritos: Interurbans, 1974.

Seyfried, Vincent F. *The Rockaway Trolley: The Story of the Ocean Electric Railway, 1886-1928.* Privately Printed, 2003.

Smith, Sarah Thompson. *A History of Ventnor City, New Jersey.* Ventnor City: Sara Thompson Smith, 1963.

Stevens, John R., ed. *Pioneers of Electric Railroading.* New York: Electric Railroaders Association, 1991.

Stover, John F. *History of the Baltimore and Ohio Railroad.* West Lafayette: Purdue University Press, 1987.

Toman, James A. and Hays, Blaine S. *Horse Trails to Regional Rails: The Story of Public Transit in Greater Cleveland.* Kent: Kent State University Press, 1996.

Waltzer, Jim and Wilk, Tom. *Tales of South Jersey: Profiles and Personalities.* New Brunswick: Rutgers University Press, 2001.

Weigley, Russell F. et al, eds. *Philadelphia: A 300 Year History.* New York: W. W. Norton Co., 1982.

Weston, Fred. *Pennsy Steam and Semaphores.* Seattle: Superior Publishing Co., 1974.

Wilson, Harold F. *The Jersey Shore.* 2 vols. New York: Lewis Historical Publishing Co., 1953.

JOURNAL ARTICLES

Alexander, Robert C. "Cape Island, New Jersey, 1860-1869." *The Cape May County Magazine of History and Genealogy,* June, 1968.

Alnutt, Brian. "The Negro Excursions: Recreational Outings Among Philadelphia's African Americans, 1876-1926." *The Pennsylvania Magazine of History and Biography,* January, 2005.

"Atlantic City Transportation Company: A Brief History of the Transportation Provided Off-Shore." Unpublished manuscript. n.d.

Baer, Christopher T. "The Pennsylvania Railroad Company: A Brief History." Unpublished manuscript, n.d., Hagley Museum & Library.

Borgnis, Mervin E. "Atlantic City & Suburban: The Pioneer to the Mainland." *Trolley Talk,* No. 122.

Borgnis, Mervin E. "New Jersey's Last Interurban." *Trolley Talk,* No. 80, August, and No. 81, October, 1970.

Borgnis, Mervin E. "Atlantic City Transportation Co.: The Miss America Fleet." *Trolley Talk,* No. 82, December, 1970 and No.83, February, 1971.

Borgnis, Mervin E. "Memories of the Shore Fast Line." *South Jersey Magazine,* Summer, Fall, 1988; Winter, 1989.

Borgnis, Mervin E. "The Life-Line to Longport." *South Jersey Magazine,* Winter, 1985.

Brill Magazine, 1907-1922.

Cook, W. George. "Railroad Steamboats on the Great Egg Harbor Inlet." *West Jersey Rails,* 1983.

Coxey, William J. "The Shore Fast Line." *West Jersey Rails II,* 1985.

Electric Railway Journal, 1889-1908. Various articles.

Ewing, Leslie H. "Story of the Arrival of the First Iron Horse." *The Cape May County Magazine of History and Genealogy,* June, 1956.

Fretwell, W. E. "Atlantic City and Longport Line." Typed Manuscript. May 4, 1937.

Glazer, Irvin. "The Atlantic City Story." *Marquee,* No.1 and 2, 1980.

Gordon, John Steele. "10 Moments That Made American Business." *American Heritage,* February-March, 2007,

Hamilton III, William P. "The Shore Fast Line." *The Bulletin,* Third Quarter, 1948.

Hamilton III, William and Francis, Edward T. "The Atlantic City Trolley Lines." *The Marker,* February, 1951.

Henwood, James N. J. "The Ocean City Electric Railroad." *National Railway Bulletin,* Vol. 63, No. 4, 1998.

Kalmbach, A. C. "Penn-Reading Seashore." *Trains,* August, 1940.

"Karel Libenauer at Atlantic City." *Trolley Talk,* April, 1971.

Kramer, Murray S. "Passaic." *Motor Coach Age,* October-December, 2005.

Maginnis, Andrew. "Brilliners." *Trolley Talk,* June, 1970.

Meier, Albert E. "Atlantic City." *Motor Coach Age,* June, 1970.

Rung, Al. "Three Months Feast, Nine Months Famine." *Trains,* June, 1948.

Street Railway Journal, 1889-1908.

Sharpe, Norvelle W. "Chamber of Commerce Records: A History of Atlantic City." Railroad Museum of Pennsylvania, Box 106.

Sullivan, Charles, et al, eds. "Atlantic City Jitneys." *Motor Coach Today,* April-June, 1997.

Taylor, Stewart F. "Raymond Loewy and The Pennsylvania Railroad: A Remarkable Association." *Milepost,* December, 2006.

Tobin, Bob. "Of Brilliners, War Boards and Fort Waynes: An Atlantic City Memory." *Electric Lines,* November-December, 1990.

Transit Journal, 1932-1942.

Wall, John. "The Big Engines That Could." *Pennsylvania Heritage,* Spring, 2004.

Wall, Bill. "New Jersey Trolleys Acquired." *Shore Line Trolley Museum Tripper,* July, 2007.

Wentzel, Don. "The Third Rail Comes to South Jersey." *South Jersey Magazine,* Summer, 1973.

NEWSPAPERS

Atlantic City Press.

(Philadelphia) *Bulletin Almanac,* 1951.

Ocean City Sentinel-Ledger.

Philadelphia Inquirer

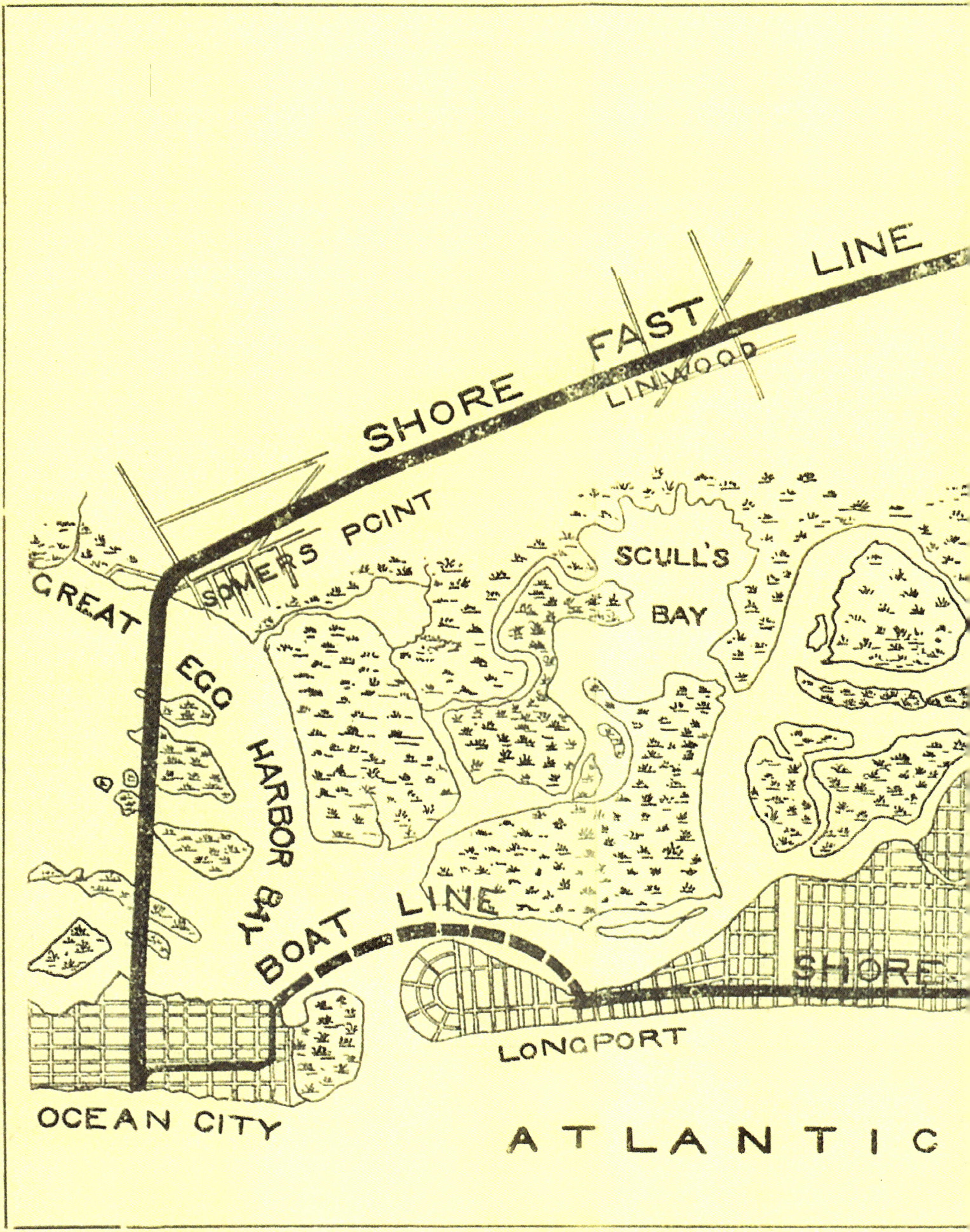

SHORE FAST LINE
LINWOOD
SOMERS POINT
SCULL'S BAY
GREAT EGG HARBOR BAY
BOAT LINE
SHORE
LONGPORT
OCEAN CITY
ATLANTIC